A Journey

In

Overseas Basketball

by Dave Adkins

A Journey In Overseas Basketball

Autobiography
Copyright © 1997 Dave Adkins
All rights reserved,
including right of reproduction.

Manufactured in the U.S.
Publisher:
Dave Adkins

Printed by:
The Town Crier Ltd.
Pella, Iowa

First Edition
March 1, 1999

ISBN: 0-9670940-0-3

Sales and Marketing: To Purchase Book

Dave Adkins
PO Box 66041
West Des Moines, Iowa 50265
E-mail: DAdkins105@aol.com

IN MEMORY OF FALLEN TRAVELERS

- Avery Adkins -

- Charlie Ammit -

- Steve Blank -

- Tim Boyd -

- Jay Brehmer -

- Robert Elmore -

- Scott Fenton -

- Vince Hickey -

- Don Leventhal –

- Paul Maaske -

- Steve Mitchell -

- David Russell -

- Robert Scrigni -

- Ian Watson -

- Owen Wells -

A Journey In Overseas Basketball
by Dave Adkins

TABLE OF CONTENTS
Foreword: Marc Hansen
Prologue: Dave Adkins
Acknowledgements

- Black for Bruton for Black
- Al Green-Cal Bruton: A Classic Feud
- Ken Cole
- The Business at Hand
- The Yank Public Servant
- Greg Norman
- Preparations for the 1988 NBL
- Tim Boyd
- Coach of the Year - Almost
- A Bad Decision
- Lynn Nance in Tasmania
- Mike Dunlap at Adelaide

Chapter 11:

- Radio Moraga
- Dicko
- Nick Nurse and Mr. V
- Bruce Chubick
- Nick Nurse and Dicko at Grand View
- Final Days in Hobart

Chapter 12:

- Sound and the Fury
- Shortage of Big Men
- Foreign to Most
- NBA - A Delicate Balance
- The CBA Dilemma
- The Marty Blake Rule
- Ray Owes
- The Transfer Fee and CBA Cash Flow
- The IBA - International Basketball Association
- Finding the Right Player - The Overseas Tryout

Chapter 13:

- Basketball Outside the School System
- Paul Rogers - An International Experience
- George Karl - *Habla Español?*
- Innocence Abroad
- Australian Amateur Junior Development

Bibliography

Appendices

Photographs
(Found at end of book)

Foreword

In the summer of 1997, a young Aussie named C.J. Bruton was declared ineligible by the NCAA, a remarkable ruling for myriad reasons. One was that Bruton had done so little, compared with many foreigners playing college basketball, to deserve it. Yes, he'd earned $9,000 two years before as an apprentice player for the Perth Wildcats of Australia's National Basketball League. But that was a little like a child's allowance next to the incomes of many of the 300-plus foreigners who go to play at American universities every year.

It was remarkable also because few Americans know the international basketball scene like Dave Adkins, who was Bruton's appointed guardian. For almost 30 years, Adkins has operated his own overseas basketball placement service. He takes American players, most of them former collegians, and finds jobs for them in leagues all over the world. He knows exactly what's going on over there - who's being paid what - which made the NCAA decision against Bruton doubly ironic. Here was an expert being told by a group of non-experts in Overland Park, Kansas, that he didn't know what he was talking about.

Pursuing the Bruton story as a sports columnist for *The Des Moines Register*, I spent many hours talking to Adkins, picking up leads and insights. At least twice a week for several months we would meet at a book store in suburban Des Moines. Dave would talk basketball and drink espresso. I would ask questions and take notes. It soon become obvious that few people anywhere have more insight into the subject of international basketball. Dave has been a head coach in Mozambique and in Australia. When he stepped down in Hobart after stringing together the most successful three years in the history of the struggling NBL franchise, his unexpected resignation moved off the sports section onto page one and became the lead news story of the day.

Dave can walk into a CBA game and, by half-time, tell you which players might have a chance in the pro leagues of Spain or Turkey, which players would be more suited to Belgium or Japan and which players wouldn't have a prayer in England. He can tell you why one of the greatest coaching performances of the last ten years - perhaps the greatest - occurred at the 1986 World Championships when Lute Olson took a bunch of collegians to the title.

In talking to Dave, it also became apparent that basketball is much more than just the NBA and the college game. The sport has exploded across the globe. Unfortunately, Americans are the last to know. If anyone is equipped to fill in the blanks, it is Dave Adkins.

– MARC HANSEN, SPORTS WRITER,
THE DES MOINES REGISTER

Prologue

I had originally intended to work with a professional writer in doing this book. However, that plan did not materialize. I, therefore, decided to write it myself. The book project was my companion for nearly two years. I enjoyed it every step of the way, but the work, of course, required effort and discipline. When I became discouraged, I was motivated to persist in completing the task by the words of biographer David McCullough, whom I heard lecture at Drake University. McCullough read passages from the diary of second U.S. president John Adams, who had made entries in his diary in the 1800's without the luxury of electric lights or heat, who had to produce his own ink, and who wrote with a quill pen. At that moment I realized in comparison how simple my task actually was and I recalled the Adams' diary when my enthusiasm waned.

I have written this book about my 30 years in the overseas basketball business. As I was writing, it occurred to me that each of the chapters could have been expanded to become a volume in itself. I had accumulated notes for years for just such a project and I was blessed with a good memory. Many life events had made an indelible impression on me and I was actually able to feel again the emotions of the past as I wrote. I believed that I had read every known biographical basketball book on the market. However, I believed also that my story was unique and worth telling. Several well-known publishers were tempted as they read the manuscript, but understandably deferred to the safer bet, celebrity-type basketball books. The rejections served as further motivation to deliver a final product. However, the selling of the book was incidental to the writing task, as I looked at the opportunity to relive the events of my life and to record them as a privilege and as an end in itself. I also wanted to pass on some of these stories to other coaches, friends, and to my family; I felt that some people would be interested. David Halberstam, my favorite non-fiction writer, could have obviously done a much better job. However, he wasn't available to assist. It was my story; therefore, I decided to tell it myself as I have learned to live my life - in my own style and within my own limitations.

It was not possible, nor practical, to present every chapter in strict chronological order. To begin in 1968, exactly thirty years ago, would not be in keeping with my intentions because this story is told as a conversation among friends over a cup of coffee. Thus, the starting point is at the Kansas City Kings Veterans Camp in 1978 when Cotton Fitzsimmons had just taken over for Phil Johnson as head coach. Through the flow of the conversation, the time and setting move forward and back between and within Africa, Asia, Australia, Europe, and the United States.

The intent is to provide a thirty-year chronicle of my experiences with people and my perception of events in world basketball. In the case of the

NCAA and Iowa State University in regard to C.J. Bruton, I am compelled to include my own opinions along with the facts. Did it ever occur to the NCAA that they had taken C.J.'s eligibility because he earned about $9,400 in the Australian NBL, yet a 4-year scholarship at a private university, such as Duke, is worth well over $100,000? As you listen to the conversation, you can draw your own conclusions on the NCAA and Iowa State. However, I firmly believe that had Bruton signed with another school such as Kansas or George Washington, with ten foreign players on its 1998 roster, he would have been declared eligible to play college basketball.

During my three decades in the overseas game as a player, coach, administrator, consultant, agent, and writer, I have developed a career and a business "outside of the loop" of mainstream U.S. college and professional basketball. Yet in my professional player placement business I have had dealings with many well-known American coaches and personalities, e.g., Bill Fitch, Lute Olson, John Lucas, Tim Floyd, Ron Adams, Tates Locke, Marty Blake, Jim McGregor, Lynn Nance, Cotton Fitzsimmons, and others. My interactions with basketball people from other countries include Lindsay Gaze, Adrian Hurley, Mike Wrublewski, David Carmichael - Australia; Harry Wrublewski - England; Rudolf VanMoerkerke - Belgium; and Nelson Serra - Portugal, to name just a few. The conversation which you hear in this chronicle, then, is about my interactions, relationships, and perceptions in discussing basketball people and events throughout the world.

This is a story of my exploration of a new world of basketball following the path of "The Great" Jim McGregor before me. As McGregor found, so I also discovered that a vast network of international hoops exists and that the United States, the country which invented and developed the game, now must take its place as a part of the big picture in the world basketball scene. While McGregor's main focus was in Europe, I have had significant basketball encounters in Australia, as well as Europe, Africa, New Zealand, and South America. I have also found interesting and commented from first hand experiences on charismatic figures from other sports such as Joel Garner and Viv Richards - cricket; Chris Everett, Arthur Ashe, and Ken Rosewall - tennis; John Walker - track; and Greg Norman - golf.

Ironically, the rise of foreign basketball powers and their threat to U.S. supremacy in major international events can be traced directly, I learned, to the generosity and at times naivete of American coaches in giving overseas teams access to any and all American tactics and techniques through the years. If the objective in all of this has been to improve the game around the world, that has happened. If the objective has been to retain U.S. dominance in the game, that dominance is no longer taken for granted. The game itself and its popularity, however, have clearly benefited from the cooperation among U.S. and foreign coaches and players.

And I also have noticed a consistent parochialism in the United States regarding the world game. For example, Lute Olson, who coached the last group of 100% amateur U.S. players to victory in a major international event in the 1986 World Championships in Madrid, himself considers the 1997 NCAA title at Arizona as his greatest coaching achievement. From my point of view, NCAA competition is only a slice of the whole in the global hoop picture and winning the world title is clearly the ultimate achievement in coaching, especially the way Olson did it with amateur players. A U.S. college coach wins an NCAA tournament every year, yet Lute Olson's 1986 World Championship has proved to be unique in international basketball history and an unrecognized American treasure in the record books. This coaching feat will probably never be repeated.

I detail the disturbing process and eventual decision by a parochial bureaucracy - the NCAA - to deny a young Australian-American player, C.J. Bruton, of his educational, cultural and athletic experiences at an American university. The whole decision making process by the NCAA in the Bruton case became an exercise in hypocrisy and a failure to recognize the evolution of basketball participation over the past thirty years worldwide. *Sports Illustrated* tracked down hundreds of foreigners who had worn NCAA Division I uniforms. Yet one prominent player - Bruton - was declared ineligible.

The focus of the book is obviously on my life in basketball. However, it would have been remiss not to openly discuss my problems and eventual victory over alcoholism and how honesty in recovery has given me a better life. Ironically I find that this experience has also allowed me to help some talented basketball players with chemical problems of their own. Their recovery has become an important part of my own journey in basketball.

– Dave Adkins, Author

Acknowledgements

I was a reader long before I was a basketball coach, player agent, or writer. Clair Bee, the former LIU coach and Naismith Hall of Famer, wrote the *Chip Hilton* series of fiction sports' stories, and I read them back in the 1940s and 1950s. Also, David Halberstam's *Breaks of the Game* was a memorable and unique non-fiction work with a basketball theme. As in the Clair Bee series and the Halberstam book, much of the information in The Bibliography was incidental background reading and was not used directly in the text of this book. Nevertheless, through the years these other books and articles, as well as certain plays, movies, and conversations, have influenced in a special way - however subtly - my opinions about the game of basketball and my perceptions of life in general.

Regarding statistics, I did not see that it was practical, nor possible, to give a per-item credit for each and every number presented and/or for information of a general statistical nature. Most of the statistical information was repetitious and available from numerous sources. I have accumulated various facts in my notes through the years and have used a wide variety of sources including interviews, sports information directors, coaches, biographies, players, foreign and domestic newspapers and magazines, books, game programs, and newsletters. I am hoping that *A Journey In Overseas Basketball* will also become a valuable resource for another writer.

I would like to recognize and thank Mr. Kevin Bailey, the talented artist who did the sketch on the cover of this book. Bailey's work appeared in *The Mercury*, the respected capital city newspaper of Hobart, Tasmania, and the voice of that unique Australian state. Thank you to *The Des Moines Register* and *Sports Illustrated* for permission to use specified material. Sportswriters Kirk Seminoff of *The Wichita Eagle* and Mark Dukes of *The Cedar Rapids Gazette* graciously supplied archival information. Thank you to *The Mercury* in Hobart, *The Townsville Bulletin*, *The Tribune Star* of Terre Haute, *The Grinnell Herald Register*, Cornell College, and Indian Hills Community College for permission to use photographs. Also, a thanks to Cal Bruton and the Geelong Cats, The Hobart Devils, and the Queensland Amateur Basketball Association for other photographs. Unfortunately, it was not possible to identify the source of the photos from Mozambique and Angola.

A thank you for expert editorial assistance from William Johnson, teacher, and Randy Mouchka, book seller. Geneva Adkins was a triple-threat contributor as a consultant, proof reader, and critic. Also I need to mention test readers Steve Addington, attorney; John Hemminger, attorney; Nick Nurse, coach; Don Gruenwald, retired coach; and Orv Salmon, coach.

Ageless Paul Morrison provided information from Drake University's basketball history.

Also, a thank you to Mark Hansen for writing the <u>Foreword</u> and for the special interview with Scott Thompson, to Dr. Carl Adkins for his work on the <u>Prologue</u>, and to the veteran coaches who endorsed the book - Bill Fitch, Ron Adams, Tom Davis, and Jim Rosborough. These four gentlemen have earned world-wide reputations in basketball because they are not only great coaches, but because they have kept their perspective. Speaking of great coaches, thanks to Lute Olson for his input. My appreciation goes to Scott Thompson for his willingness to participate in this project and to Nick Nurse for his support and assistance. Cal Bruton was a great asset in providing information and John Pfitsch, the veteran Grinnellian, shared his life story to provide important facts in the history of basketball.

A thank you to *The Town Crier*, a company whom I highly recommend and to coordinating editor, Laurie Johnson. Last, but not least, a greeting to John Lucas, Rodney Wright, and Cameron Dickinson - fellow travelers in the beauty of reality.

□ *1* □

THE KANSAS CITY KINGS, COTTON, AND THE BLACK PEARL

It was a torrid September day in Kansas City and the KC Kings were opening vets camp at Rockhurst College under new head coach Cotton Fitzsimmons. The Kings had won only 31 games in the previous season and had finished in a tie for last in the Midwest Division. Management made a good choice in its new coach as he had the enthusiasm and the savvy to turn the franchise around. Cotton was pulling out all stops to strengthen the Kings in preparation for the 1978 NBA season.

The club had drafted college basketball's Player of the Year and 1976 U.S. Olympian Phil Ford from North Carolina and had traded for Mike Evans of Kansas State in seeking an answer to the point-guard position at one time occupied by Nate "Tiny" Archibald, who had led the league in both scoring (34.0 points per game) and assists (11.4 per game) in the 1972-73 season and whose force at his position was still fresh in the minds of Kansas City fans. Although there were no budding Tiny Archibalds in camp, Cotton was looking at Billy McKinney from Northwestern and Calvin Bruton from Wichita State, in addition to Evans. Phil Ford was not present because of a contract dispute.

I was living in Kansas City at the time and was preparing to leave for overseas, as I had just accepted a job as State Director of Coaching in Queensland, Australia. Although I was not aware of any future need for a point guard down-under, I was always looking for good players and was taken by Calvin Bruton's positive attitude, his game, and his determination against great odds - the typical dilemma of all free agents in NBA tryout camps. It was "the old days" in the NBA - the camp along with coaches and players were accessible to non-club personnel. Cotton had charisma and established immediate rapport with the city and his team. He was relaxed in his work and congenial as we talked briefly before an evening practice session. The Kings' camp format included morning workouts stressing fundamentals and evening sessions with referees under game conditions. Each evening Cal Bruton battled for a job and tried to convince the Kings that his size was no obstacle to success in the NBA. Listed at 5'11, but standing side by side with my wife, Geneva, at 5'7, it was revealed that Bruton's alleged 5'11 was a four-inch exaggeration.

Cotton Fitzsimmons had been hired to build a team which would draw media attention and fans to the 17,000-seat Kemper Arena situated in the stockyard section of Kansas City. The indoor soccer team, the Kansas City Comets, regularly outdrew the NBA's Kings at The Kemper Arena. The Kings would play on Friday night and draw 6,500 fans and the Comets the next night would often fill the 17,000 seats. The soccer franchise hustled to establish local credibility, and the players did numerous instructional clinics for kids. The soccer players were semi-professional and most held other jobs outside of their sport. People in Kansas City identified with the Comets and loved their efforts to bond with the city. The Kings, however, were wearing out their welcome - seen as overpaid "fat cats" who were reluctant to do the little things that promoted good community relations.

NBA - An Easy Ticket

Aside from the struggles of the local team, the Kings, it was a great era in NBA history - for me anyway - as the tickets were cheap and the seat availability in Kansas City plentiful. More often than not, I would leave our home in Overland Park to take the twenty-minute drive and arrive at The Kemper Arena parking lot fifteen minutes before tip-off and not worry about having to stand in line for a $10.00 ticket. In fact, as I recall, Monday night games were two tickets for the price of one in the upper deck seating of the arena. It was an era of great players, pacesetters who had established the foundation for the world-wide popularity of the American pro game - Bill Walton, Doctor J, Walt Frazier, George Gervin, Tiny Archibald, Pete Maravich, and Kareem Abdul-Jabbar, to name a few.

I missed few home games that year, sat courtside many times with only 4,000 fans present at Kemper and watched the likes of George Gervin score 35 points or Walt Frazier, possibly the greatest of all defensive point guards, skillfully directing the New York Knicks of that day. Only Julius Irving, "Pistol" Pete Maravich (affectionately referred to as only Pistol in southern cities) and Abdul-Jabbar were able to consistently attract a full house at the Kansas City arena. I have vivid memorics of a massive dunk on a fastbreak by Denver's David Thompson - he had filled the right lane, received a clever pass from point-guard John Kuester, and appeared to take off at the foul line, extended, nearly tearing off the basket with the impact of the slam and causing the backboard to tremble for minutes afterward. That evening at The Kemper Arena it was snowing outside, but Thompson's dunk kept the action hot on the inside.

Another flashback, when Philadelphia was in town, Julius Irving was seated in the reception area outside of the Kings' office and I passed through that part of the arena after lunch in The Kemper Bar. Dr. J was reading a *Sports Illustrated*. The magazine looked like a paperback book in his huge hands. That time spent in Kansas City - in the seventies - was golden for me as it was a unique opportunity to experience first-hand NBA basketball, NFL football, and major league baseball, conveniently and economically.

Kansas City - Big League in Smaller Town

Kansas City was a smaller city and the players were a part of the community. It was not unusual to run into George Brett of the Royals, or Sam Lacey of the Kings, or see three or four overgrown Chiefs at restaurants or on the street in the Plaza, the upmarket shopping district in the KC metro area. I recalled stopping into The Plaza Three, a popular bar and restaurant at the time, and seeing Reggie Jackson, Craig Nettles, and Catfish Hunter of the Yankees sitting at a table having a drink - unmolested by bar patrons - the night before the opening Royal home game in the 1978 major league baseball season.

In the same place, The Plaza Three, on a beautiful spring day, I spoke with Sam Lacey, the Kings' center of that era, about endorsing the Apollo Exerciser, which I was selling. I also conversed with Nick Pinto, the 7'4 ex-Kansas State post player. Pinto was working for a KC company and handed me his business card, which identified him as "The World's Largest Insurance Producer." Dave Robisch, the ex-Kansas and NBA player, was also there on that particular day. Life was simpler then. Pathetic groupies, seeking power and meaning through vicarious identification with sports stars, didn't exist to the extent that they did in the 1990s.

In spite of the attraction of the NBA, NFL, and major league baseball in Kansas City, one of the most memorable athletes whom I watched in action there was Chris Everett at age 22 in World Team Tennis competition. I saw in her that evening at The Kemper all the ingredients of a great athlete - no matter what the sport -including extraordinary concentration, fitness, competitiveness, and skill. I expected her to be heavier, but she was extremely fit with an attractive, athletic body. Not super quick, but she was smart and had great anticipation, instincts, skills, and feel for her game.

Head-to-Head

The Kings were looking for NBA players with the commitment and character of an athlete like a Chris Everett and had hoped to find those qualities in Phil Ford, Kansas City's first-round pick in 1978. He was the Olympic point guard from the University of North Carolina, but he got a late start on the season as he had not reported to an early training camp because of a prolonged contract negotiation with the club. Mike Evans, also a first round draft choice - obtained from Denver - was hoping to prove to the Kings' management that he could do the job and that Ford would be expendable. An added boost for Evans was that he had played at Kansas State and that meant some extra local support in the form of ticket sales for the Kings. Billy McKinney, the six-foot point guard from Northwestern with his quick lefty moves, was also in the mix. Cal Bruton with strength, quickness, low-center-of-gravity, and great ball-handling skills battled Evans and McKinney to make the team. He shot well, pushed the ball, penetrated, and challenged seven-footers on the drive with professional effectiveness.

I can recall one such unique play when Bruton penetrated to the lane about ten feet in front of the basket with his sight to the goal obscured by five or six huge paint players. In fact, I lost sight of Bruton in the traffic. But then he made an exaggerated jump stop, head fake, vaulted straight up, and spread his legs wide on the way up. In making this move, the head fake and the "fake jump" with legs splayed gave him the timing to rid himself of the swatters who had long since elevated and were returning to the floor in helpless defensive position. However, with Bruton and his small stature, the shot wasn't up free yet. He then put the final touches on the move with a looping arch on the shot. The trajectory on the flight of the ball was above the height of the backboard. The basketball came directly into the basket and through the net as if it had been dropped from the ceiling.

As I watched that spectacular play by Bruton, I thought to myself - how many hundreds of hours had this guy put into his game? How many nights regardless of the weather had he dribbled a ball from his home, looking in shop windows to check his form en route to shooting practice and competition in the park in Queens?

I saw a unique sincerity and desperation in Bruton's style that in my mind distinguished him from the other players in camp. I was intrigued with the product of his dedication. Neither a surgeon nor a linguist, yet this man had the same type of commitment and time investment in his profession, his livelihood - his game, his life. And I also thought how different I was from this athlete, who was trying desperately to make the team. Bruton was 24-years-old, black, raised in Queens, had had little contact with his father, and was at the time driving a trash truck in Wichita. I was twenty years older, white, raised in the small Iowa town of Grinnell by two parents, and had just accepted a basketball job in Australia. Yet I had great respect for this young man, based on his effort in Kansas City. I hoped that our paths would cross again and that we would get to know each other. Further, I said to myself at that moment - if ever I need a guard in the future, if ever - he was the man.

In those days it was NBA or YMCA for small guards, not that different from today, except now there were more NBA jobs available with 29 franchises. Seven teams have been added since Bruton's trial with Kansas City. In my opinion, Cal Bruton and his game in 1978 would have been a first-round, NBA pick 20 years later. Cal's kid, C.J., with only a junior-college background, went in the second round in 1997. Cal Sr. at the same stage of his career when being considered by NBA teams for the draft was further along offensively, stronger, older, and more experienced. He had started for four years at Wichita State of the Missouri Valley Conference - in the days when that league meant something special in U.S. college power ratings.

Brisbane and An Overseas Opportunity for The Pearl

Predictably, Cal Bruton did not make the team. However, Phil Ford, Mike Evans, and Billy McKinney all went on to solid NBA careers. Ford, who averaged 15.9 in his rookie year, played seven seasons; Evans, nine seasons; and McKinney, who became an NBA club executive after his playing days, seven seasons.

A few months had passed from the date of the Kansas City Kings' tryout camp. I had arrived in Australia and was settling into my new job as State Director of Coaching in Brisbane, a city of 1,500,000 population and founded as a penal colony in 1824. The city maintained a pleasant pace and had a magnificent climate - similar to San Diego, California. I did some of my work in the State Basketball Stadium at Auchenflower, a suburb only five minutes from the Brisbane city center. I happened to walk into the gym one Saturday to find a group of ten young men practicing in earnest. My initial assessment was that the players were not very big, not very quick, but hard workers. I asked the coach, Bob Young, about the team. He scowled at me (another bloody Yank) and said that they were the Brisbane Bullets of the new National Invitational Basketball League of Australia - called the NIBL - and were preparing for their league opener two weeks away.

I went back to my office, made a couple of calls and was interested to hear that the other teams in the league were using "import" players to boost the local talent. However, the Bullets had no intention of bringing a foreigner. Coach Young had explained,"These are 'A' Grade League all-stars - they are Brisbane's best players. It will be a strong competition, but they should be right, mate." I began to think the opposite - that it probably wouldn't be right and that since the game had very little fan or press appeal in Brisbane, bringing a rebounder and a scoring point guard to give the team some size and "juice" - offensive punch and explosiveness - might be a good idea. I also thought that the Bullets could well be embarrassed - or worse, me - in the NIBL competition without import players. I penciled in Dan Hickert, a 6'11 playing rotation player out of Kansas State and, of course, Cal Bruton from Wichita State as top import prospects for the Brisbane team.

I spoke with the Queensland State Basketball Association president, Ken Madsen - a banker by profession and a well-known Australian basketball administrator by avocation - and he agreed that the post player for the Bullets was a good idea. He nixed the point guard. Madsen was, in a sense, in a difficult situation as Queensland's State Basketball Association President as my job as State Director of Coaching was actually concerned with junior players - athletes under 20-years old. But Madsen and I both understood that the Bullet program was the important missing piece in Queensland basketball, as strong junior players had little to look forward to in the local senior leagues, and the National League showed promise as an elite competition. In fact, this lack of strong men's competition in Brisbane was the reason that Larry Sengstock and Danny Morseu, two outstanding players and native Queenslanders, had exited for better playing opportunities in Melbourne.

I was concerned about Madsen's position both in regard to his support of my work with the Bullets and on the decision to bring the two American players. I remained adamant on the selection of an import guard as well as a post player and I was determined that somehow I would get Cal Bruton to Brisbane. The answer came the following week at a social gathering at our East Brisbane apartment. We lived two blocks from the "Yankee Stadium" of Australian cricket, The Gabba, where I saw an amazing athlete perform in the 1979-80 International Cricket Series with Australia, the West Indies, and England competing. Joel Garner, a 6'9, carved West Indian cricketer applying his physical gifts in a sport which demanded much less, was an Hakeem Olajuwan look-alike with a comparable body, wing-span, and athleticism.

Watching Joel Garner along with his world-renowned teammate, Viv Richards, reminded me of the importance of talented, colorful athletes in the successful marketing of any sport. Because of the presence of these two unique sportsmen, the West Indian team always played before packed houses and enjoyed world-wide celebrity. I had limited interest in cricket, but I had sat for three hours in the Queensland summer sun on one Saturday afternoon at The Gabba studying the fluid movements of the West Indian players, especially Garner and Richards, and I knew that Cal Bruton could impact Australian basketball in a similar manner.

With the marketing angle in mind, I talked again with Ken Madsen at the social gathering. After a few Four X's - the beer brewed in Brisbane - the idea of Calvin Bruton, known in basketball circles as "The Black Pearl," seemed feasible. Just to be sure that it wasn't to be forgotten, I called Ron Waggener that afternoon in Kansas City. I had had no idea that I would be contacting the U.S. looking for Bruton this soon after the Kings' camp. I asked Waggener - a public relations executive with an interest in basketball - to track down Calvin Bruton. Ron found him in Wichita driving a trash truck, double parking at the gym at noon to take a few shots, and in general desperately trying to find a way to do what he did best. Although Bruton was not aware of it at the time, his luck had changed. He would get his chance.

Short Notice

When I reached Cal in Wichita, I told him that he would have to leave Kansas on Wednesday - it was Sunday when we talked. All that he really wanted to hear was that someone was interested in him and that he was needed to play professional basketball. However, he did not realize at the time that it was a unique opportunity, as he was to play in the first game in the history of the Australian National Invitational Basketball League. A year later, in 1980, the competition was renamed the National Basketball League - The NBL. It has grown from an amateurish operation to the point of producing four NBA draft choices in 1997.

On Wednesday of that week I received a collect call in Brisbane from The Black Pearl who had been stymied by the U.S. Passport Office in San Francisco. His passport, used on the Missouri Valley Conference all-star trip to Brazil several years before, had expired. Bruton had acquired The Black Pearl moniker on that trip from Brazilian journalists. They had actually named Bruton "The Black Pearl of Basketball" as Pele (Edson Arantes do Nascimento), the great Brazilian soccer international, was the original and authentic Brazilian-born Black Pearl of World Football (soccer).

I spoke with the Passport Office in San Francisco to verify the urgency of the application as Bruton's plane to Sydney was to leave that same evening. The passport officer said to me on the telephone, "Basketball player? - This guy is shorter than I am." Ricky Marsh, Bruton's neighborhood pal from Queens in New York, was based in the Bay Area playing with the Warriors in the NBA at the time and dedicated his day to Cal's "chance" and drove him around the city to get his passport and Australian visa. The two ex-New Yorkers then drove to San Francisco International. Ricky Marsh embraced his close friend and Bruton boarded the seventeen-hour flight via Honolulu to Sydney.

Although he didn't realize it, Cal Bruton had achieved the impossible. He got his expired passport renewed and was issued an Australian working visa, which normally took two weeks to process, by 3:00 p.m. that day. He then caught the QANTAS international flight to Sydney with a connecting domestic service on to Brisbane. There had been a snow storm back in the Midwest and all power was out at the time of Cal's passport application. Therefore, the required police check was waived and The Pearl's most infamous steal as a 17-year-old freshman at Wichita State University did not block his drive to his goal in Australia. That "steal" was a parked car on the Wichita State campus. He explained to Wichita police later that he was just borrowing the car to take a ride around the campus. Eventually this problem was resolved through political power exerted by the Wichita State basketball program. They took care of it.

As I drove to the Brisbane airport that day to meet Bruton, little did I know that I would be repeating this process seventeen years later and meeting another Calvin Bruton on a basketball mission at an airport in another country. When Cal Bruton Sr. arrived at the Brisbane airport in the dog days of the 1979 Queensland summer, he was smiling and wearing his full length U.S. winter coat. Seventeen years later in 1995 I met college bound Calvin Bruton Jr. at the airport in Des Moines, Iowa. He too was smiling and like his father had that confident "point guard look" - and each was on his own personal mission.

When Cal Sr. boarded the plane from Sydney to Brisbane that day, he had been seated next to Australian Belinda Fedrick. She was an attractive, fit 20-year-old basketball player in the Queensland State system. She was years later employed by FIBA, the world basketball governing body, in Europe. She walked off the plane with Cal. I recalled the two of them - she the taller - coming down the ramp into the Brisbane airport together. I noticed Belinda's pained smile directed at me. Her look made an unforgettable impression, even though I did not fully understand it at the time. It was a rather dark, doubting expression masked by a pretty young face. I knew that Belinda's boyfriend was a guard competing for a spot on the Brisbane Bullet roster, Cal's new team. And I knew that it would mean even less playing time for him with The Pearl in the lineup.

The U.S. Import - Reluctant Welcomes

As time passed I was to become aware of the feelings of resentment - at times subtle and other times obvious - by most foreign basketball clubs toward the presence of American players and coaches. In Europe the antagonism toward "the American import" has been unrestrained, especially among European coaches who seemed bent on showing that they themselves don't need the hired gun from the U.S. to win games. They reasoned that their coaching prowess along with the best of local player talent was sufficient.

Some European coaches even refused to start their club's American players and did all possible to belittle their contributions. For example, Bruce Chubick, former University of Nebraska 4-year starter and CBA achiever, received "the treatment" from Dutch coach Tom Boot at Sunair in Belgium in the 1996-97 season. Chubick had the maturity and guts to survive it, but Boot appeared to be out to break Chubick's spirit. Chubick called me on a regular basis to develop strategy during his struggle with Coach Boot. The coach's tactic did not work. In fact, Bruce Chubick through his persistence and effort earned the respect of opponents aware of the problematic situation - the American player was offered a contract and continued with another club the next year. He developed into a top producer in Belgium with Tom Boot no longer coaching there. When Bruce Chubick was cut by the Sunair Club at the end of the 1997 Belgian season, four other teams in that league contacted me as Chubick's agent regarding his services. He had won the battle with the coach and the Sunair Club.

However, in Australia, the feelings of resentment were more subtle. They were born by public silence and mixed feelings about the U.S. players. On the one hand friendships developed, but the American players were still on Australian turf. However quiet, resistance and bitterness of the Australian-born coaches, players, and some administrators toward the Yanks were real and pervasive. The Aussies grudgingly knew that they were being forced to accept the reality that professional basketball had a much better chance for survival in Australia with the market appeal of the talented American players who would enhance the strength of the participating teams and draw media interest. Australian basketball had tried it on its own before without imports and the league had folded rapidly.

The Phantom Replacement

This was not to say that life was unbearable for the visiting players. There were many pleasant moments. Some American players and coaches forged enduring personal and professional bonds in overseas competition. However, it was the exception rather than the norm. Most relationships were surface at best and were conditional upon player production. U.S. players must never forget why they were there in another country - to do high quality work, to do it consistently, and to give the team a dimension not available from the local players. Assuming otherwise can mean a quick trip home. Demands on the local players - anywhere overseas - were always far less than on the U.S. import, who must constantly compete with the "phantom" replacement just one international phone call away. Replacing an import player during the season has always proven to be a disruptive process, but at times the move has paid off. The real problems of foreign teams in a losing mode normally can go much deeper than simply replacing their Americans, but the replacement has remained one of the few alternatives available to the club once the season has begun. NBA-type, in-season trades did not exist in overseas pro ball.

Most foreign teams have had an obvious shortage of local talent and many non-productive players occupied playing rotation spots. The teams farthest down the league ladder have the fewest talented locals and must rely more on the U.S. import than the league leaders - normally well-stocked with their country's national team players and outstanding young prospects. On the one hand, the American can be an asset in strengthening a team and giving the game more appeal to the media and fans. However, the downside of the American-player equation was that the import players also took playing time, opportunity, and glory from Australian, European or South American players in their own countries. The same applied to American coaches overseas - they have taken the job of a local.

From the beginning the Australian displeasure with the presence of American players, however repressed, was strong. League administrators, usually a step or two ahead of general club awareness, had planned from the beginning the eventual "Australianization" of the NBL. The strategy was a sound idea philosophically and an honorable attempt to maximize opportunities for Australian-born players. However, the policy could have gone too far and could have helped sink the NBL, as the league passed its 20th birthday with three member teams folding in 1996. Only two of the remaining eleven teams could consistently show a profit.

Contraband

The events that followed through the years regarding attitudes toward Americans in Australia had been reflected by the expressions and body language of the Queensland girl, subtle yet definitive, when she had walked into her home city with "contraband" basketball talent. However, the cultural exchange through the flow of basketball players among countries of the world has gone both directions with Americans playing in overseas professional leagues and, in doing so, stealing glory from local players. Simultaneously the young foreign-born players have been taking U.S. scholarships and opportunities from American college players. Some talented foreigners have even been able to take it a step further in earning NBA jobs and big, American-dollar paychecks. The Brisbane airport scene that day in 1979 was a microcosm of the foreign basketball business and local reaction to the American import player.

Sixteen years later in August 1995 when I met C.J. Bruton, Calvin Thomas Bruton Jr., at the airport in Des Moines, I saw a bigger version of Cal Sr., but the same large hands with long fingers and the Bruton body frame. On this occasion, C.J. was coming from his home in Perth, Australia, to the U.S. as a "foreigner" to play basketball at Indian Hills Community College. The Bruton-to-Bruton bloodline had stretched 10,000 miles and over seventeen years and I was still very much involved with their basketball careers. Ironically C.J. Bruton was making his start in the United States at a junior college in Ottumwa, Iowa, the home town of the NCAA official whose influence would alter C.J.'s career and impact his life. Ottumwa was only 60 miles from my home town of Grinnell where I developed the values and personality which would propel me to a career "outside the loop" of the U.S. basketball system.

□*2*□

GRINNELL, GRINNELL, GRINNELL; ZELMO BEATY AND THE GREAT JIM MCGREGOR

Going back in time to the 1940s and 1950s to my hometown in Iowa - this was where my story in basketball actually began. John Pfitsch, the Grinnell College coach, was my link to Dr. James Naismith, who invented the game, and Coach Phog Allen, who contributed so much to its growth and popularity. I lived two blocks from the Grinnell College campus. Although I did not ever attend Grinnell, the school played an important part in my early life. I can still hear the final stanza of the school song - "Grinnell, Grinnell, Grinnell" - and I associate these words and the college itself with my formative years. I have heard *The Alma Mater*, as the song was called, hundreds of times at the college's football and basketball games and its sounds still echo through my soul.

Growing up in a small town had definite impact - both positive and negative - on my personality and life choices. My mother and father were born in Grinnell, raised in Grinnell, and will spend eternity there. My dad died in 1967 on the evening of the NCAA Finals in which UCLA defeated Dayton. Fortunately, I was home for the weekend and we spent the evening together watching Lew Alcindor and the Bruins overpower Don May and the Dayton Flyers. My dad died in his sleep early the next morning about five hours after the Bruins had collected their trophy.

Avery Adkins, my father, was from a family of nine children - one dying in infancy. An older brother, Roy, was an outstanding athlete and set a state record in the time of 2:02.2 in the 880-yard-run in 1922. The other Adkins brothers concurred that my dad had more talent in track than Roy, but he did not develop it. He became a barber and a rabid sports fan who never moved away from Grinnell. However, my mother, Irene, has seen other parts of the world, as we traveled together in Europe in the summer of 1967, after my father's death. She also visited my wife and me in Australia on her 82nd birthday in 1988. She quit driving when she turned 89, and in her nineties she has maintained great clarity and interest in life. She never missed University of Iowa football and basketball games on TV and was very pleased that I had coached Steve Carfino and Jerry Dennard, two former Iowa players, in Australia.

Exotic Travel

When I was growing up in this small midwestern town, I had little interest or knowledge of life in other countries. I was, however, enthusiastic about family trips to Chicago and St. Louis. My dad made every effort to arrange an annual car trip during the summer to see major league baseball. We were particularly interested in the Cardinals as Jackie Collum from Grinnell was a pitcher on the St. Louis roster. My dad was very proud the day at Wrigley Field that Jackie relieved the starting pitcher after 2/3 of an inning and allowed only one run to the Cubs the rest of the way. Chicago held on to win, 3-2, but Jackie Collum, "the lion-hearted lefty from Grinnell, Iowa" - as the post-game story read, drove the Cub right fielder to the wall at Wrigley in the ninth inning for the last out of the game. Collum often pinch hit and always batted for himself, as his 5'7 stature was a tough strike-zone target and he had power to go with an effective swing. When Collum retired from major league baseball, he moved back to Grinnell.

I still have the images of two Hall of Famers from that era etched in my memory - Jackie Robinson and Stan Musial. I saw Robinson, the first black player in the major leagues, in his 1949 MVP season in a three-game series against the Chicago Cubs. His thick, strong body and his aggressive, pigeon-toed, base-running technique were memorable sights at Wrigley Field. Also, I can still see Robinson taking a big lead at third and then faking a charge to the the the plate in a successful effort to rattle the opposing team's pitcher in his wind-up. Jackie Robinson's Brooklyn Dodger team were bitter rivals of "my team" - the St. Louis Cardinals - which featured the great hitter, Stan Musial. Crouched at the plate in his famous coiled batting stance, I saw Musial on more than one occasion drive the ball out of the old Sportsman's Park in St. Louis for home runs. This was the late 1940s - an era which was truly a different America, so different that it seemed like a dream.

Chicago and St. Louis were exotic destinations for me and Iowa City wasn't far behind. I saw my first NBA game at the University of Iowa Fieldhouse during the 1953-54 season, my freshman year in high school, when the Philadelphia Warriors played the Milwaukee Hawks. That evening I watched Neil Johnston, who was signed as a free agent by Philadelphia out of Ohio State in 1951, score on an array of hook shots - off the board - up to fifteen feet from the basket. Johnston's game would be classified as "ugly" by today's standards, but he was effective. Neil "Gabby" Johnston led the NBA in scoring, rebounding, and field-goal percentage during his career. In the 1955-56 pro campaign, he was the league's leading scorer (25.7 ppg) and took the Warriors to the NBA championship. Johnston and his all-star teammate, Paul Arizin, became members of the Naismith Basketball Hall of Fame.

I vividly recalled these two great players in Iowa City that evening -

Johnston, the balding, long-armed scorer, and Arizin, a live-bodied 6'4 small forward with the career 22 ppg average. On other trips to Iowa City, I was privileged to watch the great Tom Gola of LaSalle and Frank Selvy of Furman, the nation's leading scorer in 1954 at 41.7 ppg, in the College All-Star - Harlem Globetrotter tour. Discontinued in 1955, this event gave me the opportunity to see All-Americans from the pages of *Street and Smith* come to life on the floor at the old University of Iowa Fieldhouse.

Outside of these sporting adventures and an occasional drive to Minnesota, my early life was insular. I never gave any thought to leaving Grinnell. In fact, I thought that I would probably stay there forever. I was born, raised, and attended high school in Grinnell, Iowa, but have broken family tradition in adult life by living elsewhere. However, I imagined that my mother, much like Jim McGregor's mother, tried her best to understand why I didn't stay home and build a life. McGregor was the original overseas coach and agent. When I spoke with Mrs. McGregor at age 90 in Portland, she was still wondering when her son, Jim, would come home and settle down.

Jim McGregor had a profound influence on my wanderings in the world of overseas basketball. My first contact with McGregor was in 1973 when he called me in Mozambique about collecting a fee for him on ex-NBA player Greg Howard, whom he had sent from the Italian island of Sardinia to a Lourenço Marques club. And we had further contact in 1975 when I flew into Chicago from Topeka to DePaul University where "The Great" Jim McGregor, as he was called in Europe, was running a camp.

Our Town

While McGregor was a West Coast guy originally, I used my roots in the Great Midwest as a springboard to some color and experience in other parts of the world. I associated Grinnell, Iowa, with Thorton Wilder's play *Our Town*. Wilder depicted the drama of small-town life and gave the audience access to the lives of people both living and dead in the fictitious town of Grover's Corners, New Hampshire. There was a memorable scene in this play where Wilder's deceased characters were sitting - looking from afar - in rocking chairs and commenting on the living and their ongoing problems.

In keeping with Wilder's central theme of paradox in *Our Town*, I noted this particular paradox in the play - that small-town life was so insignificant in the big picture (the world) that its insignificance made it most unique and thus significant. I could identify with that paradox, and like the Wilder's characters in Grover's Corners I was so preoccupied with my own life in my own small world (in Grinnell) that I cared little, and knew less, of anywhere else. Also, in places like Grover's Corners and Grinnell, people recognized every face on the street. I could see and feel images of fallen and forgotten

Grinnellians of the past, still an active part of my memories, as I was reminded of their lives by their grave markers. When visiting my own father and grandfather's final resting places at Grinnell's Hazelwood Cemetery, I could recognize more names there than of people on the main street of the town.

Grinnell College

Grinnell, Iowa - the town, formerly my town, (Our Town) - was a very conservative corn belt community of 9,000, but unique in that it harbored an elite, liberal arts college - Grinnell College. The school has received criticism from counselors in the state's high schools for admitting miniscule numbers of Iowa students - normally 98% of the Grinnell College student body was selected from out of state and from foreign countries. At one time Grinnell competed in big-time college athletics and was a member of the Missouri Valley Conference but took a similar course as the University of Chicago, preferring the academic high road to the major-college athletic philosophy.

I lived only a couple of blocks from Darby Gym, a World War II Public Works Administration (PWA) project, and I spent a great deal of time shooting baskets at Grinnell College facilities. I passed long hours in Darby and in the old Women's Gym, a real relic and the site of Grinnell games in the 1930s. Drake, Tulsa, and Oklahoma A&M (renamed Oklahoma State University in 1958) played at Grinnell, which was a member of the Missouri Valley Conference from 1918-1939; Grinnell never won the title but was competitive. According to school and conference records, Grinnell College finished third in the eight-team league in its last MVC season (1938-39), right behind co-champions Drake and Oklahoma A&M coached by the legendary Henry Iba, with an 8-6 conference record and 14-7 overall. Before they left Missouri Valley Conference competition, the Grinnell Pioneers recorded a 83-173 conference record and 131-222 overall.

I was told by my mother and father that they took me to a game at the old Grinnell College gym in 1940 when I was two years old. Scott McLeod, a 1937 Grinnell grad, was back on campus just before taking a job as a special agent with the F.B.I. He apparently rolled a basketball across the floor from the Grinnell's team bench to me - one of my few basketball experiences which I do not remember. Scott McLeod worked for the F.B.I. for seven years and later served as the U.S. Ambassador to Ireland from 1957-1961.

There had been some rich basketball history - mostly forgotten - at Grinnell College. For example, Henry Iba, who was elected to the Naismith Memorial Basketball Hall of Fame in 1968, brought his nationally ranked Oklahoma A&M teams via the long train ride from Stillwater, Oklahoma, to

Grinnell for Missouri Valley Conference play. Iba and Oklahoma A&M competed against Grinnell in the league play from 1934 - Iba's first year at A&M - through 1939, the year that Grinnell abandoned big-time college basketball. Iba coached college basketball for forty-one years compiling a 767-338 record (69% winning) and also led three U.S. teams in Olympic competition in 1964, 1968, and 1972. In addition to his magnificent achievements, Henry Iba was remembered as the head coach of the first American team to lose an Olympic game - in 1972 to the Russians in Munich.

I recalled that Mr. Iba was also involved in a controversy while serving as athletic director at Oklahoma A&M. Drake University was playing the Aggies at Stillwater, Oklahoma, in October of 1951 in a Missouri Valley Conference football game. John Bright, Drake's All-American tailback, had released a forward pass downfield and was watching the flight of the ball. Wilbanks Smith, an A&M defensive player, intentionally hit Bright in the face after the play. Smith's late hit broke Bright's jaw and virtually ended the Drake star's college football career. It seemed obvious that Wilbanks Smith, who was white, was on a mission to intentionally injure John Bright, a black man. The blow to Bright's face was one of the all-time, dirty plays in college athletics.

Neither Henry Iba, as athletic director, nor the Missouri Valley Conference took any disciplinary action against Smith or the Oklahoma A&M football program. Drake was outraged and dropped out of the conference in protest after the football season in 1951 and Bradley University did the same as a sign of support of Drake's position. Paul Morrison, the long-time sports information director at Drake, recalled the Bright-Smith incident. Morrison said, "It seemed intolerable that Iba did not issue an apology or that the conference took no disciplinary action. Drake left the Missouri Valley in 1951, and Bradley followed, as a result of this situation."

John Pfitsch and Phog Allen

The first basketball coach whom I knew personally at Grinnell was John Pfitsch. He came with his University of Kansas background to Grinnell College in 1948 as a well-credentialed head basketball coach. John Pfitsch was a direct link to the origins of the game of basketball; he had been the assistant coach at the University of Kansas under Coach Phog Allen, who had played at KU for Dr. James Naismith, who had invented the game in 1891 at the Y.M.C.A. College in Springfield, Massachusetts. Phog Allen had also coached Adolph Rupp, the Kentucky coaching legend, at Kansas.

While at the University of Kansas, Pfitsch had worked on Phog Allen's coaching staff against the Henry Iba teams at Oklahoma A&M. I can remember first seeing Pfitsch, who was also an assistant football coach, on a hot, late-summer day in August of 1948 at a Grinnell football practice. I had taken the five-minute walk from home to watch "the college" in pre-season workouts. On that same day I can recall also watching Dick Ullrich, a Grinnell graduate who had played in the College All-Star Game at Soldier's Field and also with the Chicago Bears, working with the kickers. At the time I didn't realize it, but Grinnell College athletes - like Dick Ullrich - with National Football League playing experience were, indeed, rare. Another Grinnellian, Ben Douglas, was a great athlete in the Missouri Valley Conference - football, basketball, and track. My dad showed me a letter from Ben Douglas on hotel stationery while the former Grinnellian was playing with the NFL's Brooklyn, New York, franchise in the late 1930s. I recalled that Douglas mentioned that he was getting limited playing time and wasn't happy in that situation. Yet another Grinnellian, Morgan Taylor, perhaps the most successful of all Grinnell College athletes, won medals at three consecutive Olympic Games. He captured gold, bronze, and bronze respectively in his 400-meter hurdle speciality at Paris in 1924, Amsterdam in 1928, and in the 1932 competition in Los Angles. Ironically, Taylor's 52-second flat clocking for third place in '32 was faster than his winning time of 52.6 in '24. The 1924 Paris Games also included gold medal winners Harold Abrahams and Eric Liddell from Great Britain. Abrahams, who won in the 100 meters event, and Liddell, who struck gold in the 400 meters, were featured in the classic movie, *Chariots of Fire*.

In 1998 I drove down to Grinnell from Des Moines and spent the after-noon with John and Emily Pfitsch. On that day, John Pfitsch told me his life's story. I learned that he was the son of a Lutheran medical missionary, who was a graduate of the Medical School at Johns Hopkins University. John Pfitsch was born in India in 1919 and returned to Texas with his family at the age of five. A 5'3 ninety-seven pound graduate of Pfluegerville High School in Texas, he was admitted to Texas Lutheran Junior College at age 16 and was promoted from football team manager to regular kicker and defensive safety.

Enrolling at the University of Texas to complete his final two years of college, Pfitsch was on the Longhorn basketball bench in his senior year in 1940 for a two-game series in Austin with the University of Kansas coached by Dr. Forest "Phog" Allen. So impressed with the Kansas disciplined offense, Pfitsch walked into the KU dressing room right after the game, introduced himself to Phog Allen, and announced that he wanted to come to the University of Kansas to learn how to coach basketball. Allen pumped Pfitsch's hand and said, "Son, you just said the right thing and you are talking to the right guy. If you want to come to Kansas, I will find a place for you."

The 21-year-old John Pfitsch accepted Allen's initial invitation and arrived at Kansas, a school with an enrollment of 3,000 students, in the fall of 1940 to learn all that he could about coaching basketball. Pfitsch had had no contact with Phog Allen since that brief conversation after the Kansas-Texas game nine months before. Since arriving on the Kansas campus, two weeks had passed and the young Texan had yet to see or talk with Allen. He was becoming apprehensive, but Allen's secretary encouraged him to be patient and said that Dr. Allen was a busy man; however, she advised Pfitsch to attend a meeting of physical education majors at 4:00 p.m. on the next day. There were 250 students at the meeting. Dr. Allen was in charge - welcoming the students, confirming to them their choice of Kansas and the field of physical education, and introducing his staff. Pfitsch sat at the back of the room and was startled to hear Phog say, "And I would like to introduce the new freshman basketball coach at the University of Kansas - Johnny Pfitsch from Texas. This is a young man with a bright future in basketball. Please stand up, Johnny."

John Pfitsch stayed at KU and worked for Allen for two years, then spent the next four years as an officer in the U.S. Army in Europe. Returning to Kansas after the war, Phog Allen named John Pfitsch as his first full-time assistant coach at the start of the 1945-46 season. In February of 1998 Pfitsch attended the One-Hundred-Year Anniversary of Basketball at the University of Kansas. He was honored as a Kansas Basketball Legend. Coach Pfitsch recalled this experience with Coach Allen as follows:

"Dr. Allen was really good to me. He did everything possible to help me become a basketball coach. He was, of course, a legend, having taken KU to the Final Four three times - 1940, 1952, and 1953 - winning the NCAA Championship in 1952. He was gregarious - always talking and always teaching. He was a certified osteopath and taught a popular Sunday School class at the Methodist Church in Lawrence. He included a summary of the previous night's game along with his Bible stories, so he always had a large part of the Methodist congregation present at Sunday School. It was misunderstood that he was a rigid disciplinarian as a coach. He did not have a 'winning at all cost' philosophy. He saw basketball, especially Kansas basketball, as the way to becoming a person of character. He didn't punish players and he relied on a positive personal relationship with the members of his team. He was never abusive. He taught the fundamentals of the game through a simple practice plan using three or four drills - a dribble-pivot drill, a 3-2 and 2-1 fastbreak drill, and a defensive footwork exercise using the boxer shuffle."

Pfitsch continued:

"All offense was taught five-on-five in a half court setting and he called the Kansas defense 'a stratified man-to-man with zone principles.' Practices were well-organized and he followed the same routine every day, but the sessions were not extensive, nor particularly hard. He stopped play frequently during practice to explain things and everyone listened to every explanation. He was a great story-teller and believed that his own inspirational pre-game and half-time talks were important in his team's performance. At times, the players were confused about his pep-talks and questioned the purpose of some of the speeches among themselves. But they always respected him."

Pfitsch stated that Allen held the NCAA career record for the most years employed as a basketball coach. He started coaching at Baker University in Kansas in 1905, and had other coaching jobs at Haskell Institute and Central Missouri State. He was eventually forced by state retirement laws to resign from his University of Kansas job in 1956 after thirty-nine years as the Jayhawks' head coach. He turned sixty-five in 1950, but he then lobbied and convinced the state legislature to push the mandatory retirement age to seventy to allow him five more years on the KU bench.

Again in 1956 and this time at age seventy, he asked the Kansas legislature for an extension, as he wanted to coach Wilt Chamberlain. On this occasion, it didn't work and Coach Allen left KU disappointed and bitter, as Dick Harp succeeded him as head coach. In his forty-eight year coaching span, Allen's teams had established a 746 win 264 loss record (74% winning). John Pfitsch remembered that Dr. Forest "Phog" Allen and Harry S Truman, the thirty-third President of the United States, attended high school together in Independence, Missouri, where county records showed that Truman was born in 1884 and died in 1972; while Allen was born one year later in 1885 and died in 1974. Roy Williams, the current Kansas head coach, has included as a pre-season ritual with his teams a visit to the gravesites of Coach Phog Allen and Dr. James Naismith. Both were buried in Lawrence.

Commenting further on his experiences with the legendary Phog Allen, John Pfitsch said:

"He was an interesting man. At one point in his coaching career he became so upset with the number of injuries in college athletics that he quit his coaching job, went to the school in Kansas City and became certified as an osteopath. Returning to KU, Dr. James Naismith hired him back as coach, and Allen incorporated his osteopathic philosophy into the training of his own teams and also taught this system to physical education majors who carried it all over the country in their careers."

"Allen," Pfitsch said, "was a strong believer in taking measures to prevent injuries and during the half-time of all games, his trainers gave sacroiliac adjustments to the players. He was so well respected in the area of athletic training that he was hired by Knute Rockne to treat the Notre Dame football team after Fighting Irish games. Rockne flew him to every game - no matter where they played - and few people flew commercially in those days. And Dr. Allen was a crusader. He tried hard to get the rules changed and the basket raised to twelve feet. He even arranged an exhibition game between two NAIA teams using the twelve-foot baskets. But his theories were disproved in this game as the higher basket didn't equalize opportunity for the smaller players; the big guys still got the rebounds and the team with the taller players won the game. He had also been instrumental in basketball becoming an official Olympic sport."

John Pfitsch confirmed that Phog Allen had great respect for Henry Iba, the Oklahoma A&M coach. Pfitsch said that Allen had coached Adolph Rupp, who graduated from Kansas in 1923 and went on to a forty-one year career including four NCAA titles at Kentucky; however, Phog Allen seemed to show more admiration for the work of Henry Iba than for the work of Rupp. Pfitsch conjectured that this could possibly have been due to the fact that Allen and Iba were working in the same part of the country although not in the same conference, as Oklahoma State did not join the Big Eight until the 1958-59 season - after Allen's retirement. Dr. Forest "Phog" Allen worked as a head college coach a record forty-eight years (48 years: 746-264-74% winning); Adolph Rupp (41 years: 876-190-82% winning); and Henry Iba (41 years: 767-338-69% winning).

These three coaching legends represented the heart of the origins, the history, and development of coaching basketball as a profession through their personal achievements and through their proteges. Adolph Rupp, the Kentucky coach, had learned his basketball from Phog Allen at Kansas as had Dean Smith, the North Carolina Tarheels' coach, and Ralph Miller, who had great success at Wichita State, Iowa, and Oregon State. Further, the NBA's Pat Riley had played for Rupp at Kentucky, while George Karl of the Seattle Supersonics and Roy Williams of Kansas had played for Dean Smith at North Carolina.

Regarding the Iba chain of success, Don Haskins of the University of Texas-El Paso, Eddie Sutton at Oklahoma State, and Jack Hartman from Kansas State had all played for Coach Iba - and Tim Floyd at Iowa State had worked as an assistant coach for Haskins at U.T.E.P. Phog Allen and Henry Iba produced unparalleled successes in their own college programs in addition to the spin-off of former players who became some of the game's greatest coaches in their eras.

Phog Allen coached the Kansas Jayhawks to the 1952 NCAA Championship winning the title game, 80-63, against St. John's in Seattle. The

6'9 All-American Clyde Lovellette was the leading scorer, and Dean Smith, the future North Carolina coach, was a guard on the KU team. In those days, John Pfitsch recalled, the U.S. Olympic Team's players and coaching staff were decided by a one game play-off between the NCAA Champion and the AAU Champion with the winning team's coach automatically becoming the Head Olympic Coach and the losing team's coach, the Assistant Olympic Coach. Six players were then selected from each of the two teams competing in that play-off game.

That year - 1952 - was an Olympic year, and Kansas, the NCAA champ, lost to the Peoria Caterpillars, the AAU champ, to determine U.S. representation in the Helsinki Olympics. Six Kansas players and six Peoria players were selected. John Pfitsch chuckled at the irony when he told me how unknown Fred Warmble, the Caterpillar coach, by virtue of the Peoria victory over KU, had been named Head Coach and the famous Phog Allen, Assistant Coach, for the 1952 American Olympic team.

Ironically, Ron Bontemps of the Peoria Caterpillars and former Beloit College star player - an opponent of John Pfitsch's Grinnell College Pioneers - was considered the top U.S. player. Pfitsch and Allen had a disagreement about Bontemps. Pfitsch said that Ron Bontemps was a great player at any level of competition. However, Phog Allen disagreed. He told Pfitsch before the Olympics and was adamant that Bontemps was not good enough to play at KU. However, after the Helsinki event, Allen - forgetting his previous assessment of the player - reported enthusiastically to Pfitsch that "the guy from the little college in Wisconsin, what's his name, turned out to be the best player on the Olympic team. I would have liked to have had him at Kansas."

Thus, John Pfitsch with his University of Kansas coaching background, was well-prepared to handle the head coaching job at Grinnell College. He had decided to leave Phog Allen's program to test his own mettle as a head coach. Pfitsch left KU with a Master's Degree and spent two years at Midland College in Nebraska as head coach in four sports - football, basketball, boxing, and track - as well as head of the physical education department. He went from Midland College to Grinnell in 1948.

Grinnell vs. Beloit

In the 1949-50 season, John Pfitsch's second year at Grinnell, I attended one of the now-forgotten, great basketball contests at Grinnell College in 1950. I was there in the front row at Darby Gym and have never seen a more competitive game. Beloit College, coached by Dolph Stanley, was the Grinnell opponent. The Grinnell Pioneers had long since abandoned Missouri Valley Conference play and had gravitated to the Midwest Conference, a group of private, liberal arts colleges with academics as their first priority. Beloit College fit into the Midwest Conference in terms of enrollment and educational philosophy, but was considered an outlaw of sorts because of the school's ambitious coach and powerful basketball program.

At Beloit College, Coach Stanley's basketball team was clearly at another level during its first stint in the Midwest Conference and during his tenure recorded victories over Division I opponents including DePaul, Loyola, Marquette, and Louisville. Beloit actually participated in the National Invitational Tournament(NIT) at Madison Square Garden in 1951 - the smallest school in that tournament's history. At the time, the NIT was on a par with the National Collegiate Athletic Association (NCAA) in regard to prestige in American college basketball. In contrast, the home team Grinnell College Pioneers had a pretty good small college basketball program with no ambitions beyond competitiveness within the Midwest Conference.

Thus, it was on that clear, cold winter evening in January of 1950 that Grinnell was severely over-matched and appeared to be preparing to be run off the court by Beloit. Grinnell Coach John Pfitsch - employing the Kansas A.P. offense and the stratified man-to-man defense with zone principles - relied on a balanced attack featuring 6'4 post-player David Dunlap. Beloit countered with Ron Bontemps, the aforementioned 1952 U.S. Olympic team star, and Johnny Orr, transfer from the University of Illinois, who later gained coaching fame at the University of Michigan and at Iowa State University.

I can recall that the Beloit team huddled arrogantly at its foul line at time-outs early in the game in lieu of conferring with its coach at the bench. However, as the game progressed and Grinnell remained more than competitive, that changed. In the final minutes, Dolph Stanley was doing everything possible to hang on to what at the start of the evening seemed to be an easy victory.

The two teams fought hard and traded baskets and the lead all night long. Bob Bigelow, Grinnell's muscular 6'3 off-guard, put the clamps on Bontemps the second half and held the Beloit star to only four points. Grinnell fell behind mid-way through the second half, but rallied to close the gap in the last six minutes of the game with a full-court press used to combat stalling tactics employed by Coach Stanley. Beloit finally won, 77-75. *The Cyclone*, the college yearbook, reported that it was a "moral victory" for the Pioneers. Those counted, of course, in the Grinnell philosophy. Grinnellian Dave Dunlap outscored Olympian Ron Bontemps, 21-20.

I rehashed this game with Johnny Orr in his office at Iowa State in 1981, and he remembered vividly the Grinnell game and also recalled the name of a player from another era - Calvin Bruton. Orr remembered Bruton and his match-up with Michigan All-American Ricky Green. Bruton outscored Green, 15-10, and also outplayed him on this occasion. Orr was referring to his 1976 Michigan team's NCAA Regional tournament one-point win (74-73) over Wichita State which featured Bruton and 6'10 Bob "Mo" Elmore. Michigan advanced that year to the NCAA Finals before losing to a great Indiana team, 86-68. That year was golden for Coach Bobby Knight and the Hoosiers, who rolled to an undefeated season with 32 consecutive victories led by National Player of the Year Scott May. Indiana's 1976 NCAA Title could be remembered by many, but the Grinnell-Beloit game, virtually forgotten, I recalled as a little-known classic in U.S. college basketball history.

Another brief anecdote on Dolph Stanley - I played a year of AAU basketball in 1959-60 with a team sponsored by Sanitary Farm Dairy of Cedar Rapids with Bill Seaberg, the former Iowa Fabulous Five guard, the player-coach. We played forty games competing in the Iowa AAU League, also matching up with college freshman teams around the state. We lost only once the entire season and that was in the finals of the Iowa State AAU Tourney. The winner was to represent Iowa in the National AAU at Denver, but two former small-college stars, Dick Wright of Loras and Dick Keel of Coe, were the best players of the day and led their team to victory over Sanitary Dairy with University of Iowa players Bill Seaburg, George Seaberg, Nolden Gentry, Dick Ritter, and Frank Mundt in the line-up.

One of our key players was Jerry Leggett, who was a great point guard for Dolph Stanley in the late 1950s after Beloit had been bounced out of the Midwest Conference in the wake of winning 40 consecutive conference games. Leggett, a heady competitor, later became a successful high school coach at Quincy, Illinois. Leggett said that Coach Stanley had purchased a new set of home uniforms in the 1957 season. The Beloit team wore those uniforms for the first time and lost the home opener. Leggett said that Dolph came in the Beloit dressing room right after the losing effort and ordered, "Let'em lay." And Leggett said that those beautiful, new, gold uniforms were never seen again.

A Tough Decision: Drake or Cornell

Grinnell College was a positive influence on my own basketball development, and I was a first-team all-state player in high school. In the Grinnell spirit and tradition, I was interested in academics as well as athletics. As a high school senior, I was recruited by several mid-Division I schools and was offered a scholarship by Drake Coach John Benington. I started my freshman year at Drake, but lacked the maturity to stay with the task. Leaving Drake was traumatic, and it was a situation which impacted my life for years. Yet my decision to quit Drake was the best that I could do under the circumstances. I needed a strong, authoritative voice in my life at the time - someone whom I respected to sit me down and firmly reinforce the importance of staying the course on personal decisions.

In retrospect, I was stuck in some personal conflicts and could also have used some ongoing psychological counseling to grow and get through this phase. However, I felt strong guilt about quitting Drake and that made an indelible impression on my life. The positive side of my own loss of self-respect - which turned to self-loathing - was that I have been able to help some other players at similar junctures facing problems in their lives.

My high school coach, Paul Maaske, had been named head coach at Cornell College after my senior year in high school. Maaske had lived only a block from my family in Grinnell and his wife had kept in contact with my mother and dad after I had enrolled at Drake. Today the ethics of that situation would be controversial, but I was vulnerable. However, I am not blaming Maaske nor any one else. I eventually gave in and ended up at Cornell College, known as a college division team or Division II NCAA in those days. Maaske actually came to the Drake campus one Saturday evening, picked me up at the dorm in a Cornell College station wagon, and drove me back to my home in Grinnell that night. I enrolled at Cornell College on the following Monday. I graduated from Cornell in 1962.

Although I probably would have logged playing time at Drake, I never found out for sure. Leaving Drake left a strong imprint in my unconscious that I had backed down from a challenge and that I had been irresponsible in doing so. The whole matter of choosing a college had been traumatic because of my immaturity and lack of direction. Neither of my parents had gone to college and I really had too much incidental advice from friends with no reliable voice of experience, which I desperately needed. I had originally decided to go to Grinnell College and there had been a story in the local paper about this decision. This was obviously a confusing process for me and one that was to influence the course of my life in some strange ways. I carried this emotional baggage, which became insidious, for the next twenty-five years until I finally was forced to face it and deal with it.

Ron Altenberg

At Cornell College, I did have the unique experience of playing one year of basketball with a world-class athlete and a great college basketball player. Ron Altenberg, my roommate, had been a star at any sport which he tried. He was a natural. In football - he was an All-State halfback at Marion High School in Iowa and had attended the University of New Mexico on a football scholarship. His blinding speed, once clocked at 9.5, took him to a third-place finish in the university-college open 100-yard-dash at the Drake Relays, and his great hands made him a threat every time he lined up on the football field.

But Altenberg was a small town guy who got homesick, left the big-time football at New Mexico and returned to Iowa and Cornell College - only seven miles from his hometown of Marion. Also, his first love in sports was basketball, and in 1960 he led tiny Cornell to the Final Four of the

College Division NCAA Championships at Evansville, Indiana. En route, Altenberg, with his 28-point-per-game average and his incredible athleticism, engineered the upset of the number-one-rated college division team in the country - Prairie View A&M and 6'9 future NBA All-Star Zelmo Beaty. (I played the 1958-59 season with Ron Altenberg. I was, however, not a member of the 1960 Cornell team, as I had dropped out of school for a year.)

In pre-season practice games against the University of Iowa, Ron Altenberg outran, outjumped, and outscored the Big Ten guards in Iowa City. When he finished his college degree, he was invited to play in an exhibition game for my old AAU team, Sanitary Farm Dairy, against the famed Phillips Oilers of the National Industrial Basketball League (NIBL). At the time, the Oilers and other top NIBL teams paid their players about the same as the NBA teams and they attracted the pro level of talent. In typical Altenberg style, he stole the show by scoring 32 points on his grooved, long-range jumper. It would have been 45 points with the NBA distance three-point line rule. The Oilers couldn't stop his rocket drives which always ended with his hand near the top of the square above the basket.

Also in typical Ron Altenberg style, the Oilers signed him to a contract right after that exhibition game in Fort Dodge, Iowa. Ron and his wife, Francis - a Marion girl - then moved to Bartelsville, Oklahoma, where player-coach Gary Thompson capitalized on Altenberg's astonishing athletic ability. Thompson had been an All-America selection at Iowa State University and a U.S. representative on the 1959 Pan-American Gold-Medal team before establishing himself as a star and player-coach with the Oilers.

The Roland Rocket

I saw Gary Thompson play several games as the legendary "Roland Rocket" at tiny Roland High School and as a great college guard at Iowa State. As a college player, Thompson was strong and had outstanding spring in his legs. He could create his own shot because of his quickness, jumping ability, and superb release. Also, he had an accurate long-range 1990s jump shot, unusual in the 1950s. In fact, Thompson's game, body, and athleticism were of the 1990s. Gary Thompson was a combination guard, as he played both the point and the shooting guard. Since the Rocket was such a great perimeter shooter and scorer, teammate Lyle Frahm, also a talented player and exceptional athlete, played many minutes at point guard to free-up Thompson to use his scoring ability. He led the Iowa State Cyclones to a huge upset, 39-37, over Wilt Chamberlain and the Kansas Jayhawks at the ISU Armory in January of 1957.

The Roland Rocket was a first-team all-conference selection in the Big Seven Conference (with Oklahoma State added in 1958 to form the Big

Eight) in 1956 and 1957; he was named to the All-American team in 1957; and he was a Gold-Medal winner with the U.S. National Team in the 1959 Pan-American Games in Chicago. An unfortunate injury kept him out of the 1960 Rome Olympics. Thompson's game and playing style would have allowed him to earn those same playing distinctions forty years later - he was that good, his game was that advanced, and he was that competitive.

I spoke with Gary Thompson, a successful Phillips Petroleum Company distributor, at his Ames office in 1997. Outside of wearing glasses, he looked about the same - as solid and compact as in his playing days. In fact, when I shook hands with him, I could still see much of the Roland, Iowa, high school athlete - as if he were climbing off of a tractor on the family farm to talk with a visitor from the city. I was particularly interested in his impressions of Ron Altenberg. Thompson said that he had never seen a player run like Altenberg "eating up the floor with huge strides." Modern players who NBA scouts say run the floor well were for the most part not in Ron Altenberg's league in that department. I felt that both the 5'10 Gary Thompson and Ron Altenberg had the talent and the game to have been NBA players in the 1990s. Altenberg was just six-feet tall, weighed 165 pounds, but had amazing legs that took him places very fast and very high. He was one in ten million. I doubt seriously if Ron Altenberg ever played against anyone at any level who was more athletically gifted than himself. Like his game, his life went fast also. He died at age 50 of cancer.

Zelmo

After Ron Altenberg had graduated from Cornell, the highlight of my college basketball experience was making the 1961 all-tournament team in the NCAA Regional Tournament along with Zelmo Beaty, the future NBA All-Star from Prairie View A&M in Texas. Zelmo and his unbelievably talented teammates flew with the Cornell team from Omaha up to Brookings, South Dakota, with South Dakota State University as the tourney site. I can recall the Prairie View players coming into the plane with their heads down and making a direct route to the back seats. They were sleek, trim athletes with their heads shaved ala the 90s and each neatly dressed in a suit, white shirt, and tie. They were an impressive group of athletes - on and off the basketball court.

On arrival the Prairie View coach, Leroy Moore, had some complaints about the team's hotel assignment in Brookings. He felt that they were getting second-class treatment. His team was rated number one in the nation in College Division and they were favorites in the NCAA Regional Tournament. They played Wisconsin-Whitewater in the opening game and Zelmo Beaty eliminated an opponent with an aggressive elbow less than two minutes into the game. (Zelmo as an NBA rookie did the same thing to Bill Bradley - then a high school player - in a summer league game in St. Louis, according to Bradley in his book, *Life On The Run.*) However, Prairie View lost in the final to host team South Dakota State in home cooking at its best, or worst.

I averaged 21.3 points per game for the season with most of my scoring done from the deep perimeter. In reality, with today's three-point rule, it would have been 27 or 28 per game. I liked the sound of the story on the tourney in the Brookings paper - "Dave Adkins of Cornell 'rained in' 56 points in the two games and was a unanimous all-tourney selection along with Zelmo Beaty of Prairie View." (After all these years gone by, I still liked it.)

I can recall two events on the flight back from Brookings to Omaha. The Prairie View coach, Leroy Moore, told our coach, Paul Maaske, that his school would no longer compete in the NCAA Tournament and would opt to go to the National Association of Intercollegiate Athletics (NAIA) Tournament. Prairie View did just that and won the NAIA the next year in 1961-62 with a 27-3 season's record. The other event was that I suffered the after-effects of a post-tourney celebration and got very sick on the flight. I ignored it at the time, but it was an ominous sign of developing personal problems.

Sharm Scheuerman

A sidelight to my days at Cornell was becoming acquainted with and befriending Sharm Scheuerman, the head coach at the University of Iowa from 1959-1964. I met Sharm when Cornell scrimmaged Iowa in the pre-season. He was originally from Rock Island, Illinois, and was a three-year starter on Iowa's great teams of the late 1950s. Sharm was the point guard on the Iowa team which made two-consecutive Final Four appearances in the 1954-55 and the 1955-56 seasons. The Hawkeyes played Bill Russell and the San Francisco Dons in the 1956 NCAA Finals at Northwestern University. Iowa jumped out to an 11-2 lead to start the championship game, but then Russell and reality took over as the Dons held Iowa to 32% shooting en route to an 83-71 victory. Russell scored 26 for the winners and Sharm Scheuerman from his point-guard position had 11 for Iowa.

After completing his eligibility, Sharm was the Iowa freshman coach under head man Bucky O'Connor. Bucky was a popular and successful coach for the Hawkeyes but was tragically killed in a freakish one-car accident on a beautiful spring afternoon in April 1958 while driving from Iowa City for a banquet speech in nearby Waterloo. I remember hearing the newscast regarding Bucky's death as I stood at the front desk of the dorm at Cornell picking up my mail on that day.

Sharm confirmed to me, "I was only 24 when I got the Iowa head job, a year younger than Bobby Knight when he started with Indiana." A few weeks after O'Connor's death, Scheuerman became the youngest head coach in Big Ten Conference history and the fourth youngest in NCAA Division I records according to various sources. Only Phog Allen (age 22) at Kansas, Branch McCracken (age 22) at Ball State, and Stan Morrisson (23) at Pacific were younger. Scheuerman at 24 and Bob Knight (25) at Army were fourth and fifth respectively on the youngest coach list.

Sharm recruited and coached Don Nelson, the ex-Celtic and NBA coach-administrator, the same Don Nelson who took an unprecedented action by announcing in 1997 - three years in advance - that his son, Don, would become head coach of the Dallas Mavericks in the year 2000. That is, if the NBA still existed, if Dallas still had a team, and if Don Sr. still had clout there. Three years can be two lifetimes in the NBA.

Don Nelson was a great college low-post player. Although only about 6'6, he was very strong, had great hands, and had the talent and instincts to score in traffic against bigger opponents. He put together three extremely productive years as a Hawkeye - 15.8ppg-10.0rpg (1960), 23.7ppg-10.8rpg (1961), and 23.8ppg-11.9rpg (1963). I only saw Nelson struggle one time as a Hawkeye - against Paul Silas of Creighton. I wrote Don Nelson a letter in 1988 and asked him to drop a line to Cameron Dickinson, who was having major personal problems at Southeastern C. C. in Nebraska. Nelson, who had other things that year to do as head coach of the Golden State Warriors, responded immediately and sent a positive message to Dickinson.

Also, Coach Sharm Scheuerman recruited the incredible Connie Hawkins who came to Iowa and never did play because of confusion and controversy around his alleged involvement with gamblers. He was later cleared of these charges. With no college playing experience, Hawkins led the American Basketball Association in scoring 26.8 points per game in 70 games in 1967-68 and later became an NBA legend with the Phoenix Suns. Freshmen were not eligible at Iowa; however, Connie used to put on a ball-handling and dunking exhibition just prior to the tip-off in varsity games. He would wrap-up his show by casually floating in and dunking a ball with each hand.

It was a different world in college recruiting in those days in the late fifties. Iowa would not have had a chance to sign Hawkins in the maze of college basketball in the 1990s. Connie would have gone to the NBA directly out of high school or would have played one season with a Big East Conference team before turning pro. Iowa's recruitment of Hawkins was so innocent that it would seem implausible today. Sharm Scheuerman said that Arlo Wilson, an advertising executive in New York City and brother of Iowa sports information director Eric Wilson, had contacted Iowa about Bill Burwell, a senior-post player at Boys' High School in Brooklyn. When Iowa visited a Boys' High practice session, Coach Mickey Fisher informed Sharm

Scheuerman that Burwell was definitely going to Illinois; however, junior Connie Hawkins was another great prospect on that same team. Iowa talked with Hawkins and Sharm felt that the early contact, which was unusual in those days, had given the Hawkeyes an inside track.

However, Hawkins went to the University of Colorado in the summer after his senior year in high school, but returned to New York before the end of the summer session. Connie's brother, Fred, called Sharm and asked if Iowa would still take Connie, who later traveled from New York to Iowa City by bus to enroll in the fall of 1961. Hawkins stayed in school for about eight months and then left Iowa in 1962 amidst rumors of affiliation with Jack Molinas, former NBA player banned from that league for life for gambling on professional games. Hawkins was eventually cleared of charges, but it was a costly experience to "The Hawk" as he was also banned from the NBA. In time the ban was lifted and he was finally allowed to sign with the Phoenix Suns at age 27 in 1969. However, from the time he left Iowa in 1962 until signing a $20,000 per year ABA contract for the 1967-68 and 1968-69 seasons, he played sporadically - in the short-lived ABL and later with the Globe-Trotters - and made little money. Fortunately Connie Hawkins did put together seven successful NBA seasons after the gambling controversy was settled in averaging 16.5 points over a 499 NBA game span. After his retirement as a player, he was hired by the Suns as the club's director of community relations in Phoenix.

Connie Hawkins' only college coach, Sharm Scheuerman, was involved in a player personnel position with Athletes in Action, and I entrusted C.J. Bruton to him to play AIA's 1997 college tour. In a unique moment at Carver Hawkeye Arena before the Iowa-Athletes in Action game in Iowa City in November 1998, Sharm Scheuerman was introduced to the Iowa fans. Just how many present that day knew the facts of his career and the full impact of his era on Iowa basketball history - including two consecutive Big Ten titles along with the the the two Final-Four appearances - I don't know. I made certain that C.J. Bruton knew all about Sharm's background prior to the AIA tour and told C.J. to listen when Sharm Scheuerman was talking about guard play. I was pleased that I myself was aware - it made the moment special as Iowa has been back to the Final Four only once, under Lute Olson in 1980, since the back-to-back appearances of The Fabulous Five (Sharm Scheuerman, Bill Seaberg, Bill Logan, Carl Cain, and Bill Schoof) in the fifties. I still asked Scheuerman questions about Connie Hawkins and implied that Sharm was reborn in AIA program to atone for tactics used in Connie's recruitment. But, the truth was that Iowa and Sharm were in the clear and the gambling charges were also later disproved. Sharm maintained that the only thing that Iowa did for Connie was to buy him a bus ticket from New York to Iowa City. I believed it - it was a different world then.

If Iowa's recruiting plan had succeeded, Hawkins and Don Nelson, who was a great college post player, would have been on the same Iowa team. But it was not to be and tragically the Iowa point guard in that era, Bobby Washington - after he had completed his eligibility at Iowa - shot and killed an Iowa City bartender and served a prison term at the Fort Madison, Iowa, penitentiary until his release and apparent rehabilitation.

In spite of all the off-court confusion with Hawkins and Washington, Sharm held Iowa together and finished his five-year stint with a respectable 72-69 record and a nationally ranked team to his credit. His 1960-61 team got off to a 12-1 start but lost four starters - Ron Zagar, Dave Maher, Tom Harris, and Frank Allen - at semester because of academic problems. With only one starter in tact - Don Nelson - I remembered when Scheuerman took a makeshift team to Indiana and upset the Hoosiers, 74-67. Joel Novak, who became a district court judge in Des Moines, took over the point-guard position after the eligibility debacle. That Iowa team finished 18-6 overall and 10-4 for second place in the Big Ten, including a 61-60 loss to conference champion and NCAA Finalist, Ohio State. Ralph Miller succeeded Scheuerman at Iowa. Dick Schultz, long-time NCAA exec, worked for both Sharm and Miller as an assistant coach. Schultz then replaced the highly successful Miller (95-51) as Iowa's head coach in 1971 and had a 41-55 record over his three-year tenure.

Sharm was still the head man at Iowa when I graduated from Cornell in 1962, and I learned much basketball from him while attending Iowa practices. I coached the next five years in Iowa high schools - at West Liberty and Prairie City - and I gained some valuable experience in coaching and in small town living. I actually recalled those days from 1962-67 as more troubling than productive with some hints, which I was ignoring or denying, that in spite of some limited personal achievement my "social drinking" was becoming a not-so-subtle, disturbing area of concern to me.

Iowa High School Coaching Jobs

I was fired from my first job at West Liberty in 1963 after one year because of my general lack of respect for the unwritten laws of being a teacher and coach in a small town - by drinking in the local tavern and coming to work hungover - and because of my involvement in an alcohol-related automobile accident. The Rock Island freight train won in no contest over me and my 1961 bright red Ford sedan. Jack Register, the railroad detective, told me that I had hit the train forty-one feet back on the engine and that I had luckily turned into the train rather than turning on impact in the direction that the train was traveling. The luck of my quick turn into the engine allowed the car to bounce back and clear the tracks rather than being sucked under the train. Immediately after the impact of the collision, steel to steel, I can recall sitting in the red Ford about four feet from the tracks - barely in the clear - with scores of lumbering freight cars rattling past in front of me. In races with freight trains, ties go to the train. The car looked like an accordion from the front bumper to the windshield. I was, obviously, extremely fortunate to survive the collision.

Out of control in regard to my drinking at the time, I had no business in a teaching job. The West Liberty school district agreed with me. I thought back to the episode after the NCAA Tournament in Brookings, South Dakota, when I became sick on the airplane after an evening of beer drinking celebration. The events at West Liberty were the first time that I had become blatantly aware of a developing pattern of personal problems related to alcohol. It was disturbing.

News and rumors of the accident spread rapidly in the small town. It didn't take long for the school officials to hear the stories. I can vividly recall the West Liberty school superintendent summoning me one evening to discuss my escalating problems. As we sat down to talk I was in a fog emotionally and in deep denial, but I heard him say something about "firing the basketball coach." I looked around the office and there were just the two of us - one superintendent and me - and I was the only basketball coach present.

I tried to smooth it over with a profane response and the superintendent raised the stakes and refused to recommend me for other jobs. I decided to see if he meant it. I made a hasty trip to California, interviewed for a high school coaching job in Garden Grove, California, and found that the telephone service back to West Liberty was in good working order, and in the superintendent, I was dealing with a man of his word. He advised the California school to look elsewhere for a coach - good professional advice at the time.

I could not escape the reality of my irresponsible behavior and problematic situation. After several months of futile job applications, I finally decided to schedule a meeting in West Liberty to address my career problems. On a cold, gray Sunday afternoon in January of 1964, I drove back to West Liberty, Iowa, and met with the same superintendent who had fired me and in the same office where the firing had taken place about seven months prior. I made amends for my past behavior and convinced him that I was sincere in my efforts to get back into teaching and coaching.

Today I understand that the man had done me a favor by forcing me to be accountable and to look hard at my own behavior. Even though I was sincere about my desire to work again in a school system, I had not yet admitted the source of my troubles, which would eventually become evident, nor was I able at the time to accept complete responsibility for my past actions. I was in denial of reality, still blaming circumstances and other people. In my mind the problems were a result of a series of bad breaks and misunderstandings which showed that I had not come to terms with the truth and was still denying my self-destructive behavior. But that Sunday meeting put the West Liberty situation behind me professionally for the most part, yet I was to meet this same school superintendent again under some very strange circumstances - eighteen years later.

After the meeting, the superintendent agreed to give me a more positive recommendation, and I was able to re-group and was given a second chance. I then accepted a job in Prairie City, Iowa, an agricultural community with a population of under 1,000. Prairie City - it was really not a city, but more of a retirement village for area farmers located 20 miles from Des Moines. Doug Bauer, a Prairie Citian turned professional writer, noted in his book, *Prairie City, Iowa: Three Seasons at Home*, that one could travel 150 miles from there in any direction and find only more of Iowa. I enjoyed my time there and made some friends in the town, but I knew my stay would be short-lived. My home town of Grinnell with a population of about 9,000 was, in comparison, a metropolis.

I coached both boys' and girls' varsity high school basketball at Prairie City and the events of the four years there were again bittersweet experiences. I knew at the time that I could do more with my life, yet I was producing modestly in a class B high school of 150 students. My mind-set at the time was much like players today who talk of NBA, yet have not distinguished themselves anywhere - in college or overseas. They dream of millions yet do not have or do not use their talent to bank thousands, or anything in many cases. I was the same way at the time; I dreamed of bigger and better things but struggled daily to deliver on the simplest of professional tasks. However, I was buoyed by the words of Forddy Anderson at Walt Shublom's Clinic of Champions in Kansas City in 1965.

Anderson had been fired at Michigan State and had just become the first-ever basketball coach at John F. Kennedy College in Wahoo, Nebraska - now defunct. Anderson stuck his head into a room of young high school coaches and made an indelible impression on me by stating bluntly, "You are right where you are supposed to be. Each of you has the job that you deserve. If you want to move up, prove it by your work and your behavior." Ouch. In other words, Coach Anderson was saying to me - grow up, work hard, be responsible, quit complaining. The poignant advice which that day cut through my own blind-spots also applied to many other coaches and players who had not developed the honesty to face their own shortcomings and do something about them.

I looked at my job much differently from that point on. I still heeded Forddy Anderson's words and a similar message from John Wooden - "Don't tell me, show me." I have repeated these words to myself when my own motivation was low. In my business today, if I slowed down, the player placement process would grind to a halt. I preferred the consistent business activity, but I knew that as Forddy Anderson revealed to me years before I had to generate it through my own efforts and energy.

After the five years in the Iowa public schools, I decided in 1968 that I was going to do something different with my life. The superintendent of schools at Prairie City at the time, William H. Logan, had previously taught on a U.S. military base in Korea. He suggested that I investigate this type of job. I applied with the U.S. Department of Defense Schools and was subsequently offered a teaching and coaching job on Okinawa. I had also considered going into the U.S. Air Force and spent a day taking tests at the USAF Recruiting Office in Des Moines. I was 29 and past draft age, but I seriously considered the Air Force alternative. I passed the test and became eligible for OTS, but I eventually accepted the DOD teaching job.

Before leaving for Okinawa, I drove my 1962 Corvair on a three-week solo trip in the summer of 1968 from Grinnell to Michigan through Canada to New York and then down the eastern seaboard to Tallahassee. Driving across the Florida Panhandle into Mississippi, Alabama, and Georgia to New Orleans, I began to experience a sense of freedom and became more sold on my decision to take the job on Okinawa. The Corvair trip was a warm-up and confirmation of better days ahead.

I had clearly made some mistakes but also I had done much better work at Prairie City in my second job than I had at West Liberty. Yet, I still did not get the full message and had not given up on the idea that my problems with alcohol would pass. I was misled by another insidious symptom of alcoholism - its cyclical nature. The craving was a matter of body chemistry in the alcoholic and can disappear after a period of abstinence, yet could - and usually did - return unexpectedly.

I was feeling pretty good but not aware that I was still in a dangerous state of denial as I packed my bags and boarded a plane from Travis Air Force Base in California to my new job with the U.S. Department of Defense Schools on Okinawa. The largest island in the Ryuku group surrounded by the waters of the Pacific Ocean on the east and the East China Sea on the west, Okinawa is about 80 miles in length and 15 miles across at its widest point. I felt reborn when I stepped off the plane at Kadena Air Force Base at 4:00 a.m. in the pitch dark, heavy night air laced with the strong musty smell of the tropics and ocean salt water. I was glad to be there.

□ *3* □

OKINAWA, MIDDLE TENNESSEE AND OFF TO MOZAMBIQUE

On the island of Okinawa, I was working in a larger high school, about 1,500 students, as a physical education teacher, basketball coach, and athletic director. The students were dependents of American military and civilian personnel based on Okinawa primarily to sustain the war effort in Viet Nam. Although the work itself was challenging, one of the benefits to the job was the opportunity to spend time in Hong Kong, Taipei, Tokyo, and Bangkok. The routine became to travel to Taipei over Thanksgiving, Hong Kong and Bangkok during Christmas vacation, and Japan at spring break. Okinawa was a great experience and opened my eyes to the world out there. I also was becoming aware that I, like Jim McGregor before me, wanted more space and a less conventional structure in which to work.

Hong Kong and Arthur Ashe

Although my focus had always been on basketball, my interest was piqued by news of an international tennis tournament in Hong Kong during the Christmas holidays in 1969. I had read in the English language newspaper of the tournament and saw both Arthur Ashe and Stan Smith in the lobby of the Hong Kong Hilton where I was staying at the 1969 rate of U.S. $18.00 per night. I talked briefly with Stan Smith, who was soon to be inducted into the U.S. Army, and learned that the U.S. Davis Cup Team players - Ashe, Smith, Bob Lutz, and Donald Dell - were playing an exhibition sponsored by the Hong Kong Lawn Tennis Association. Later that day, I took a cab to the Cragengower Cricket Club, the site of the tennis matches. I arrived there about noon - well in advance of the first match scheduled for 1:30 p.m. - on a warm, sunny December Hong Kong day.

The atmosphere was serene, the court grasses manicured, and the sporting environment polite and pleasant. There were two rows of folding chairs around the court and a small section of bleachers on each side with a modest crowd present creating a personal, if not intimate, sporting atmosphere. The match between the Americans and Hong Kong's first Davis Cup team was an exhibition and the setting - the city, the club, the participants - were far more interesting to me than the results, which I have since forgotten.

At the time of the Hong Kong tourney, Arthur Ashe was in his athletic prime at age 26. I felt that I knew Ashe even though I did not meet him, nor speak with him. I could not put down *Levels of the Game*, a book in which John McPhee described a 1968 Forest Hills singles match between Ashe and Clark Graebner. The author McPhee used the net on the tennis court as a dividing line to contrast the lives of the two players - their backgrounds, playing styles, and race. Knowledge of the material in the book was the source of my insight into Ashe's presence and personality. I knew that he was born in Richmond, Virginia, was the son of a police officer, and that a Ronald Charity had helped Arthur Ashe learn to play tennis. Charity had taught himself the game and Ashe became a protege.

Also I knew that Dr. Walter Johnson, a Lynchburg physician, had provided Ashe with training opportunities at a time when very few blacks played the game and available facilities were segregated and scarce. Seeing Arthur Ashe gave me some inspiration in that I felt I had in some small way experienced excellence, though vicariously, in watching him play at close range. I carefully observed his playing style for over three hours and made notes on his mild, yet aloof, polite demeanor and his athletic explosiveness. He was so smooth, quick, and precise - along with possessing deceptive power.

Kubasaki High School

Overall, I had a positive experience on Okinawa with no major problems - a criteria which I used at the time to judge my life, given the reality of past experiences. I enjoyed teaching physical education, coaching the Kubasaki High School Dragons basketball team, and doing some work in sports administration as the high school athletic director. My high school team competed in a company level army league, since there were no other American high schools on the island. The highlight of the season was the Far East Invitational Tournament held in Yakota, Japan, in the spring of 1969. Fifteen American high schools from Japan and one from Okinawa, my team, competed in a single elimination tournament. Kubasaki was defeated in the semi-finals, and it was apparent that the lack of high school competition during the regular season had hurt our chances.

However, I learned an important coaching lesson going into the semi-finals of that tournament. I tried to put in a special combination defense in one practice session before the big game. The principle was sound - match up with Johnson High School in its 3-2 offensive set out of a 3-2 zone defense, but switch to aggressive, straight man-to-man defense on the point guard's initial pass to the right wing and stay in the 3-2 zone on that possession if the first entry pass from the point went to the left wing. It was a simple enough concept - but the players were young, did not have time to digest it, and had not practiced it. Dumb move by the coach.

Our opponents scored a couple of wide open lay-ups against this defense, which set the tone for the game. In the half-court set my players became confused because of our defensive plan. It was a tough loss, but a great lesson and one which saved me other unnecessary problems in future years. Also, another factor in our inability to win that tournament was that we played more like a college team and had adapted to the physical play in the army league. Our playing style did not translate well against high school teams and the tighter refereeing.

I was ready to return to the U.S. after two years on Okinawa (called "The Rock" by GIs). I contacted Jack Gardner, the "gray fox" of University of Utah basketball, about a graduate assistantship. I got Gardner's telephone number from directory assistance in Salt Lake City and called him at his home on a Saturday afternoon to discuss my interest in Utah. How innocent and straight forward that all seemed - I doubt that any Division I head coach of note has his home number listed these days, especially at a school like Utah. Coach Gardner was enthusiastic about my coming to Utah but did not have a grad assistant's spot available. Gardner suggested that I come to Utah at my own expense and work my way into an assistantship in the second semester. I considered the Utah situation, but explored other possibilities and eventually headed to Middle Tennessee State University on a fellowship in a new doctoral program, which paid all tuition and housing.

Middle Tennessee State

When I arrived in Murfreesboro, Tennessee, I was in good form knowing that I had made some definite personal and professional progress in the Okinawa job. I was in great physical condition as I had started running on a daily basis in Prairie City and had increased the intensity of my workouts on the outstanding military facilities on Okinawa. I had quit drinking entirely for nine months while writing a master's thesis during the 1969-70 school year, along with carrying the responsibilities of the teaching-coaching job.

However, this change of social habit had been precipitated by the advice of a Japanese M.D. at the army hospital. He looked at my blood tests on a routine physical and asked, "How much do you drink?" Before I could create a satis-factory excuse, he said, "You stop immediately or you will have serious prob-lems." I again became aware of the cyclical nature of alcoholism - although I did not classify myself as alcoholic at that time. The craving, however subtle, ebbed and flowed and it was possible to stop drinking for extended periods without really establishing a base for long-term recovery. I was not using alco-hol, but also I was not addressing my past problems which were associated with my drinking. I learned that I was able to stop drinking for extended peri-ods until life, as I perceived it, became untenable and then I would drink again.

I was able to stop using alcohol for nine months with little difficulty, but it was to be the lull before the storm. Going to the bars and clubs had been the center of my social activities at every juncture of my adult life, and I therefore searched the military base libraries to find information which proved that I could return to regular, controlled use of alcohol some day. I did, of course, finally find this medical opinion - probably presented by an alky doctor. I was confident that with a little time to rest off the grog, I would be able to return to being a typical social drinker and go on to bigger and better things in the world. And then like "old Uncle Charlie," I would at about age 50 get religion, put a plug in the jug and hum hymns at work. But I queried - if my drinking wasn't an issue, why was I preoccupied with it?

In 1970 Middle Tennessee State University was known as a regional university with an enrollment of about 9,000. The school was in a growth cycle and had gone through several stages of development from its origins as a teachers college. Located in Murfreesboro, about 40 miles south of Nashville, the Blue Raiders played Division I college basketball. Upon arrival at Middle Tennessee State University - just back from Okinawa - I immediately went to the gym and met Jimmy Earle, the head coach. The timing was good for me as his top assistant, Don Newman, had just taken a job in business in Chattanooga and his other full-time man, Butch Clifton, had gone to Georgia Tech as an assistant coach. That left the head man Earle with only two graduate assistants - Bob Blankenship, who had been a successful high school coach in Atlanta, and Ray Rich, who had limited coaching experience at the time.

After talking with Jimmy Earle, it was decided that I would also work as a grad assistant with the Blue Raider team, a member of the Western Kentucky-dominated Ohio Valley Conference. Jimmy Earle had taken over the reins from Ken Trickey, who had gone to Oral Roberts as head coach and then to Iowa State. Trickey's teams at Middle were run-and-gun types. The Blue Raiders were led by Willie Brown, a scoring machine, who was later tragically killed in New Haven while working as a cop, and Booker Brown, a seven-footer from Kansas City. Book, or "Senator" as Coach Earle called him, was among the nation's leading rebounders averaging 16.5 rebounds per game under Trickey in the 1968-69 season. There were some rumors among former Middle Tennessee players that possibly creative statistical techniques had boosted the Senator to higher office on the national rebound stat lists, but who knows.

Maury John

Trickey, of course, had a great run (118-23) at Oral Roberts and later a very bad run at Iowa State. He was as poor a fit at Iowa State University as his predecessor, Maury John, whose outstanding career was cut short by cancer, had been good. Coach John took over the Cyclones in 1971 after a

5-21 season under the retiring Glen Anderson. I can recall catching a ride with Maury John from a Cornell College basketball camp in Mount Vernon to Iowa City in July of 1973. He was in the process of turning around the Iowa State program with 12-14 and 16-10 records in the books in his first two seasons at the Big Eight school.

At that time Coach John seemed to be in good health and was very upbeat regarding his Cyclone basketball team. He was in particularly good spirits that beautiful July day because he had just played well in a round of golf with some other coaches in Mount Vernon. However, he was diagnosed with cancer of the esophagus only five months later in December and died in 1974 - after the basketball season. Ken Trickey was hired in 1974 and in his two seasons rode the Cyclone program to successive 10-16 and 3-24 records. He left Ames with twelve games remaining in the 1974-75 season with assistant coaches Gus Guydon and Tommy Smith taking charge for the balance of the season.

Jim McDaniels at Western Kentucky

While at Middle Tennessee I can recall a road trip to Austin Peay University in Clarksville, Tennessee, in February 1971. After the game Jim Freeman, the Sports Information Director at Middle, said that a wire service had just reported that Jim McDaniels, the Western Kentucky seven-footer, had made a verbal agreement to play with the Carolina Cougars of the old ABA. This was, of course, against NCAA rules. McDaniels denied this report. But after Western had qualified for and participated in the Final Four that year, the NCAA investigated and stripped the Hilltoppers of their trophy and their check, and their place in the record book was vacated.

Villanova, another Final Four qualifier in 1971, met a similar fate as its star player Howard Porter had also committed to a pro team during the college season. Jim McDaniels, Big Mac, averaged 26.0 points per game in his rookie year in the American Basketball Association in 1971-72 with the Carolina Cougars, but was never a force in the NBA. I spoke with Phil Johnson, the Kansas City Kings' coach, at a summer instructional camp at Rockhurst College just before the ABA dispersal draft. In 1976 four ABA teams were absorbed by NBA clubs. ABA players were made available to NBA teams in a dispersal draft. I asked Coach Johnson about Jim McDaniels as a possible dispersal draft choice for Kansas City. Johnson replied, "Who wants to pick up a seven-foot shooting guard?" He was referring to Mac's preference for the perimeter shot. The Kings selected Ron Boone in the draft from the Spirits of St. Louis and Phil Johnson's statement made sense at the time - over 20 years ago. But today the 6'8 and 6'9 guys who can shoot the perimeter shot and run the court made the seven-foot guard concept a reality with the 6'6 and 6'7 two-guard already commonplace in both college and pro competition.

Stories around the Ohio Valley Conference reported that a six-foot version of Jim McDaniels had presented his credentials to take the ACT at a regional testing site at Cumberland Community College in Tennessee prior to Big Mac's admission to Western Kentucky. A score of 15 was the magic number in those days on OVC eligibility - and as the legend went "little Jim" scored high enough for "big Jim" to make some waves at Western and on the national basketball scene. It was probably just a story - apparently never investigated, but believed and repeated by many fans in the South. That was a solid Western Kentucky team coached by Johnny Oldham - Mac, Clarence Glover, Jim Rose, Rex Bailey, and Brad Dunn were the nucleus - probably the best team in Ohio Valley Conference history.

Tennessee State vs. Kentucky State

One of my more memorable basketball experiences in Tennessee occurred outside of the Middle Tennessee basketball program. I had an important exam in psychology scheduled and could not justify taking the time to go on a three-day, two-game road trip with the team. However, after the test, I walked over to the gym and Mason Bonner, a freshman guard from Birmingham, was working out. He yelled to me and asked if I was interested in driving to Nashville that evening to see the Tennessee State-Kentucky State game. I agreed to go, picked Mason Bonner up later that day, and drove the 45 minutes from Murfreesboro to Nashville's Jefferson Street area and the Tennessee State University campus, the site of the basketball arena called Kean's Little Garden.

Kentucky State and Tennessee State, both predominantly black schools, were rated number one and number two respectively in NCAA-Division II competition at the time in January, 1971. The Thorobreds of KSU featured the scoring machine Travis Grant, and a seven-foot freshman post player, Elmore Smith. The home team TSU Tigers had power forward Leonard "Truck" Robinson, post player Lloyd Neal, guard Ted "Hound" McClain, and shooter supreme Ron Dorsey. Each of these players went on to professional careers in the National Basketball Association with the exception of Dorsey who played only with the Carolina Cougars in the American Basketball Association.

The talent level on the two teams was obviously superb and was matched only, and at times exceeded by, the enthusiasm of the fans and the intense atmosphere in the jam-packed gym. Students pounding out primitive sounds on large bass drums set the pace and provided the lead for the wild, deafening cheers for the home team. The game setting at Kean's Little Garden in Nashville that evening was comparable to the scenes, which I was to later experience, at the Sporting Pavilion in Lourenço Marques, Mozambique, and the frantic crowd there packed 10,000 strong into the 7,000 seat arena to witness those Academica-Sporting playoff matches.

The game itself that evening in Nashville and the level of competition matched the general atmosphere and enthusiasm of the victory-hungry Tennessee State team and followers. Each and every point was cheered and the game could not have been more closely contested. With four seconds remaining in the game and Tennessee State leading by one point, 71-70, Kentucky State coach Lucius Mitchell called a time-out with his team in possession of the ball. It was obvious that the Thorobreds would try to free Travis "Machine Gun" Grant for one of his patented, automatic, baseline jump shots.

Playing the ball in from the foul-line extended in their own front court, the Kentucky State guard faked a pass to the other guard and then drilled a pass directly to Grant who had come across the foul lane after having received a screen from Elmore Smith. Thus, Grant caught the ball on the baseline - about 15 feet from the basket. It looked like money in the bank for Kentucky State. However, these three events seemed to occur nearly simultaneously with only a possible split second lapsed between them as 1) Kentucky State fed the ball to Grant 2) Grant caught the ball cleanly in favorable scoring position, and 3) what seemed like a thousand Tennessee State fans poured onto the floor with the ten players and two referees engulfed in the mass of humanity.

It was the last that I saw of the ball. I did not see Grant get his shot off and recall only the final horn sounding with the two referees doing their best to reach the safety of their dressing rooms. KSU Coach Mitchell could not believe what had happened and stood by his team's bench bewildered at the mass confusion on the floor, never receiving an adequate explanation of the course of events. Tennessee State won by a single point, 71-70, in what I consider another one of the great and forgotten games in U.S. college basketball history. What a wild game with a bizarre finish.

Johnny Neumann

Also, while at Middle Tennessee, I took advantage of opportunities to see some Southeastern Conference games at Vanderbilt University in Nashville. Johnny Neumann, who was a sophomore at the University of Mississippi, scored an immaculate 40 points against Vanderbilt in 1971 in one of the greatest individual performances that I had ever seen. *Los Angeles Times'* columnist Jim Murray once described the style of Pete Maravich, who holds the NCAA record of 44.2 points per game over his career at Louisiana State University, as a race against the clock.

In contrast, I saw discipline and patience in Neumann with no apparent urgency to score at any cost in his game that night. The Vanderbilt defense put extra pressure on Neumann through double-teams early in the game, but he kept his poise and was never in a hurry to get his shots. He was a skilled 6'6 forward who scored from all angles that evening, led the nation in scoring at a 40.1 clip in 1970-71, and then turned pro, jumping to the American Basketball Association after that season.

Neumann sustained his professional career in the U.S. for eight years including two seasons in the NBA and then played in Europe. In 1994, I received a telephone call from Johnny Neumann, who had played and coached in Europe, inquiring about a coaching job in the Australian NBL - as I recall, he was in Cyprus at the time. All of the NBL coaching jobs were filled, and I did not hear back from him.

Red Murrell

Johnny Neumann's performance at Vanderbilt reminded me of a similar individual scoring show by Red Murrell at Drake in 1958. I was a freshman at Cornell College and still curious about the Drake basketball program, as I had been a scholarship player there briefly. I drove to the old Drake Fieldhouse to see the Drake-Houston game on February 3, 1958. Murrell, a strongly built 6'4, was scorer supreme. According to Paul Morrison, long-standing sports information director at Drake, Murrell was born February 23, 1933, which made him a 25-year-old senior in 1958. However, some would dispute that age, even though Murrell himself provided the information on a conference registration form. He was back to school after time in the army as well as a stint at Mobery Junior College and Chillicothe Business College. Morrison said that Chillicothe was not included in the MVC background information. For the record, Red was 25. He was built like a tight end, a good jumper, and he had an unorthodox, but very effective jump shot, releasing the ball far behind his head and always falling away from the basket. It was impossible to block the shot as the defender had to fight through Murrell's extended legs in order to get at his muscular upper body.

Red Murrell could be classified as a "gunner" without a conscience and was always on a mission to score regardless of the number of shots required or the percentage. On this occasion, the University of Houston was primed to stop Murrell and on Drake's first two offensive possessions the defense triple-teamed Red. Totally out of character, Murrell rifled two great passes from the top of the foul circle, as he appeared to be preparing for his patented fall-away jumper, to a wide open Bob Tealer to stymie the Houston defensive plan.

On these plays, Red worked into shooting position and it looked as if he - to no one's surprise - was about to take on the Houston triple team with 25-foot, fade-away jump shots. But at the last split second, he drilled the pass on a line to Tealer for Drake lay-ups. The two passes set the tone of the game and Murrell scored 51 points that evening in leading Drake to victory. Johnny

Neumann, Red Murrell, and Pete Maravich were three of a kind - big time scorers, gunners, capable of consistent performances and whose style of play can seldom be seen in college basketball today.

Academics

Overall, I had an excellent experience at Middle Tennessee - both in the doctoral program and in basketball, and I enjoyed the Nashville area. I had been an "A" student in high school and a disinterested one in college, but was reminded of my academic inclinations when I wrote the master's thesis on Okinawa in which I conducted physical fitness testing over an eight-week period with students at Kubasaki Middle School. I did all of the statistical work in the thesis - without a computer or even a calculator - by hand using arithmetic formulas to establish means, medians, t-scores, and levels of statistical confidence.

I had made periodic calls to Dr. Christine Foster, my advisor at Northeast Missouri State University, via the short-wave Mars Radio System. I stood in line on Sunday mornings at the radio station on Kadena Air Base to make the overseas call for updates and advice on the ongoing thesis. My effort and achievement in completing the Master's thesis on Okinawa had given me the confidence and motivation to do the doctoral study, which provided a much needed intellectual awakening for me.

In a psychology class at Middle Tennessee, I was influenced by George Kelly's theory of personal constructs and his discussion of the *elaborative choice* - which I interpreted as meaning that, essentially, each of us chooses his/her own life's path and each choice sets in motion a series of events which can be difficult to rescind. I was reassured by Kelly's work and liked what was unfolding in my own life, both academically and in basketball. Also, I was guided somewhat by novelist James Norman Hall's philosophy of risk-taking, as it related to personal growth in subjecting yourself to the destructive, as discussed in his work, *In Search for Paradise*. I had been following Hall's philosophy - though unknowingly - by taking risks in moving around in the world to accept jobs, which yielded little security, but did boost self-esteem and enhance my life experience.

James Norman Hall's comments were of particular interest to me because he was born and raised in Colfax, Iowa, only six miles from Prairie City. He used to catch a late evening freight train through Colfax and ride the 30 miles to Grinnell where he would jump off the train and roam the Grinnell College campus. He would then catch an early morning, west-bound freight back to Colfax for a day of high school classes. Hall was a highly-decorated pilot in World War I and gained fame as co-author with Charles B. Nordhoff of *Mutiny on the Bounty*.

I had a clear head most of the time in Tennessee and was occupied with school and basketball; therefore I kept my drinking under control for the most part. I was at my best in making the Dean's List with a 4.0 point grade average in the first semester of the doctoral study. Although my longer term objective was to become a small college basketball coach and athletic director, I was more interested in my minor field of psychology and took all the graduate courses available dealing with human behavior - motivation, personality, and pathology. An awareness that I had wasted academic opportunities as an undergraduate made me want to apply myself in the doctoral program. In particular, I had had a good start in learning French at Cornell and still maintained interest in the serious study of a second language. I was thinking that the opportunity to learn a foreign language would be an attraction in considering my next job. Further, even memories of high school Latin study retained some intrigue for me.

While my academic work was going well, the basketball team at Middle Tennessee that year was so-so (11-15), led by Kenny Riley from Pearl High School in Nashville. Riley was built like an NFL tight-end and took pleasure in blatantly goal-tending a perimeter shot or two by opponents each and every game to the consternation of Coach Jimmy Earle.

A goal-tend by Riley, especially in tight games on the road, was certain to upset the coach and send him into a rage. But the bench players took great pleasure in the play and the reaction of the coach - sort of a passive retaliation for not recognizing their talents. The ode of the average player worldwide and his rallying call from the usual position on the bench has always been, "I am better than the guys playing ahead of me." That blind spot in self-appraisal kept them going and sustained their hopes. For example, at the Los Angeles summer league - one might hear an unknown free agent player (or his agent on his behalf) state, "I scored 38 on Cedric Caballos" or on some other unsuspecting NBA guaranteed salary player who stopped by the Long Beach Pyramid to break a sweat and find some action after the game. This constant challenge on the basketball court can be compared to the frontier days in the Wild West with the quickest gun always being tested and the reporting of the event afterward usually exaggerated and inaccurate.

Edd Bowers: The Mozambique Decision

While at Middle Tennessee in the 1970-71 academic year, I decided to take a drive down to Florida over the spring break and en route stopped in Atlanta. I made my way to Underground Atlanta, the night spot scene in the city, and as I wandered through that area, to my surprise I heard my name called. I looked up and saw an old friend, Edd Bowers - the football coach at Grinnell College. Edd told me that he had just returned from a sabbatical in Mozambique (Africa) and said that the Academica Club of Lourenço Marques, the capital city, was looking for a full-time basketball coach. As we discussed the situation, I became interested in the job and Edd agreed to contact Academica and to recommend me.

There were no fax transmissions or e-mail, and international telephone service seemed out of the question in 1971, so Edd Bowers wrote a letter on my behalf. I also sent an air-mail inquiry from Murfreesboro, Tennessee, to Lourenço Marques, Mozambique, in care of Teotonio Lima, the Portuguese administrator at the Academica Club in Lourenço Marques; and about six weeks later I received a reply by mail with a contract offer. However, in the meantime, I had re-applied with the Department of Defense Overseas Schools and received an offer to return to Okinawa. The job back on Okinawa presented the most short-term security, as I had been there before, and also I would have been working in the American system of education. However, I was concerned that I would be making little progress in the repeating of a previous experience by going back to Okinawa and discussed my concern with Dr. West of the Middle Tennessee psychology department. He assured me that the experience would be different this time around even though the physical setting was the same.

I subsequently went to Arnold Air Station in Tullahoma, Tennessee, to take a pre-employment physical for Okinawa. I was examined by a young Air Force doctor who queried my plans. I told him that I had already spent two years on Okinawa, but that even though I had enjoyed the previous experience there I was still thinking about the Mozambique offer. Ironically, the doctor said that his parents had worked as missionaries in southern Africa and that he found that part of the world interesting. In addition to his medical training, the doc was a good enough salesman to pique my interest in Mozambique and after the physical I walked over to the personnel office at Arnold and withdrew from the Okinawa job. I was aware that I was taking a big risk in choosing to go to Mozambique and passing up the Department of Defense School situation, which offered more certainty. The liberal arts value system again proved to be a part of me - the two in the bush better than one in the bag - and the possibilities generated in taking the risk much more appealing than the certainty. I felt animated driving back to Middle Tennessee from the air base, knowing that I had made the right decision and definitely had an adventure in store in my new job in the Portuguese state of Mozambique.

□ *4* □

AFRICA, A WAR, AND A U.S. OLYMPIC DEFEAT

Before leaving for Africa, I drove to Iowa after completing the summer school session at Middle Tennessee. I spent a few days in Grinnell to see old friends and to reassure my mother of my decision to go to Africa. My father had passed away three years before and I was feeling some guilt because of my mother and about leaving the country again. I was also aware that several of my high school classmates were still living in Iowa and doing well - one had developed a successful stadium-seating company and another was moving up the ladder in management with Merrill-Lynch. Their successes made me think, but I sensed - not without some doubt - that I needed to take a different path in my life even though at that time I had no particular long-term objective. However, I also vaguely felt that these choices were right for me. I looked at the job in Mozambique as a personal challenge and as an experiment - even having recurrent thoughts that life, itself, was an experiment.

It was September 1971 and I was off to Africa to coach the Academica Club basketball team in Mozambique's capital city of Lourenço Marques. I spent a week in New York trying to get my visa for Mozambique without success and then another ten days in Lisbon, Portugal, doing the same. I was somewhat overwhelmed with the rapid daily changes in my life accompanied by strong interplay of emotions - somewhere between fear and pure excitement. Overall, I remained positive with growing interest in the challenges ahead in the Portuguese world even though at the time I was confused and frustrated with the language. I was finally issued a visa in Lisbon and flew the 13 hours from Lisbon to Johannesburg, South Africa, en route to Lourenço Marques. I stayed a few days in Joburg, as the South African city was called by ex-patriot Americans and Europeans, getting my bearings and enjoying one of the great cities of the world - a Sydney or Toronto on the African continent. But unfortunately - unlike Sydney and Toronto - Johannesburg was a city with insidious political problems.

While staying at the Victoria Hotel, a three-star accommodation and popular among traveling Portuguese, I was intrigued by the calm, controlled, manageable pace of Johannesburg. I thought how lucky I was to be there and how interesting my life was becoming. Every now and then my positive feelings were replaced by fear and uncertainty, as I did not know a single person in that part of the world. However, as I boarded the plane at the Jan Smuts Airport in Johannesburg, I felt confident knowing that I had accepted this challenge and relieved that it was finally time to take the one-hour flight to Lourenço Marques and get to work. I arrived in Mozambique at 11:00 p.m., but there was no one from the club to meet me at the airport. I took the fifteen-minute cab ride to the downtown area and checked into the *Turismo Hotel*. I slept well and woke up the next morning in a new world - and wondering what I was doing there.

I can recall standing in front of the Turismo Hotel on the morning of Sept. 16, 1971, my first day in Lourenço Marques. I experienced a 10-15 second panic attack - momentarily doubting my decision to come to Mozambique. I felt very alone at the time. But somehow the feeling passed, not to reappear until several years later - in a psych ward, a more appropriate place in which to deal with emotional flare-ups. I looked around the busy street that day in Lourenço Marques and as I took a deep breath, I felt a little more stable and was somewhat reassured that I was exactly in the right place for this time in my life. It was too late to turn back, and after all, it was only an experiment.

The Academica Job

At noon that day two student officials from Academica picked me up and took me to temporary quarters at *Casa Universitaria* - a dormitory at the University of Lourenço Marques. I was introduced to Professor Teotonio Lima, the head administrator at Academica. He asked me two questions in our first meeting - what did I want to be called - coach, or professor, or Mr. or what? I said that I would take coach. He also asked what would I need in the way of equipment to work. I replied that I needed an office, a typewriter, and a telephone. They seemed to be logical requests. He fixed me up with the office immediately. I had plenty of room to work - in fact I was the only one occupying an office on the third floor of the building, and from the looks of the place the only one who had occupied it in the past ten years. But it was okay, as I liked the privacy and the quiet.

However, the typewriter became a small drama. A few weeks later Teotonio delivered a World War II model of a manual typewriter which must have weighed twenty pounds with a carriage at least thirty-inches long - and Portuguese characters, of course. I was intending to do some fitness testing with university students in the writing of my doctoral dissertation, a comparative study of fitness levels among college students in different parts of the world. However, I was to be stymied by a quixotic university administration which gave me green light, red light, no light, etc. for two years. But I did eventually finish the testing at the University of LM and also did complete my degree in 1975. With the office and typewriter intact, I had my work space. I never did get a telephone.

My main job at Academica was trying to figure out a way to beat Sporting, the best team in Portugal (and Africa) at the time. Teams in Mozambique were allowed to use one foreign player and the Academica club had already selected the American player prior to my being hired. I had had plans to bring a former Middle Tennessee player, but Richard Almstedt of Monmouth College in Illinois was already on the Academica payroll. He was a 6'9 post player who had played the prior year in Luanda, Angola. He made the most of his limited athletic tools - he always trained hard and proved to be a good scorer and rebounder.

Also, the club asked me to practice with the team and dress for games as a back-up if necessary. In checking the local league rules, Academica officials found that teams could use only one foreigner on the floor at a time, but could have two dressed for games. Thus, if Richard Almstedt needed a rest, I could insert myself in the line-up, and at 32 I was still in reasonable basketball shape physically, but far past any real passion to play. However, I agreed and filled in when Almstedt was in foul trouble. I was able to end the playing commitment as we neared the playoffs - two of our players in the army returned to Lourenço Marques. But the task to consistently whip Sporting required a near miracle, which I was not able to produce, either playing or coaching.

We traveled to the Mozambique city of Beira for week-end exhibition games in preparation for the regular season. After the last game on Saturday evening, we all set our alarms for 4 a.m. to take the six-hour drive in a van to the Gorongosa Game Park, considered one of Africa's very best game reserves. Fifteen people, including players, club officials, and the American coach were jammed into one, open-top van. It was a hot, miserable trek but worth it all. Totally non-commercial, Gorongosa was wild and primitive consisting of a vast area of bush, swamps, pools, and open plains. Lion, elephant, zebra, impala, wildebeest, sable, gazelle, and water buffalo called the Gorongosa reserve home.

Our creative Portuguese van driver managed to actually corner a huge lion among the ruins of a deserted rest camp. He drove to within five-yards of the animal which responded with a deafening roar. The lion was obviously upset and our open-air van created the perfect opportunity for its next meal - jungle curb service. It was actually the beast's choice - our party would have been totally defenseless. Finally, the driver relented and vacated the potential disaster. The deserted camp site was called *Casa dos Leões*, the House of Lions, as the King of Beasts favored the shade and cover of the dilapidated buildings.

I learned that the old camp had been constructed in 1940, but was abandoned because of a malaria epidemic in the area. Upon our return to Lourenço Marques, I told the story of the cornered lion to a Rhodesian big-game hunter at the *Por do Sol* bar at the Hotel Cardosa. He shook his head in disgust and related his own experience in wounding a water buffalo in the Mozambique bush. Two years later the Rhodesian was hunting in the exact area where he had previously grazed the animal and the same water buffalo was waiting for revenge. The white hunter nearly lost his life in the animal's charge, but managed to somehow ward off the vendetta and retreat to safety.

In addition to the league opponents, we had an occasional exhibition game with personnel off U.S. naval ships deployed in the Indian Ocean and docked in Lourenço Marques over a week-end. In one such exhibition which was played on a Sunday morning, the American officers invited the Academica team back to the ship for lunch after the game as a public relations exercise. I rode back to the American ship with a couple of officers for a tour and then lunch.

The game had been more social than competitive, but it was nice to interact with some other Americans. As we were eating lunch, I saw a sailor who looked familiar. I asked one of the officers if there was anyone on board with the surname of Beck. He replied that there was a guy from Iowa by that name. I had gone to high school with Don Beck, and as I recall, he had joined the navy at age 17 or 18. I don't think he really remembered me, as he was a couple of years older, and about 15 years had passed since I had last seen him. It was strange to see someone from Grinnell, Iowa, in Lourenço Marques, Mozambique. As a further goodwill gesture, the officers arranged to have four cases of American beer loaded into the trunk of my car. I appreciated the gesture, but decided to use the six-packs as gifts to Portuguese friends around the hotel and at the university.

There were eight teams in the Lourenço Marques league, and it seemed as if we never quit playing - tournament after tournament, cup after cup, and finally the highlight was the playoffs with the winner of Lourenço Marques playing the winner from Beira, the other major city in Mozambique. The eventual champion then competed for the National Championship of Portugal which included a four-team field. Two teams represented the host city - which rotated annually between the champion from Portugal, Angola, and Mozambique. The eventual National Champion then represented Portugal in the European Cup competition. In 1972 Football Club of Porto won the title in Portugal; the city of Porto was therefore the site of the Nationals. But that really didn't matter to me or Academica because we got whacked by Sporting via assistance from a referee named Freitas Branco and never got out of the Lourenço Marques playoffs that year.

Academica vs. Sporting and Freitas Branco

The Finals of the Lourenço Marques Provincial Championship in 1972 came down to Sporting versus Academica. The games were played at the Sporting Club Pavilion, a concrete and fiber-glass structure which seated 7,000 but accommodated 10,000 in big games. There was a standing-room section around the top of the arena and in one section, two tickets were sold for each seat thus stretching the capacity of the building. The Sporting facility had been constructed in 1960 as an open-air arena, but a few years later the club had added a fiber-glass roof with a six-foot open space around the entire arena for "air-conditioning." The floor was a rough wood, but with decent footing. It was maintained at a minimal standard - never very clean with no chemical seal as was commonly used in the U.S. The locker rooms were small with only one shower head available and there was always a pungent mildew smell in the dressing room area. The 7,000 seats in the building were concrete slabs. The facility was no frills, spartan, but the best in Mozambique, and functional.

Sporting was clearly the premier club in Lourenço Marques with aggressive leadership, which had put in place an effective junior development program along with their dominant senior men's team known as the Lions. Having recruited some very good talent, Sporting was led by Mario Albuquerque, a 6'5 swing player, and Nelson Serra, a 6'2 combination point and shooting guard. They had depth and shooters. The club also arranged to have Jan Hoeks, a 7'2 South African, in Lourenço Marques during the week of the tournament.

Sporting put Hoeks and his family up at the Cardosa Hotel as the South Africans enjoyed a basketball working holiday at the expense of the creative Sporting Club administration. Hoeks lacked finesse but compensated in head-locks and sharp elbows. His size combined with exceptional aggressiveness for a big guy made him a factor. Bespectacled with a full head of blonde hair, he was not well-coordinated, but was a physical threat on the court swinging his long arms and throwing elbows - tactics learned in schoolboy rugby in his native South Africa.

The big man was a good athlete and was very strong with a sinewy body. If he had come through the U.S. system at the time, Hoeks had the physical tools and the competitiveness to become an NBA player. Off the court he was an intelligent, personable man, but as a basketball player he was very raw with no real previous coaching and therefore little skill.

There were four teams participating in a double, round-robin tournament format. Sporting beat us (Academica) by two in the first round with neither team losing in succeeding rounds, and we squared off for the final and deciding game with a huge, volatile crowd present. The title was to be decided by the cumulative margin of victory in the head-to-head meetings of the two teams - since Sporting was undefeated and Academica had only the two-point loss to Sporting in the tourney. Thus we, Academica, needed a three-point victory in the second game to win the Provincial title and advance to the Nationals in Luanda, Angola.

The Sporting boosters, known as *Macaricos* (translated "blow torches" and implying their extreme emotional pitch and volatility), were everywhere. The atmosphere was raucous. Every point was celebrated and cheered - it was a truly great match-up and the two bitter rivals came down to the final seconds of the big game tied.

Quen Gui, a Portuguese of Chinese descent and Academica's best perimeter shooter, nailed a 23 footer with the clock running down and put us up 76-74. Everyone in the place was on his or her feet including the players on both benches. However, Freitas Branco, an army sergeant and one of the referees, took exception to the Academica bench players - who while cheering Gui's field goal were apparently on or over the sideline. The referee waddled with delight from the other side of the court, making a beeline to our bench and defiantly signaling technical foul every step of the way. Branco, a pal of Sporting's president - Moura - known as the club *padrinho* (godfather), definitely took over the game. He exhibited pure glee in calling the technical for an obscure infraction, if there had been an infraction, which indicated to me that this referee had an agenda.

To make that clear - we scored, went up by two, and then Sporting brought the ball in and looked up court with about four seconds remaining. Referee Branco, on the far side of the court, gave an enthusiastic technical to the Academica bench after our last basket and the clock stopped with two seconds remaining. Sporting called a time-out and Nelson Serra was selected to shoot the two technical-foul shots. But, of course, a huge factor in all of this was that the first game of the tournament between these two teams had been won by Sporting by two points. Thus, if Nelson hit both foul shots, the game would go into overtime and Academica would have had another chance to "win it all" with a three-point victory margin.

But Nelson made the first foul shot and intentionally missed the second which gave Academica a one-point victory in the game, but in considering both games (as was the system), Sporting's two-point win in game one sealed the title for them. The word pandemonium was an understatement to describe the mass of humanity that erupted onto the court after Nelson's second *lance livre* (foul shot) caromed off the side of the basket.

Comment: the next day I happened to be at the crowded Lourenço Marques airport and I saw Freitas, "The Referee," and Moura, the energetic president of Sporting, chatting and wearing huge smiles. I have had a recurring dream over the past 25 years of Moura handing Freitas a plain manila envelope stuffed with 1,000 escuda bills. They were probably just old friends, and I would have witnessed the same camaraderie between these two if Academic had won. Like hell. We wuz robbed - Mozambique style.

Lisbon - 1997

I took a sentimental journey to Lisbon, Portugal, in January of 1997 - twenty-five years after the controversial Sporting-Academica game - to look up former Lourenço Marques basketball players and coaches. I called Mario Albuquerque and he arranged a lunch with Rui Pinheiro and Luis Pena, a former Sporting coach. Mario told me that his son, *Joao*, would pick me up at the hotel and bring me to a meeting point in a downtown Lisbon office building. That day I was informed by the hotel desk clerk that there was someone in the lobby to see me.

I had remembered Joao Albuquerque as a blonde, five-year-old who often fell asleep with his head against the window of the *machibombos*, a word of African derivation referring to the city buses in Lourenço Marques. He was now twenty-eight and a great looking Portuguese man. Joao had heard many stories about his dad and Sporting, and seemed fascinated that I myself was one of the characters of the past coming to life. When we arrived at the office building, I recognized everyone immediately - Mario, Rui, Luis Pena, and Quim Neves, the former Academica center. It was an interesting and emotional conversation and I had not seen any of these people since Mozambique - exactly twenty-five years prior. And "Freitas Branco" (the referee) were the first words spoken by Quim Neves - before hello - after all of those years.

All-Star Tour

My first year in Lourenço Marques ended on a low emotional note as a result of that loss to Sporting. It was hard to forget as *Sportinguistas*, the rabid Sporting Club supporters around Lourenço Marques, took great pleasure in taunting me as I walked down the city's streets. However, eventually the gloom lifted as the Portuguese Basketball Federation put together some games at the end of the 1972 season which gave birth to the All-Star Tour, a team comprised of the American players who had played that year for Portuguese clubs in Portugal, Angola, and Mozambique. I coached the team on a ten-game tour which started in Lourenço Marques and finished in Luanda, Angola.

This was a nice group of people and talented basketball players. They blended well into a solid unit considering the short preparation time. Jim and Kit Jones, 6'8 twins from Beloit College, had been playing with clubs in Lisbon and they were a formidable post-wing combination. Kit was a strong, skilled high post player and Jim was a rangy wing player who could shoot the perimeter shot, which had attracted Dallas of the American Basketball Association to draft him. Robin Clark was a 6'2 guard from Coe College and a solid, all-around backcourt player. Rob had a great sense of humor and was at a stage in his life where basketball and laughs were his top priorities, as he was postponing a career in financial management in which he eventually excelled. Richard Almstedt was the 6'9 post player who had played for me that year at Academica and he gave us more size and inside scoring. But our two best athletes were Mahlon Saunders of Decatur, Illinois, and the University of North Dakota, and Dale "Flash" Dover, a Harvard graduate and son of a New York City cab driver. The All-Stars were unique also in that several of these players had learned the Portuguese language. Kit Jones was fluent and Jim Jones, Dover, and Almstedt communicated in Portuguese without hesitation.

Mahlon was a strong, sleek 6'4 inside-out player while Dale Dover was a combo guard in a running back's body. In our initial team meeting, Dover, who had nearly single handedly taken his Porto team to the Portuguese title over Sporting of LM that year, was talking about "not having my burners on yet." I was concerned about the comment and also noticed a negative reaction to it from the other players. I met with Dale that evening in the Girassol Hotel and asked him to play team basketball during the tour and to kick on his passing burners. He agreed immediately and did an excellent job throughout the tour - he got his points but normally when others weren't open. A foreign language major at Harvard, Dale Dover was also a very gifted athlete. Although he did not shoot consistently well from the perimeter, he could get to the basket on anyone. After his basketball playing days, he became a foreign service officer and was in Sweden the last I heard.

The All-Star Tour gave me a personal lift from the camaraderie of the players and also enhanced my professional status, as the team was a big story in the Portuguese world. We played before packed arenas every game. Also, we put a good lick on Sporting, and then I switched benches and coached my Academica team against the All-Stars in a hotly contested one-point win to the Americans. I received another benefit from the All-Star portion of the tour in the city of Lourenço Marques - a Portuguese guy who owned a car dealership in the city asked me for an All-Star jersey for his son after the tour. I picked up one for him and in return got free service on my car for the next two years.

As we were preparing to leave Lourenço Marques and as the other six players checked in at the LM Airport for the flight to Beira to continue tour games, I was caught waiting for permission from Academica, my employer, to leave the city and participate further with the All-Stars. Finally, at the last possible minute an Academica Club student-director appeared and gave me the signal to proceed and board the plane with the team.

In the northern Mozambique city of Beira, the two games were routine victories by large margins. I was interviewed there by a journalist who published a full-page story about my year with Academica. In that interview I confirmed that I was more interested in working with mature players than developing high school age Portuguese players. This story was to have some impact on my next year's contract. Academica, my employer, didn't like the part of the story about my preference for coaching senior players, and not the juniors, but Sporting did.

After the Beira games, we again boarded Deta, the Mozambique national airline, and flew further north into the war zone to the city of Nampula for two games with Portuguese military teams. This was a village carved out of the jungle. There was a block-long main street which led to the military base and the gym, packed with 4,000 males on a night off from hunting Frelimos, the liberation group or terrorists - depending on which side you were on.

When our traveling party left the hotel to walk to the arena, we were joined and followed by at least 100 people of all ages who gazed with interest but said nothing as we strolled in a solemn, silent procession to the game. It was a haunting spectacle, but not nearly so haunting as the scene in the Portuguese officers' club with soldiers sitting at tables lighted by candles and composing letters to loved ones back home in their beloved Portugal. The morale was obviously low and the army's assignment most difficult - often called a war of attrition as Frelimo hacked away at the will of the Portuguese. The basketball game had been scheduled to entertain the troops and to provide some color in a otherwise gray routine.

Early in the evening and prior to our first game, I decided to take a walk around the town of Nampoula and ended up again at the officers' club. It was getting dark and I bypassed the club and innocently wandered deeper into the base facility itself. I approached a building protected by a high barbed wire fence and was stopped dead in my tracks as a guard stepped from the shadows and stuck a hostile rifle barrel in my ribs. After a very tense moment I was able to explain who I was and that we were playing at the base gym in about two hours time.

At first he was uncertain and not impressed, but I suggested that he be my special guest at the game. It worked out for both of us - I got back to the hotel alive and the guard proudly occupied a chair at the end of the All-Star bench at both of our games. I was relieved, as I could see the headlines in my hometown newspaper, *The Grinnell Herald Register* - "Former Local Basketball Player Shot as Spy in Africa." My new friend, *Jose* - the Portuguese soldier, also had a sense of humor. Immediately after the game and while I was talking to one of the opposing players, he came up behind me and stuck his index finger as if it were a gun into my ribs - again. Then he roared in maniacal laughter. As I said, our mission was to entertain the troops and this guy got his money's worth.

We won the first game easily - by 30 points, and right afterwards I was approached by Gui and Quim Neves, Academica players at the time in the army based in Nampoula. Both were scheduled to play in the next day's game. Gui said that their commanding officer had told him that if his team came closer to the All-Stars than the team which we had just played, he and Quim along with their teammates would get a weekend pass to Lourenço Marques. There was apparently competition between the respective commanding officers associated with the two teams which had been selected to play the All-Stars.

Since the NCAA had no jurisdiction in foreign countries (in those days), much less in the Mozambique jungle, I told Gui that I would poll our team and let him know. Our American players all liked Gui and respected Quim's abilities, so we cut a deal. The next night was the same procedure - the quiet parade to the gym, the packed house of lonely soldiers, and a 28-point win to the All-Stars with Gui's group the real winners translated to the weekend pass. In fact, I called a time-out with about five minutes remaining and reminded my players to keep it under 30 - the "magic" margin in order to earn the weekend pass. Gui nailed a jumper which left the score 130-102 with time running out. Both benches cheered and a section of the arena, apparently Gui and Quim's outfit, roared. It reminded me of an NBA game when the home team hits the free Big Mac shot.

And, of course, my pal, Jose, the rifle-toting guard from the previous night, was again in his reserved seat at the end of the bench. However, on this occasion, he required two extra seats for his *amigos*. I said, of course, "No problem." At mid-court after the game, once again he caught me with the finger in the ribs with full approval from his two friends as my hands went up in response - although by this time not really surprised.

The tour then proceeded to Luanda, Angola, for a final two games. The highlight of the Luanda stay was the excellent beach (*praia bonita*) and the attempt by the Luanda basketball directors to get our players drunk on a game-day tour of the *Cueca* Beer Brewery. At that time in my life, it was one of the few occasions that I said no to an offer of a cold beer. I really wanted the win first and a beer afterwards. Our team concurred and we got both in that preferred order.

The All-Star tour ended in Luanda and the players dispersed to Portugal and home to the U.S. I took an indirect route back to Lourenço Marques. I walked off the plane on a scheduled stop in Ian Smith's city of Salisbury, Rhodesia, and had a week's holiday in that beautiful setting. Since independence in 1979, the place has been renamed as Harare, Zimbabwe, and has become known for its continuing social and economic problems.

Eartha Kitt in Rhodesia

While in Salisbury, I read in the morning paper that Eartha Kitt was performing in the city that Saturday. I sensed the possibility of a unique evening and attended the performance at a movie theatre adapted to her live-stage performance. On the front page of the Salisbury newspaper that day there appeared a disturbing cartoon illustration. The cartoon portrayed a white man tuning in his TV set which showed an image of Kitt. The caption stated

"Picture's a little dark today." She evened the score that night with her opening number in which she all but seduced a white waiter-character in the scene.

It was a memorable, courageous performance in an unusual setting, with negotiated racially integrated seating in the theatre for this special appearance by Kitt. Also on that African tour, Eartha Kitt was arrested in the South African city of Bloemfontein, capital of the Orange Free State, for violating *apartheid laws* at a public park. After the week in Salisbury, I returned to Lourenço Marques. With the basketball season over I had an opportunity to enjoy the city and the beach, to study Portuguese, and also to take a trip and spend some time in the Republic of South Africa.

Back to Lourenço Marques

The sleepy seaport city of Lourenço Marques, since 1976 called *Maputo* after the revolution and under a Marxist government, was a pleasant mixture of European (Portuguese) and African culture during the sixties and early seventies. Located on the shores of the Indian Ocean, the city had an excellent climate, beaches, and numerous sidewalk cafes - *cafes ao ar livre*. Lourenço Marques was a holiday mecca for English-speaking South Africans and Rhodesians seeking a foreign adventure in Mozambique, a country with a different language and different social values. It was a common practice for the male visitors to do things that they could not do back in South Africa and Rhodesia - mix freely with people of other races and seek the companionship of the black African women working in the Lourenço Marques bar district.

The two major basketball clubs in this city of about 400,000 had established their downtown social headquarters using the cafes *Scala* and *Continental* as their meeting places. Located across the street from each other on the busy main street of Lourenço Marques, *Avenida da Republica*, the two popular cafes attracted supporters from Sporting and Desportivo. They gathered with other club mates to drink their espresso coffees, called *bicas*, and glare across the street at the rival club members. This was the tradition. However, at the time, Academica was actually Sporting's main rival. Desportivo was waiting for a resurgence through the return of its hero Frank Martinuque, an American scoring point guard from the University of Vermont who had given them hope in the previous year against the stronger Sporting team.

Desportivo's Phenotype Error

In the meantime while Desportivo was waiting and talking of Martinuque's return, the club was doing little else to rebuild its team. However, a well-meaning Desportivo fan tried. At one point in the 1972 season, this Desportivo booster had visited friends in the Chicago area and somehow had seen a local league game at the YMCA. He saw a prototype of Martinuque, 6'3 with blonde hair and square shoulders, playing in this local YMCA competition. He immediately assessed the player as another Martinuque and made hasty arrangements to bring the American to Lourenço Marques on the next plane in time to play against hated rival Sporting on the very next Saturday evening.

My notes from Doc Dolan's Sports Psych graduate class at Northeast Missouri State defined "phenotype error" as the assumption by a coach that a player of a particular stature or appearance would be the best player. In the fifties, the phenotype error was associated with white boys in thin, wiry bodies and crew-cut hair. Some of that physical description could play and others could not. In the nineties, the phenotype definition applied to African-Americans who looked like the basketball players on television, but did not necessarily have the ability to go with the image. Unfortunately, the error not only influenced perception of the player by others but the player's perception of himself, as evidenced by the hundreds of "never weres" who show up to participate in CBA and IBA free agent camps each year.

To continue, Pete, the YMCA player who definitely fit the category of a phenotype error, was the unsuspecting American recruited right out of the Chicago YMCA by the Portuguese club supporter to resurrect the Desportivo team. The two of them - the recruiter and the phenom recruit - took the 30-hour trip to Lourenço Marques from Chicago arriving the day before the Saturday game. They were greeted at the airport by scores of enthusiastic Desportivo fans as well as official club board members, who whisked Pete away from the airport by limousine to an undisclosed hotel - a secret hiding place - until game time. But the local press was hot on the story.

The Saturday *DIARIO* had three-inch headlines - "Ghost of Martinuque Returns to LM" and worse yet 10,000 bought tickets for the 7,000 seats at the *Pavilhao do Sporting* to see the second coming of Frank. Latent Desportivo fans - underground club alumni - came out of the woodwork to witness the resurrection of their beloved team. It was truly a huge throng that packed the arena that Saturday evening and poor Pete, at best an average ex-Division II guard, was suffering from jet lag, culture shock, and limited basketball talent. The confident pre-game Desportivo taunts for revenge over the recent Sporting dominance subsided rapidly as the beleaguered American player began and ended his Lourenço Marques basketball career with two paltry field goals in 40 agonizing minutes of play. He finally got into the scoring column with one minute remaining in the first half - as Sporting demolished the phenom himself and the Desportivo dream of rebirth.

I made it a point to find Pete after the game, but he was so overwhelmed that I doubt his subconscious has allowed him to recall any of the "Mozambique Experience" - it must have seemed like a bad dream. The problem was, of course, that Frank Martinuque was a solid, skilled, former Division I player from the University of Vermont, and Pete, who resembled Frank in appearance only, was a YMCA player. The same type of mistake can occur in different proportions in the first round of the NBA draft. Remember Bob Bigelow, a first-round pick from the University of Pennsylvania of the Kansas City Kings in the 1975 NBA draft? That was my point - no one else did either. For more information, contact Joe Axelson, the Kings' G.M. at the time.

The Polana Hotel

When I wasn't coaching or talking basketball, I spent considerable time in my room at the *Girassol Hotel*, and also at the swimming pool and bar at the *Cardoso Hotel* and the *Polana Hotel*. I lived in the *Girassol,* which meant sunflower in Portuguese, the better part of three years. I enjoyed traveling light during this part of my life and could carry all of my possessions in one suitcase. However, of the three hotels mentioned, the *Polana* was the most famous and had a fascinating history. It was named *Polana* in honor of the African chief whose *kraal* (village) was near the site of the hotel, which was opened in 1922. The Polana was built on top of a cliff and overlooked the Indian Ocean far below. It was truly picturesque and smacked of colonialism at its best - luxury and superb service.

I heard stories from the Polana manager, Victor Bodis, and the bartender at the Polanabar, Cesario de Freitas, about the hotel's World War II history. I learned that Allied and Axis agents and officers, who were staying at the hotel on leave from the war, would be in the dining room or in the bar at the same time without incident. History showed that important military information changed hands at the famous hotel in Mozambique, which remained neutral during the war. The Polana was a favorite of British author Graham Greene, who used the hotel as a setting for his book, *The Human Factor.*

A short distance from the Polana, a colorful ex-patriot Italian opened a popular restaurant called *La Bussola* (the compass.) I heard rumors that Napoleon, the restaurant owner, had been incarcerated at some stage after the revolt of 1974 in a jail on Mozambique Island, once a major clearing house for the Portuguese slave trade. I knew Napoleon and always enjoyed stopping at La Bussola for some good Italian food and a drink on off-nights from basketball. He was a fiery, out-spoken character who never hesitated to assert his opinion. At that time with the war raging in the north of Mozambique, it was a good idea to limit public discussions of political issues. You could never be sure who was listening.

The Sporting Job and a Trip to South Africa

A month had passed since the controversial Sporting-Academica game with Sporting going on to lose eventually to Porto in the finals of the 1972 championship of Portugal in Europe. I had always respected the Sporting players, as I got to know them well in the frequent matchups between our two clubs. However, I felt that my job was to defeat them as often as possible and I never really thought I would ever coach the Sporting team.

I was planning another year with Academica, and I figured that the storm had passed and it was time to discuss the upcoming 1972-73 season. When I brought this up with Teotonio Lima, the Academica decision maker, he had other ideas regarding my future with his club. He didn't beat around the bush as I heard him say, "Coach, maybe you go home to the States now." Once again, as in a past life in West Liberty, Iowa, I looked around the room and I was the only coach present. But having anticipated this possibility and experienced professional rejection before, I immediately developed a back-up plan. I knew that I preferred to stay in Lourenço Marques for at least another year. I had befriended a *Sportinguista* and former player, *Bebe Carreira*, who became instrumental in my accepting a contract with Sporting, Academica's archrival. He was actually delighted that Academica had shown me the door.

Bebe was also helpful in my getting my final check from Academica. At the time I was paid U.S. $800 per month in local currency. That was a big salary in Lourenço Marques and went a long way in the economy. The paymaster at the university office was always livid on my payday, and made no effort to hide it. When I showed up each month to draw my hard earned escudas, he would go into a tirade when he saw me coming with my stamps in hand to stick to the paperwork to make it all Portuguese official. I sensed that he had no appreciation for the level of skill required to coach a basketball team. I think that I might have ruined that guy's life, at least for a year, by appearing at his office on a monthly basis to get paid.

But Bebe went with me to pick up the final check, as I was now "Sporting property." He finessed the receipt of the money while at the same time not only inserting the dagger but twisting it frequently in the dialogue with the paymaster. I was pleased to get paid without another scene, happy to have another year in LM, and content to have Mario Albuquerque and Nelson Serra on my side for a change. At that moment I knew that I had become a better coach and that my prowess and basketball reputation would be enhanced.

With the immediate future reassured by the Sporting contract and with two months remaining before the start of training for the 1972-73 season, I drove my 1966 English-built Vauxhall on a trip through the Republic of South Africa. Driving from Lourenco Marques to Nelspruit, South Africa, I then headed down the coast through Natal and the Transkei, the Independent Black Homeland located between the Kei and Mtamvuna Rivers on the Indian Ocean. The road to Umtata, the capital of the Transkei, was unpaved and a very rugged, dusty day's drive. I spent that night at Port St. John, an isolated coastal village tucked away on the east coast of South Africa, and then went on to Cape Town, with overnights in East London and Port Elizabeth.

The scenery was beautiful and varied, changing from the rugged mountains near Nelspruit to lush beaches of the Indian Ocean in the Natal province - and finally to the distinctive Table Mountain landmark of Cape Town. After spending three days there, I traveled through the *Karoo*, the dry steppe country of the Cape Province, and made my way north up through the Cape to Bloemfontein, the capital of the Orange Free State. From there I drove into the Transvaal and continued on to the sprawling metropolitan areas of Johannesburg and Pretoria.

While in Pretoria, the administrative capital of the Republic of South Africa, I decided to look up Bob McGovern, a friend and former U.S. Consulate officer from Lourenço Marques, then stationed in Pretoria. I stayed for about two months during the South African winter and enrolled for a Portuguese course at Leif College in Pretoria. The study was essentially a programmed tape course with an instructor available for prompting and assistance. However, it wasn't difficult to find Portuguese conversation in South Africa. In cafes, markets, barber shops - the Portuguese dominated these businesses - I was able to keep up on news in Lourenço Marques as even the *Diario* was available at some news sellers.

I spent a great deal of time in book stores, libraries, coffee shops, and bars on my stay in the Johannesburg and Pretoria region. Thomas Wolfe's *You Can't Go Home Again* was my constant companion and I read it with genuine interest. I began to sense, yet was not ready to accept, that "home" was more a matter of one's emotions and perceptions rather than being a particular physical location. The old cliche, "Home is where the heart is," seemed to explain it best. During that South African winter, Wolfe was good company, the Portuguese study always challenging, and the time away from basketball most welcome.

One day in mid-August, 1972, I was reading the Pretoria paper and noticed a three-line article with a small headline stating "American Coach Here." The coach, Taylor Hayes from William Penn College in Iowa, was in Pretoria and scheduled to do a couple of basketball clinics. I found Taylor through the South African Basketball Association and we agreed to work together in presenting clinics to students at the University of Pretoria and at a teachers' training college.

After we completed our work, I invited Coach Hayes to come to

Lourenço Marques, as I was to return there soon. I gave him careful instructions to bring without fail the Converse film of the 1972 NBA and NCAA title games. It was a great film which I wanted to share with my Portuguese colleagues. I made plans to show the film to all of the clubs in Lourenço Marques at a university auditorium. Coach Hayes showed up without the film and there we were with an auditorium full of basketball players, coaches, and officials waiting to see the great American game via film. I got through it, but did hear a few utterings of "*bastardo Americano*" - I think they meant me, but I didn't take it personally.

U.S.A. Loses to Russia, 51-50

The next day I had just dropped Taylor Hayes off at the airport and I was walking down Avenida da Republica for my morning bica coffee. I picked up a copy of *The Noticias*, the morning paper, and read an article which hit me like a bomb. The story was about the first loss in Olympic history by a U.S. basketball team, to Russia in a disputed, but recorded, 1972 Olympic title game. The United States coached by Hank Iba had been upset, 51-50, in the Munich Olympics.

The game report in the Portuguese paper said that the United States was leading the Russians, 50-49, with three seconds left in the game. Russia started to put the ball in play, but called a timeout with one second showing on the clock. After a protest, the three seconds showed again on the official time. The U.S then deflected an inbounds pass and time ran out. However, another protest ensued and again three seconds were put back on the clock as the Brazilian and Bulgarian referees agreed that the ball had not been put in play legally. (The interpretation and call by the referees was supported by Robert Jones, secretary-general of the International Amateur Basketball Federation.) Again - the third time - three seconds showed on the game clock, only this time Alexander Belov caught the floor length pass over Americans Kevin Joyce and James Forbes and scored the winning Russian basket. Final: Russia 51 U.S. 50.

This was the first loss by a United States team ever in Olympic competition - a 63-game winning streak dating back to 1936 had come to an inglorious end that day in Munich, West Germany. The Russians stole the game and a later report stated that someone else stole Coach Hank Iba's billfold from the U.S. bench. The appointment of Iba as the head coach of the U.S. team had been controversial. He was retired from a 41-year college coaching career and he posted only two-winning Big Eight Conference records in his final twelve years as Oklahoma State's coach. Critics felt that the U.S. team needed "new blood" in its head coaching choice.

Ominous, I thought. The American team got a bad deal. Nevertheless, how could they have lost? I never dreamed that eventually the U.S. would have to use NBA all-stars to win back the Olympic Gold. John Thompson and the 1988 debacle in Seoul underscored this reality - no gold, no silver, only bronze - and hastened the involvement of the NBA in the formerly amateur event. It was not fun being overseas when the Olympic loss occurred as talk ran rampant that the U.S. dynasty in international competition was starting to crack. Foreign clubs had second thoughts regarding the value of American coaches because of that one-point Olympic defeat. And wasn't it ironic with the inclusion of the NBA in the Olympics that today the term "amateur" has become a moot issue in the most international of all American games - basketball. Yet the NCAA continued to use naive reasoning to make decisions via obsolete rules on a world game - as if applying the traffic regulations of sleepy "downtown" Overland Park, Kansas, to the Sydney Harbour Bridge or to the German autobahn.

With the loss by the American team in the Munich Olympics now digested and my having been named the new coach of the Sporting Lions, I was carefully preparing for a rather difficult season. I knew that we would have little competition from the other seven clubs in Lourenço Marques, but still we faced an eight-month league season. I was thinking "beat Benfica," the famed Lisbon club and the strongest team in Portugal, before our first practice session. The Benfica shootout was to be played 30 games hence in Luanda, Angola, the host city for the 1973 National Tournament of Portugal. I had to focus on the task of preparing a very talented Sporting of Lourenço Marques team to win the National Championship - anything short of the title would be construed as failure by the club. I knew that - it was no secret.

□ *5* □

SPORTING, THE POLICE, AND A NATIONAL CHAMPIONSHIP

As the pre-season games in the 1972-73 Portuguese Basketball Federation season began, I still did not have my Sporting Club team intact. *Luis Almeida* and *Ramao*, two starters, were in the Portuguese Army *(Tropa)* and were on assignments in the North of Mozambique where a terrorist war was still being fought - and was escalating. *Frelimo*, the Marxist backed liberation mob, was involved in a war of terrorism and attrition against Portugal in her African state of Mozambique. I was concerned about the availability of these two valuable players for important games, but we were all much more concerned about their safety. One Desportivo player, *Jose Arruda*, was blinded when he became entangled in a land mine in the Mozambique war and the fatalities were mounting by the week.

The Sporting Club had great pride and had established a winning tradition long before I took the head coaching job. Veteran players, one of the two indoor facilities in the city, aggressive management, a good junior development program - it was all in place. The goal was obvious - win it all in the National Tournament in Luanda, Angola, by upsetting Benfica of Lisbon, a heavy favorite, or the season would be regarded as a flop.

Mario Albuquerque, a 6'5 all purpose player who could beat anyone one-on-one off the dribble and used left and right hand on the drive equally well, was our leading scorer. At the lead guard, we had *Nelson Serra*, a 6'2 scoring point who also was a good passer. *Rui Pinheiro*, a talented wing shooter at a skinny 6'5 and *Luis Almeida*, a very handy 6'3 off guard along with *Ramao*, a 6'6 230 lb. bull at the post, comprised the heart of a balanced, deep squad. *Victor Morgado*, a 6'2 perimeter specialist, and *Belmiro Simongo*, athletic 6'4 post player, were the two Portuguese of African descent in the playing rotation. *Tomane* was Nelson's backup at the point and *Morais* was an intelligent guard who played little but contributed with attitude and effort. Rules allowed one import player, and I selected Terry "Tyrone" Johnson whom I had known while at Middle Tennessee.

Terry Johnson

Tyrone was a great jumper and played well beyond his 6'4 height. The Tennessean was to participate in 37 games that season but actually only played, i.e. produced at a high level, in two of these games. But fortunately he chose the most important games of the season in which to excel. I went to Johannesburg to meet Tyrone, who had flown to South Africa from Nashville via New York and Lisbon, and accompanied him to Lourenço Marques. That 50-minute flight became suspenseful from the moment we took off as we flew through a violent thunderstorm every mile of the way. The trip between Lourenço Marques and Johannesburg was routed over mountains and was always choppy, but nothing like this. At that point I wasn't so concerned about the player's talent, just prayed that he was going to get to use it and that I would be there to see it.

Tyrone was assigned a room by the club in my hotel, The Girassol, and that arrangement worked out well. The hotel catered to tourists during holiday periods and it was a surprise to the South Africans - used to apartheid - to see a black man living in the hotel. There was one incident in the hotel bar in which a drunk South African made a racial remark to Terry, who was ready to take him on with a steel comb. Fortunately trouble was averted and the guy checked out of the hotel early the next day.

Born and raised in the tiny town of Normandy, Tennessee, Terry was in culture shock for the next six months. He was a tough guy and he survived, but he seemed to need all of his focus on survival and therefore he became a constant source of concern for the club and his teammates. "Dave, what is wrong with Terry - he does not play well again." But, because of the team talent level and depth, we continued to rack up win after win in spite of Johnson's inconsistent contribution. That was not a good situation - American coach had selected American player who was not producing. Yet I knew, and the looks from Mario and Nelson told me that they knew, we were not going to beat anyone in the Nationals with Tyrone's regular season production. He was truly like a "wounded lion" at times as he suffered from homesickness and cultural confusion.

For example, when Terry took a stroll through the city and happened to end up in the bar area, he would see some very interesting, attractive black African women, but "women of the street" (*as mulheres da rua*) looking to do business with South African and Rhodesian tourists. In fact, these women would taunt him at times and this type of rejection was not helpful considering his difficulties otherwise. Terry did eventually have a relationship with a Portuguese girl which seemed to help settle him down temporarily.

Terry Johnson's racial dilemma in Lourenço Marques reminded me of the writer, James Baldwin, who moved from the U.S. to Paris in 1948. Baldwin lived as an ex-patriot American in Paris for several years before alternating his home between France and New York City. In an essay, Baldwin wrote of his experiences while on a vacation in an isolated Swiss village in the early 1950s, and how that it had never occurred to him that there were people in the world who had never seen a black man, a Negro. As the American strolled around the village streets, school children would shout names at him.

James Baldwin's experience in Switzerland was somewhat different from the problems which Terry Johnson faced in Mozambique. In the Swiss village, Baldwin was the only black while Johnson was a black American among many black Africans in Lourenço Marques. Yet both had felt rejection because they were different from the locals - in language, dress, cultural values, and behavior. However, Tyrone's homesickness did not affect his street fighting or his ability to defend himself - and me at times. One evening we decided to take in a movie in the heart of the city and I called a cab from the hotel.

The taxi arrived about 15 minutes later, but in the meantime Bebe Correira had showed up at the hotel with his car and said he would go with us and drive. The taxi driver honked his horn and I walked out and told him that we would not need the cab. Nothing more was said, but he swung his car around the circular drive at the hotel and sucker punched me square in the face from his driver's seat. I was momentarily stunned, but Tyrone jerked the other cab door open. The driver abandoned his car and took off on foot through backyards and alleys with Sporting's import player filling a lane in hot pursuit.

I got into the chase also, but my objective was to stop Tyrone, as I could see the next day's press coverage in the *Noticias* already - "American Coach and Player Jailed." Somehow I didn't think that Sporting wanted to read about this matter in the headlines especially with Terry doing about 10 ppg and me constantly telling the club "*paciencia, por favor*" - yes, please be patient with him.

The cab driver was a good runner and it took our rebounder about 15 minutes to finally subdue him. When I arrived, the cabby was on his back screaming and Tyrone was pummeling him with piston-like punches. It was clearly headed to TKO or worse, but I pulled my man off and we left the villain driver to fend for himself. Next day I learned that some of these Lourenço Marques taxi drivers routinely carried guns under their front seats, so I guessed overall we did pretty well - no gun, no newspaper report, only a bloody nose for the esteemed coach, and the continuing problem of Terry Johnson's play. The events of that evening were indications that Terry did have some loyalty toward me and hopefully that would eventually translate to better play and commitment on the court. I needed to convince him to play with the same energy and enthusiasm with which he fought.

The season moved along rapidly and we were winning, but not playing well. Tyrone's lackluster performances continued, interrupted only occasionally by a thunder dunk or a blocked shot, but invariably followed by bad hands on the break or just general lack of consistent effort. Prior to Tyrone's arrival, the Lourenço Marques referees had not seen much play above the basket and waived off dunks for about a month. Finally Sporting got in their ear and the rule was re-examined.

The club arranged a trip in the middle of the season to play two games in Quelimane in the North near the war zone. However, everything was peaceful there, except for an occasional rumble of heavy artillery fire in the distance, and we competed against local teams. Quelimane was a quiet, neatly laid out river port known as the "Coconut Capital of Mozambique."

I recalled walking in the beautiful Mozambique sunshine through the tree-lined streets to eat lunch with our players - and Nelson ordered wine. I questioned this and reminded him of our 8:00 p.m. game. He said that the game never started in Quelimane until at least 11:00 p.m. and that he would drink a glass of wine, take a nap, and be ready to play. What did I know - it was Portuguese country and culture. Nelson was, of course, right; only the game didn't start until midnight. We won and the guy who drank the wine at lunch finished with 24. I wondered how Bobby Knight would have handled the wine situation - with tact, I presumed.

I have often thought that these were unique basketball experiences and ones that I would not trade with anyone. I was thoroughly enjoying the challenge of Portuguese basketball and the overall living situation. We won the Quelimane Tournament. With that trip and the better part of the season now behind us, it was time to focus on the main event - the Nationals in Luanda. However, a rather unusual and disturbing personal situation developed just before the trip to Luanda. The bartender at The Girassol said that a man named *Luis* was asking some questions about me. About a week later I received a message to contact Luis at an LM telephone number. I called the number and it was a sub-station of the local police. Luis was not there but I left a message that I had called.

A Man Named Luis

That very evening I was at a downtown night spot called the *Kalifa*, a small and popular bar open all hours. I stopped in there about midnight and was sitting alone when I was approached by two Portuguese men - probably in their 40s. They sat down at the bar - one on each side of me - and ordered a drink. Then one of them turned to me and said very quietly in Portuguese, "I am Luis - we must talk with you about some important security matters." He showed me an ID which I didn't look at very closely. He said that after we finished our drink, we would go to his office. I agreed as I was curious, did not think that I had anything to be concerned about, and also felt that I had no choice in the matter.

We went in an unmarked police car. I knew that the feared secret police, *PIDE*, had its headquarters in *Villa Algarve* on the *Marginal*. However, we went the opposite direction from the Marginal. Luis' partner drove out of the central business area to a sparsely lighted, small, stucco building which looked like an LM police station, but did not actually have a sign identifying it. We parked behind the building and entered the back door into a very austere hallway. Then they led me into a windowless room with a table and four chairs and only an overhead light. Luis and the other cop, whom I never did officially meet, sat down and motioned me to do the same. I sat across from Luis and the other guy sat to my right. Luis spoke in Portuguese throwing in an occasional definitive English word spoken with a heavy accent.

Basically, I was told that they needed answers to some questions about my identity and my activities in Mozambique and South Africa over the past two years. The Portuguese police apparently had a file on me as Luis worked from a manila folder. He said that he had information that I had been associated with the Academic Association at the university, which had been a source of concern for authorities because of the controversial political activity there.

I was aware of the political activity and debate among a particular group of students at the University of Lourenço Marques. However, I responded that my only connection with Academica was the basketball team which I had coached in 1971-72. I had to admit that Luis did make an interesting point when he referred to the physical education program which included a priority for training Africans - age 21-25 - selected through competitive examinations to become physical education teachers.

The program - administered through the physical education department associated with the university - taught theory and activity courses with the objective to certify these students as teachers. After completing the training, the African students returned to their villages in the rural areas outside of Lourenço Marques to teach children individual and team activities as well as lecture on habits leading to a healthier life style. I did have contact with and access to these African students periodically, testing their level of physical fitness for my doctoral dissertation.

The Lourenço Marques police were making the connection between my contact with the African students and their subsequent return to the villages where terrorist groups were recruiting personnel for their war against the Portuguese government. I was concerned as I realized that the police were making a legitimate connection in theory and probably in practice. But I explained - and I could see that my interrogator had started to anger - rather unconvincingly that my only contact with the students had been in Lourenço Marques at the physical education facility which was located about two miles from the main university campus. Luis, with a rank smelling cigarette in the corner of his mouth, scrawled several comments in his records as I spoke and then conferred with his partner speaking rapidly and incomprehensibly in a harsh, colloquial Portuguese. My confidence was wavering as the process continued and the smoke was getting to me.

The police officers were chain smoking through this entire questioning episode. The stark room with its sparse and uncomfortable furnishings had just the four chairs - one unoccupied - and the wooden table. The overhead light beam barely penetrated the unrelenting cloud of smoke hanging over the table and added to the surreal nature of the experience - truly Kafka revisited. "Grinnell Boy Sentenced to 20 Years for Espionage in Mozambique." Luis looked me directly in the eye and asked, "*O senhor conhece o missionario Americano chamado Anderson?*" - Did I know the American missionary named Anderson? Yes, I did know Anderson and his wife, as I had met them at a dinner one Sunday evening at the house of the American Consul General.

I knew what was coming next. "*O senhor visitou a missao na selva?*" Had I visited the mission located in the country? Yes, I had visited the mission - I went there to look at the possibility of putting up a basket and backboard for the African students at the mission school. Again, I saw the point in the questioning. The police did not trust the missionaries. Political activities in the rural areas outside of the city were a source of concern for the police and they knew that missionaries throughout the country were trying to educate and enhance the lives of native Africans. And in their own way and through their own Marxist philosophy, Frelimo - the terrorist, liberation group - perceived themselves as doing the same thing. Thus, the police seemed to be focusing on the theme of my contacts with people - Africans and the missionaries - living in the country areas, the bush.

The time passed and it was 3:00 a.m., yet the questioning was unrelenting. I was asked if I ever had had conversations with some Portuguese, whom I did not know or did not recognize their names. The next name mentioned - *Sergio* - definitely got my attention. Luis continued and insisted that I had been seen several times with this African guy named Sergio - what was my relationship with him?

Sergio was an interesting and rather mysterious character whom I saw from time to time around Lourenço Marques. He was an African of light complexion - nearly mulatto - who resembled in facial features the American boxer George Foreman. Sergio was trilingual - speaking English, Portuguese, and the local African dialect well. He was intelligent, but slippery and vague about his occupation, and he traveled frequently in and out of the country. Since Sergio spoke English, he was able to converse with Terry Johnson, the black American player with Sporting. Sergio spoke

English with an accent in a rapid, staccato manner. In contrast Terry responded in a slow Tennessee drawl, barely audible at times. Thus, they would often look at me for a third-party English translation as they had trouble understanding each other.

When I ran into Sergio, it was at The Girassol or occasionally in the downtown night club district, but the relationship between Sergio and Terry was surface at best. I didn't mention Terry Johnson's name to the police, but I replied that I knew Sergio from The Girassol Hotel and *Mona's*, a Portuguese boarding house and bar across the street from The Girassol. I had sold Sergio a three-stool, bamboo bar which I had purchased for use in an apartment. I remembered the day that I helped move the bar and stools from the hotel to Sergio's downtown flat. Sergio had a sense of humor and quipped, "We need some African labor to move this. Where's Terry?" I told Terry Johnson about it later and he found it quite humorous.

Luis pressed the issue about my relationship with Sergio, as I had to admit that I had spent time on several occasions drinking and talking with him. One Sunday he and I had driven out to *Costa do Sol*, the beach area, to a small motel and bar called *Casa Praia* (Beach House.) We spent an hour or so there and then Sergio disappeared into an office with the owner for 30 minutes discussing a business deal of which I knew nothing. I finally confirmed that I knew this guy, Sergio, socially, but I knew nothing much else about him. Luis then raised the ante and yelled at me, "Yes, you only knew him socially, but we know that he asked you to deliver a package for him to Angola. Is that not true?" I hesitated before answering, as I did not want to antagonize my interrogators further, but also I wanted to be firm in my answer. I was clearly on their home court. I replied that I had been to Luanda about six months before on the All-Star basketball tour, but that I had no knowledge of any package.

Another hour passed and the room was so full of smoke that it was becoming difficult to breath and my eyes were burning. They then queried me about the trip in 1972 to Nampola, what exactly was I doing there and had I been on any military installations? Their police records were accurate and that question was concerned with the basketball tour with the All-Stars. Yes, I had been in the Portuguese officer's club, but I didn't mention the business with the rifle in the ribs. However, Luis had that information also. The free passes to the game didn't keep Jose, the Portuguese soldier, from making a report on our encounter. Not only was I on their home court, I felt that I was now about ten points down.

The interrogation continued. What was my official relationship to the U.S. Consulate, as they knew that I went there regularly. I replied, "I just stop there each day to read the American newspapers and to say hello to friends." Luis asked why I didn't read the Portuguese papers - and I said that I did read

The Noticias and *The Diario* to keep up with the latest criticism of my coaching and to practice my Portuguese. That proved to be a good answer, as the two police officers smiled and Luis said in heavily accented English, "It is good you learn Portuguese. But is very difficult language." I nodded agreement.

I anticipated a question about my relationship with the ex-patriot Italian, Napoleon, the owner of the La Bussola Restaurant. I had heard around the local bar scene that Napoleon had had previous run-ins with the Lourenço Marques police, but that was all I knew about it. I replied that I liked to stop at La Bussola once in a while for a drink and to eat Italian food. Luis instantly countered, "Why do you eat Italian. Don't like bacalhau?" *Bacalhau* was a strong tasting codfish which the Portuguese prepared in various *molhos* - cooking oils. I lied for the first time in the questioning, *"Sim, gosto de bacalhau muito."* I felt that I had to affirm that I liked the Portuguese codfish dish. I didn't know if he was serious or not, and I wasn't taking a chance at this point. Luis glanced at his partner and back at me with a wry smile on his face. He seemed pleased with my comment about the bacalhau.

Actually, I enjoyed the place, and Napoleon, a very intense Italian, was always good for some local news. Luis' partner seemed particularly interested in recording my comments on Napoleon and the two compared notes without conversation for several minutes. Finally, I was informed that there was one more question and then they would decide what to do with me. I knew that each question asked had had some degree of legitimacy, through incidental connection between me and their concern over terrorism in the North of Mozambique and in Lourenço Marques itself. I knew that if the police wanted to trust their imagination they could arrest me on these circumstantial connections to my contact with the University of Lourenço Marques, the Academica Association, the African physical education program, the American missionaries, Sergio, and Napoleon.

As I reviewed in my mind the questioning, I became more and more concerned about being detained and the last question did nothing to ease my thoughts. What had I been doing in South Africa for a two-month period and did I associate with any U.S. Embassy employees in Pretoria? South Africa was very concerned about the war effort in Mozambique as the two countries shared common borders and the spread of terrorism was a very real threat. Although the two countries were neighbors geographically, their governments had conflicting racial policies. The separatist policy of apartheid was strictly enforced in the Republic of South Africa, while there existed a more liberal mingling of the races in Mozambique. Even though both countries shared the concern and effort against terrorist groups, they had a mutual distrust for each other's ultimate motives.

In regard to the query about South Africa, I anticipated that Bob

McGovern's name would come up. I replied that I had spent two months in Pretoria and that I had stayed with Bob McGovern, a foreign service officer at the U.S. Embassy. McGovern was single, had a big house, and invited me to stay with him. I detected through the smoky haze in the room a definite reaction to my comment about McGovern, followed by a brief burst of back-and-forth comments. I was preparing myself for the worst.

Luis sighed and gave me a strange look and then said that I, the American basketball coach, had been very stupid. Luis muttered through clenched teeth, "If you know nothing, why do you associate with all of these dangerous people?" I think he really meant indiscreet, not stupid, but he was referring to my interactions with some of these "colorful" people and especially McGovern, who had been considered controversial when based in the American Consulate in Mozambique because of an alleged affair with the wife of a prominent Portuguese.

They asked several more questions about McGovern and wanted to know my last contact with him in Mozambique. I told them that the last time I spoke to McGovern in Lourenço Marques he was preparing to travel to South Africa to take a steamer from Cape Town to Houston. He had mentioned that he was planning to take some good books and a case of scotch along for company. Then after a three-month leave in the U.S., he had returned to South Africa and was based in Pretoria at the U.S. Embassy there.

The police officers made some final hasty notes, looked at each other, and Luis nodded his head toward the door. I started to get up and he said to me, "*Nao. Fica.*" Stay put. I sat back down, but it felt good to move my body and stand - if only for a few seconds. They picked up the files and their cigarettes and walked out without a further word to me. I heard the door being locked from the outside and at that point I wasn't feeling very optimistic. I waited for about an hour - it was now 5:00 a.m. - and finally I heard the key in the lock and the door open. Luis said, "*Vamos.*" And we left the building and went back to the car.

It was still pretty dark with the dawn just starting to break on the horizon. As they drove me about a mile to a main intersection, I noticed that we had passed a sign on the street which said "*Xipamanine*" - an African township known for its open-air market. At the intersection they told me to get out and catch a cab back to my car still parked at the Kalifa. I did that and did not hear from the police again in an official capacity, but I did run into Luis two more times. The first was in a memorable situation at a volatile scene at a basketball game and the other at the Lourenço Marques Airport.

I caught a cab back to the hotel, went to my room to shower and changed my clothes, which were inundated with smoke. I gave up on the idea of sleep. I grabbed a cup of coffee in the dining room kitchen, which opened at 6:00 a.m., and sat beside the swimming pool to clear my head and my lungs and to get my bearings. I was reflecting on the evening before and though relieved at being out of police custody, I knew they could reappear again at any time. While sitting by the hotel pool that morning in Mozambique, I thought back to my days in Prairie City, Iowa, with the pick-up trucks lined in front of the only restaurant in town - the Please-U Cafe. Farmers had come "to town" for their morning coffee with little else to do on bleak winter days.

I was a long way from Prairie City now - actually on the other side of the world. I was also a different person leading a much different life. And there was an even stranger postscript to the questioning episode with the police - Sergio did later ask me to deliver a package for him in Luanda and I, of course, refused. I heard rumors that Napoleon had run into further problems with the police and had been incarcerated. Also, the Academic Association became even more controversial and was eventually closed by the police after a night raid on the Academica offices. The physical education program for the African teachers was cut-off from university funding, and missionaries were asked to leave Mozambique.

When I was working in Africa from 1971-74, the backdrop for the entire Lourenço Marques scene was the threat of terrorist activity as the action moved closer and closer to the capital city. Terrorist origins were in the North of Mozambique with most of the earlier activity near the city of *Tete*, but the threat slowly spread south to Lourenço Marques. The Marxist backed *FRELIMO* (Front for the Liberation of Mozambique) was originally led by *Samora Machel*, Joaquim Chissano, and *Eduardo Mondlane*, who founded the radical student group called *Nesam* in Lourenço Marques. The war was a constant source of anxiety and concern for Portugal which used her state police force, *PIDE* - later replaced by Security Police under the direction of the Minister for Overseas Territories - to disperse and control threats to the central bureaucracy and stability of the country. Luis was just doing his job when he questioned me and was obviously with the Security Police and possibly a PIDE official.

Luanda and the Nationals

But my thing was supposed to be basketball, not foreign politics, and I was doing my best to focus on the National Tournament. We moved through the provincial competition in Lourenço Marques and Beira with no drama and arrived in Luanda ready to challenge Benfica for the National Championship of Portugal. As I heard so often in LM on the streets and at the *Por do Sol Bar* (Sundown) at the Cardosa Hotel, "But Dave, Benfica is a team of professionals. Sporting does not have a chance." Bulletin board stuff, but we didn't have a bulletin board at Sporting. I used strong motivational words which I embodied and carried to my team through my own upgraded competitive approach to this tournament.

There was no question that Benfica was a formidable opponent. Known as a football (soccer) power throughout Europe, the *Estadio da Luz*, Stadium of the Light, was built in 1944 and later upgraded to accommodate 120,000 fans. The Benfica Club of Lisbon played basketball in the same facility as the football and ingeniously scheduled basketball games to coincide with the end of football games. Thus a soccer match with 80,000 in attendance would end at 5:00 p.m. and the basketball game would start at 5:30; therefore the basketball arena with a capacity of 4,000 was usually full of rabid fans from run-off business from the football match.

After arriving in Luanda and checking into the *Universo Hotel*, I went with the team to the site of the next evening's game. I was shocked to find that we would be playing outdoors on a slick, concrete floor surrounded by 7,000 erector-set-like bleacher seats. I smelled trouble, and the scent was strong and my senses correct as we lost our opener to Benfica by twelve. The tourney format was four teams in double round-robin competition with comparative scores as tie breakers - a similar format to the previously discussed Academica-Sporting game decided by head-to-head scores when both teams had identical records in terms of wins and losses.

The American players participating included Ken Grabinski of the University of Iowa with Sporting of Luanda, Rob Clark of Coe with Football Club of Luanda, Sebern Hill of U.S. International with Benfica, and Sporting's Terry Johnson of Middle Tennessee. I was the only American coach in the tournament and in Portuguese basketball at the time.

Gary Ferguson, who had played for Bill Musselman at Ashland College, was also in Luanda during the tournament. He had been on a team which did not make the Portuguese final four teams. I asked Ferguson about his experiences playing for Bill Musselman, whose teams had led the nation in team defense four consecutive years from 1968-1971 in Division II college basketball. Ferguson recalled that in his senior year, Ashland had suffered its first loss of that season on the night before the start of Christmas vacation. Parents had driven hours to see the game and pick up their sons for the holidays.

Ashland lost. Musselman was irate and demanded that the players give up their Christmas and stay at Ashland to practice. The coach, players, and parents negotiated into the early hours of the morning. Finally it was agreed that the players come back to practice the day after Christmas - three days earlier than originally planned. The team returned to a four-hour practice session in weighted vests. Ferguson said that the players literally crawled off the floor - and Ashland did not lose again in the regular season that year. Bill Musselman later coached at the University of Minnesota, the CBA, the NBA, and at the University of South Alabama. Musselman's teams won an unprecedented, four consecutive CBA Championships from 1985-1988 with his 1987-88 Albany team establishing a 48-6 regular season record.

Then in Luanda it started to rain and rain and rain (*chuva, chuva, chuva.*) It rained for three days with no games played and finally the tourney site was moved to a brand-new high school gym. Although still under construction, the facility was finished by round-the-clock work. (In Luanda that would mean about 6-8 hours a day.) We had our last two games on a real floor and indoors - out of the continuing rain.

On game night, we had to fight our way into the gymnasium through throngs of people frustrated that their tickets were canceled. There were only 2,500 seats in the gym and 7,000 tickets had been sold in advance in anticipation of the games being played at the outdoor court. Needless to point out, there were some angry people without a way into the game.

When we entered the gym, there were our opponents, Benfica, and their coach, Teotonio Lima - my ex-boss at Academica. "I think it is time you go home to the States, coach." The Benfica group was leisurely, actually cavalierly, sprawled on the floor at one end of the court watching the evening's first game. I have never been presented such a psychological advantage in all my life by an opponent. I was wild, grabbing our players and yelling, "Look at them, they think they have this won, they don't respect us." Finally, Mario Albuquerque, always cool and sensing that I was overdoing it, said, "Ok, Dave. We understand. Now shut up so we can play." I couldn't believe he had said that to me - his coach.

Mario was right, of course, so I shut up for a while and did our team PLAY. We rocked them with our surprise 3-2 zone which we had practiced in the afternoon heat that day on a secret outdoor court. I had second thoughts about putting in the zone on short notice, as I recalled the disastrous results of my last minute plan with the Kubasaki Dragons in Japan in the Far East Invitational. I decided that this was different, as the players were more experienced and we had played some 3-2 zone earlier in the year. Also Rob Clark - the American player with Football Club of Luanda and member of the All-Star tour - was there and assisted the Sporting players with proper defensive shifts relative to the ball.

The new high school gym seemed a little narrow, so I knew we could overplay on the wing and make it difficult to pass to Benfica's perimeter shooter, Sebern Hill. We planned to play him tight and force him to put the ball on the floor. Also, in that it was a last-minute decision to practice on game day, I had to think of the effect on our veteran team, which was set in its routines. But as Nelson Serra said that afternoon, "I don't like to practice in the sun, but this is different - this is Benfica."

Another huge key for us was our pre-game meeting standing on the dance floor in the bar of the Universo Hotel where I challenged Terry

Johnson in front of all of his teammates. The timing was perfect as the pressure was on and the stakes were high. I simply said, "Well, Terry, are you going to play tonight or not - we need to know whether to count on you in advance." (I was considering something else to do that night if he had responded no.)

Terry grimaced and shook his head. I said, "Say it, Tyrone, tell us." He finally muttered, "Yes, I'll be ready." I breathed an internal sigh of relief - you never know what some of these guys are going to do or say regardless of the situation. Also, as the team meeting broke up, Mario Albuquerque and Nelson Serra pulled aside Rui Pinheiro, the talented 6'5 wing shooter with a tendency to take bad shots. The two veterans, Mario and Nelson, asked for and received a commitment from Rui that he would play for the team and not for the fans. So we had the pieces in place and the twelve-point margin established through the first-round loss to Benfica didn't seem to be much of an obstacle - probably just added motivation.

The game started with several fast breaks on which we did not score, but we had legs and we had spirit and I knew it would come - and it did. Nelson was struggling. I was impatient and told Tomane, the backup point, to get in for Nelson. Tomane said, *"Nao obrigado, paciencia, Dave, paciencia."* (The guy, a substitute, said no thanks and be patient - to me - the American coach.) So I figured Tomane was probably right as Nelson nailed a perimeter shot and I said, "Way to go, Nelson." And I walked confidently in front of our bench, as I had seen American college coaches do on TV. The next day the press in Luanda gave me credit for exercising good judgment and patience in the early stages of the game when we were not scoring. I graciously accepted the praise.

The Benfica players, apparently carrying on a tradition from Lisbon, liked to remind our guys that their girl friend, or wife, was, they understood,"very good" and probably very busy right now - only stated more graphically. At that very moment, Terry went elbows above the rim and took the ball down along with two Benfica players ending up on the floor. And in a scene captured on film and shown in the news reports at movie theatres across Africa, the two Benfica players decked by Terry on the rebound jumped up and challenged him. Terry Johnson calmly turned and motioned them to "come on"- a real classic when seen back in Lourenço Marques while basking in the glow of the victory and sharing it with friends and supporters.

The Portuguese news service used some ingenuity by including the Dirty Harry line "Make my day" as the caption on the Terry Johnson-Benfica altercation. Final score: Sporting 102 Benfica 77. I liked that very much. Mario pulled me aside afterwards and said, "Dave, you made a smart move in using the zone and the team meeting at the hotel was important.

But I think that we could have scored 150 if you had not slowed it down in the second half." I never had to worry about losing my humility with Mario around.

Another overseas basketball season had passed and this time we had won a National title with a 35-2 season in the books - monumental stuff. After two years in Africa, I decided to take a trip back to the U.S. to my hometown of Grinnell. On the trip back, I spent a week in Lisbon and then flew to London for a few days before heading to New York and then on to Chicago and Des Moines. I became immediately frustrated in Grinnell as my celebrity was in Africa but my body was clearly present in Iowa. I rejected a contract renewal offer from Sporting and asked for a ridiculous raise, which they did not seriously consider. This could be translated as a very dumb move on my part, especially in that I was starting to miss the LM scene.

Time passed and I began to think that my days in Mozambique were not to be repeated. But as I was driving south from Grinnell to Oskaloosa in central Iowa, I looked up into the bright July Iowa sun and saw a commercial jet winging eastward - toward Africa I thought. I headed directly to Western Union in Oskaloosa and wired Celia, a Portuguese friend and employee at the U.S. Consulate, *"Celinha, por favor, fale com Desportivo. Quero treinar Desportivo. Tenho que regressar a LM - DA"* - Yes, indeed, I wanted to coach Desportivo and I had to return to LM - please help me. She called Desportivo, and I did return and also unknowingly laid the groundwork for Overseas Basketball Services (OBS), my recruiting and overseas placement business.

Mahangalene, a basketball club in the Lourenço Marques league, asked me to find a good U.S. player for them for the 1973-74 season. John Pfitsch at Grinnell College told me that Eric Bundgard, a 6'6 inside-out player who had started school at the University of Colorado and finished at St. Olaf College, was interested in playing in Mozambique. Eric drove down to Grinnell from Northfield, Minnesota, that summer and we agreed that he and his wife, Kim, would travel with me back to Lourenço Marques and Eric would play for Mahangalene.

Desportivo and Chester Brown

My ability to recruit a quality American player was a selling point to Desportivo in their decision to offer me a coaching contract. I selected Chester Brown, a 6'10 Middle Tennessee player, to boost the hopes of the club's faithful. I figured that Desportivo had potential because they had had success in recent years, but they definitely needed a revival of spirit - winning was the key. They had no indoor practice facilities, which had been a huge advantage for me at Sporting, but I didn't really care at that point. I wanted to get back to Lourenço Marques and coach regardless of the details. So I made the arrangements and met Chester Brown and Eric and Kim Bungard at Kennedy Airport in New York. We were off to LM with a twelve-hour stop-over in London. When we arrived in England, I took Chester via train from Heathrow Airport to downtown London. We wandered around Picadilly for a few hours and stopped in a pub or two to get out of the downpour. I hoped Chester remembered that experience - it was raining, chilly, and vintage London.

When we boarded the South African Airways flight from Heathrow to Jan Smuts Airport in Johannesburg, Chester created a stir among the passengers in the economy cabin. The apartheid laws did not apply to the South African Airlines service, but most of the passengers were citizens of the Republic of South Africa and lived under that country's racist system. The passenger list was sparse with many open seats. Chester had been assigned a seat next to a young, attractive South African girl. As he smiled and began to take his seat, she quickly headed him off and said that he could have more leg room in an entirely vacant row across the aisle from her. I watched the incident carefully and concluded that it was ironic that a white South African girl had directed the black American man to another seat in an airliner from a country which practiced apartheid. Yet, it was actually good sense for Chester to have a complete center aisle of the 747 to himself. He was satisfied with the seating arrangement and didn't comment on the matter. Many passengers were first startled and then intrigued by the presence of this 6'10 black athlete trying to get settled for the 13-hour flight to Johannesburg. However, everyone was pleasant, and among the economy passengers Chester became a celebrity of sorts during the flight.

Back home in Lourenço Marques at The Girassol Hotel, I felt the emotion of seeing my old team Sporting in the headlines and off to the European Cup to play Heidelberg, Germany. This was the result and the reward of our winning the Nationals the previous May in Luanda. All that work and now the old Sporting standby, *Luis Pina*, was back at the helm as coach. I was in the meantime trying to find hope with my new team at Desportivo. I was also trying to forgive myself for my own arrogance in contract discussions with Sporting. I could have been preparing the Sporting team for the European Cup in Germany; instead I was staying in Lourenço Marques and working to field a respectable team with Desportivo.

We played a game against Sporting just before they left for Europe; they whacked us by 20 points. Chester Brown showed promise but also showed that he wasn't in shape. I confirmed to everyone that I was happy in my new job by getting kicked out of the game via my second technical. The technicals were due to personal frustration and had to do with being mad at myself for my own lack of wisdom in walking away from a championship team to a cellar dweller. As a result of clouded judgment caused by my arrogance in the Sporting contract discussions, I have learned to become more patient with unrealistic players and also with their potential employers in contract negotiations. Some players just don't understand that the club determined his market value, not the player himself.

With Sporting in Europe and my new team practicing on its outdoor, lighted court, in Lourenço Marques, I was pushing Chester to get in shape and looking forward to the the arrival of Frank Martinuque, the Desportivo idol of the past. Frank was returning along with brother Ted, who had been a big scorer at St. Peter's College and had agreed to play with the new Benfica of Lourenço Marques club under Portuguese coach *Alexander Franco*. Coach Franco was a busy man on the LM scene, coaching Benfica, writing sports stories for the *Diario*, and working for the local movie theaters translating English dialogue in the Hollywood films to Portuguese subtitles.

The Martinuque boys were good players and made positive contributions in what was to be a very short stay in Mozambique. One Friday evening at about midnight, I was driving home to the Girassol from downtown and noticed that Ted Martinuque was walking in an unsteady manner along the street. I was familiar with the half-stagger. The next day I saw Ted and asked him what he had done the night before. He said, "Not much. But I did go downtown to a couple of bars and everybody was drunk last night. I couldn't believe it."

Part of the conditioning plan on Chester Brown was to get his 6'10 body in game condition through some extra individual workouts on weekends. One Sunday morning we were at the club, which also included an Olympic-sized swimming pool, working hard in the white hot, Mozambique sun on basketball fundamentals. After a couple of hours, I suggested that we call it a day, have a cold drink, and take a swim. "Do you swim, Chester?" The big guy replied, "Yeah, coach, I learned in class at MTSU." I have found that it can be unwise to take a player's word at face value and never to question his opinion of his level of fitness, talent, college statistics, or potential. They were always forthcoming on these matters, but lacked objectivity in self-assessment.

I was surprised to find that this lack of objectivity in self-assessment also applied to swimming skills. I was wary about Chester in the pool and I carefully watched as he ambled toward the deep end. I yelled a warning, "Deep end, Ches." He turned, smiled and then flopped his long body into the crowded pool. Ten minutes later I noticed some commotion and there was Chester - all 6'10 feet of him flailing away frantically in the center of the large pool - far from the safety of the deck. I ran to the pool side and caught the attention of three young Portuguese who calmly swam over to him and summarily hauled him ashore. Ches was exhausted, scared to death, and spitting water. As he lay on the deck recovering, I thought of the body box that I had seen available for emergencies at the U.S. Consulate in case a deceased American citizen needed to be shipped home. I was grateful not to be faced with the challenge of packing 6'10 inches of basketball player into six feet of body box.

Chester recovered from the swimming incident and joined Frank Martinuque to bring early season glory to our Desportivo team, but not before two interesting situations developed: Sporting returned from Europe and we were ready for them, and Greg "Stretch" Howard made his appearance on the LM scene fresh from a short season in Sardinia.

Sporting Christmas Tournament

Sporting had returned after losing a very close two-game series with Heidelberg. One game had been played in Germany and the other in Porto, Portugal. Sporting had used its normal lineup with Terry Johnson back from the Tennessee summer. In Lourenço Marques there was an annual Christmas Tournament at the Sporting Pavilion. We - Desportivo - were playing very well with Chester working into shape and Frank Martinuque giving our offense some direction along with support from *Manuel Lima*, a veteran post player. *Fernando Lobo*, an 18-year-old guard with an accurate perimeter stroke, was an unexpected producer also.

We were matched up with Sporting in the finals of the two-day tournament. It was just before Christmas in Lourenço Marques and the days were very warm. The scorching heat of the day retained by the arena was increased by the body heat of the packed house. The setting was perfect for the Sporting *macaricos* to ignite the fuse. It was an eerie night and the Latin emotions were at a boiling point. The evening game schedule included a double-header. There had been a brief sparring match in the first game between a 6'7 Italian guest player and Barry Smith, a six-foot guard from the University of Houston playing with the Portuguese *Ferraviario Club*.

The problem had started when the two players collided on a drive to the basket. The bearded Italian got off the floor and tried to convey "Everything is ok, *amigo*" and gave his cultural equivalent of a pat on the rear by gently tapping the American Smith on both cheeks. At that point the cultures and players clashed. Barry Smith thought he had been slapped. He danced in place, and threw an educated left hook and caught the *Italiano* flush on the cheek. Rather than attacking Smith, the big Italian - incidentally a strong player - stepped back and appealed to his 10,000 Latin brethren with magnificent gesticulation, arms extended and palms up as if to say, "What did I do?" That gesture by the Italian had the force of a knock-out punch. The crowd roared like a pride of hungry lions and booed Smith the rest of the game. Thus the fuse was already burning when Desportivo and Sporting took the floor for the main event.

The situation which developed between Barry Smith and the Italian was a microcosm of the difficulties involved in professional players and coaches adapting to different cultures, especially one as unique and racially confusing to American black players as the colonial Portuguese setting in Mozambique. I understood through personal experience the feeling of being entirely alone, not knowing anyone, thousands of miles from friends and family in a country that speaks an entirely different language - along with being booed.

Barry Smith had come directly to Mozambique from Coach Guy Lewis' high-profile basketball program at the University of Houston. It was impossible for Smith to be prepared for life in Mozambique after four years in Houston. Ferraviario, Barry Smith's employer in Lourenço Marques, had arranged a small sleeping room for him at the club headquarters in downtown Lourenço Marques. He had little interaction with the other Americans in town and had become virtually isolated. Outside of the 12-14 hours a week required of his basketball job, he spent most of his time in his room.

During that era, there was no television, and all radio broadcasts were in Portuguese, with the exception of the British Broadcasting Company news which was transmitted through a South African station. Also, many of the black American players had come to Africa seeking some contact with what they had perceived as their roots, but they usually became discouraged as they received little encouragement from the *Mozambicanos* themselves. Mahlon Saunders from the University of North Dakota used to become annoyed walking down the streets of the city as black African youngsters would stop, point, smile, or even laugh, as if they were ridiculing him. I doubted that they were always ridiculing, but the American players got tired of this type of attention. James Baldwin, the writer, had had an experience similar to that of Mahlon Saunders with children on the streets of a village in Switzerland, and Terry Johnson from Middle Tennessee had tasted rejection by African women. I feel certain that this type of situation was perplexing to the Americans.

The Africans of Mozambique did not know who these strangers of the same color were or where they were from, but they did know that they (the Americans) were different from themselves and not one of their own. The Africans also reacted to the fact that the American black players had nice clothes, cash, and moved freely in the LM social scene. Further, the black American and black African, because of differences in language, could normally not communicate with each other. Most Africans working in the city of Lourenço Marques spoke some Portuguese. However, they were as likely to speak *Afrikaans* - the South Africa Boer language, based on Dutch - as English.

Learning the Portuguese language was a huge challenge for these young American athletes and few even tried. In English most of them spoke as intelligent, college educated men, but in Portuguese, if they learned any of the language at all, they found themselves communicating at a crude, primary school level. It was most frustrating to attempt to speak and have the listener laugh or appear baffled. I have been through this process myself in learning both Portuguese and Spanish and know the shock to one's self-esteem, already being tested in adjusting to the strange culture. Thus most avoided the new language entirely and sought refuge with other American players or other English speaking people in the city.

I spent three years in Mozambique and valued the experience, yet I was always aware of extra stress in my life associated with the drastically different lifestyle. In spite of the fact that I was in my early thirties at the time, ten years older than the players, and had previously lived overseas, I went through a similar adjustment. In contrast, these young Americans had come directly from their college campuses with limited travel experiences. Most had seen only their home towns, their college towns, and cities of collegiate basketball opponents.

Thus, the Italian-American sparring match in the first game on that steamy Lourenço Marques evening had set the stage for the main event - Sporting vs. Desportivo. The game started with spectators on their feet yelling, and about six minutes into the first half, Chester Brown and Nelson of Sporting went after a loose ball. Chester momentarily lost his cool and kicked Nelson in the stomach. Bad move. A fight was averted somehow, but the atmosphere had passed the volatile zone into explosive. But we were able to stay focused and built a 20-point lead on the Lions through our running game and the Martinuque-Brown combination on the pick-and-roll.

Exactly one minute before the first half ended, the power in the building went off. The packed house was suddenly as dark as the African jungle and, momentarily, completely silent. Then apparently someone decided that we needed some light on the subject as a fire was ignited and bright flames illuminated the far end of the basketball pavilion. Manuel Lima, my center and also an under-cover police officer, grabbed my arm and held me in place for a brief moment. I found out about Lima's police work one night when he and I were returning from a downtown bar. He had been driving and hit a huge bump in the street. His glove compartment flew open and I saw a large holstered revolver there. Anyway, Lima told me, "Is best you and Chester leave right now, Dave." I couldn't have agreed more.

I was concerned about Geneva Alofs, an American whom I had been dating. She was a U.S. Consulate employee from Grand Rapids, Michigan, and was sitting at the game with Ted Martinuque. Fortunately they were already outside when Chester and I made our way out of the arena with the assistance of Lima and another guy who was holding a large flashlight in one hand and a dark object in the other hand. He was giving Lima instructions and actually seemed to be in charge of our two-man evacuation. When we had cleared the arena, I thanked Lima and turned to the other guy to also thank him. He looked familiar - and then I knew - it was Luis from last year's all night question-and-answer session. He smiled, casually checked the clip in his hand gun, said to me in Portuguese, "Dave, why are you always in trouble?" Then he disappeared back into the turmoil of the arena.

The game was canceled and we returned to The Girassol for drinks. While we were sitting at the hotel bar, Geneva received an urgent call and had to go to the U.S. Consulate (about midnight) as she had back-up communicator duties. She returned from the Consulate about an hour later and told me that there had been another Frelimo threat to blow up a Lourenço Marques dock building. This threat had coincided with the fracas at the game. The terrorist activity in the North and the continuous threat of war was moving closer and closer to the capital city of Lourenço Marques. A deadly situation seemed to be taking shape. Portugal had serious, and now pressing, problems in Mozambique.

Stretch Howard

But the next week, it was business as usual. On Monday at practice I looked over to the edge of the lighted, outdoor Desportivo practice court and noticed a very large, impressive-looking man standing and watching our practice. He introduced himself as Greg "Stretch" Howard and was trying to find the Academica Club. I thought, "Oh no," because the guy was a carved 6'10 and my man Chester was also 6'10, but not carved.

Greg Howard had been a first-round draft choice by the Phoenix Suns in 1970 and had played in 92 NBA games, 44 at Phoenix in 1970-71 and 48 in Cleveland the next year. He had also played in Italy and had come to Mozambique directly from Sardinia in Italy courtesy of Jim McGregor, overseas super-agent of that era. McGregor called me later and asked me to help collect his agent fee on Stretch from Academica. I explained that a collection effort was a little sensitive given the current history of the rivalries involving Sporting-Academica and Desportivo-Academica and also considering my past experience with the Academica club.

Greg Howard was, of course, very talented and impressive on the court, especially compared to the talent level in our league. The Mozambique fans loved him and he was a big drawing card, but Academica didn't improve much as a team. It appeared that just possibly Greg's heart wasn't in club objectives. An Academica Club director called me at the hotel and said that he needed to meet with me urgently. I figured that the call had to do with McGregor's money, but that wasn't it. He asked me what was wrong with

Greg Howard and went on to say that Greg liked to drink a glass of gin - a large glass - at a sidewalk cafe across the street from the Academica Club headquarters, at breakfast time. I said that he shouldn't worry because Academica doesn't practice until later in the day. (I had learned about scheduled drinking from Nelson in Quelimane.)

Greg finally got his game going and Academica was looking good for a playoff spot, but then the NBA giant disappeared into the African darkness. Unannounced, he had taken a midnight flight back to Europe. While Academica was trying to figure out the disappearance of its *Americano*, Desportivo was likewise trying to figure out its American - me, the coach. I could see that the country's politics were rapidly taking center stage and I began to discuss this with club officials. With the departure of Greg Howard, the heating up of the terrorist activity, and rumors of impending doom to the Portuguese in Mozambique, Chester Brown had decided to return to the U.S. and the Martinuque boys also made their exit plans.

Eric Bundgard, who had played some very good games for Mahangalene, had already gone home to Minnesota with his wife, Kim. But in my delivery of Eric to the Mahangalene club the seed for a future business had been sown. When I had introduced Eric to the club president, the Portuguese proudly and secretly passed me an envelope containing a 1,000 escuda bill (worth U.S. $30 in 1973) for my recruiting efforts. I humbly accepted the "fee." It was several years later that I associated those 1,000 escudas with a market demand and making a living through recruiting U.S. players for foreign clubs.

Mozambique Exodus

At this point, my run in Lourenço Marques society and basketball was coming to a conclusion. However, as this final season continued, Geneva Alofs - the U.S. Consulate employee - had become the focus of my third year in Lourenço Marques. We enjoyed each other's company and took some spontaneous trips to see the African wildlife in Krueger Park, about a three hour drive from Lourenço Marques.

Also, in the spring, we flew to Salisbury, Rhodesia, and then back to Lourenço Marques where we drove Geneva's 1965 Mustang through a similar route which I had taken alone two years before - Nelspruit, Durban, Port Elizabeth, Cape Town, and back north through the Orange Free State into the Tranvaal to Johannesburg. We enjoyed the wildlife parks, the beaches, and comfortable hotels. In the cities of Cape Town and Johannesburg we took in plays, concerts, and ate at ethnic restaurants in the thriving and apparently secure Republic of South Africa.

But on a Sunday morning in April of 1974 in Johannesburg, as we listened to the British Broadcasting Company special report, it was revealed that a military coup in Lisbon had occurred and this change of government spelled an end to Portugal's involvement in the war in Mozambique. This meant of course that all hell would break loose in Lourenço Marques as Frelimo would become bolder and bolder. We drove pensively to Swaziland before returning to Mozambique. As we discussed the past year together and the shocking news from Lisbon regarding the coup, it became clear that the Mozambique experience was coming to a sudden end for both of us.

I decided that I needed to conclude my relationship with Desportivo and the club agreed, as the promising start of the season had been overshadowed by the political turmoil in the country and the return of key players to the U.S. Geneva and I had some serious matters to discuss regarding the possibility of our future together. We were not yet ready to be married. I decided to return to the U.S. to my hometown in Iowa to write my doctoral dissertation from the data collected in Lourenço Marques at the Physical Education Institute. Geneva resigned from the Foreign Service, which had moved her furniture and car to Mozambique from her previous assignment in the Netherlands. However, the resignation left her with the responsibility of shipping her own possessions back to the U.S. without financial assistance from the U.S. State Department, her employer.

Also, State Department regulations made it illegal for her to sell her imported car at a profit. Her sharp, 1965 Mustang was a rare commodity and had solid market value. It was the only Mustang that I had ever seen on the streets of Lourenço Marques. We finessed the Mustang transaction as I bought the car from Geneva and then sold it to my old friend, Sergio. We often thought of the possibility of Sergio approaching Samora Machel, the new Mozambique leader after the revolution, to buy the Mustang and then Sr. Machel using the car in official functions driven by chauffeur through the streets of Lourenço Marques. Samora Machel was killed in 1986 returning to Mozambique from Malawi in a suspicious plane crash over South African territory.

Concerning Geneva's furniture, stereo, crystal from Europe, etc., my former Sporting player, Mario Albuquerque, was working for a company which specialized in international shipping. Another friend and Sportinguista, Basil, known as "*O Grego*" (The Greek), was also in the shipping business and worked with Mario to make the arrangements to ship Geneva's things back to the U.S. Like clock-work, a crew of African workers arrived at Geneva's apartment and packed her possessions into four huge shipping crates. As the truck, loaded with all of her earthly possessions, pulled away from the apartment, she sadly muttered, "I doubt that I will see those things again." I knew Mario was a great player and reliable friend, but I also was doubtful.

Preparations for departure from Mozambique were hectic and emotional. I had spent three worthwhile years there and had established some enduring friendships. As we were clearing immigration at the Lourenço Marques Airport on the day of our departure, a uniformed Portuguese police officer brusquely waived me out of line and into a small office. I had no idea of what was going on, as I was led to an airport police security office. There in a cloud of cigarette smoke was Luis, calmly going through a manila folder - my file.

This personal drama resembled the arrest scene in *Midnight Express* where the American student was apprehended in the airport by the Turkish police. Luis gave me a blank look and then deadpanned a question, "How much did you receive for the Mustang and why didn't you sell it to me?" Before I could answer, he gave me a slight smile and hand shake and said, "*Boa sorte, amigo, adios.*" Good luck, friend, good-bye. I was momentarily shaken, but gathered myself and made my way through immigration onto the plane where Geneva was anxiously waiting. We were both relieved as the Deta Airlines plane lifted off on May 16, 1974. We looked down at the city of Lourenço Marques - possibly for the last time - and the scene of a memorable chapter of our lives.

We flew on to Johannesburg to spend a quiet week and then made arrangements to return to the U.S. via Nairobi, Frankfort, London, Montreal, and Chicago. We arrived in London and spent two weeks going to every play and concert available. We both felt a need to get back in touch with the English world and what a glorious place to do it - in London's West End. We attended one memorable play which was performed at the Garrick Theatre. The drama, *That Championship Season*, was written by Jason Miller and starred Broderick Crawford as coach of a high school state championship team which was having its twenty-year reunion. While four players of note and the coach were gathered together and in their cups, old conflicts among them and past frustrations in each player's life surfaced.

They had labored under the illusion that the winning of a high school state championship would propel them to success in their adult lives. This did not happen as they had become respectively a corrupt politician, an alcoholic, a ruthless miner, and failed high school principal seeking political office. The coach, who had espoused the importance of winning, had quit basketball saying that it was no longer a white man's game.

I was able to identify with the mid-life theme of "letting go of the dream" which surfaced in the dialogues and also with events of the men's lives including alcohol abuse, unresolved personal conflicts, career failure, passage of time, and general disillusionment with life. They first had had to remove their inhibitions with alcohol in order to express themselves and the drunken dialogues led only to further conflict. I identified with that also.

At that play, I reflected on my own life and my involvement in basketball, especially the last three years in Mozambique. I also warily looked to the future. I was aware that I had been strongly impacted by the Lourenço Marques experience and I wasn't sure that I really wanted to be returning home. It had been a good run and I had left Mozambique with some valuable gifts - a fiancee, enduring friendships, vivid memories, and a life-long interest in the Portuguese language.

Also, I had been living the past three years in a unique city which was a mixture of European colonial and African culture, a setting which no one would experience again in Mozambique. I had mixed feelings about returning to Grinnell, the site of my own championship season drama. A positive was that I was glad to be with Geneva; however, I was concerned by her candid comment and probing question during the flight from London to Montreal, "You seem to be troubled, aren't you drinking a little too much?" She actually said that to me. I was shocked, but secretly I too was concerned. Alcoholism always tells the drinker that he is o.k., but I denied that I was alcoholic. I just drank a little too much at times. Oh, well. I would figure it out eventually - maybe back in Grinnell.

□ *6* □

HOME AGAIN, A DOCTORATE, AND DOWN-UNDER PART I

We returned to the United States in June 1974 with Geneva spending time with her family in Grand Rapids, Michigan, and me going back to Grinnell. Eventually she came to Iowa and worked for Grinnell College in the alumni office while I did overseas player placements and began work on my doctoral dissertation. I spent several months putting together the dissertation data from Lourenço Marques and Geneva typed it on an electric typewriter, in a pre-computer era. We then drove to Murfreesboro, Tennessee, to Middle Tennessee State University where I met with my doctoral committee. The dissertation was eventually approved, conditional on my making a couple of minor revisions, after several meetings that week.

Geneva and I came back to Iowa from Tennessee and the next few months in Grinnell were eventful and focused on three developments: Geneva's possessions arrived from Lourenço Marques; the official certificate I received for a Doctor of Arts Degree from Middle Tennessee; and a meeting with Jack Thurnblad, the Carleton College coach back from a three-month sabbatical in Australia.

Geneva was living in an efficiency apartment across the street from Grinnell College and I was renting a similar place about a mile from there. One Saturday noon we were having lunch at my apartment and the phone rang asking for Geneva Alofs. It was a call from the Rock Island Railroad informing her that four packing crates had arrived in New York from Africa and were en route by rail to Grinnell. The news and subsequent arrival of her possessions were the source of a small celebration, nostalgia for Mozambique, and a prayer of thanks for Mario Albuquerque, who had orchestrated the entire shipping project.

Nine months, 10,000 miles, two ocean crossings later, and everything had arrived in good condition. A prayer was also in order for scores of innocent Portuguese in Lourenço Marques: a shocking wire-service story reported that a terrorist group had opened fire with automatic weapons at rush hour near the Lourenço Marques Airport with a reported 75 civilians killed. This atrocity was the final straw in what had been Portugal's waning interest in her African state of Mozambique.

We had barely unpacked the shipment from Lourenço Marques when I received a letter from Middle Tennessee State University informing me that the dissertation had been officially approved. Originally I had planned to use the doctorate to get a job in higher education and become a small college athletic director, basketball coach, and teacher. Even though I have never pursued that original plan, I have received personal benefits from the discipline which was developed in the process of earning the degree and in the writing of the dissertation. My major in physical education focused on athletic administration, but I had a strong minor in psychology which has proven valuable in better understanding human behavior - that of my own especially.

Probably the most important benefit of the doctoral study has been the development of my habit of disciplined, daily reading of which I preferred non-fiction and biography. This discipline has also enabled me to persevere in the serious study of two foreign languages. I cannot imagine taking a business trip to Australia or Europe without the companionship of a cache of good reading material and my business-personal diary which I keep in both Portuguese and Spanish. Protecting myself from the boredom of airline travel in this cocoon of books, articles, notes, and correspondence, the flying time became productive and a 14-hour flight from Los Angeles to Sydney can pass rapidly.

The professional credentialization in earning the degree has also come in handy at times even though I do not work in higher education. I seldom use the educational title of Doctor and for good reason. Right after receiving the doctoral degree, I used "Dr. D. Adkins" in booking an airline ticket from Chicago to L.A. Half-way through the flight, a steward approached me and confirmed my name as it appeared on the ticket. He then asked me if I would take a look at a passenger who had apparently fainted. I explained and vowed to never use the Dr. title again on any type of reservation. However, I did give some effective "medical" advice in that situation - "Give him some space, loosen his collar, apply a wet towel to his face, fan him." Like magic, he came around.

First Thoughts of Australia

Soon after the excitement of receiving Geneva's possessions and the good news on the dissertation had subsided, we had dinner with Edd and Eleanor Bowers. They mentioned that Jack Thurnblad had just returned from Australia. Thurnblad, like Bowers, had been a productive coach at a highly-selective liberal arts college, Carleton College in Northfield, Minnesota. Edd was at the time Grinnell College's head football coach while Thurnblad was Carleton's head basketball man. It was Edd who had provided my initial contacts for the Mozambique job at Academica and now was pointing me toward another opportunity. I decided to give Jack Thurnblad a call and then drove up to Northfield to spend the afternoon with him to discuss Australian basketball. After our meeting he agreed to recommend me for a job in Australia, so he wrote Ken Madsen in Queensland to introduce and recommend me for future openings.

I was enjoying the stay in Grinnell, but I knew it was time to leave again, as I did not want to commit to a job there. While in Africa and in preparation for the return to the U.S. and Iowa, I had read Thomas Wolfe's *You Can't Go Home Again.* I again referred to this book and found Wolfe's insights helpful as I realized I had been holding onto an old dream in regard to home. Grinnell, as home, was an idealized picture in my own mind of safety and security. Thus, my visit was only temporary, like everything else in reality. As Gary Player, the South African golfer, once said - "Everything in this life is on loan."

In spite of my continuing interest in overseas hoops, I had no overseas offers and it seemed that at the time I needed to do what was in front of me; take a sales job and get moving with my life. I was acting on the information which was available to me and not necessarily the way that I wanted it to be. The Australia situation was still preliminary and I needed to make a living.

I have used the same line of reasoning and the principle of "today's information, not tomorrow's dream" in working with basketball players looking for overseas playing opportunities. I advised them to find a job, stay in shape, and wait to hear from me regarding possible job offers. Sometimes the chance doesn't develop for months and sometimes not at all. I do my best to tell players the truth when I cannot help with their careers - an important service to them. Most, of course, don't want to hear any comment from me in conflict with their own pictures of themselves. But, on occasion, I have sensed that the player was relieved to hear that I could not help him, and he, therefore, was temporarily safe and would not have to worry about going overseas into the abyss of the unknown. I have learned the power and sense of living in the present on the basis of today's reality, not tomorrow's dreams, or fantasies. It was a difficult concept to convey to a young basketball player or to an old coach holding onto a dream - which often was only that.

Grinnell had been a good stop. I had had the opportunity to renew old friendships and spend time with my mother, but it was time to make decisions and Australia still seemed only a remote possibility. When I had committed to the doctoral program at Middle Tennessee, I was thinking vaguely of seeking a job at a U.S. college in teaching and coaching. On this occasion I wanted something that I could leave on short notice, Australia was definitely a top priority, but so was making a living.

On the Move

I worked as an area representative for the Physical Fitness Institute of America. PFIA was an umbrella marketing organization for the sale of a piece of exercise equipment called the Apollo Exerciser, which was a clone of a previous product called Exer-Genie. The product was incidental to the concept of physical fitness and to the sales strategy, which involved physical fitness lectures to clubs and organizations in my sales area. My doctorate was a ticket to these speaking engagements, which were booked by a public relations staff out of the company's home office in Incline Village, Nevada. I liked the physical fitness field and the contact with business people, the lecture was informative, and the sale of the product generated income.

I learned much about selling from Dean Miller, the sales manager for the Apollo organization. He was a former coach and later became a successful real estate broker in Incline Village, Nevada. I was selling physical fitness. I believed in the value of daily exercise and therefore was successful in the job. The work required mobility and I was involved in a series of address changes. We moved from Grinnell to Topeka, then Kansas City, Orlando, and back to Kansas City over the next two years.

While living in Topeka and before the other moves within the U.S., Geneva and I decided to get married and did so on July 16, 1976. We were married at the Simpson College Chapel in Indianola, Iowa, and then had a dinner and reception with family and friends in Des Moines. We flew to Jacksonville the next day and spent four days looking around Central Florida for an apartment and office space for the exercise equipment business. Winter Park, a suburb of Orlando, was our choice for our Florida home. We then flew back to New York and embarked upon a honeymoon trip to London, Copenhagen, and Amsterdam. While in Copenhagen, I visited the basketball association there. This European hoop setting stirred my juices and reinforced my interest in getting back into overseas basketball on a full-time basis.

En route by public bus transportation from our hotel to the local basketball association office, I met an American player who was contracted by a club in Copenhagen. In my brief talk with him during that bus ride, I was reminded of another side of the game - a downside. The kid had been so high that he could barely focus and this was at 10:00 a.m. The bus incident reminded me of the death of Bob "Mo" Elmore.

Death in Europe

I recalled the tragic death of a great college player at Wichita State University in Europe. I contacted Kirk Seminoff, a veteran sports writer who had covered Shocker teams for years. Seminoff, of course, remembered

"Big Mo" and provided background information to me from the newspaper's archives. *The Wichita Eagle* reported that Bob Elmore had been found dead in his apartment in Italy on November 25, 1977, of a massive coronary associated with the presence of heroin in his blood. The death drew extensive media attention in Wichita, Kansas, and two *Eagle* and *Beacon* writers, Julie Charlip and Don Williamson, wrote a comprehensive six-part series, which began on January 15, 1978, on Bob Elmore's death.

I had had several talks with Elmore's teammate and childhood friend, Cal Bruton, in Brisbane, Australia, in 1979 about the 1975-76 Wichita team. Bruton recalled the "New York Pipeline" headed by Steve Shalin, a banker and coach of the famous Salukis AAU team. Shalin had a talented group of high school players in Saluki uniforms that year. Included were Bruton, Elmore, Rudy Jackson, and Ricky Marsh, who later logged NBA time with Golden State. Jackson and Elmore were aggressively recruited by Wichita State and the 5'7 Bruton was thrown into the deal at the insistence of the 6'9 Rudy Jackson. Steve Shalin saw that the three committed to Wichita State. Bruton and Elmore became first team All-Missouri Valley Conference players, while Rudy Jackson didn't pass entrance requirements and ended up at Hutchinson Junior College. As Bruton recalled, Jackson had further problems at Hutch when someone attempted to change his transcript after a break-in at a college administration building. Bruton said that Jackson was later drafted by the Knicks and subsequently played a few seasons in Europe, with limited success.

Bob Elmore and Cal Bruton attended Junior High School 231 in Queens, New York, together but Elmore played at John Adams High School and Bruton at Springfield-Gardens. Thus the two New Yorkers went back a long way. They were junior high classmates, high school basketball rivals, Saluki AAU teammates, and eventually through Steve Shalin became teammates at Wichita State University. Bruton and Elmore were explosive college players and expectations were high at WSU heading into the 1975-76 season. The parts were in place for a conference title run - the mercurial Bruton at the point; powerful 6'9 Mo at the center spot; talented 6'7 Robert Gray at the power forward; 6'5 Cheese Johnson, a slick scorer, at the small forward; and an athletic 6'3 German import Bob Trogele, the off guard. The team finished 22-10, but fell short in a first-round NCAA loss to Michigan.

One warm Queensland summer day in 1979 as we drove to a junior basketball camp, Cal Bruton remembered the disappointment of being cut by the San Antonio Spurs after a promising training camp including several solid performances in NBA exhibition games. He thought that he was going to stick with the Spurs, but that didn't happen, and Bruton said that even suicide had crossed his mind in more desperate moments. Bruton knew that

Bob Elmore had also experienced shock and disappointment after being cut by the New York Nets in 1977.

According to *The Eagle* series, Giancario Asteo, the Italian coach, was not aware of Elmore's use of drugs and WSU Athletic Director Ted Bredehoft told writers Julie Charlip and Don Williamson that Elmore didn't use drugs while a Wichita State player. Cal Bruton, the prominent teammate, disagreed. Bruton had been the point guard and leader of that Shocker team with Bob Elmore at Wichita State in 1975-76. The Shockers won the Missouri Valley Conference and lost a 74-73 first-round NCAA Tourney game to Michigan at Denton, Texas, on March 13, 1976. Bruton roomed with Mo on the NCAA trip and stated that Elmore had actually used the night before the Michigan game in the team hotel. Bruton said that Mo justified his using at that time as it relaxed him.

Cal commented in a hand-written fax (April 17, 1998) to me on the Michigan game as follows:

"...He (Elmore) was in foul trouble and did not play the last 13 minutes of the first half. He played well in the second half. He scored 16 points in the second half and scored our last eight out of nine during the final 10 minutes...His last trip to the line with us 1-up, he missed giving them their chance and Ricky Green made no mistake."

Green hit the game winner from the corner as Bruton had outplayed him all night long. Bruton finished with 15 points (6-13 fg) and held Green to 10 points on 4-17 shooting. Elmore finished with 18 points - 16 in the second half - and had 7 rebounds. Years later, Michigan coach Johnny Orr told me that "I thought Ricky Green was quick, but that damn Bruton picked his pocket all night long. He was unbelievable against Green."

Elmore was named to the all-conference team in 1976-77, his senior year, at W.S.U. before going to camp with the Nets and then accepting the Italian contract. In spite of Elmore's achievements as a college player, Bruton was, of course, aware of Mo's drug habit and its effect on his performances at WSU. Cal Bruton told me from his home in Perth, Australia, in 1998 that he had been constantly frustrated with the situation at Wichita State, because Mo Elmore was a great talent who was hindered by his deadly habit. Thus, Cal Bruton concluded that the team never was able to reach its full potential. He thought that the Shockers could have gone all the way in the NCAA Tourney with Mo at his very best. Sadness for the loss of his teammate and friend since junior high, Mo Elmore, along with the frustration and the facts of the Michigan game all were still fresh in Calvin Bruton's mind 22 years after the final gun in his team's 74-73 defeat, his last game as a college player.

Agents: Take Your Chances

Thus with renewed interest in overseas basketball, yet tempered by the memory of the bus experience of seeing the player high on drugs, we returned to Florida from our trip to Europe. I then received a call from Jim McGregor in Italy. I made plans to meet him in Chicago at DePaul University on a Sunday morning to look at some players he had lined up for a tryout.

After the workout at DePaul, we took a cab to a downtown hotel and spent a couple of hours discussing our careers to date and opportunities in overseas basketball. He asked me if I was interested in coaching a touring team in South America for three weeks. I had to decline, as I was still obligated to my sales job and also just married. I did not want to make an abrupt change of direction at that moment. As a result of the Chicago meeting with McGregor, I started to get active in contacting players even though I continued in the sales work.

At the time, in the late 1970s, I knew of only a few others involved in the overseas player business - McGregor, Jim White in California, Richard Kaner in New York, Herb Rudoy in Chicago, and me, to a lesser degree. In those days it was not difficult to find and sign players. Today there are hundreds of would-be overseas agents with lists of players, and like NBA agents, a small percentage with employed clients. First-round draft picks needed agents with NBA experience and legal back-up. However, players destined to play overseas prior to an NBA career or overseas exclusively needed help from ethical professionals experienced in foreign basketball markets.

On the down-side of the agent business, there were successful player agents who used their NBA client lists to attract and sign ex-college players with no hope of playing in the NBA. These agents then stockpiled the players rather than actively working to find them employment. Their strategy was that if a foreign club or other agent approached one of their stockpiled players about a job, a fee split was in order. Also, there were those with no authentic, direct overseas experience or contacts who signed players and then called others in the business for assistance and, of course, a 50-50 fee split. These types relied on the electronic supermarket and hoped that the player's name on a fax or e-mail transmission would attract the attention of a foreign club looking for a player.

Regardless of the communication technology available, I preferred to know my overseas basketball contacts personally, which meant periodic travel to accomplish this. I have found that the three means of business communication were in order of effectiveness - personal contact, telephone calls, and written correspondence, including faxes and e-mail. A legitimate overseas agent can do a great deal to enhance opportunities for qualified players, for he should know who fits where and the player's legitimate market value. Further, an effective agent will speak candidly to the player about the market facts. There were probably as few reliable players as there were trustworthy agents. A contract can be only "a piece of paper" to many irresponsible parties in the overseas game. However, the exceptions who have done their best to honor an agreement have made foreign employment a viable situation for players, clubs, and agents.

While still living in Grinnell in July of 1975, I again set in motion my efforts in player recruitment. I drove to the Milwaukee Buck Veterans' Camp at the University of Wisconsin-Parkside to watch David Russell, a 6'7 forward from Shepherd College in W.VA. Junior Bridgeman was, via a trade, the Bucks' first rounder in 1975 and he was getting most of the attention. I signed Russell to a player-agent agreement over a couple of beers at the hotel after the Bucks' evening workout and then contacted Jim McGregor regarding the player's availability for European duty. I subsequently received a call from an interested Dutch club, but the David Russell story and his young life came to a tragic end via an automobile accident in Europe soon after.

A Dangerous Game

Russell joined Bob Elmore, Wichita State, and Steve Mitchell, Kansas State, as fatalities among U.S. players in Europe during that era. As discussed, Elmore, the 6'10 Wichita State star, died in Italy in 1978 with the autopsy reporting heroin in his system. Steve Mitchell led Kansas State to the Big Eight Conference title in the 1972-73 season and averaged 15.1 points and 8.9 rebounds for Coach Jack Hartman. Drafted in the third round, Mitchell went to a Phoenix Sun camp. He was cut by Phoenix and then played successfully in Europe for five years. Various media sources stated that he was found dead in a friend's home in Italy in 1978 reportedly of natural causes associated with an asthmatic condition.

Although each of the three tragic deaths of former U.S. college basketball players - Dave Russell, Bob Elmore, and Steve Mitchell - had been reportedly related to different causes, adjustment to life in a foreign country for young American players has always been a challenge. In those days, overseas basketball was known as "the eight hour week" as players had too much time on their hands. Alcohol, drugs, and undisciplined living were too often the time fillers.

For players uncomfortable in a foreign culture, marking the days off the calendar was common. I saw Jo Jo English, who averaged 15 points in 21 games with the Adelaide 36ers in 1995, in the lobby of the Melbourne Hilton Hotel with his headsets on, oblivious to the activity around him. He had been hired on short notice as a replacement player, and I heard that he was having problems adjusting to Australian life. Jo Jo and his headsets reminded me of Moses Malone, the 12-time, NBA-All-Star, who had come directly out of high school in Petersburg, Virginia, to the pros in 1974. Malone was an unsophisticated kid trying to protect himself from an adult world. He, like Jo Jo down-under, used his headsets for temporary protection from a strange environment and as "I.V.'s" tapped into the safety and security of reassuring sounds.

Times have changed since the overseas deaths of the three American players in the 1970s. Many European teams have implemented daily training schedules more intense and requiring more of the players' time than U.S. pro and college teams. The heavier workload has kept the import busier with more of his energy required in basketball. Drugs and alcohol were, of course, still abused. Ultimately, the choices made outside the gym reflect the player's character and motivation; and these choices can ultimately determine his fate overseas regardless of his abilities on the court.

The McGregor Letter

I had stayed in contact with Jim McGregor since our first conversation in 1974, when he asked me to collect the fee in Lourenço Marques from the Academica Club on Greg Howard. We renewed that original contact and met face-to-face for the first time via the meeting in Chicago two years later. Coach McGregor was the only basketball personality who extended me congratulations on my taking the director of coaching job in Australia in 1978.

Upon receiving that letter, I became aware for the first time that I was actually in the process of putting together a career and a life in overseas basketball, outside the loop of U.S. hoops. McGregor's message reinforced that I was not just wandering around the world debating in my mind if I should be back in the U.S, home again, to follow a conventional path. That confirmation from McGregor, who actually worked in the overseas game, helped me to see the value of what I was doing, as I had no peer group to consult. The letter was an affirmation of my decision to go overseas again and helped remove self-doubt.

I had learned in our Chicago conversation that Jim McGregor was from Portland, attended USC, and earned his fame as the Whitworth College (WA) coach by taking a team to the N.A.I.A. championships and in some part by drawing 12 technical fouls in a game with Puget Sound. McGregor said that in that game he had charged onto the court and apparently informed the referee that it was either "sodomy or a foul." McGregor swore that he was assessed a technical for every step it took him to reach the bench.

He spoke of building the Whitworth program into a small college power and reached the quarterfinals at the NAIA Nationals in Kansas City in 1953.

When McGregor returned to the Whitworth campus after his triumph in Kansas City, it was masked good fortune that the college president fired him. He was able to create - the thing he did the best - a far more interesting and profitable career from a base in Gorizia, Italy. I was finding out the same thing in my own life through various overseas basketball experiences. I doubt that anyone in the history of the sport has traveled more miles and had more fun in basketball than the great Jim McGregor, who also wrote a book, now retired in Palm Springs, California.

Florida

After my exercise equipment sales work in the Topeka area, the Chicago meeting with McGregor, and my marriage to Geneva in 1976, we had relocated to Winter Park, Florida. The move to the Orlando area was job advancement as I became a sales manager, along with my own selling work, over a seven-state area in the southeastern U.S. I did several keynote addresses at major conventions in Orlando, Tampa, Naples, and Miami, again using the soft-sell lecture approach to the topic of physical fitness for the busy American and offering the opportunity for the convention visitor to take home in his suitcase an Apollo Exerciser.

Lecturing on physical fitness from a podium to qualified buyers was an effective sales strategy. This was an occasion where the title of Dr. was a huge asset. I would give the lecture, sell the concept of daily physical fitness through use of the Apollo Exerciser, close the individual sales after the lecture, and provide a two-hour physical fitness workshop at the convention site on use of the equipment. I did my best to suggest a wide range of effective fitness activities to supplement the Apollo program. I also knew that in spite of good intentions most would lack the discipline to stay with any physical fitness program for very long.

Ed Jucker

Although I had a hectic travel schedule in covering my seven-state sales territory, I did have time for an interesting basketball experience while living in Winter Park. Each day I drove past Rollins College en route to my office downtown. I had read in the paper that Ed Jucker, the former University of Cincinnati coach, had been named the new coach at Rollins, an NCAA II school. I stopped at the Rollins gym one day. Jucker was there and in the process of moving into his office. I introduced myself; he was cordial and wanted to talk basketball.

I noticed a framed photograph of Jucker's 1960-61 NCAA Champions and called attention to that great college team. Coach Jucker picked up the photograph, pointed to a blonde Cincinnati player with a crewcut, and commented, "Wiesenhahn was the key in the 1961 championship game against Ohio State. He held John Havlicek to four points. That gave us the chance to win." Jucker showed me the clipping which affirmed that Havlicek could manage only one field goal in five attempts in that title game, while Bob Wiesenhahn had 17 points and 9 rebounds.

Ed Jucker and the Cincinnati Bearcats won back-to-back NCAA championships in 1960-61 and 1961-62 beating the same team - Ohio State - in the final tournament games. Jucker was passed over as National Coach of the Year award in both of his Cincinnati teams' championship seasons; Fred Taylor, the Ohio State coach, won the award both years. Ironically, the 6'4 Wiesenhahn had an abbreviated NBA career and played only the 1961-62 season averaging 2.0 points per game with the Cincinnati Royals. John Havlicek went on to figure heavily in eight NBA championships with Boston, was the Celtics all-time leading scorer, and was named to the Basketball Hall of Fame in 1983.

The Big O

No, Oscar Robertson was not on either of those Bearcat title teams - or any other NCAA champion, for that matter. He was drafted after his college eligibility by the Cincinnati Royals in 1960 and averaged 30.5 points and 30.8 points in the NBA in the two years that Jucker's teams were busy winning their NCAA championships. I saw Oscar play three times in the flesh - once against Drake University in 1957, once with the U.S. team in the Chicago Pan-American Games in 1959 at DePaul University, and once as a pro with the Cincinnati Royals versus the Hawks at Keel Auditorium in St. Louis in 1965.

Drake held him to 16 points, less than half of his 35-point average, on that December night in 1957. He blended into the team with the talented U.S. Pan-Am Gold Medal winners, but was also the leading scorer at 16.5 points per game and shot 57% from the field, a sensational percentage in those days. Jerry West was the team's second leading scorer at 11.3 points.

I watched the "Big O" as he backed down the St. Louis Hawk defense and hit a 15-foot game winner on that Sunday afternoon in St. Louis in December 1965. He had the ability to get the shot that he wanted off the dribble; he was confident and deliberate in making his moves; and his behind-the-head release was unblockable as well as being deadly accurate. Robertson, who averaged a double-double (33.8 points and 15.2 rebounds) in his 88 game college career, consistently demonstrated basketball skills otherwise unknown in the history of college basketball.

In my opinion, Oscar Robertson was the greatest collegiate individual player of all time; he could score, shoot, pass, dribble, ball-handle, rebound, and defend, and he did it all with great consistency at the highest level. He continued his incredible production in the NBA as he was named to the All-NBA First Team on nine occasions and averaged a triple-double (scoring, rebounding, assists) in both the 1961-62 and 1962-63 NBA seasons. Although he was obviously a gifted athlete and possessed a strong body at 6'5, Oscar was a perfectionist in all basketball fundamentals. He relied on execution as he scored, passed, and grabbed his impressive rebound totals (15.3 per game), a result of great fundamental body position, timing, and quick hands.

I was a regular at Rollins College that year and witnessed some good games under Jucker played with various opponents including Stetson University coached by Glenn Wiles and North Carolina-Charlotte under Lee Rose. I also ran into Jim Bouton, the ex-Yankee pitcher, in Winter Park at the gym and also at the travel agency one day. He was working out on the Rollins campus preparing for a comeback. However, we left Florida a year later to return to Kansas City; five months after the move from Florida in January 1977, we decided to spend 30 days in Australia on a business holiday. The key event in the trip was meeting with Ken Madsen, a banker and the president of the Queensland Amateur Basketball Association in Brisbane.

First Trip to Australia

We managed to stay a few hours ahead of a major snowstorm in flying from Kansas City to Los Angeles. We spent a night at an LAX (airport) hotel and then flew to Sydney from Los Angeles. Our hotel in Sydney was near Kings Cross, the center of the city's seamier nightlife, but we enjoyed a three-day visit and then rented a car and drove to Port MacQuarie, New South Wales, and then on to Brisbane. I called Ken Madsen, who had received Jack Thurnblad's letter, and Madsen invited us to dinner at his home with his wife, Allison. Bob Young, a junior coach in the Brisbane competition, was also present that evening.

Ken told me that Ian Watson, an Aussie Olympic player, was currently working as Queensland State Director of Coaching and that he would be offered a contract renewal in September (1978). However, he also said that Ian and his wife, Sue, might reject the offer and return to their home in Melbourne. It was agreed that I would stay in touch on the matter and that evening I did express interest in the job should Ian vacate. Geneva and I liked Brisbane, but it seemed rather uncertain at the time that we would return there in the near future. The next day we flew from Brisbane to Melbourne for a week and then to Adelaide before returning to Sydney for our flight back to the U.S.

In Melbourne, I had gone to Albert Park, the headquarters for the Victorian State Basketball Association. Court One at Albert Park was still using the scoreboard from the 1956 Melbourne Olympics, and the other 16 courts generated revenue and provided facilities for thousands of players of all ages through the years. I met Lindsay Gaze, the legendary "first man of basketball" in Australia and the most knowledgeable of all Aussies in the international arena. As the years passed, I would get to know Lindsay well through Melbourne-Hobart games. However, on this occasion, our conversation was short and he confirmed that there would be little opportunity for me on the Australian basketball scene. Like all coaches, he was just defending his turf.

Portuguese in Kansas City

That trip down-under gave me some insight into the Australian basketball system; I assessed that they were just getting started and noted that they had no national league, professional competition. Back in Kansas City, we had purchased a nice townhouse adjacent to Corporate Woods, a rapidly developing business complex. We liked the Kansas City area even though I did from time to time feel a surge when Australia or Europe or Africa was mentioned.

This feeling was reinforced by an event which occurred in Kansas City in November of 1977. I experienced very strong emotions while walking through the shop area of the Crown Center Hotel in downtown Kansas City. I ran into Nelson Serra, George Sing, and Morais, three players from Lourenço Marques, who were in Kansas City to represent Portugal in an international tournament sponsored by the NAIA. I was shocked and in disbelief to actually see these guys again. They had exited Mozambique right after the revolution in 1974 and were living in Lisbon.

The Portuguese team was in town for a week. I spent considerable time with Nelson and also placed Rod Littlepage, a 6'11 post player from Drake, with the Porto Club, whose president was along with the team for the Kansas City tournament. Geneva and I took Nelson, Carlos Lisboa, and another Portuguese player to the Chief-Bronco National Football League game at Arrowhead Stadium on a sunny, December, Sunday afternoon. However, the temperature dropped at least 25 degrees during the game and these guys were most impressed with the severity of midwestern winter weather and the challenge of life in the Northern Hemisphere. After the game, we all went back to our townhouse for dinner and I played a tape from *Radio Mozambique*. I shall never forget the emotion in our living room in reaction to the distinctive sounds of Lourenço Marques radio. My mind was racing in a very intense moment.

The hot Kansas City summer passed rapidly. In September 1978 I had just returned home from a Royal-Yankee game at Royals Stadium and received a call from Ken Madsen in Australia. He said that Ian Watson had decided to return to Melbourne and I was being offered the Queensland State Director of Coaching job. I accepted without hesitation. Geneva said, "I don't believe you did that," then added, "Yes, I do." Shortly after, she was as enthusiastic as I, as we were putting our house on the market and making plans to store our furniture. It wasn't easy to pick up and leave on short notice, as we had enjoyed Kansas City, but my gut kept saying, "Queensland next stop." On December 15, we left Los Angeles en route to Auckland to spend a week in that seaport city located on New Zealand's North Island before continuing to Brisbane.

□ *7* □

DOWN-UNDER

We arrived in Brisbane in the middle of the Queensland summer in December 1978 and my first task was to work with Ian Watson, the outgoing director of coaching, in planning and supervising the Queensland State Junior Camp scheduled for the Gold Coast in January during the school holidays. The live-in camp included under-16 and under-18 boys and girls billeted in cabins in a complex on the Pacific Ocean. Also included were a spartan basketball facility, the standard steel quonset but with a good wooden floor, decent lighting, and six baskets mounted on wooden backboards.

I can recall especially the accommodation - a crude tourist cabin with no air-conditioning, no screens on the windows, and a dirty floor - which slept four people. Our cabin was across the street and only about fifty meters from a popular local night club. The music was loud and motorcycles roared in and out until the wee hours. Then the sun would shine in the open windows a couple hours later and it would be time for another fourteen-hour day at the camp. What a week. I learned much about the structure of Queensland basketball and also the talent level among junior players. I was impressed with both. But also I was determined to move the camp site the next season as far away from that night club as possible.

Ian Watson had been in the state director's position for two years. He had established the foundation for a productive junior development system including coaching education courses as a part of a state and national coaching accreditation scheme along with instruction to junior players through local, regional, and state camps. As a player Ian, the son of Ken Watson, a well-known Victorian basketball administrator, was a solidly-built, lefty point guard who had distinguished himself as a heady, competitive leader of the 1976 Australian Olympic team. He was an intelligent man, trained as a mathematics teacher, who had established good rapport with the state basketball community in Queensland. Tragically, Ian Watson died of cancer about three years later in Melbourne.

As I got further into the job in Queensland, it was clear that the junior program was in place, but the senior-level, competitive basketball presented few opportunities for aspiring players. For example, Larry Sengstock and Danny Morseu, two Queenslanders who became prominent Australian National Team players, had exited their home state at age eighteen to participate in the country's strongest competition in the Victorian Basketball Association (VBA) in Melbourne.

In retrospect, both Morseau and Sengstock were, at age eighteen, big-time U.S. college-level talents, Division I impact players in the Big Ten or the Big Eight Conference. At age twenty-two they were serious NBA prospects, draftable players, but that was a different era with little interest from or exposure to the American pro league. I saw a pressing need to fill the void at the top end of the Queensland state basketball program. I employed two plans to accomplish this task: build the Brisbane Bullets, just established as a charter member of the National Invitational Basketball League, and create a more competitive program for existing A grade teams, comprised of players eighteen and older with the desire to continue competitive basketball.

Key Arrivals

With the arrival of Cal Bruton and Dan Hickert, recruited as reinforcements to the local stars, the Brisbane Bullets were completing serious preparations for the league opener versus the Canberra Cannons. The NIBL, National Invitational Basketball League, was the latest attempt in Australia to establish a high level men's competition with a national scope.

Other efforts had failed because basketball was not a grass roots Australian sport and few people down-under knew, or cared to know, anything about it. "The Yanks can keep their bloody game, mate; I am off to the footy match at the MCG" - referring to the 120,000 seat Melbourne Cricket Ground and site of Australian Rules Football, known as the "national religion" of Australia. The grass roots issue in basketball has never been resolved in Australia and the game still labored with fan appeal and the development of a sound financial base for the Australian professional league, the NBL.

Bruton and Hickert, the 6'11 ex-Kansas State post player and survivor of one of Jim McGregor's whirlwind rail and bus tours of European markets, arrived with little practice time before the first game. McGregor used to take the San Marino All-Stars on an annual tour playing games against European clubs with the objective to place in jobs his entire touring team. He selected eleven post players and one point guard to pass the others the ball.

Hickert was hesitant to accept the Brisbane job, as he had heard stories and seen firsthand the random cutting of U.S. players in European jobs. When I located him to discuss the Brisbane Bullet opportunity, Big Dan had to climb his 6'11 frame down from a tractor on the family farm near Bird City, Kansas, to take my call. When I rang McGregor about Dan Hickert, he replied, "Yeah, I know Dan, Dan, the Rebound Man - decent player, great person."

Hickert had been in Brisbane a week before the opening game and Cal Bruton had parked his trash truck, for the final time, in Wichita and had flown into Brisbane only 36 hours before tip-off of the first National League game in Queensland basketball history. However, the Black Pearl made the best of his limited adjustment period before competition by going directly from the airport to the gym. Auchenflower State Stadium, another quonset but with two courts and an acceptable wooden floor, was the home of the Bullets and had a seating capacity of only 1,000. Auchenflower had survived the Brisbane flood of 1975. There was a momumental high-water mark still visible at the top of the square on one of the backboards on Court #1 - a spot on the board probably untouched by human hand until the invasion of National League players competing against the Bullets.

Harold Peacock Sr., president of Queensland Basketball Inc., the financial arm of the Queensland state system, and I met Cal Bruton at the Brisbane Airport on that rainy Queensland summer day in February 1979 and drove him to the gym. Mr. Peacock was known as a successful, creative businessman. A former Australian rules player from Adelaide, Harold Sr. had become involved in basketball in Queensland. He used his business expertise to work with banker Ken Madsen to develop an effective plan in financing the building of indoor gymnasiums throughout the entire state. Peacock was intrigued by Calvin Bruton's personality and then impressed with his work ethic. Cal was a little leery of Harold and was apparently getting a message from his instincts. Bruton told me a year later that he thought that Harold would like to "own me."

En route from the Brisbane airport, Cal Bruton immediately asserted his need and desire to get to a gym with the Bullet game coming up the next evening. He had just arrived after a 30-hour trip and was not in great condition as he had not played in a structure since the Kings' NBA camp five months prior. I recalled Harold giving me an approving quick glance when Bruton said, "Take me to the gym; I want to loosen up and shoot for a half an hour." Both men - the American player from New York and the Aussie rules businessman from Adelaide - shared a common respect for the value of hard work. Peacock had built his life and businesses that way and Bruton his basketball career in the same manner.

Harold and I watched the young guy from Wichita State via Queens, New York, light up the drab Auchenflower setting with his smile and obvious passion for basketball. The thirty-minute shoot-around evolved into a three-hour, one-man workout and upon leaving the floor Bruton pronounced himself "ready" - for whatever was ahead.

The Brisbane Bullets

The first two import players in Brisbane Bullet history were truly opposites in many ways. Dan Hickert was a 6'11 farm boy raised in Bird City,

Kansas, who became a limited action player as a walk-on at Kansas State under Coach Jack Hartman. Dan was an accounting major and maintained a controlled, conservative approach to basketball and life. Cal Bruton, on the other hand, was a flamboyant and creative player. At 5'7 he had to compensate with total commitment from a young age in order to excel in the big man's game and to survive on the streets of Queens in New York.

Bruton started as a freshman at Wichita State in an era when WSU basketball enjoyed consistent national rankings. He was a two-time, All-Missouri Valley Conference selection and played a dozen exhibition games with the San Antonio Spurs in 1976 before being cut. Bruton was devastated and depressed for several months after his experience with the Spurs before resurfacing and re-committing to another try at professional basketball.

The Bullets placed Dan and Cal in a holiday flat, actually a large motel room with a kitchenette. Living together, they got along very well, until one day Dan came to me and said, "Doc, (named by Bruton) Cal took some of my pictures." That was a mistake. Dan was a perfectionist and a dedicated photographer. Hickert had meticulously arranged his hundreds of new photos in a special filing system. Bruton decided that he would send home a few in which he had appeared without clearing it with Dan.

Big Dan was irritated and I thought immediately of team dissension and disaster. But I conferred with Cal. It was agreed that Bruton return the photographs and then Cal would trade his prized gold chain necklace to Dan for rights to future pictures taken by the elongated photographer. Once that business was settled, I can't recall another harsh word between the two. Dan stood up for Cal at his wedding in 1979 and the two have remained friends for life. Both settled after their NBL playing days in Perth, Western Australia.

On another occasion, Cal called my office and said that he needed to talk with me. Later in the day, I met him in the city and asked him what was up. He said that he wanted to get a haircut and wasn't sure how to go about that in Brisbane. He didn't like the idea of walking into a barber shop unannounced. I was sure that I wanted no embarrassing situations for Cal and had already talked with my own barber in East Brisbane about the Black Pearl. We jumped in the car and drove over to East Brisbane where I introduced Cal to the barber, who was beaming. The barber, an Australian in his sixties, proudly did the hair cut and then asked for Bruton's autograph afterwards.

In the first Brisbane Bullet game contested at Auchenflower Stadium versus the Canberra Cannons on February 4, 1979, local standouts Colin Varian, Bruce Fitzgerald, Grant Simmons, Robert Wood, Albert Navruk, and Barry Freeman were joined in the Bullet line-up by the two U.S. imports, Calvin Bruton and Dan Hickert. The team was coached by Bob Young, called Bimbo by locals, and a veteran junior coach who was clearly challenged by the NBL level of play.

Coach Young always wore a tormented look, especially when I was in his presence. I sensed that he would have preferred to go 0-18, which would have killed the continuation of the franchise, than compete and win some games with the inclusion of the two Yanks. He was somewhat agreeable to the inclusion of the 6'11 Hickert but "saw no need to bring an American guard." In fact, Bimbo resisted at every turn any attempt to enhance or upgrade the Bullet program. Harold Peacock called me about a third of the way through the season and asked me to replace Young as the head coach. I was tempted, but I felt that the team was coming together and that there were feelings enough already from locals about the prominence of outsiders in the Bullet organization. My instincts were good in this matter, as Cal Bruton learned later in his career the perils of replacing an incumbent Australian as coach. He was still paying for it in terms of NBL coaching opportunities.

Two hundred curious faithfuls filed into the Auchenflower gym on opening night of the 1979 National Invitational Basketball League season. Hickert controlled the tip versus 6'10 Cal Stamp, player-coach from Wake Forest, and the Pearl had the ball pushing it into the Bullet offensive zone. One quick cross-over move and he lost his man. He pulled up from about 23 feet and the little New Yorker released the first shot in Bullet history - and it was a brick. As the ball caromed hard off the rim at a sharp angle, Bruton turned to the small, captive audience and loudly claimed "Jet lag." In another quick movement he threw his gold chain necklace for safe-keeping to Cass and Bill, two ex-patriot Canadians sitting in the front row. In tossing his prized gold chain to strangers, Bruton had demonstrated unconditional trust in the Bullet fans and thus began a relationship from which both he and Brisbane Bullet basketball received significant benefits.

Through that initial interaction with the fans and the following ragged, but promising performance, Cal Bruton and the Brisbane Bullets took their first steps in National Basketball League competition in Australia. Despite losing their first four games, the team rallied and miraculously finished 10-8 in league play. Calvin led the league in scoring with a 32-point per game average. The first edition of the Bullets survived and provided the groundwork for what was to become one of the most successful franchises in Australian basketball history.

The Yugoslavian Incident

During the 1979 NBL season, the Yugoslavian club champion, Cibona, under head coach Mirko Novosel, came to Australia to play a five-game test series with the Australian National Team. Cibona also had scheduled some exhibition games with club teams around the country. The Yugoslavs' tour was sponsored by Basketball Australia, then known as the ABF - (Australian Basketball Federation) which had arranged games throughout the land down-under and thus gave people in all the major cities a chance to see high-level international competition.

Harold Peacock Sr. was the president of the Gold Coast Basketball Association. He had used his influence to get the Cougars, the men's team participating in the Brisbane A Grade competition, on the Cibona schedule. Harold invited Cal Bruton and Dan Hickert as guest players to join the local Cougar team spearheaded by two sets of brothers, the Granthams and the Goldfinches. The Cougars were a dedicated and controversial group which was despised by the Brisbane bureaucracy. The feeling was, of course, mutual.

Mr. Peacock was an entrepreneur and a risk taker in his business life, which carried over into the promotion of basketball. Locals often said that Peacock was always after "his pound of flesh" in business dealings, but he also had a sense of humor. He added some color to the Cougar-Cibona game by tipping the local newspaper that he had received a bomb threat from a dissident, ex-patriot Yugoslav group protesting the appearance of Cibona at the Gold Coast. Police were alerted, but Harold assured all concerned in the local press and on the radio that any and all security measures would be taken at the game. That little touch was enough to stir the kettle of interest and, of course, assure that the Gold Coast gym was standing room only to fans who paid a special, premium price for tickets to the big game.

Geneva and I drove Cal and Dan the 60 miles down to the site of the Yugolsav game in Southport on the Gold Coast in the morning. Harold Peacock never missed an opportunity to further the cause of local basketball. He had scheduled a full slate of clinics utilizing me along with Bruton and Hickert to give pointers to his junior players in the local basketball association. After the clinic work, we all had lunch together about 2:00 p.m. and then Dan and Cal disappeared into the beach scene at the coast.

About three hours later, Geneva and I stopped at Harold Peacock's home. His wife, Shirley, was busy chastising him for his ingenuity in causing a possible international incident at the game because of the bomb threat story. Big Dan and Cal were sleeping on Harold's patio and I was impressed with their dedication and professional preparation in resting for the big game that evening. But it wasn't quite as it appeared.

Before a fully packed house, Cal Bruton scored 41 from all angles and was sensational. On one occasion, he took an outlet pass from Hickert and weaved his away through the entire Cibona team, scoring on a clever runner over a 6'10 rival. The local Australian players did well, Cibona won a closely contested game by five, and Big Dan finished with four points and four boards.

I learned later that evening that Cal had taken Hickert to a beer garden in the afternoon. They drank their pre-game meal and had consumed a couple of pitchers of the cold 4-X Queensland beer. Thus the nap was needed to sleep off the grog. When I questioned the two, Bruton laughed and Dan, serious to a fault, said that "Yes" he had drank a few glasses of brew, "But I felt fine during the game; didn't bother me at all." I looked at Cal and said that we really expected a little more than four rebounds and four points from our 6'11 U.S. import. Dan was shocked at his numbers.

As State Director of Coaching, I saw the Bullet program as the flagship in the entire state basketball network and a program where aspiring Queenslanders could play at the highest level in the country and remain at home. However, Coach Young had other ideas. At the end of the season, I attended an important meeting with the Brisbane Basketball Association board with my ally, Harold Peacock Sr. present. Bob Young opened the session with his accounting books on the table and said that it was not feasible for the Bullet program to continue. Further, he stated that the projected NBL fee of $25,000, which would cover equalized airline and hotel expenses for league teams for the next season, was out of reach for the Bullets. He concluded his report declaring that the team should be dropped from the National League.

I was silent, momentarily reflecting on my basketball experiences on Okinawa, at Middle Tennessee, and most recently in Mozambique. I thought of the effort it had taken to leave Kansas City and come to Queensland to do this work. I did not want to come up short in Queensland. I knew how critical the continuation of the Bullets was to the growth of Queensland basketball. Harold Peacock glanced at me in this silence and I said,

"I don't think we can retain Cal Bruton, but I can find another point guard. Also, we need a little more muscle in the paint for next season, and we should probably look carefully at David Claxton to coach the Bullets (as Bob Young had stepped down right after the 1979 season.) We will be better next year and should attract more sponsorship money. Queensland basketball is riding a winner."

Harold was elated at my response and at the end of the meeting, I knew that the Bullets had survived for at least another season.

The Australian-American League

In addition to the NIBL and the Bullet program, which did not directly benefit all of the senior players in the six local basketball clubs in Brisbane, I concocted a plan to put some color (and pain) into the lives of the likes of Lang Park, Northwest Districts, West Mitchelton, Maine, the Gold Coast, and Toowoomba. These were the senior "A Grade" Brisbane clubs, the top level of senior men's competition, but completely amateur. The project was challenging, as it did require unpaid club personnel to do some selling and fund raising. Previously, these local clubs had never made much effort to raise money. There had never been a need of this magnitude.

The Australian-American Amateur Basketball League was chartered in March 1979. With the unflinching support of Harold Peacock Sr., we eventually received endorsement from the leaders of the six Brisbane clubs. However, the University of Queensland basketball club was a casualty. At the crucial AAABL membership meeting, I was introduced to Struts, the University club rep. At the first mention of the deposit required, Struts and his club disappeared into the Queensland night air. The league went forward. I had made arrangements with National Associaton of Intercollegiate Athletics (NAIA), which had 400 small colleges as members. Harry Fritz, the Executive Director of the Kansas City based NAIA, selected six guards and six inside players from member schools. Thus, the twelve NAIA players, along with Coach Red Myers of Erskine College in South Carolina as head of the NAIA delegation, traveled to Brisbane for an eight week special basketball season in U.S. summer-Australian winter.

The plan worked well. The local clubs raised the cash, bought the airline tickets, and shared responsibilities among club members to billet the visiting NAIA players. When they arrived in Brisbane, a press conference had been scheduled. Each of the six participating clubs drew from a hat the names of a visiting American guard and forward to participate in its club's team through the eight week basketball program.

I learned that the "magnet" to attract the Queensland press to a basketball event in 1979 was free booze. The local press had shown virtually no interest in basketball until this press conference. We scheduled it at noon so that all of the local media types would be up and around. It was held in the heart of the city so that no one would be inconvenienced, and, of course, the bar was open and gratis as advertised. The Australian-American Amateur Basketball League thus got off to a good public relations start. The league program included a home and away regular season schedule followed by play-offs and a title game. (See Appendix B re: AAABL participants.)

Outside of a few early complaints about homesickness from the young American players and Lenzy Houston from Tusculum College in Tennessee losing his patent leather, size-15 dress shoes in Sydney, the AAABL went off with few hitches. The competition definitely impacted local play, interest, and thought processes regarding competitive basketball. I also eventually tracked down the size 15's for the player. Lenzy Houston was to return to Tusculum College in Tennessee to earn his degree. I was able to open some doors for him to continue his basketball career in Australia where he and his family took up permanent residence. He found a niche and has been an asset as a player and as a coach in the development of basketball in the state of Tasmania.

The next year, 1980, the AAABL was introduced to North Queensland. We therefore had a six-team Northern Division and a six-team Southern Division in Brisbane. North Queensland, with Dan Slattery of Townsville as the catalyst, embraced the league and dispatched the visiting players on an energetic clinic program in the local schools. In 1981, the AAABL continued in Queensland and I also set up the same program in Perth, Western Australia. There were about 70 NAIA players that year traveling to Australia to play basketball in the innovative hoop program. This competition formed the framework for the Queensland State League, which was to include a network of teams competing throughout a state geographically the size of Texas. The State League later involved the participation of Queensland teams in the Australian Continental Basketball Association (CBA), a national Division II competition. The same development occurred in Western Australia, as the AAABL stretched the local clubs and stimulated the interest which led to the Western Australia State League.

I saw the experiment as the first step in bringing higher-level competitive basketball to all areas of the state of Queensland. Two of the competing teams in North Queensland, Townsville and Cairns, were to become members of the professional Australian National Basketball League. The competition also has impacted hundreds of developing young Aussie players through the years. It was a creative program backed by reliable people - players, coaches, administrators, referees, sponsors, and fans - who took positive action.

Stars from Other Sports

Even though usually occupied with basketball business, I took some time to attend other sporting events while in Queensland to continue to broaden my base of understanding of Australian sport. John Walker, the international track star from New Zealand, was participating in a track and field meet at the newly constructed Queen Elizabeth II track facility built for the Commonwealth Games in Brisbane. At the time, Walker, who was a muscular, impressive athlete, was considered the best middle-distance runner in the world. As I watched Walker run a strong 1500 meters and win easily, I again thought of the West Indian cricketers, Joel Garner and Viv Richards and of Cal Bruton and the marketing aspect of Australian sport. Walker was a world-class athlete and attracted sponsorship money and fans in track and field, as did the West Indians in cricket and Bruton in basketball. I saw the same type of "star impact" at the South Pacific Tennis Classic in Milton, Queensland.

The marketing magnet of this event was Australia's Davis Cup star Ken Rosewall. I drove to the Milton Tennis Stadium, only a few blocks from the Auchenflower State Basketball Center, at 7:30 a.m. on a Queensland October morning in 1979 to see the revered Rosewall hit practice balls in preparation for the tournament. He was a mature player and an established star in world tennis, yet he was out there alone, early in the morning, continuing to perfect his stroke. I was the only other person near his practice court at that hour. I focused on Rosewall's form and admired his concentration, skill, talent, and dedication - traits necessary to excel in any competitive sport. I noted that like John Walker, Joel Garner, Viv Richards, and Cal Bruton, Rosewall had something special, more than athletic ability. He obviously loved his work and had that "something extra" - the rare, precious commodity of athletic charisma which people around the world paid good money to experience.

The Black Pearl to Geelong

When the smoke cleared after the 1979 National Basketball League and Australian-American League basketball seasons, Geneva and I took a break and traveled to Perth, Adelaide, and Sydney to ponder a one-year contract extension from the Queensland State Association. We took the time to relax after a very hectic ten months in Brisbane. It had been a period of non-stop basketball activity - NBL, AAABL, Junior Championships, camps, coaching courses, etc. We eventually decided to stay in Australia for another year and I began to gear-up in the recruitment of a replacement for Cal Bruton, who had signed with the Geelong Cats in Victoria.

I did not think the Brisbane Bullets at that time in their history were well enough organized to handle Cal Bruton and his plans to bring his family from Wichita to Australia - his bride, Trish, and their two young boys, Elliot, age eight, and Calvin Thomas Bruton Jr. (C.J.), age four. Later a third son was born in Australia, Austin David Bruton, Geneva's and my godson. Rex Stewart, former player and a director in the Geelong Basketball Club, had flown up to Brisbane and had discussed Cal Bruton's contractual situation with me.

Although at the time Geelong was not a member of the National Basketball League, it was that club's objective to upgrade its program and make application to the NBL, Australia's top league. It was to be Cal Bruton's job to provide the impetus on and off the court for this Geelong plan to be accomplished. The club was fully prepared to do whatever was necessary to recruit the Bruton family, and offered a multi-year agreement to utilize Cal's unique abilities in its long-range basketball plan. As much as Geneva and I hated to lose Cal from the Brisbane scene, it was in his and his family's best interests to move to Geelong. Rex Stewart and the Cats were better able to accommodate the Brutons than the home team Bullets of 1980.

When Cal Bruton was being recruited by Geelong for future employment, he visited that Victorian city of 150,000 as a personal guest in the home of Rex Stewart. Ben, Rex's six-year-old son, was fascinated by the Black Pearl. The young Aussie could not take his eyes off of this unique

American black man with the great smile. Young Ben would watch intently and then talk excitedly to his father, Rex, and mother, Val, regarding Bruton. Rex later said the thing that impressed Ben the most about Cal was his hands. The Aussie kid was intrigued with Bruton's long, graceful fingers and extra large hands - never mentioning the color of his skin. The trip was positive for club and player. Bruton agreed to report to Geelong for the 1980 Australian season.

U.S. Player Self-Promotion

In an attempt to replace The Black Pearl, I recruited Brian Banks from the University of Nebraska, an All-Big Eight point guard, who had played for Coach Joe Cipriano. Dan Hickert, from Kansas State University also in the Big Eight Conference, returned. He was joined by Tom Gerhardt, who had been a bench player at the University of Illinois, and Mike Haddow, a shooter from the NAIA power Grand Canyon.

Gerhardt, a powerful 6'7 forward, sold his candidacy for an import spot in Australia with a color photograph of his reverse slam with elbows at rim level. The Mayne Basketball Club's player-coach Robert Wood saw the photograph and said that he could use that kind of athleticism in his team's line-up. Mayne agreed to underwrite Gerhardt's airline ticket to help their club and also to assist the Bullet financial cause. However, Gerhardt and Coach Wood didn't see eye-to-eye.

Gerhardt left Mayne and Wood was convinced that "the slam" photograph was a sham. Gerhardt later admitted use of the old gymnastic springboard trick. Ingeniously placing the springboard in front of the basket, Gerhardt took a short run and sprung from the board to a height which made possible the impressive reverse dunk. A friend doubling as a photographer snapped the picture, which was a big factor in the contract offer. Although the photo was effective in stretching his leaping ability, Gerhardt was a good player, a strong, productive athlete with a positive competitive spirit.

However, there have been cases of similar self-promotion projects in which the job applicant demonstrated a lack of character or was a farce as a player, or both. I sent a capable 6'7 forward with ties to the state of Iowa to a second-division job in South Australia. He performed well for a while and then told the club that he would play better if his wife was with him. The club agreed to give him the money for an airline ticket. When the player received the cash, he arranged a ticket for himself back to the U.S., sneaked out of Australia without notice, and left a note for the club president stating that he didn't think the club could have been so dumb as to give him the money. Ironically, I attended a high school state tournament in the U.S. in which this player, along with others, was inducted into that state's basketball hall of fame. And, of course, this player had included his "professional career" in Australia as part of his basketball playing background.

Another innovative attempt to forge pro basketball credentials occurred in Iowa in 1997. I was driving from my office to the post office one morning and received a call on my car phone from police officer Mike Stueckrath. The Des Moines policeman said my name had been mentioned in a criminal investigation and that I should come immediately to the downtown police station. Stueckrath informed me that a college basketball player had been arrested in Kansas with a stolen car and that this player said I had given him the car as an inducement to sign a player-agent contract. I recalled that this player had called me a few months before and I had advised him to go back to school. In my opinion, he was a good athlete but had no legitimate chance to play overseas pro ball because of his size (6'2), his position (off-guard), and his lack of production at the college level.

I called the player's coach from the police station and told him the story. Further investigation found that the young man had taken the car from a local dealer's lot and had - sadly - concocted the agent contract story. I heard later that the troubled player had also borrowed some stereos from the school's dormitory.

Another young man alerted me by telephone to his Division I basketball career and his 18-point per-game average in his senior season at a Missouri Valley Conference school. I spent some time with him. He was pleasant and strongly built. First impression was that maybe he had some potential. However, after checking his official stats, I found that the decimal had been misplaced. He had actually scored at a 1.8-point per-game clip. End of story - end of career hopes. Why do they do this type of thing? Official stats are the starting point for any background check on a player.

Player misrepresentation problems of this type could happen anywhere. In my discussions in New Zealand with Maurice Woodhouse and Nenad Vucinic, administrator and coach respectively in the city of Nelson, they told me of an American player who had express-mailed to the Nelson Basketball Club an impressive highlight tape in an attempt to attract an offer. Replete with statistics and the impressive play demonstrated in the tape, the club bit and sent him a ticket.

The American arrived in New Zealand. As time passed, it became clear that he was not the player in the tape, although there was a physical resemblance. The club cornered the bogus player who admitted the scam and that the tape actually showed another player. In retrospect, the situation was humorous, but at the time the club was irate. It can be an expensive lesson considering the tight budgets of many clubs. They have to do what they can to avoid mispresentation of talent levels by players and agents.

Bill Palmer and Ken Richardson

In the early years of the Australian National League, the import player rule was changed from no limit in 1979 to four foreigners per team in 1980. Eventually the rule reduced foreign content to the current two overseas players per team. The two-player limit has been pretty much a standard around the world with the exception of the ACB, the Spanish pro league, with three foreigners permitted. In 1980, the Brisbane Bullets used foreigners Brian Banks, Mike Haddow, Dan Hickert, and Tom Gerhardt along with local players Bruce Fitzgerald, Colin Varian, Chris McGraw, and Robert Wood. David Claxton was named head coach after a minor drama with the Brisbane Association. They had objected to Claxton's appointment because of an old feud between Brisbane and the Gold Coast, Claxton's former team.

We were underway in Brisbane again and the 1980 Bullet team advanced to the four-team play-off held in Launceston, Tasmania. West Adelaide, behind the play of Ken Richardson and Ricky Hodges, sunk the Bullets in the opener. Brisbane recovered to win the consolation game against the Nunawading Spectres, anchored by today's NBL General Manager Bill Palmer, and Commissioner of Referees Gary Fox. Palmer, a 5-man, and Fox, a lefty wing player, were the leading scorers for the Spectre team.

Bill Palmer was the first high-quality American post player to commit to Australian basketball, and Palmer has made the full commitment. After his playing career with Nunawading, he married an Australian girl and later became the long-standing General Manager of the Australian NBL. While a player at Stanford University, Palmer had an adventure on a Pac-10 (Pac-8 in those days) road trip. A great story teller, Palmer told of how he and a couple of teammates had been out past the midnight curfew having a few beers. They returned to the team hotel. Just as they called for the elevator, one of the Stanford coaches, who had also been out on the town, weaved through the hotel lobby en route to the elevator. Noticing large human statues used for hotel decor, Palmer and his two pals disguised themselves by assuming a position imitating the pose depicted by the statues. The coach, in his cups, noticed nothing irregular, even glancing at the statues by the elevator and making an approving grunt. He disappeared as the elevator doors closed and the Stanford players were in free.

Another great player who participated in the 1980 NBL play-offs was Ken Richardson of West Adelaide. Richardson was a sinewy built 6'6 inside player from Ohio Northern University. His game was quickness, strength, and persistence. Bill Palmer described Richardson as "slippery." Richardson was at the end of his career when the NBL was just starting; however, he was named to the first all-league team in 1980, but retired as a player after the 1982 season. Ken Richardson came to Australia when the sport was amateur and he worked as a paper-chopper to make ends meet when starring for West Adelaide. He was known as a "boy" and loved to have fun on road trips, or at home games. He teamed with Terry Aston, as bench assistant, to complete a successful stint as player-coach of the Bearcats. After his playing days and a couple years as an NBL coach at Geelong, Richardson took a job on an oil rig off the Australian coast.

The AAABL, the league involving the NAIA college players, continued in June and July of 1981 in Brisbane and also U.S. players were dispatched to North Queensland including Rockhampton, Mackay, Townsville, Ayr, Herbert River, and Cairns. Dan Slattery, Townsville administrator, provided the lead. Slattery worked with the Northern clubs to develop a program to utilize the visiting American players in doing regular school visits to promote and teach basketball. The high profile presence of the Americans teaching basketball in the Queensland schools annoyed some of the other sporting bodies such as rugby, cricket, and Aussie rules football. In Australia, there was heated competition among the major sporting bodies to recruit the best young athletes for their particular sport. The school coaching program was an aggressive and effective technique to attract new talent to basketball.

Coach Red Myers

Red Myers, the athletic director and head coach at Erskine College in South Carolina, was the official National Association of Intercollegiate Athletics representative in the Queensland league in 1979 and 1980. Red worked hard and performed a valuable service as the liaison and troubleshooter between the clubs and U.S. players throughout the entire schedule. Returning to Erskine College, Red Myers was eventually removed as head coach by the college president.

Apparently, the school administration arranged a retirement ceremony for the displaced coach, who did not take kindly to the idea of retirement, who did not attend the festivities, and who had already agreed to work as an assistant coach at nearby Lander College. I didn't hear what the college president did with Red's retirement watch. Red Myers was a throw-back to another era, a disciplinarian who taught teamwork, shot selection, and defense. He was tough on his players, but they respected him and played hard. I can recall asking Myers to name a couple of coaches whom he respected. The first name mentioned was Ben Jobe, a Tennessee State graduate who carved out a career in some of America's well-known black colleges and universities.

Before Myers left Erskine College, David Claxton, the Brisbane Bullets coach and later National Team assistant, spent several weeks on campus at the South Carolina school learning the defensive schemes of the veteran Myers. The basketball world was shrinking and defensive philosophy used successfully in South Carolina was now being employed in Queensland.

With no fax machines or e-mail yet, grueling 30-hour plane trips were the medium to access learning and to develop new ideas regarding the game through the Australia-American connection.

As 1980 came to a close, there was a changing of the guard in the Queensland State Association. Ken Madsen stepped aside as president for newcomer Barry Neilsen. Also, it was mutually agreed that I not continue in the State Director's job. We felt that with the advent of the NBL and the AAABL and their impact, it was necessary for clubs to settle for a year and build. I was ready for a break from the two years of non-stop basketball work and felt satisfaction in the contribution which I had made to Queensland and Australia basketball. I was ready to go home for a while, but I somehow knew I would come back to work in Australia again.

□ *8* □

ADIOS AUSTRALIA - HELLO
OVERSEAS BASKETBALL SERVICES

Geneva and I returned from Brisbane to the U.S. in September of 1980. I began in earnest the recruitment of key American players for NBL teams from a home office in our new condo in Des Moines. In addition, I spent two years working for a private, liberal arts college, Buena Vista College, as the Des Moines area and also foreign-student recruiter.

When we were making the final inspection before moving into our condominium, I noticed an employee from the condo management company doing some last minute cleaning of our new place. I had a chill when I recognized him: it was the school superintendent who had given me my walking papers 18 years before in my first high school coaching job. He did not recognize me, but I later introduced myself and thanked him for his strong and correct action in removing me from my ill-fated attempt to assume adult responsibilities in the workplace. He was obviously no longer in the school business and had paid, ironically, like myself, a penalty for a serious, lingering problem with alcohol.

In my new job I called on area high schools to interview prospective students and also took two extended student-recruitment trips to Hong Kong, Bangkok, Kuala Lumpur, and Singapore to assist the college in penetration of the foreign student market - so important to the cash flow in U.S. private colleges. Also in 1980, Joel Grau, the head basketball coach at Buena Vista, resigned. I decided to apply for the vacated head coaching job and was positioned well because of my employment with the school. However, cooler heads prevailed and we decided that the move from Des Moines, a mid-sized city with a metro area of about 300,000, to Storm Lake, a northwest Iowa town of about 10,000 and somewhat isolated, would not work for the school or for us.

While ambitious U.S. college coaches used foreign players to strengthen their teams, foreign students, non-athletes, who paid full tuition, were high priorities for admissions offices in many American colleges and universities. During my two years at Buena Vista, I became acquainted with the foreign student recruiting market through the two Southeast Asia recruiting trips. The first was a group project with twenty schools represented and the second I took alone to follow up previous leads in Hong Kong, Bangkok, and Kuala Lumpor.

Many U.S. colleges and universities must rely on the full-tuition students from overseas to lend diversity to their campuses and also to provide hard cash to their budgets. When I was with Buena Vista in 1980-81, we worked with figures which showed there were about 4,500 foreign students enrolled in Iowa's 2-year and 4-year institutions of higher education. Buena Vista wanted a piece of that business and was especially interested in the diversity angle, as private school competitors jokingly referred to foreign students at BV as students from outside the surrounding tier of counties. Universities in major U.S. metropolitan areas, such as USC in Los Angeles, may have as many as 3,500 foreign students enrolled as regular students or studying to pass the TOEFL test of English proficiency for future admission. College admissions figures showed that the state of Iowa had approximately 7,500 foreign students enrolled in 1998.

Foreign governments and industries subsidize talented students through formal contracts. Thus the subsidized foreign student can be required to return to his home country after completing a U.S. college degree. He/she then worked for the sponsor for a specified period to pay back the advance used for the cost of the American education. Branches of the U.S. military have employed a similar strategy and have used college tuition benefits as incentives in recruiting programs.

Commuting to Australia

Although I was working full-time in student recruitment, my main interest during these years in Des Moines was still overseas basketball and particularly the Australian NBL. I could feel the warmth of the 1,000 escuda note in my hand for delivery of Eric Bundgard to the Mahangalene Club in Mozambique in 1973. More importantly, I recalled the satisfied look on the face of the club administrators, knowing that their team would be better with Eric's presence and their bragging rights enhanced. Thus, from that experience in far-off Africa, I learned and remembered well the payment and the smile, both indicating a market for the delivery of qualified American players to overseas clubs. Overseas Basketball Services, my basketball recruiting business, was starting to take shape.

At the time, I did most of my business in Australia and kept close contact with the NBL. I flew back there each year during the period of 1980-1984 to the NBL Finals in addition to taking a special trip to Perth to coordinate the AAABL-Western Australia program. I was living in Iowa, but my main focus and the better part of my income was coming from down-under.

The trip from the Midwest to Australia can be grueling, especially when the destination was Townsville in North Queensland. I could count on thirty-six hours travel time. Also, in crossing the international date line, there was a twelve-hour time change. I would leave home at 2:00 p.m., U.S. Central Standard Time, and arrive in Townsville at 2:00 p.m. - two days later, Eastern Standard Time in Australia. I would always go directly from the airport to the hotel to make calls to set up a schedule for that afternoon.

I forced myself to stay up until 11:00 p.m. on that first day and then, without fail, would crash. Four or five hours later, I would waken hungry. I was normally able to find a twenty-four hour cafe open. After an early morning snack, my routine was to return to the hotel, take a 4 a.m. swim in the pool or work out in the hotel's exercise room, and then catch up on my business back in the U.S. via telephone. Because of the time difference, (early morning in Australia was early afternoon, the previous day, in the U.S. For example, 8:00 a.m. Wednesday in Melbourne was 4:00 p.m. Tuesday in Iowa), I learned to accept and respect the discomfort and unreliability of perceptions distorted by travel fatigue. I took a second and third look at all important business decisions. I knew that I would sleep for eight hours during each twenty-four hour period, but in short naps rather than consecutively. This abnormal, daily routine allowed me to maximize my work time on trips down-under, only to return to the U.S. weeks later to re-adapt.

While I took these trips on a regular basis down-under on basketball business, it was unusual in those days for Australian club representatives to travel to the U.S. to recruit import players. An exception was Ian Loxton, who was representing on a U.S. trip a Victorian Basketball Association club in need of two American players for the Melbourne-area competition. I arranged to have David Johnson, a 6'8 forward from Drake, and Frank Kaminsky, a 6'10 forward-center from Lewis University, available to meet Ian in Des Moines. He interviewed the players and offered them contracts for the season. Both went to Australia. Johnson did a good job, but Kaminsky returned home to Chicago before the end of the season.

Why did Vincent Price Leave?

When I drove Loxton back to the Des Moines airport to take the first step of his long trip home, I recognized Vincent Price, the actor, in the airport restaurant. I had seen Price star in *Diversions and Delights*, an Oscar Wilde monologue, in Brisbane in 1980. The play was presented at a downtown movie theater at 5:00 p.m. on a Friday afternoon. I was curious and decided to attend, along with only about a dozen others. I could recall a rather strange occurrence, which has remained a mystery.

Right after the intermission, about ten minutes into the second part of the play, Price left the stage and did not return. I was thinking about that situation when I called Price's presence in the restaurant to the attention of Ian Loxton. I introduced myself and Loxton to Mr. Price, mentioned that I had seen the Oscar Wilde performance in Brisbane, but unfortunately did not pursue the reason for the early exit from the stage. Price remembered the performance and was reasonably cordial in our brief conversation. Mr. Wilde had starred in the *Diversions and Delights* monologue in Paris in 1899. There had been an announcement printed on a page in the original program, which had been copied - 81 years later - in the Brisbane version of the program. This message stated that Mr. Wilde was suffering from an infection of the inner ear as well as other maladies and that the audience would have to take his health problems into consideration.

My guess was that Vincent Price's early departure was simply following the script from a precedent set when Wilde was forced to leave that Paris stage back in 1899 because of the ear infection and other maladies. At that juncture of his life, Oscar Wilde was in poor health, which was associated with his two years of hard labor on a conviction of sexual immorality. He had just returned to the theater after the incarceration at Reading Gaol, but died the next year in 1900.

While my experience with Oscar Wilde and Vincent Price didn't open any doors for me in Australia, my continuing interest and respect for the NBL did. I received a call from Robbie Cadee, a former National Team and St. Kilda Club player. Cadee was a wiry lefty who had played the point and triggered the feared St. Kilda 1-3-1 half court trap. With long arms, quickness, and good anticipation, he was a key to the effectiveness of Coach Brian Kerle's defense. Robbie was the new coach of the Bankstown Bruins in the NBL and was searching for U.S. reinforcements. He was looking for a point guard and a power forward. I sent Donnie Ray Cruse, who had played with Lang Park in the 1980 AAABL. Cruse had an established track record as a reliable person and consistent player in Australia. With the guard slot filled, I looked hard for a productive forward - a 4-man.

In browsing the 1980 NBA draft, I noticed that Kelvin Henderson of St. Louis University had been Portland's 4th round selection. I tracked down Henderson through the Billiken coaching staff and then flew to St. Louis the next day to see him work out. An old college friend, Jim Adams, met me at Lambert Field and drove me out to the housing project where Kelvin lived with his family. The three of us then proceeded to a high school gym and I observed as this thin, nearly emaciated figure, ran through drills and demonstrated his athleticism.

Henderson was obviously talented, but not in very good shape and probably not eating regularly. I decided to sign Henderson and made arrangements with Bankstown to fly him through Des Moines en route to L.A.

and Australia. When Kelvin arrived in Des Moines weeks later, I bought him a big steak, worked him out, and did my best to prepare him for the overseas responsibilities. He proved to be a valuable player for Bankstown. I understood that Henderson married an Aussie and still played in the state league in South Australia. Later he tested the restricted use of naturalized players in the NBL and lost in the courts.

The Naturalized Player and The Bosman Rule

Even though an Australian citizen, it was necessary that a naturalized player - a foreigner who had become Australian - met the qualifications to play for his adopted country (Australia) as a National Team player. This involved citizenship, which can take up to five years, and also a FIBA waiting period of three years. FIBA, *Federation Internationale de Basketball*, is the governing body of international basketball. This bureaucracy with administrative control of world basketball competition has offices in Munich, Germany. After meeting these FIBA criteria, then and only then could a naturalized Australian play as a local in the NBL.

Classification as a local player has become an important economic consideration in Australia, and in other foreign countries. American players thus classified no longer have to compete for the two-player import spots on a team and were instead competing for the other eight local player squad positions. In other words, naturalized Americans - those American-born players who become Australian citizens - have an asterisk beside their rights as Australian citizens. For example, all citizenship rights were granted except running, jumping, and shooting a basketball in an NBL uniform and drawing a paycheck as an Australian citizen.

There was a similar situation in Europe which dealt with this same issue Kelvin Henderson fought in Australia. The Bosman Rule allowed all players with European Community passports to play in other countries in Europe as local players without restriction. A European soccer player with the surname Bosman had asked for a clearance from his Belgian club to take a job in the Netherlands, which already had its limit of foreign players. Bosman appealed to the European Court of Justice and was awarded the freedom to play without restriction in the Netherlands. This ruling opened the doors in Europe for participants in other sports as well; therefore, basketball players with passports from the 15 European Community countries (Western Europe, including Austria, Belgium, Denmark, Finland, France, Great Britain, Germany, Greece, Holland, Ireland, Italy, Luxembourg, Portugal, Spain, and Sweden, not Eastern Europe) could play without restriction as to nationality in other European Community countries.

For example, 6'11 Spencer Dunkley had played four years of college basketball at the University of Delaware. He had averaged 19.2 points in his senior year and was subsequently selected in the second round of the 1993 NBA draft by the Indiana Pacers. However, Spencer Earl Dunkley was born in Wolverton, England, and traveled on an English passport. He therefore became eligible through the Bosman Rule to play in Greece as a local player - not counting against the two import player per team limit.

In this scenario, top clubs in Greece have been known to pay the right players seven-figure per-season salaries. The better players in England would make considerably less than in Greece - only 50,000 to 60,000 pounds per season. Thus, a player like Dunkley would have received a financial windfall through the Bosman ruling. Not only had his market value soared overnight, but he had more job security as a Euro-player and did not have to compete for his job with U.S. imports. However, in Australia, Kelvin Henderson lost his case over a similar issue in the courts. It was confirmed that that country's naturalized citizens could not play as local players without a substantial waiting period, a possible delay of several years. This waiting period was critical and consumed valuable income-earning years in the short life of a professional athlete. *The Bosman ruling was the first major step toward an open-market, free-trade policy in international basketball. The Henderson decision was the opposite - it further isolated Australian basketball.*

Australianization

The Henderson Decision was important in the NBL's apparent plan to eventually and totally "Australianize" the league. However, while the Australian league had improved through the years and was developing some outstanding players, the country had less than twenty-million people. The small population and loss of outstanding athletes to other professional sports can be cited as reasons that the NBL had yet to yield a sufficient number of high-level Australian players to provide strength and depth to all eleven NBL teams. In short, there were not enough top level Australian basketball players to go around.

The ruling on Henderson protected the contracts of Australian-born players of lesser ability than the naturalized American players and in doing so reduced the available pool of talented players, therefore weakening the overall strength of the NBL. Ironically, Malcom Speed, the former chairman of the NBL and attorney by trade, was a staunch and outspoken advocate of the elimination of the instant eligibility of the naturalized player for NBL competition. It was clearly Mr. Speed's objective to Australianize the NBL even before it was a consensus among league teams. He worked hard to promote this policy and had made definite progress toward this objective, as noted from the results of the Henderson court case.

I agreed that there was some merit in Speed's and the NBL's position, as the naturalized Yanks were taking roster spots and contracts away from young Australian prospects. This in the eyes of some Australian administrations was impeding the overall development of basketball down-under. However, earning court time and being handed it through a rule are two different matters. If a young Aussie "can play," he should have no trouble in proving it on the court and beating out the older naturalized Americans. There have been some truly weak Australian players drawing paychecks in the NBL; they would not have made the team without the Henderson Decision to aid and abet their mediocrity.

Apparently Mike D'Antoni, former NBA player and Italian League coach, had the same opinion of the 'Lega' in Italy before the Bosman Rule opened up all Italian professional basketball jobs to players with European passports. D'Antoni, who has moved on to the NBA as an assistant coach, spoke with Jim Patton in *Il Basket D'Italia* about the local talent issue in Italy. D'Antoni felt that there were too many average (Italian) players with no incentive to improve and that these players were holding back the standard of play. These local players weren't afraid of losing their jobs because of the lack of competition.

However, the Bosman Rule changed that situation for clubs which can afford Euro-players. Mike D'Antoni's comments applied to Italian basketball but perfectly described the dilemma in the naturalized player dispute in Australia and the ramifications of the Henderson Decision. Kelvin Henderson had become an Australian citizen and wanted to play in the NBL as an Australian thereby becoming a threat to an NBL roster spot held by an Australian-born player. As in Italy, the local player was secure because of the lack of competition for his job, but the import could lose his job at any time and on any whim of the club. Most contracts have included a "performance clause" which has allowed the import players to be cut with or without a severance package.

Henderson thus challenged the rule which required the FIBA player certification three-year waiting period. In other words, Henderson was saying that I am an Australian citizen and I therefore have the right to play basketball as an Australian right now - immediately. I should not have to wait the additional three years, which penalizes me financially and shortens my career. NBL officials had implemented the FIBA rule requiring the three-year waiting period. This rule applied in all countries to naturalized players requesting eligibility to represent their adopted country in Olympic or World Championship competition. Apparently, FIBA had implemented the restriction to protect Olympic competition from "ringers" who otherwise could receive special concessions for a hurry-up citizenship just to play in a major international competition. The three-year waiting period applied after the naturalized player had completed the actual citizenship requirement - in itself a three to five-year process.

The NBL had obviously adopted the FIBA rule as part of its eligibility requirement to throw up obstacles for naturalized Americans and to thus protect playing time for Australian-born players. Reportedly under-represented in the courts, Henderson lost the case, and the impact of natural-ized Americans on the NBL had been instantly and drastically reduced. Although pressing 40, LeRoy Loggins and James Crawford can still impact NBL play and have continued 20-point-per-game production in spite of their advanced years. Other naturalized Americans caught in the Henderson Decision could have done the same thing.

Thus "The Term of His Natural Life Rule" was in place. I have named the rule after events in Australian history when Mother England was export-ing convicts, many guilty of minor crimes, to Australia. If the convict sur-vived the incarceration, he normally had no money to return to England and therefore spent the rest of his life in Australia. Released convicts became an important source in populating the country. This matter was the focus of the Australian classic, *For the Term of his Natural Life*, written by Marcus Clarke. Rufus Dawes, the convict in Clarke's book, had been wrongly accused of murder and robbery. He was convicted and transported on a prison ship from England to Van Dieman's Land, modern-day Tasmania, to serve his sentence. Kelvin Henderson, like ex-convict Rufus Dawes, was sentenced to a "life-term" in Australia without the full-citizenship rights.

Summer Season

Unfortunately, Mr. Speed left his NBL chairman's job in 1997 to take an administrative job in Australian cricket, which at the time was facing the possibility of a major player strike. Speed also engineered the idea of the "summer season" in NBL basketball to avoid head-to-head television com-petition with football - Australian Rules and the Rugby codes.

The original NBL discussions and negotiations centered on a $3,000,000 per season, revenue-generating plan from television. Channel Seven was to pay NBL clubs this amount for rights to the telecasting of league games. The cash was a strong incentive for the NBL to change the league schedule from the winter to the Australian summer, thus adopting the European schedule with games played from September through May. Unfortunately, the deal with Channel Seven did not materialize. Malcom Simpson, retired Adelaide 36ers president, summed up the situation at the Chicago Bulls-Phoenix Suns game at the United Center in January 1998 as follows:

"I am very concerned about the NBL and its current course. Things don't look good. NBL merchandise sales, the TV disaster, and decreasing game attendance are all sources of major concern. The original NBL proposal emphasized a $3,000,000 TV-rights package from Channel Seven. Now ABC will carry some games with absolutely no revenue to the NBL clubs. In fact the league may have to pay ABC to do the games."

With the switch to the summer season in motion, clubs were screaming foul as their crowds in 1997 had fallen off drastically. Another NBL season ran January through July 1998 as the problem of poor attendance persisted. This was a transitional season, known as the "short season," with the monumental switch to the European and U.S. calendar occurring in September 1998 with the season ending in April 1999.

There was no lucrative NBL television contract in place and I was concerned as to what would transpire and what teams would be left standing. The loss of three league teams in 1996 due to financial problems was fresh in the mind of NBL supporters. It was so clear that three other NBL clubs were struggling financially at the end of the 1998 season - Canberra, Newcastle, and North Melbourne. Subsequently, the expected merger between North Melbourne and Southeast Melbourne took place in July of 1998, reducing the NBL to ten teams. However, the new franchise at West Sydney pushed the league membership back to 11 teams for the 1998-99 season.

The NIBL Model

Although it was unintentional, the original business structure of the Australian National Basketball League was similar to the old National Industrial Basketball League (NIBL) in the United States. American companies recruited ex-college players to work as legitimate employees and also to represent the company team in a very high level of basketball. Company teams such as Phillips Petroleum recruited the player, put him into a two to three-month job-training program, and then brought him to its home office in Bartelsville, Oklahoma, to play for the Oilers in the NIBL. At the time - in the forties, fifties and sixties - players would routinely select the amateur NIBL over the professional NBA because of the opportunity to play a similar level of competitive basketball and also to progress in a job career. Many U.S. Olympians were selected from NIBL teams at the time.

In my opinion, the Phillips Oilers model with legitimate work responsibility in the playing contract made a great deal of sense for the clubs in the Australian NBL, who have pushed their team salary cap - along with other operating expenses - to a point of near financial collapse. The rising salary cap seemed to be a case of the clubs chasing their own tails. The intent of increased spending on player salaries was originally to compete with mid-level European clubs for U.S. imports.

The severe Australian personal income tax structure along with the eroding

Australian dollar in the world market can make the competition with European clubs futile. In this scenario, an Australian $100,000 gross salary became approximately (depending on exact exchange rates) U.S. $40,000 net income, a lower-mid European salary for a U.S. player.

In addition to the foreign player competition factor, the talented Australian, especially National Team players, has become the highest paid player in the NBL. And although the value of the U.S. dollar is of less concern to the Australian, he still faces the factor of the local tax burden and that comes into play if a European club is attempting to contract the Australian player. That has seldom happened. However, Andrew Gaze has played in Italy and Greece. Andrew Vlahov of the Perth Wildcats and Mark Bradtke of the Melbourne Tigers, both Australian National Team players, have drawn European pay-checks briefly in Belgium and Spain respectively.

Also, Paul Rogers from Adelaide went into the the 1997 NBA draft and was selected in the second round by the Lakers. Rogers, who had an English passport, subsequently passed on NBL offers and took a reported U.S. $500,000 per season job with Real Madrid in Spain. It was unlikely that he would have earned more than U.S. $100,000 (gross) per year in an NBL job. As Australian-born players continue to improve, some will spurn NBL jobs - as in the case of Rogers - for employment with the higher paying European clubs. Should the Bosman Rule ever apply to Australians, the NBL would be in chaos and basketball down-under would be in deeper trouble.

English League Solution

In the Budweiser League in England, the teams approved the use of up to five non-English (import) players per team effective in the 1997-98 season. The impetus for this rule change from the original two imports to five came from the frustration of club ownership in negotiating contracts with National Team calibre, English players. An added factor in England was the impact of the Bosman Rule: a high-level player with an English passport became a valuable commodity in countries which paid higher salaries than in the U.K.

The English club owners saw that they also would be wasting their time and money if they tried to compete with, for example, Greek or Italian clubs which paid eight or ten times more than the highest English salaries. Although they opened their league up to more foreign players and risked alienation of the local press and fans, the first year with the new import player rule in England was judged a success. To the credit of club officials, England put an end to the idea of putting itself out of the basketball business because of escalating player salaries, a policy which could set the standard for future FIBA rulings on player limits in professional basketball competition around the world.

Immigration officials expressed concern about the new import rule in

English basketball and passed a regulation that only three work permits per team would be issued. The limits on the work permits has placed a higher premium on the naturalized English player, who can participate in the Budweiser League without a work permit, but lacks the punch to attract Euro offers. Ironically, while England has come to rely on naturalized Americans to fill important roster positions, Australia through the Term of His Natural Life Rule had cut off the flow of Yanks to their league.

Although English basketball found a remedy to its salary cap problems, as they knew they could bring American players of a reasonable talent level to their shores for much less money than signing their own National Team players, Australia had yet to find a solution. The Australian problem was quite simply how to maintain a high-standard, attractive, cost-effective basketball product to avert the financial collapse of the NBL. Naive Australian administrators look to "chasing the sponsorship dollar," as they say, as their savior.

Truth was that sponsorship must be a two-way street and the sponsor must see that he was getting his money's worth in investing in NBL teams. The critical criteria for the potential sponsor was the fan appeal of the game, which had fallen dramatically in 1997 and 1998. I would think that the NBL would be much more attractive to potential investors and sponsors in the Australian business world *if* National League clubs were proving to be financially viable through their own sweat and ingenuity. I have noticed a subtle, self-defeating part of the Australian make-up, a product of their own country's socialism. Some of the clubs seemed to prefer not to go "all out" to develop their own path. Deep in their hearts they thought that they would be rescued by the government, or a sponsor in this case, or both.

I felt that the NBL was on the right track in the early years. The clubs recruited American players who, along with the Australian players, worked part-time or full-time jobs to offset the expense to the club. The most productive Americans in early NBL history were the likes of Cal Bruton, LeRoy Loggins, James Crawford, Dave Nelson, etc., all of whom had the desire and motivation to do whatever necessary to continue their careers in high-level basketball competition.

Everyone could win in the Phillips Oilers' model. The clubs would be given financial relief; the players would be forced to use more than their basketball talents and thus better become prepared for life after sport; and the media and fans could better identify with that rare mix of humility and athletic greatness in the player's lifestyle.

The evolution of the modern Australian pro league - and the crisis associated with the change of seasons, lack of TV revenue, dwindling fan support, and club financial problems - has created obstacles with difficult solutions. The Australianization of the league has been a factor. Consistent with

Mal Speed's leadership and advocacy of this "only Aussie" policy, Chuck Harmison, general manager of the Illawarra Hawks, saw the elimination of the American import as the solution to his club's ongoing struggle to make ends meet financially in the NBL. Harmison told Bret Harris in *The Australian* that since the Australian players have shown great improvement through the years, the American players have become more and more dispensable.

Although overstated - import players still dominated the individual statistical categories in the NBL - and eerily patronizing, there was no question that Harmison was correct in regard to the point that Australian players had improved since the inception of the NBL in 1979. Ironically, I can link the improvement of the Australians with their competition against the American players, both import and naturalized, to NBL competition. Would the total elimination of the foreign player (the import doesn't have to be American, but always has been) become the final nail in the coffin of NBL basketball?

The "national league concept" failed prior to the National Basketball League's use of import players starting in 1979. The strongest teams in the NBL have the most depth in Australian talent. Weaker teams with less Australian player production rely more on the U.S. import, which keeps them competitive. In fact, the 1997 NBL champion - the Melbourne Tigers - had the combination of high level Australian talent (Gaze and Bradtke) ably supported by Americans Lanard Copeland and Marcus Timmons, who became the difference for the Tigers in their title run.

The Tigers won fifteen straight games once Timmons was signed. It was safe to say that without Copeland and Timmons, the Melbourne Magic with the best Australian talent in the NBL, including NBA first rounder Chris Antsey, would have won the title hands down. The same formula applied to 1998 NBL title winners, the Adelaide 36ers. First-year coach Phil Smyth combined strong Australian talent with two veteran Americans with NBA experience, Kevin Brooks and Darnell Mee.

The dilemma in Chuck Harmison's statements about eliminating the import player from the NBL was as follows: although the level of play among Australians has risen admirably through the years, there were still not enough impact-type Aussies to supply an eleven-team professional league. That type of local depth dropped off after the top teams and the others were left to rely on the U.S. import to compensate.

There seems to be help on the way. Ian Stacker, the Townsville Suns head coach, emphasized aggressiveness and a positive attitude in upsetting the heavily favored Americans for the 1997 FIBA World 22-and-Under title in Melbourne. Coach Rick Majerus of the U.S. chose to drop off the Australian perimeter players to concentrate on Chris Anstey, the NBA seven-footer, and the athletic Sam McKinnon.

Unfortunately, that strategy backfired as the Aussies scored five first-half three-pointers. A few of the younger Australian players have moved past NBL competition - Anstey to the Dallas Mavericks and Paul Rodgers to Real Madrid. Simon Dwight, a smooth 6'9 forward, looks to be the next Australian signed by an NBA team. Although the Under-22 World Title was a remarkable achievement and a strong endorsement for progress down-under, the disappointing performance of the Boomers in the 1998 Athens World Championships was quite another matter. Australia, considered among the early favorites in Athens, lacked the quickness and cohesiveness to be a threat to a high placing. The frustration continued as Australia had never taken a medal in men's basketball at the Olympics or World Championships. Playing on its home court and with Longley in the line-up, the Boomers could break through in Sydney 2000.

Regardless of the talent on the horizon, in order to continue the privilege of playing NBL basketball in Australia, the individual teams must find answers to their financial issues. I can see the Phillips Oilers' business structure with players working off-court (in civilian jobs) as a solution to the futility of unrealistic budgets followed by financial collapse of individual teams, as in Hobart, Gold Coast, and Geelong in 1996, and eventually the league itself.

The Old Days in the NBL

In a time when the NBL was less complicated, Australian clubs were aware that I was qualified to select import players with my experience in the NBL and also by my presence in the U.S. I had strong interest and understanding of the NBL along with first-hand access to qualified American players. It was a much larger world in 1981 than today as few NBL teams sent personal representatives to the U.S. on recruiting missions. Today NBL coaches take these recruiting trips which can be confusing and often non-productive because of the finite requirements for a good NBL player today - teams needing too much for their money and seldom getting it.

Between 1980 and 1984 I did a great deal of business in Australia from my base in Des Moines and sent players to Australian club officials including Michael Osborn (Adelaide City Eagles), Robbie Cadee (Bankstown), Terry Ryan (Canberra Cannons), John Scott (Illawarra Hawks), Bob Turner (Newcastle Falcons), Barry Barnes (Nunawading Spectres), and Val Graudins (City of Sydney). Also, I had an extended transaction with Mal Simpson, the Adelaide 36ers' president of the past 15 years, but then a young administrator with the local Adelaide club, Sturt. (See Appendix B for list of players sent to foreign jobs by Overseas Basketball Services.)

Mal Simpson called me from Adelaide and said he was looking for a power forward for the Sturt Club in Adelaide. I had just recently run an overseas job tryout camp at Lincoln High School in Des Moines and had several players available. Bruce Kucera, an athletic 6'8 forward from Rockhurst College, came to mind. I contacted Bruce and he was ready to go. However, there was at the time a rigid immigration process in regard to work permits in Australia and one of the requirements was a police clearance.

Bruce told the truth and stated that he had been involved in a marijuana case with the Kansas City police. This report was enough for Australian Immigration to deny the request for a visa. But Bruce was persistent and convinced me that his problem had been a most unusual situation. He was able to support that claim with a letter of recommendation from the President of Rockhurst College. As I recall, there were other prominent people providing letters of support also.

Simpson was loyal to Bruce's application and after about three months of correspondence and deliberation, the player was granted a visa. He spent two years with Sturt and did a satisfactory job down-under. Mal Simpson eventually became the long-standing President of the Adelaide 36ers, one of the flagship teams in the NBL, and guided that club to consistent production and an NBL title in 1986 under Coach Ken "King" Cole.

Pop Wright and Lewis Lloyd

I did my best to select players for overseas jobs from colleges in Iowa, as I had been living in Des Moines. The Missouri Valley Conference competition was at my doorstep with Drake as a member school; also Iowa State of the Big Eight and Iowa of the Big Ten were within easy driving distance. That year, Drake had two prominent seniors, Lewis "Black Magic" Lloyd, who was drafted and eventually played seven years in the NBA, and Rodney "Pop" Wright out of Dunbar High School in Baltimore. Pop Wright scored 39 and Lewis Lloyd 37 in their final collegiate game vs. Tulsa in 1981. Lloyd was a mercurial 6'6 scorer-rebounder and Wright a talented 6'4 off guard. I had basketball and personal dealings with both of these Drake players.

The first time I met Pop Wright was at the Holiday Inn South in Des Moines in December of 1981. He had just returned from an unsuccessful tryout with the Harlem Globetrotters. I received a call from Pop, who was staying at the Holiday Inn as a special guest, although the hotel didn't know of his privileged status at the time. I had a 20-minute talk with Wright in the hotel lobby. I can remember two things clearly about that conversation: Pop Wright was an impressive looking athlete, thin, but strong and possessing a certain charisma, and he asked me to loan him $400 to pay his motel bill. The Holiday Inn was managed by a Drake University booster club member and I heard later that he absorbed the cost of the stay. I balked on the loan, but did call Bob Turner at the Newcastle Falcons of Australia about Pop's availability.

I had already placed George Morrow with Newcastle for the season. George was a first-team All-Missouri Valley Conference selection and had been drafted by the Celtics. He was a strong 6'8 post player, established himself in the NBL as the league's leading rebounder and spent two years in a Newcastle Falcon uniform. George returned to the U.S. and became an assistant under Tom Apke at Creighton and Appalachian State, and he still stayed in regular contact regarding players. I can place "George Morrow" with his size and game today in Europe, South America, or Australia. A paint player of his quality was always in demand.

I admit that I did not do a thorough job in screening Rodney Wright for the Australian NBL. Since he was playing in Des Moines and I had seen him in action several times, I did not doubt his talent. I made the mistake of assuming he was okay and low risk off the court. I had talked with a couple of people around the Drake program and received no negative comments. However, Pop was not ready for Australia and the Aussies were definitely not prepared for him. I received some warning signs when he came over to our condo for assistance on some immigration paper work. He was wearing a tight stocking cap and my wife, always cordial to players, commented, "Pop is definitely different."

Everything was set and the Drake player was ready to fly from Baltimore-LA-Sydney. On the morning of his departure, I received a call from the airlines asking if I would accept responsibility to pay for extra bags for passenger Wright (seven extra bags) - I refused. He eventually made it to Australia and played in eight NBL games averaging 22.0 points and hitting a mid-court game winner for Newcastle on the road at Launceston, Tasmania. I received a call from Cal Bruton and he said something to the effect that I must be losing my touch in player selection because this guy Wright did not fit - anywhere. Summarily dismissed from his job in Newcastle, Pop Wright returned to the U.S. to continue escalating his deadly hard-drug habit. He was shot in a drug deal on the streets of Baltimore and later arrested in Des Moines passing stolen checks. He was attempting to cash the checks at a bank one block from the Drake campus. A former Drake player worked at the bank and immediately understood what was happening when Pop appeared with the stolen checks. The police were summoned.

Pop Wright began to come to his senses when he was being roughly handcuffed while spread-eagled on the floor of the bank; the cop affectionately whispered, "We gonna put you away forever, mother--." The words penetrated and were important in making Pop realize that he was wasting his life and this could be some serious prison time. At that point in the handcuffing, Wright broke down and cried. Fortunately, a layer of his denial had been cracked. He spent a short time in jail and then a year in a drug rehab program including a half-way house. After the rehab, he returned to Des Moines for another try at a life.

Pop's running mate on the court, off the court, and at their apartment, which they called the ghetto, was Lewis Lloyd. Sweet Lew had his own problems even though he was a productive NBA player. This guy averaged 30 points as a junior and 26 points as a senior at Drake and went 17.8 ppg, 13.1 ppg, 16.9 ppg, and 12.4 ppg in his four best NBA years at Houston. But he was drug-tested out of the league and finished his career in 1989-90 with Philadelphia and then Houston.

Lewis was a scoring machine without a conventional jump shot. He specialized in runners down the lane, got up and down the court well, and just had a knack for putting the ball in the hole against anybody. He was a great college player and was at one point on his way to becoming an NBA all-star. When Lewis was with Golden State, I saw him score 18 points in the first quarter and 26 in the first half against Isaiah Thomas and the Detroit Pistons in Oakland. He was so exhausted with his first-half effort that he was able to play only a few minutes in the second half of the game. But Lewis Loyd also ran into the drug road-block.

I ran into Pop and Lewis in Des Moines in 1990 at an AA meeting at Mercy Hospital, and I could not believe the change in Mr. Wright. I honestly thought that he would never get it. He looked good, and more importantly, was demonstrating his progress through his sobriety and productive living in Des Moines. I discussed Pop and Lewis with John Lucas and said that Rodney Wright was a miracle of all miracles in the drug-alcohol recovery world. I developed a new relationship with Pop and tried in vain to assist Lewis in a comeback via an Athletes in Action tour.

Curt Forrester and Tad Dufelmeier

At about the same time that Pop Wright went to Newcastle, I had been introduced to Curt Forrester, a hard nosed and versatile 6'6 forward from Grand View Junior College and Stetson University. Sy Forrester, Curt's father, was the A.D. at Tech High School and Curt was working as an assistant there to head coach Mel Green, former Drake University assistant. I recruited Curt to play with City of Sydney in a contract extended by club official Val Graudins. Curt was ready to go, but his dad, Sy, said that I should replace his son as Mel Green's assistant coach for the last three months of the season as part of the deal. I agreed and spent three enjoyable months with Mel Green and Sy Forrester working in the basketball program at Des Moines Technical High School.

Curt flew off amidst hugs from his family and tears from his girlfriend on a snowy winter day in January 1981 to sunny Sydney. He was a productive player in the NBL first as an import and then, having married an Aussie, became a citizen and played as a naturalized player before the "Natural Life Rule" was implemented. Curt Forrester was known for his toughness both on and off the court. He did not back down. While running a meat delivery service to supplement his basketball salary, he settled more than one delinquent account with his famed left cross. Also, Curt was known to have escorted an angry club owner by the shirt collar out of the Sydney dressing room after a tough King loss. There was another Forrester on the horizon, Corey, a sturdy teen-ager now growing up down-under.

Curt Forrester was instrumental in my recruitment of Tad Dufelmeier, a talented point guard and high school teammate of Forrester at Tech. I had called Tad and asked him to come to the downtown Des Moines YMCA for a workout in January 1982. He sounded apprehensive on the phone, as if he wcrc bcing conned, but he showed up. I can still see him dribbling the ball around the empty gym and glancing up warily into the balcony. I entered the gym unseen by Tad and watched as the guy became more and more certain that he had been had. But it was real - he had been a productive point at Loyola of Chicago averaging about 15 points his senior year and also was a 90% foul shooter. I made the deal with the Canberra GM, Terry Ryan, and Tad flew out weeks later to join the Canberra Cannons of the Australian Capital Territory. Although he lost his front teeth in an on-court collision, Dufelmeier had a successful NBL career as an import and then as a naturalized player. Like Curt Forrester, he has made Australia his permanent home.

Sydney Kings and the NBA

Sydney had three ex-NBA players in the lineup at various times in the 1980s - Owen Wells (Houston Rockets), Ronnie Cavenall (New York Knicks) and Wayne Kreklow (Boston Celtics). Wells came to Australia on a holiday after some good paying jobs in the European circuit and 33 NBA games on his resume. Bob Turner, the Newcastle coach, heard that there was an American basketball player working as a waiter in a local restaurant. Turner followed up and found an ex-NBA player less than a mile from the Falcons' homecourt.

Wells continued that year in his waiter's job and also signed a contract with Newcastle for the 1981 NBL season averaging 24.0 points. Owen Wells went back to the U.S. after the year with Newcastle and then returned to Australia as player-coach with Sydney in 1983. He led the team to the best regular-season record in the NBL in his dual role of player and coach, was named league MVP, and duplicated his 1981 point production with a 24.0 point per game average. However, Sydney lost early in the playoffs to West Adelaide. Ronnie Cavenall, a seven-footer out of Texas Southern, was Owen's post player. After the playoff loss, Cavenall was immediately cut by Sydney. He returned to the U.S. and eventually stuck with the New York Knicks in 1984-85 and then was up briefly with the Nets in 1988-89.

Owen Wells played ten games for Sydney in 1984, averaging 28.0 points. He then retired as a player but stayed in NBL coaching until mid-year 1987 when he was replaced at Sydney by Ken Cole. At the end of the 1988 NBL season, Wells left Australia for a job in Saudi Arabia and it was reported that he died a few years later of AIDS. Wells' sexual orientation was well-known among some American basketball players in Australia, but did not seem to disturb his effectiveness as a professional player and coach in the NBL. As a player, Owen Wells was talented, an athletic, 6'6 swing-guard, who was an effective scorer, rebounder, and defender.

I sent Wayne Kreklow to Sydney mid-way through the 1985 season in an attempt to give a talented team some chemistry. Kreklow was a great scorer as a combination guard at Drake and was a member of the 1981 Boston Celtics NBA title team under Bill Fitch, a coach with playing and coaching roots in Iowa whom I have known for over 40 years. Kreklow was angered that the Celtics had not offered him a guaranteed contract before veterans' camp prior to the 1981-82 season and refused to report to Boston. Even though the Celtics extended Kreklow a share of the title money in 1981, it was not enough to convince the ex-Drake star to give the NBA another shot. He finished the 1985 season with the Sydney Kings averaging 18 points over a 15 game NBL span. Wayne Kreklow was a talented 6'4 scoring guard and he had the tools to develop an NBA or a great overseas basketball career. However, after the season in Sydney, he returned to the U.S. to take a job as a college volleyball coach. To my knowledge, Kreklow never played professional basketball again.

Tiny Pinder

Kendall "Tiny" Pinder was a teammate of Kreklow on the 1985 Sydney team. Tiny had been an outstanding player for Norm Sloan at North Carolina State and had joined the Harlem Globetrotters' number one unit in a world tour after leaving N.C. State. He played in Australia with the Trotters, talked with the Sydney Kings, and decided to stay. Tiny, a carved 6'8 athletic player, led the league in rebounding and scoring in 1985. He later played on Cal Bruton's Wildcat title team in Perth in 1991.

Unfortunately, Tiny had recurring problems with the Australian police, related to rape allegations. He spent two years in jail in Western Australia and, at age 39, the Illawarra Hawks gave Tiny another chance in the 1995 NBL. Even then, his body looked about the same as ever and he would have been a valuable role player assuming there were no further problems.

However, trouble seemed to be following Pinder and he was again incarcerated, this time for a parole violation. I sat with this man-child during an Illawarra Hawk game in August 1995, just before his trial. He seemed to deny guilt in all situations and acted lively and normal in the two hours which I spent with him.

Three Legends

On the lighter side of down-under hoops, three legends, LeRoy Loggins, James Crawford and Ricky Grace are prominent NBL producers whom I introduced to Australian basketball. Loggins and Crawford were products of the AAABL in Brisbane, the league involving local clubs and college players from the NAIA in the United States. These players have continued to put up numbers as Loggins started the 1998 NBL season at a young 40 years of age alongside Cal Bruton's 21-year-old son, C.J. Crawford at 39 still can get the Wildcats 20 points and 10 rebounds against any opponent, and Grace, the youngest of the three, was in his prime as an NBL backcourt leader.

Loggins, a rail-thin swing guard, was a skilled, athletic, energetic star out of Fairmont State (NAIA) in 1981. Crawford played his college basketball at tiny Cumberland College in Kentucky. Before enrolling at Cumberland, James Crawford had played at Livingston University in Alabama under Coach Ken "Stump" Bracket, whom I knew at Middle Tennessee. Stump had been a key figure as a recruiter in the Middle Tennessee turn-around in the seventies, but unfortunately he developed cancer. Crawford said that the Livingston players had actually carried Coach Bracket to the bench from the dressing room for games until the disease cut his life short. Both Loggins and Crawford came directly to Australia from their senior seasons on their respective college campuses, Loggins to Brisbane and Crawford to Geelong.

I can recall two great plays by Loggins, one when he was 22 and the other 16 years later at 38. In the 1980 AAABL on a Sunday afternoon game at Auchenflower, Lang Park was matched up with the Gold Coast, LeRoy's team. Chris McGraw, a raw boned 6'7 and only eighteen years of age at the time, was last man up the court on a Gold Coast fastbreak when his teammate Bruce Fitzgerald stole the ball and hit McGraw with a pass.

Chris was pretty much all alone, drove casually to his basket, and prepared to go up to dunk the ball. He was a good jumper and the ball was even with the top of the square when LeRoy Loggins came flying down the court and with great ease leaped to reject the dunk attempt and blocked it cleanly. Chris McGraw and everyone else in the gym were amazed at the play by Loggins. LeRoy floated in like a seagull to make that play.

And in 1996, sixteen seasons later, I was watching Brisbane and Sydney at the Sydney Entertainment Center with 9,500 in attendance. Sydney had taken a commanding first-half lead behind the scoring of Melvin Thomas and Isaac Burton, but Brisbane slowly worked its way back. With 20 seconds remaining in the game, Sydney was leading by one point. Shane Heal was bringing the ball up against the Brisbane man-to-man press. LeRoy stole the ball and quickly turned the steal into two critical points for

Brisbane. It was a quiet, immaculate steal as Loggins left his man, approached Heal's blind side and picked the ball clean. LeRoy finished the play with a soft dunk and Brisbane held on to win.

Shane Heal, the Kings' point guard, left Sydney at the end of the 1996 season to become only the second player in Australian basketball history after Luc Longley to receive a guaranteed contract in the National Basketball Association (with the Minnesota Timberwolves). Heal played the 1996-97 season with the T-Wolves, but in an unexpected move was released by Minnesota in November 1997 and returned to his home club in Sydney.

Like Loggins, James Crawford has seen many changes in the Australian NBL since his arrival in Geelong in 1980. I can recall James coming to Brisbane for the AAABL in 1979 as a college junior at Cumberland College in Kentucky. He played with the Mayne Tigers and was billeted with a family from that club. One Sunday afternoon Crawford walked into Auchenflower for a Mayne game with a child in each arm and the young Australian mother and father smiling at his side. After handing the kids back to their parents, he took the floor and put on an amazing exhibition of an assortment of moves based on his "pogo-stick" jumping. He became famous for catching an offensive rebound with both feet on the floor and in a flash going back up for a ferocious slam. Crawford also showed an accurate 16-foot jumper, usually using the glass.

In the eight weeks of AAABL play in Australia that summer, Crawford had proven to me that he had a future in overseas professional basketball. I kept close tabs on his play as he returned to Cumberland College for his senior year when he earned NAIA All-America honors under Coach Randy Vernon. I rang Coach Vernon after the college season and told him that I wanted to work with James and that I could guarantee him employment in Australia. The Geelong Cats, coached by Tim Kaiser and later by player-coach Cal Bruton, were building a sound foundation in Victorian Basketball League competition preparing for entry into the NBL. Crawford joined Bruton, Steve Kalockinski and Ray Shirley in the Geelong Cats lineup, one of the most talented foursomes on any team in Australia basketball history.

I remember visiting Geelong in the early 1980s and finding James Crawford huddled in a heated shelter on a Holden automobile dealer's used car lot. He worked part-time as a car detailer to supplement his basketball salary. Crawford also worked in Rex Stewart's sportswear factory in his first year at Geelong. But times have changed and the guy from Peach Tree, Alabama, has become an NBL legend by putting together year after year of all-star play and whose game could be compared with that of the ex-NBA star, Larry Nance. Crawford has built a nice life for himself and his family on the shores of the Indian Ocean in Perth. He always had a reputation for being "tight" with his money - players do not understand it was a compliment - and he now has something to show for his financial discipline.

Ricky Grace had the strongest college background of the three legends. He was a key player with the powerful Oklahoma Sooners which lost to Danny Manning and the Kansas Jayhawks in the 1988 NCAA Finals. Grace averaged 15 ppg and played both guards at OU in the backcourt with NBA star Mookie Blaylock. I first saw Grace at a Quad Cities' CBA camp and invited him to stay with me in Des Moines while working out for Cal Bruton, who was recruiting a player for his Perth Wildcat team in 1990. Grace and Bruton went head-to-head for two days at a high school gym and Grace was awarded an NBL contract with the Wildcats. Quick, smart, and a lefty, Ricky got a 10-day call-up with the Atlanta Hawks in the 1993-94 NBA season and played for Perth vs. the Houston Rockets in the McDonald's Cup. He has been a key contributor to Perth's three NBL titles in 1990, 1991, and 1995. Like LeRoy Loggins and James Crawford, Ricky Grace continued as an effective player into the 1999 season and had accomplished a great deal on and off the court in his Australian professional career.

Cyclones

In addition to the decision by Loggins and Crawford to play in Australia, I also received a call from Chuck Harmison in early 1982. Chuck had been a double-figure scorer for the Iowa State Cyclones in the Big Eight Conference and had played in Belgium after graduation. Shortly after my conversation with Harmison, I took a trip to Melbourne. I met with Barry Barnes, the Nunawading coach and later the Australian National Team's head man, at the Travelodge at Tulamarine Airport. We discussed Harmison's potential as an NBL player and how he might fit into the Nunawading lineup.

I liked Harmison's size (6'7), his basketball skills, and his under-rated athletic ability and conveyed this information to Barry Barnes. Soon after, Chuck Harmison was wearing a Nunawading uniform and sustained a fifteen year, 386 game playing career in the Australian NBL, retiring in 1996. Skilled, fundamentally sound, and consistent, Harmison was one of the most productive and best-liked import players of all time in Australia. He was named General Manager of the Illawarra Hawks in 1997 and was working with Coach Brendan Joyce to build a winner necessary to fill the new 6,500 seat arena in Wollongong.

Soon after Harmison's arrival in Melbourne, his Iowa State teammate Dean Uthoff called me on a Saturday afternoon in February 1983. He said that he wanted to play in Australia and asked if I would assist in the process. Uthoff was the all-time leading rebounder in the Big Eight Conference and at 6'11 and 275, I knew he was employable.

I drove to Marshalltown the same day that Uthoff called and watched him play in the Iowa State Amateur Athletic Union Tournament. We spoke after the game and I agreed to find him a job. I called Rex Stewart at Geelong that evening and he was interested. I informed Uthoff of the job prospect and asked him to meet me halfway between Cedar Rapids, his home, and Des Moines at the Grinnell College gym for a brief workout on Monday. He agreed and I drove down to Grinnell. Uthoff did not show up.

I was informed about a week later that he was, in fact, already in Australia and playing for Nunawading. The club had made direct contact with Uthoff through his former Iowa State teammate Chuck Harmison, whom I had placed in Australia with the Nunawading club in the previous year. I was unhappy about that situation and asked the club for remuneration. The club refused to pay me. This misunderstanding was recorded as the only blemish on my otherwise perfect collection percentage for players delivered to NBL teams since the league began in 1979. In those days, I did not require a player-agent contract and operated on good faith with players and clubs.

In this situation, I had assumed that Uthoff was sincere in asking me to help him find a job. The Nunawading club took advantage of the situation. They had heard of Uthoff through Chuck Harmison, who innocently tried to help his college teammate. The club then approached Dean Uthoff directly, but Uthoff apparently did not inform club officials that I had been working on his behalf in finding employment in Australia.

Uthoff went on to play productively in Australia until his retirement in 1996 from the Sydney Kings' active player list. Uthoff had been drafted by San Antonio and had some of the qualities necessary to play a back-up role in the NBA. He worked hard with the weights, was always in great shape, and did some things on the basketball court very well - block outs, defensive rebounds, and fast-break outlet passes. As a solidly packaged 6'11 and weight-trained 275 pounds, Uthoff was a force in NBL play.

When I was coaching at Hobart in 1986, I recall telling Jerry Dennard, the former Iowa player, to take a charge when Uthoff wheeled blindly into the paint for a shot. Dennard was fearless on the court, but had reservations about getting steam-rolled by the big man and never got around to following those questionable instructions from his coach. Dean Uthoff never did progress much with his shooting skills; nevertheless he was a consistent and valuable NBL player, especially after becoming naturalized and playing as an Australian. Big Dean reminded me of Kent Benson, the Indiana post player who spent 11 years in the NBA, in that he was productive, but didn't really play as big as his size dictated. Lynn Nance recruited and coached Uthoff at Iowa State. Nance said that Dean worked hard during practice, but put little effort on skill work after the required training time. Dave Corzine, a similar player who spent 13 years as an NBA back-up center, was Uthoff's nemesis at the San Antonio training camps. Uthoff admitted, "Corzine really gave me problems." And Uthoff did the same to NBL opponents.

Thus, during this period in the early 1980s I was busy with the overseas recruiting and the college admissions job. We had settled in Des Moines and had purchased a condominium. On the surface, my life looked to be in order. However, I was having some serious, recurring personal problems and was about to embark on the most important phase of my adult life.

□ *9* □

PSYCH WARD TO HOBART - A NATURAL STEP
WITH STEVE CARFINO

While browsing in a book store at a shopping mall in Des Moines, I noticed the title, *Where Did Everybody Go*, an autobiographical work about alcoholism by Paul Molloy. I had previously read a review of the book and recognized the title. I examined the book, opened it and read a few words, put it down, and left the store. For some reason, however, after walking away, I returned and bought Molloy's book, which described his struggle and eventual recovery from alcoholism.

I drove back to my home and could not put the book down until I had read every page. I could identify with Malloy. He was an educated and apparently successful columnist for the *Chicago Sun-Times*, but there was something drastically wrong with his life. I was educated and had achieved in basketball and business, but I knew that there was something drastically wrong in my life. Malloy had denied his problems with alcohol and nearly died. Eventually, after several failures at living sober, he completed a treatment program. He struggled, accepted the reality and the severity of his situation, struggled further, and eventually began to live a sane and sober life.

I was inspired by Paul Molloy's story, but I was still drinking on a daily basis, yet doing my best to live responsibly. This was, of course, impossible. My pattern was to get my work done and then "relax" by drinking a few beers at a neighborhood bar with other business people. I would then go home for three or four stiff martinis before dinner. We ate out frequently and the after-work drinking routine also included wine and often after-dinner brandy. The depression and the general state of my mental health had become a serious issue and I was aware that I was going downhill, but I did not know why. I felt terrible, had little energy, and was starting to look exhausted with dark circles under my eyes.

I finally decided to test myself and wrote out an agreement (with myself) not to exceed three drinks per day for a ninety day period. I meticulously recorded my daily consumption of alcohol. During that time I took a three-week trip to Southeast Asia on a recruiting trip for Buena Vista College. I planned my three drinks per day taking into consideration the time change in crossing the international date line. I did not exceed the three-drink limit for the 90 days. However, on the 91st day, I got very drunk and the old drinking pattern continued. It never occurred to me that trying to control my drinking was an obvious symptom of a problem with alcohol.

Eventually, I began to attend some AA meetings in Des Moines in 1983 and decided to stop drinking on my own without going through a treatment program. I went 99 days without a drink and then relented on a business trip to Providence, Rhode Island. The exercise equipment manufacturer sponsoring the trip had arranged for a day's outing on Rhode Island Sound. It was a cloudless summer day and drinks were served all day long. I was miserable on that boat, but did not drink. When the dinghy came out at the end of that hideous day to pick us up to return to shore, I felt that I had been rescued from a shipwreck - only I was the wreck. That evening I drank two beers and broke my 99-day run of staying dry. At the time I did not understand that there was a significant difference between staying dry and living sober.

Upon returning to Des Moines, my heavy drinking resumed; eventually I entered a treatment program at Iowa Methodist Hospital, but dropped out after ten days. I then entered the Mercy Hospital alcohol-rehab program on an outpatient basis and completed the five-week program. I stopped drinking on November 11, 1983, and finished the hospital rehab in January 1984. Ironically, my sobriety date of November 11 was my mother's birthday. After treatment, I began to attend AA meetings in the Des Moines area on a daily basis and have not taken another drink. In my case, similar to Paul Molloy's, I had used alcohol for a long period of time, twenty-four years, on a daily basis to deal with life and life's problems. The process eventually became pathological - physically, mentally, emotionally, and spiritually. I struggled daily in early sobriety and experienced unpredictable mood swings going from okay one moment to deeply depressed the next.

I wasn't drinking, but my perceptions got worse. I continued to suffer acute and debilitating depression and entered the Lutheran Hospital in Des Moines in January 1985. It was then that I faced some troubling personal issues, which I had until then either buried or denied. I had thus begun a very slow and thorough recovery process with continuing AA participation and commitment to honesty as the key. Through my drinking pattern, I had avoided mid-life issues, especially the issue of my own mortality. While in recovery, I was eventually able to come to terms, at least philosophically, with my own death, thoughts of not-being, without the issue impeding my daily living. Although the recovery process was confusing and perplexing at the time, enduring relationships in reality through AA, around the world, and sobriety itself have made my life real, more enjoyable and much more productive.

Dr. T

I began to make some progress in the psychiatric ward at Lutheran Hospital, euphemistically called Mental Health Unit, but I knew exactly where I was. Through the guidance of a psychiatrist, Dr. Walter Thompson, I learned and accepted what I had to do to get honest and made a serious commitment to do whatever was necessary to develop emotional stability and build a solid foundation in mental health. I had penetrated the denial of my situation and knew that I was in a serious struggle to stabilize my depression and regain emotional balance. It was a long, difficult process. One day Dr. Thompson told me, "You have a lot of time in your life left, but you need to get moving. Don't expect too much. It will take patience and constant effort." This was great advice and exactly what I needed to hear at the time. However, I found that I wasn't able to spring out of the psych ward into a new life without hard work, psychotherapy, AA, recurring depression, and gradual behavioral changes.

Dr. Walter Thompson was a source of inspiration for my understanding and learning to live with chronic depression. One day at the hospital I asked him if I would ever "get out of here and get well." He paused, looked me in the eye, and said, "That is up to you. How hard do you want to work at your recovery?"

I replied, "Whatever it takes."

He countered, "Prove it."

I often think of Dr. T's profound Socratic question-and-answer teaching method and its penetrating message of responsibility for self. This doctor-patient dialogue was clearly a turning point in my life and a further lesson that all good things took patience, sustained effort, set-backs, and time - usually a long time.

Alcoholism and Will-Power

In the recovery process, I did a great deal of reading about alcoholism. I became fascinated with the literature available. I was able to use the information along with my experiences in treatment, psychotherapy, and the wisdom of other recovering people to build my own path to a sober, productive life. I studied a large body of confusing information about alcoholism and have been able through trial, error, and personal experience to simplify my life and my own daily routine in recovery. I fully agreed with the American Medical Association, American Psychiatric Association, and other professional medical organizations in the world that called alcoholism a disease. I saw it as chronic with identifiable stages and symptoms, genetic predisposition, and progression, with very low rates of recovery and predictable outcomes.

Further, I accepted that this disease can run in families and that recent research had shown the genetic link. Also, I have found that drinking for an alcoholic is but a symptom. When an alcoholic stops using alcohol, life normally becomes untenable because the chemical becomes a solution as well as a problem. I had used alcohol as a solution to life's problems for 24 years.

When I stopped, I was left to seek answers in reality, answers buried deep and not readily available to me. It was necessary for me to stop the use of alcohol in order to deal with my previous behaviors, which were for the most part in direct conflict with a rather rigid value system. But I found that my values were in place, my behavior was not, and the truth was buried in twenty-four years of denial.

Few alkies, even with treatment, stay sober very long. Authoritative studies say 5% or 6% can sustain sobriety up to five years and then the percentage dropped again. Living sober was most difficult because of the physical craving, common in about 12% of the U.S. population and the characteristic which distinguished the alky from the social drinker. The craving could be over-powering, but it passed. I heard Jimmy Swaggert, the fallible TV evangelist, who spoke of the alcoholic simply lacking will power and discipline. There was an appropriate saying in AA that will power as a tool for the alcoholic to stop drinking was as effective against alcoholism as it was in the control of diarrhea.

My recovery has required a total behavior change. This started with a brutally honest examination of past behavior (the wreckage of the past) along with eventual acceptance of responsibility for indiscretions associated with my alcoholism. Commitment to the AA Twelve-Step Program, professional help in early sobriety, and continuing daily effort to live in harmony with my values with an emphasis on personal growth have been the key ingredients. Today, I don't drink alcohol or do drugs; I do behave in harmony with my values; I do associate regularly with other recovering people; I do go to AA meetings and I do embrace the Twelve-Step AA Program; I do work with newcomers in AA; and I do remember to keep my expectations down and my efforts up in life's activities. This program of daily discipline has worked well for me.

Several years after treatment and the subsequent hospitalization for depression, I was walking through the skywalk system at the Mayo Clinic in Rochester, Minnesota. My mother was in the hospital for surgery and I was in Rochester for the week. I inadvertently ran into Dr. Thompson, then teaching psychiatry at Mayo. I found myself giving him a big hug and thanking him profusely for his part in my recovery. He was a dignified, reserved, black man and I know that my sincere and spontaneous greeting moved him as he walked away on the crowded noon-hour skywalk with his two colleagues busily asking him, "Who the hell was that?"

Easing Back into Coaching

Also while in the hospital psych ward in 1985, I felt a strong internal urge to get back into basketball. Maybe it was just that my head was clear enough to know that I had had a good start in basketball and I had some issues to resolve in that area of my life. After I was released from the psych ward, Sy Forrester at Tech High School in Des Moines gave me my first sober opportunity as an assistant to coach a winless seventh-grade girls' team. The highlight of that experience was when one of the girls on our woeful team made two consecutive free throws. The bench went crazy.

For additional involvement in basketball at the time, I did volunteer work at the Boys' and Girls' Club as a coach and also with a local AAU men's team. This team, composed of some good ex-college players, had been organized with the objective of delivering an anti-drug message through basketball. When I agreed to coach the team, I wasn't quite sure what I was getting into. We played a college exhibition schedule and the general manager and founder of the organization gave a testimonial speech at the half-time intermission of games regarding his own recovery from alcoholism and cocaine addiction. The intentions of the group were positive, but unfortunately the team founder continued to struggle with the cocaine and found it difficult to sustain a clean and sober life style.

I coached this AAU team on a tour to Bradley University, Eastern Illinois, Western Illinois, and in the Iowa State AAU Tournament, which we won. Overall, I appreciated the opportunity to do some coaching. However, I was relieved to end the relationship as I saw drug and alcohol education as a serious topic whose message needed to be delivered with maximum credibility by people with solid sobriety. Few, if any, of the players in this group were actually in recovery. Most of them had never had alcohol and drug problems, although a couple were using and were borderline. The leader of the group could not maintain sobriety, and I, though dedicated to recovery, was very new at life without alcohol. In short, it was a strange and disturbing experience with basketball egos being fed through identification with a higher cause. On the lighter side, as the team traveled from game to game in a van with the chain-smoking, cocaine addict at the wheel and me, unstable at best, at his side, I smiled to myself. I could identify with the scene from *One Flew Over the Cuckoo's Nest* in which McMurphy (Jack Nicholson) had commandeered a school bus from the insane asylum to go on a joy-ride with his fellow disturbed inmates.

I made the best of the situation and knew that it was only for a few games. We defeated Western Illinois and Eastern Illinois and then played Bradley University in Peoria, Illinois. Bradley was a school rich in basketball tradition with a strong record of achievement in the Missouri Valley Conference. When Ken Trickey was coaching at Iowa State, a local sportswriter was discussing the ISU schedule and mentioned Bradley. Trickey's famous rhetorical question came in response, "What's Bradley?" These words were an appropriate epitaph to Coach Trick's two-year, 13-win/40-loss legacy at Iowa State. He never lived down that comment among area sportswriters and Iowa State fans.

Jim Bain and Bradley

We played the game at the old Robertson Fieldhouse, the scene of scores of famous moments in Bradley basketball history. Our opponents on that 1984-85 team were coached by Dick Versace and included freshman Hersey Hawkins, Mike Williams, Voise Winters, and point guard Jim Les. All of these players and the coach also eventually drew NBA paychecks. Bradley had, obviously, a formidable group of athletes with capable leadership on the sidelines from Versace, who appeared to have just come from his hairdresser. Tony Barone was Versace's assistant who went on to head jobs at Creighton and Texas A&M. It was a pre-season game and we were only a touring AAU team. We got little respect from anyone, even though we played Bradley tight for 30 minutes before losing by 15.

Jim Bain, a Big Ten referee who worked a national college schedule, and his partners ignored several obvious goal tending violations by Bradley and that set the pattern for the evening. In fact, it seemed that Bain - not a popular man among University of Iowa followers - was enjoying the course of events. He cast an occasional smug glance down at me, a mere AAU coach, from the elevated court to the player benches 4-5 feet below the playing surface.

Referee Bain had been involved in a highly publicized controversy in the 1981 Iowa-Purdue game. Iowa eventually lost by one point, 66-65, with Bain's phantom call on an Iowa player, Kevin Boyle, putting Dan Palombizio on the foul line for the winning free throw with no time on the clock. Replays showed that Boyle had been eight feet away from Palombizio on the play. Lute Olson, the Iowa coach, had sharply criticized Bain. The conflict escalated to a topic of national interest among basketball fans around the country, especially intense in Iowa City and the Big Ten Conference. The Big Ten Commissioner, Wayne Duke, reprimanded Olson for his public criticism of a referee, but Duke also admitted that Bain had violated a conference rule by working three college games in a twenty-four hour period on the weekend of the Iowa-Purdue game. The beleaguered official sued an Iowa City business which had sold Jim Bain Fan Club t-shirts showing a picture of a referee with a rope around his neck. Also, Bain canceled a speaking engagement in Davenport, Iowa, after the season when he allegedly received death threats.

In my experience as a coach on the bench with high school, college, and overseas pro teams, I have seen referees who seemed to think that everyone in the gym had bought a ticket to watch them blow their whistles. Recognition from the public rates high on the list of motives for participation in athletics, even for referees. In the case of an athlete, the need for recognition can drive him to better performance. However, the recognition motive for the referee must be kept in check through personal discipline as it can come into conflict with players and coaches in an emotionally charged atmosphere. The best referees compete to achieve a high standard of professionalism and to enhance the playing situation, not to show up the coaches and athletes. After all, fans have paid to see the players and coaches in action, not the referees. In my opinion, referees who lack the discipline and restraint to defer the center stage to the teams and who are on the floor to show up players and/or coaches are in the wrong business.

I survived Bradley, Bain, and the tour in general even though I was shaky and unstable at the time. I did learn from that experience that I wanted to continue to pursue a job in basketball. After the tour, I contacted Mike Wrublewski, the long-time owner of the Sydney Kings, and Rex Stewart at Geelong in Australia. I had placed several players at Geelong, including Cal Bruton, who pushed me to take the Geelong job. Cal wanted to give up his player-coach role and concentrate on playing. James Crawford and Wayne McDaniel, a 6'6 scorer out of Cal-State Bakersfield, were my Overseas Basketball Services recruits with the Geelong club.

Sydney, Geelong, and Hobart

Rex Stewart put me in touch with Bob Spurling, who was in charge of the Geelong coaching-selection process, and he expressed interest in my situation. After a couple of discussions with Geelong, Spurling called me. He said that his club had heard that I was going to coach Sydney and asked if I would pull out of that job to commit to Geelong. I said that I would, so I called Mike Wrublewski and told him that I was going to accept another job in the NBL. Two weeks later, Spurling called with the news that "things had changed" in regard to Geelong club ownership. Steve Jackson, a local in the electronics business, had taken control of the club and was not interested in hiring me as coach. Thus, I was 0-2 at this point in my efforts to coach in the NBL.

I decided to persist in search of another job and placed a call to David Claxton in Brisbane. I had supported Claxton in his successful effort to become the Brisbane Bullet head coach in 1980. He was doing the television commentary on Bullet home games at the time and was therefore well-informed about coaching changes in the Australian league. Claxton told me that the Hobart job was open and he agreed to call, on my behalf, the Hobart club president, Wayne Monaghan. That phone call set in motion the events of the next three years, as I was hired as head coach of the Hobart Devils in the NBL. However, the Devils were barely in the league and marginally competitive at the time. The Hobart team had gone 8-73 in league play in the previous three years under a series of coaches.

My predecessor with the Hobart Devils was Charlie Ammit, known as a "fly-in" coach. He took care of his commercial painting business as his full-time job and then would catch a flight from Sydney to arrive in Hobart on Thursday evening for one practice before weekend games. He was one of the NBL's colorful personalities and reportedly carried a fifth of whiskey along with his game plan in his briefcase. I heard from a player that Charlie was coming down on the elevator at a Brisbane hotel for breakfast when he ran into Ollie Johnson, the Devils star player in 1985. Charlie reportedly said, "Good morning, Ollie. Good to see you up early on game day." Ollie was, of course, just returning from a night on the town. Coach Ammit endured a 2-24 mark with Hobart in the year prior to my arrival.

Looking back, it probably took someone right out of a psych ward to take on this job, and I qualified. Hobart's Wayne Monaghan rang me with the Hobart offer: a salary of $6,000, airline tickets for my wife and me, and the use of a Mercedes. I later found the car perk to actually be a bright yellow, 1962 model which was not in running order. When I first saw the Mercedes, it wouldn't start and the back seat was littered with empty beer cans. Apparently a former player had used the car during his stay in Hobart. Also, upon arrival in Tasmania, I found that the club was on the brink of financial collapse and I was responsible for soliciting sponsorship dollars, the life blood of cash flow in overseas club basketball. I had knocked on many doors in the exercise equipment business in Florida and didn't mind working in this capacity temporarily, to help get the club on its feet.

I recall my first day on the job, as I got out of my car in downtown Hobart to make calls on businesses, potential club sponsors. I experienced the same intense surge of panic that I had felt my first day in Mozambique 15 years before. It was a reminder that I had much work to do on myself, as well as in the coaching of the team. Monaghan had assured me that once we arrived in Hobart and people got to know us, doors would open. I trusted Monaghan; however, after accepting the modest offer from Hobart, I still had some doubts, and it took time to come to the conclusion that Australia was the right move.

The decision to go back to Australia had been a dilemma because I had simultaneously in August 1985 been offered more conventional employment as the Director of Admissions at Park College near Kansas City. That job paid $30,000 - $24,000 more than the Hobart coaching job. It also meant that the 200-mile shift from Des Moines to Kansas City would be much more convenient than the commitment required in the overseas move to Hobart, Tasmania. The Park College job involved a routine relocation, the Hobart job upheaval. However, we had begun to accept upheaval and uncertainty as normal and necessary in this phase of our lives and in this decision-making process.

Time was getting short and I had to give Hobart and Park College an answer. Geneva and I had used a legal pad to record the positive and negative points about each job. We would add comments periodically during the two-week window we had established in making a decision. We had listed 25 reasons why we should go to Kansas City and only one advantage to the Hobart job. The Kansas City list was essentially of a material nature and the one-item Hobart list was emotional. When I discussed Kansas City, I spoke objectively and without much feeling; but when I talked of Hobart, I became animated and enthusiastic and felt a wide range of intense feelings. In my life at that stage, common sense had little chance against emotion.

The time had finally come when I had to make a decision. I recall that on a Friday I got up early and drove to downtown Des Moines. I parked about four blocks north of the Marriott Hotel and began to walk to the hotel for a 7:00 a.m. coffee and read of the newspaper. About a block from the hotel I saw a familiar, large figure walking toward me on the same side of the street. I recognized Steve Waite, a former University of Iowa starter under Lute Olson, and stopped to chat with him. I told Steve that I was making a decision that day on a coaching job in Australia and that I was considering Steve Carfino for the import point-guard job. Waite had played with Carfino at Iowa and was very positive and enthusiastic about him as a player and as a person. Waite described Carfino as "a great guy with NBA basketball talent." I thanked him for his comments on Carfino and walked directly to the hotel, with the answer becoming clearer with each step. Upon arriving at the Marriott, the decision was made and I looked at the meeting with Waite as a sign to take the plunge and go to Hobart.

I called Park College and spoke with the acting president to inform him of my decision. For some reason the college administrator was upset and upbraided me for "leading him on" regarding my interest in the job. He also said that he would see that I didn't ever work again in college admissions. He was right. I didn't work again in admissions. I tried to assess the future impact of that veiled promise, but it was too late to reconsider. I was excited as the momentum had changed and I was ready to go to Australia again.

The chance meeting with Steve Waite hastened my decision to take the Hobart job and set in motion two months of selling furniture, condo, and cars, all of our material possessions. We had moved a few times before and had even lived in Australia, but this relocation was particularly difficult. I was struggling in early sobriety and going through some huge emotional and perceptional adjustments, and my wife, Geneva, was feeling my instability.

When a couple had purchased and loaded our living-room furniture into their truck, Geneva and I both felt strong emotions as we looked around at our lonely, vacant condo. The clock was running, another phase of our life was passing, and we had decided to "travel light" in the Hobart venture. Later that day we drove to the downtown Grand Avenue Bridge over the

Des Moines River. Each of us had written on inflated balloons with magic marker issues to "let go of." We took turns releasing the balloons into the brusque wind and prayed aloud that the issue would be resolved. The balloon exercise was very positive for us both. I will never forget it.

We arrived in Hobart in September 1985. Peter Loone, a Hobart Devil sponsor and reliable member of the club-management team, met us at the airport. He drove us through the city of 200,000 to his Cambria Villa Motel in New Town, a red-brick suburb of Hobart. The next day, club president Wayne Monaghan had arranged a press conference at a local hotel and I met the board, sponsors, and writers from *The Mercury,* the capital city daily newspaper in Tasmania. The honeymoon year with the local media had officially been launched. The press had witnessed debacle after debacle called Hobart Devil basketball for three years netting the 8 wins and 73 losses. I sensed that no one thought that anything would change, save for names and faces in the pre-season rhetoric.

I had planned a long build-up to the season and knew that it would take at least three months to put together a team. It was one of those deals: the team was 2-24 last year, but the bad news was that everyone was back. I felt that it was my job and that it was necessary to see that everyone "was not back" and to bring in some new players - Australian born especially. I hoped that Steve Carfino and Jeff Acres, a versatile and skilled 6'7 forward from Oral Roberts with one previous season of overseas experience, could carry the load offensively. We had one major off-court problem, as well as the obvious on-court obstacles, to overcome: the club was broke and could not pay the players during the 1986 season. Everyone understood the financial realities in advance, but the club emphasized that if the team was successful, the 1987 season would be different in terms of player payments.

Jim Rosborough, Lute Olson's assistant coach at Iowa and Arizona, called me to recommend Carfino. Coach Ros said that Steve, who had worked in the sporting goods business right after graduation from Iowa, realized how much he had missed playing. He just wanted a shot, like many other guys. However, unlike many pretenders, Carfino had authentic talent and came from a great Big Ten college background. The financial problem at Hobart didn't seem to bother Steve Carfino. He had been out of school over a year and was hungry to play organized basketball again at any cost - or at no cost, as the Hobart situation presented. In a brief interview with Carfino at The Highlander Inn in Iowa City, I was impressed with his interest, his presence, and his charisma. He was a great-looking athlete with poise, a trademark of Lute Olson's graduated players. Most players can come across with some surface polish when necessary in limited contact situations, but Steve Carfino was sincere and convinced me that he really wanted to give the Hobart job his best effort. He didn't know me, but relied on Coach

Rosborough's advice. (I did not bring up the topic of psych wards with Rosborough in telephone conversations or with Carfino in our first meeting.)

Deno

Every morning my first month in Hobart, I would walk from our room to the Cambria Villa Motel office. The motel was owned by Peter Loone and his wife, Pat. I used the office to make calls across Australia to give my hollow sales pitch about playing time, challenge, and opportunity with the new Devils. One key call was to Jerry Dennard in Adelaide. I had placed "Deno" as an import player with the Newcastle Falcons a couple of years before and he had done a respectable job for them. However, the Falcons were looking for more offense and cut Dennard, who returned to California. He later called me in Des Moines from his job in a group home in Chowchilla, California, and asked for another playing job. I knew that he wouldn't attract an NBL offer, as he was not a great scorer, but would be valuable to a state league team. After making a few calls, a club in Adelaide agreed to hire Dennard.

Jerry Dennard had been a junior college All-American at Merced in California and was considered to be a blue-chip Division I prospect. He was heavily recruited and finally signed at Iowa, but was hampered by a back injury early in his junior year. When he took the floor the first time as a Hawkeye, he received a thunderous, standing ovation from 14,000 rabid supporters in the old Iowa Fieldhouse. That moment was to be the highlight of Deno's career in the Big Ten; it went downhill from that point on. He was a mobile 6'9 guy with long arms and a strong, but thin body, and he had guts. His game was power-forward, but he didn't have the bulk to bang in the Big Ten. Also, his playing time was limited and at the end of his senior year in 1984, Jerry Dennard was not a factor in the Iowa program.

Even though he got little recognition as a player at Iowa, I remembered his story. I contacted him through Sharm Scheuerman and Coach Jim Rosborough to set in motion the job in Newcastle in 1984 and his life in Australia. At one point he balked on some required paperwork for immigration. I called Ros and asked that he emphasize to Deno that he may be finished before he starts if he can't follow important directions. From that point on Jerry Dennard did his best to be responsible in our dealings, except years later in a tryout with Townsville. When I told him to cut his pony tail for the tryout, he agreed, but then failed to do it. The club was looking for veteran leadership and the strange hair-do didn't fit its picture. It was a factor in his not receiving an offer in an aborted NBL comeback effort.

Deno became the key player in the turn-around of the Hobart program, but not without considerable planning and cooperation from several people in Hobart. Wayne Monaghan, Peter Loone, the Honorable Michael

Hodgman, and many other Devils faithfuls pitched in to help in the recruitment of Jerry Dennard.

Michael Hodgman, known as "the mouth of the South" in Australian politics, was a colorful, talented politician and a huge asset to the Hobart Devil basketball program. During that time in Hobart, a *clintonian rumor* circulated that Mr. Hodgman had received a clandestine note at his hotel in Canberra while Parliament was in session and he was busy conducting the Australian nation's political business. The note said something to the effect that "I am an admirer and have always wanted to get to know you better. Should you be interested in pursuing this matter simply wear a red rose in your lapel at the session of Parliament on Monday morning."

When that Monday arrived, as the story went, Michael "Mickey" Hodgman reportedly burst through the doors in his dark suit with a red rose in his lapel. He glanced around the chambers apparently to see if his admirer was present. It took him only a few seconds to realize that he had been duped. Several journalists, who were clearly aware of the significance of the red rose, were most likely authors of the note. However, the fact remained that without the assistance of Mr. Hodgman, the Devils would not have had the services of their new Aussie. Without Dennard in the lineup, we would have been in deep trouble. Hodgman was the Devils' sixth man and came to our aid on many occasions throughout my tenure as the Hobart coach, as did another Tasmanian politician, Hank Petrusma.

When I called Jerry Dennard from the Cambria Villa office that morning in October 1985, he was living in Adelaide, South Australia. He had that year been playing state league and his basketball form in general was going downhill. He told me that he was engaged to be married and wanted to come to Hobart as an import player. I felt that I needed a player with more offense in that spot and Jeff Acres had already been selected. As I spoke with Deno, I thought how valuable he would be as a naturalized player, thus not counting against the two foreign-player limit in the NBL. At the time, a naturalized player could suit-up immediately upon receiving his Australian passport with no FIBA waiting period.

In the next three weeks, the club began to take action. It was a team effort to land the prized recruit. I presented my naturalization plan to Wayne Monagahn, who flew to Adelaide to sell the idea to Jerry Dennard and Robyn, his fiancée. The couple were married on the next Saturday in Hobart at the home of Jacky Mildred, an active club sponsor and manager of Olivetti. The first thing Monday morning the newlyweds met with Michael Hodgman, who arranged to have Deno's permanent residency established immediately with the promise of only a three-month wait for official Australian citizenship. The naturalization of Jerry Dennard meant that a 6'9 all-purpose player would be in the Devils lineup instead of a 6'3 lesser talent. Just one week before the official opening of the 1986 NBL season, Jerry Dennard became an Australian. He also became a pivotal acquisition for the club in lifting the team out of the NBL cellar and into some temporary respectability.

Devil of a Time

Official practice started on December 1, 1985, with the new version of the Hobart Devils team intact. Steve Carfino and Jeff Acres were the U.S. imports with Jerry Dennard and two Brisbane rejects, 6'11 Murray Shiels and 6'9 Paul Simpson, positioned to play key roles. Local Tasmanians included the Stanwix triumvirate: Brendan, Warren, and Darren. Dan Van Holst Pelakaan, who had played at the University of Toronto, rounded out the Hobart team. However, there was a behind-the-scenes crisis which threatened the viability of the franchise.

I had been working as a club rep in calling on former and potential new sponsors from a "hit list" compiled by the club president, Wayne Monaghan. As I pounded the Hobart sidewalk each day, I learned that the Devils had not been particularly popular among local business people nor did the club have what was called good credit. In fact, the former club administration had taken out a loan to cover expenses from the previous year and bank payments were delinquent. Also, rent payments to the Warrane Basketball Center, the team's training site, were past due.

The Devils were under the auspices of the local basketball association which actually held the NBL franchise for the Hobart team. The Devils was the team that many locals loved to hate. In fact, the local league, probably the weakest senior men's basketball in all Australia, was the focal point and main interest of the Warrane Stadium crowd and of local basketball administrators.

I sensed that it was with some pleasure that David Scott, the facility administrator at Warrane, informed me that the Devils owed $1,500 in back rent and could not train there until paid. I finally negotiated 6:00 a.m. training times until the debt was paid off. The Devils' program and its new coach were clearly second-class citizens in the eyes of the locals at Warrane; however, we did get an early start on our rebuilding process.

Thus, as I called on Hobart businesses, I began to form a clearer picture of what I was up against as a coach who had come to Tasmania with some hope and a vague dream of succeeding in the NBL with this team. Finally, I requested a meeting with Wayne Monaghan and Peter Loone. I asked them a very important question, "Are we actually going to be able to pull this off and afford the NBL pre-season deposits and field a team?" Time had passed and this was February with the season only weeks away. The club was already delinquent on $15,000 in NBL fees. After I posed the question, there was disturbing silence, but I trusted both Monaghan and Peter Loone and knew that they would be up-front and work to find a solution, if one existed. They finally said that Wayne Monaghan, a banker, was going to spend two days non-stop on the books and give me an answer by Monday morning. The answer came as promised and it was, "No worries, mate - just go win some games." I felt that the weight of responsibility had suddenly shifted from administration to coach, which was just what I needed to lift my efforts and spirits. I could hear the words of Dr. Thompson from the psych ward, "How hard to you want to work? Prove it."

Time passed and we were finally ready to play some real games. Hobart hosted a four-team, pre-season tourney involving Sydney, Adelaide, Geelong, and the home team Devils. We lost the opener to Geelong behind the long-range shooting of Dane Suttle, a former NBA journeyman with Kansas City, and then dropped consecutive games to Adelaide and Sydney. In the Sydney game, Tiny Pinder threw an apparent intentional elbow, as revealed by the game tape, and broke the jaw of Devil post-man Murray Shiels. We sent the tape to the NBL office, which viewed the vicious blow but chose to take no disciplinary action. It was a brutal elbow thrown by a powerful man, but the incident seemed to pull our team together as Shiels courageously played on with padded, protective headgear.

We met the Kings again in the final day of the Hobart tournament. We showed progress in winning by 18 points after being pounded by 35 by the same team on the previous day, a 53 point turn-around in less than 24 hours. I had a curious visitor that night on the bench. Rob, a member of my AA group in Hobart, strolled up to me while we were warming up for Sydney and asked how it was going. Then uninvited, but welcome, he took a seat beside me on the bench. With the Devils leading by about 20 with three minutes remaining Rob said, "Well, I think you have them." He then disappeared into the crowd. Carfino asked me about that guy sitting on the bench. I replied that it was a spiritual matter and I would tell him about it sometime, which I did.

My official NBL debut as a coach with the Hobart Devils was in Brisbane versus the Bullets. Brian Kerle, who had been very successful with the St. Kilda Club in Melbourne, was the Brisbane head coach. Cal Bruton was back with the Bullets and matched up against Steve Carfino, our prize recruit from Lute Olson's program at the University of Iowa. Brisbane was all over us and we lost 115-72. Coach Kerle made a terse comment after the game to the press. The article appeared in the early morning edition of the Brisbane paper, which I saved. Kerle said something to the effect that Brisbane did not play well, etc. That comment triggered thoughts of what Brisbane with a 35-point victory thought of us. To the average reader, there was probably nothing incendiary in Kerle's comments. However, for a coach desperate for some type of edge, it was perfect. I knew the clipping would come in handy down the road in the return game, and it did.

We had arrived in Brisbane for the Friday night game. Geneva flew up from Hobart and spent a couple of days with Cal, Trish, and the Bruton boys - Elliot, C.J., and Austin. She stayed in Brisbane while I flew on to Canberra for another game. C.J. Bruton, Calvin Bruton Jr., was eleven years old at the time and had already developed the beginnings of the Bruton personality smile, learned I imagined from the media dream, father Calvin Sr.

Early Saturday morning after the Bullet massacre, we gathered our Hobart group and headed through the quiet dawn to the airport. The Hobart party traveled in a fifteen passenger van, a virtual time machine, which gave me a mobile view of familiar Brisbane sights from the past and also the present, as we motored in the early morning light through the city to the airport. I felt a certain calm in the moment being a part of the team en route to another game. Yet, I had glimpses out the window of the van at many signposts of the past - schools, gyms, and businesses in Brisbane - where I had labored seven years before in promoting junior basketball and the Bullet program.

I had always felt a strong kinship with Brisbane, as I had spent two productive years there in the Queensland coaching director position from 1978-1980. And even though humbled and disappointed by the results of the previous night's game, I recalled my fateful meeting with the Brisbane Association after the Bullets initial year in the NBL in 1979. I knew, and Harold Peacock Sr. knew, that without our presence at that meeting there could have been a giant step taken backwards in NBL basketball or even no Bullet NBL franchise at all. We had during my era as State Director of Coaching in Queensland established the Bullets and then saved them. Also, Coach Brian Kerle had come to my hotel in Melbourne, the year before he returned to Brisbane, to get my opinions on the potential of the franchise. As I recall, I not only gave out important information that evening to Kerle at the Marco Polo Motor Lodge on Flemington Road, but also picked up the dinner tab. If I had kept the tab, I would have attached it to the article containing Kerle's comments on the Brisbane-Hobart game for added incentive.

I knew well that I had been a key figure in the whole basketball scene in the city of Brisbane and in the state of Queensland. I had done a job that no one before me had been able to do by creating programs which allowed players from the state to compete at the highest level of Australian basketball without leaving Queensland. But I had to put all that out of my mind, as we were boarding a plane for Sydney and then over to the Australian capital of Canberra for our second game of the season and another moment of NBL basketball truth.

Freitas Branco Revisited

We played much better at Canberra against the Cannons but finally lost by two in a disputed finish. Carfino played superbly in a match-up with Australian National Team point guard Phil Smyth. U.S. players thought Smyth received plenty of latitude from referees, especially when playing against a Yank opponent at the point-guard position. Carfino displayed on his wrists the bleeding "quick-hand scratches" from Smyth after the game.

In the final minute of game action with Warren Stanwix, a Hobart guard, breaking out of the pack under our basket to get back on defense, referee John Martin saw fit to tack an intentional foul on Stanwix. That meant two foul shots and possession - end of the story for the Devils on that evening. Our player, Stanwix, was about 40 feet from the ball and Martin about the same distance from the call he made. The Martin whistle reminded me of Freitas Branco, the controversial referee, in Lourenço Marques in the 1972 Academica-Sporting game and had the same result for my team. In speaking with Tad Dufelmeier and Dave Nelson, two of my recruits to the NBL, they confirmed that Referee Martin worked a lot of Cannon home games and was known as a "homer," consistent in his calls against Canberra opponents through the years. Nevertheless, Stanwix had been a part of that 8-73 history at Hobart and even though a doubtful call had swung the game, we had to learn what to do and what not to do in order to win some games. I didn't agree with the call, but I didn't blame the referee for the loss, even though it was a critical factor.

We had to learn to play harder, smarter, and with more consistency. The intentional foul with the clock running down came under the category of what not to do, but the loss provided a launching point for increased effort in game preparations and eventually in winning some tough NBL battles. However, I had too much at stake considering the bigger picture and the logistics of our move from Des Moines to Hobart to get too discouraged with our 0-3 start. We eventually broke through and got our first NBL win at home against the Nunawading Spectres coached by future Boomer (National Team) head man, Barry Barnes.

Off the court I spent my days working for Pat Ogg at Merino, an Australian company which manufactured disposable catering items for the hospitality business. Pat hired me as a sales rep to call on local restaurants, bars, hotels, etc. He had two children playing junior basketball and I was given time off on an occasional afternoon to spend with his daughter, Sandra, and her under-16 team. Pat himself was involved with the Hobart and Tasmanian Association and he had done me a favor by providing some temporary employment. Even though cordial to me, Pat had certain feelings about the Devils from their past debacles. In my coaching job initially, it was not hard to keep people happy because a win or a loss, depending on loyalties, would always appeal to about 50% of the basketball constituency in Hobart. The Devils were the team whom many loved to hate, or hated to accept.

Tall Poppy

In Australia, there existed the "tall poppy" phenomenon, which was a metaphor used for people who rose above the others in their endeavors, as in a poppy that had grown taller and stood above the others in a field. And then it was the "job" of others - peers, competitors, and the press - to observe this growing poppy and at the opportune moment cut it down to restore it to the size of the others. The term applied to those in the news, especially in politics, sports, and business. While the tall poppy mentality was consistent with the principles of socialism on which the land down-under was founded and had been governed, it was also a part of human nature everywhere, as in human envy or jealousy. In extreme cases tall-poppy thinking could become pathological. I was to gain first-hand knowledge of tall poppy as the Devils program was always under extreme scrutiny by the media and the public, in waiting.

Hobart, the capital of the island state of Tasmania, was a small city of about 200,000 perched on the banks of the magnificent Derwent River and overlooked by seasonally snow-capped Mount Wellington. In fact, locals referred to Tasmania as a country, not just a state. Tasmania was often left off commercial maps of Australia, as happened on the large electronic information board at the Commonwealth Games in Brisbane in 1982. Indignant Tasmanians roared in protest as the Games opened with the image of the Apple Isle, Tasmania, missing from the map of Australia. Predictably, mainlanders showed no mercy and replied that it was no big deal as they thought the island state had sunk into the waters of the Bass Strait.

I learned that Tassie, as it is known to locals, was discovered by the Dutchman Abel Tasman in 1642 and was populated in large part, like Australia in general, by ex-convicts, prison employees, and British soldiers. Originally used as a penal colony, the island setting was perfect to house and contain convicts exported from the United Kingdom in the 1800s. Hal Colebatch, a political scientist at the University of Tasmania, pointed out in his lectures a significant difference between the settlement of the United States and the settlement of Australia.

Colebatch emphasized that while both countries' early white inhabitants came from Mother England, those in America came to seek personal freedoms and escape governmental control. Those who came to Australia were dispatched by and were dependent upon the government, either as convicts or as British public servants looking after the convicts. Mr. Colebatch concluded that America, and eventually the United States, was born from conflict with governmental control; Australia from reliance on government.

This fundamental attitude toward governmental dependence can be traced as the critical philosophical difference between Australia and the United States - socialism vs. capitalism. Yet with the passage of time, the welfare mentality of socialism has become an insidious element and threat to life as it was intended by the early settlers in America. Today, the English are called "POMES" (shortened to POMS) by Australians, taken from the lettering on the sides of prison ships of the past - P.O.M.E. - Prisoners of Mother England.

In general, Australians held ambivalent feelings toward England. The Royal Family seemed to be quite popular down-under, but on other matters Australians have shown antagonism with no mercy for Mother England. Stories abound that depicted the Australian position in regard to the POMS, as for example, the story of the three travelers who were forced to sleep in the stable at the country inn. During the course of the night the Yank (American) and the Pakie (Pakistani) appeared at the innkeeper's door complaining of the smell of the sheep. Later on that evening the sheep appeared complaining of the smell of the POM (the Englishman). This was a typical Aussie story regarding POMS.

Parochialism - It's Everywhere

We found Hobart to be a pleasant place to live with a slower pace, a stimulating cooler climate, beautiful and varied scenery, and a parochial cultural mentality. I viewed "parochial" as meaning narrow in scope and more of a defining term than necessarily derogatory. New Yorkers were called parochial, as many lived within the walls of one of the world's largest, most cosmopolitan cities. However, most New Yorkers seldom ventured outside of the city nor saw the need to develop a broader scope or a world view. While Sydney and Melbourne were enormous cultural melting pots as Australia's business centers, Hobart life and the perceptions of Tasmanians in general were distinctly separate from those of mainland Australia. Thus, when the NBL teams from the mainland come to Tasmania, a win was a cause for over-reaction and a Tasmanian "national celebration" by Devil supporters throughout the state, with regret, but unflagging hope for eventual team failure from Devil detractors - either point of view parochial.

As the 1986 season progressed, we were able to pick up a win here and there, but most importantly, we stuck together as a team and showed consistent improvement. Team chemistry was good and the club, along with Steve Carfino and me in solo efforts, was able to convince Tasmanian and veteran player Peter Mann to return to the Devils team. Mann had been steadfast and productive in the infamous 8-73 Hobart Devils era. He knew from his experiences in playing with Melbourne clubs that the first three years of

Devils basketball were a bad dream for him as a serious player, and one he did not wish to repeat. When I was hired at Hobart, Mann was cautious. He stayed away to assess the situation. Steve Carfino and I did a basketball clinic at the high school where Mann was teaching physical education, and we all had a chance to get acquainted. Carfino and Mann got along well. When the local hero, as he was called in the press, finally agreed to play, he gave the team on the court a real boost with his perimeter shot and his work ethic. However, Peter Mann was also a great asset in the arena of Hobart basketball politics. He gave the New Devils some needed local credibility, and his presence on the team temporarily quieted many insidious Devils detractors.

Welcome to Kingborough Stadium

St. Kilda of Melbourne came to Hobart and brought about 50 team supporters on a special club promotion. The team had recruited 6'10 Paul Kuiper from Baylor University to fill its post position and found that when he arrived in Australia he was traveling on an Australian passport. Thus, with the Devils bending every rule and deadline possible to naturalize Jerry Dennard, the Saints "fell into one" and picked up a valuable Australian player without forethought. However, they did little to capitalize on their good fortune. Ken Epperson, a handy 6'7 All-Mid-America Conference selection from the University of Toledo, was St. Kilda's key import.

Devil Fever had gone up a few degrees and we were now regularly filling, i.e. packing, the 1,800 seats at the Kingborough Stadium, located in Kingston about ten miles from Hobart. In fact, as the Hobart team began to win, there were NBL games in which the arena was at capacity by 6:00 p.m. with 8:30 tip-off. We normally had our pre-game meeting at a hotel in Hobart and then bussed the 20-minute ride to the stadium together. I recall the surge of emotion among the players and coaches on the bus as we noted the strings of cars parked on roads leading to the game site. With St. Kilda in town, a Melbourne club with a championship tradition from the Kerle days, the Devils were ready. I mean all 1,800 fans, in addition to Ron Christy, the public address announcer, were ready to assist in the slaying of the mainland dragon.

A colorful local disc jockey, Christy pushed everything to its limit in dialogue and discussion on his popular Hobart radio show and did the same thing at Devils games. Wayne Monaghan recruited Mr. Christy to do the public-address announcing at Devils home games and Christy, a great natural showman, immediately caught the fever. Whenever an opponent would step to the foul line he would be all over the shooter with various comments, taunts, noises, and screams through the microphone to distract the enemy. Even though blatantly unsportsmanlike, this was Tasmania defending her shores against mainland Australia.

That evening in Hobart was probably the most disastrous and painful game in St. Kilda's history. Christy riled the opponents. Ken Epperson got kicked out after a fight with Warren Stanwix. Kuiper, the surprise Aussie, tripped and hit his head on the Kingborough concrete floor and was taken to hospital. Wayne Larkin, the feisty Saint guard, went into the Hobart crowd after a loose ball and was punched by several well-meaning Devils fans. And worse yet for St. Kilda, Hobart really played well. Carfino and Acres teamed up for 60 points and the supporting cast took out frustrations from years gone by. Dan Van Holst Pelikaan, a 6'2 athletic reserve, stepped up and made an amazing play by dunk tipping an errant shot over several St.Kilda defenders. We won by 35 and Brian Logan, the St. Kilda club president, was livid. He told me that St. Kilda had never seen such a travesty of justice and sportsmanship. I could identify with his position, however not sympathetically, as I had similar feelings on road trips to Albert Park Basketball Stadium in Melbourne.

The St. Kilda victory gave our team more hope and a few weeks later we were head-to-head again with Brisbane in Hobart at the Kingborough Stadium, now a dreaded stop for NBL opponents. I immediately started to talk to the team about the 115-72 drubbing in our opener with the Bullets and the Brisbane coach commenting to the press, "We (the Bullets) didn't really play well," which in turn meant that the Hobart Devils played very badly. The game theme was - *Earn some respect*. Thus the trap was set, but I really didn't know if we had the "juice" and depth to get the job done.

The Brisbane Bullets were the defending NBL Champions having defeated Adelaide in a three-game series in 1985. They had six National Team players in the playing rotation - Larry Sengstock, Danny Morseu, Robert Sibley, LeRoy Loggins, Cal Bruton, and John Dorge. Sengstock, Bruton and Morseu had the physical tools to play in the NBA, and the other three Bullet players were close to that level. In contrast, to my knowledge, Tasmania had never had a National Team rep who had played for Australia in a major international event, outside of Simon Cottrell and Ian Davies, who both had fled the Apple Isle at an early age. These guys in Brisbane Bullet colors that evening had Olympic Games and World Championship playing experience; they were known in Australia as "Internationals."

It was obviously tough for Hobart that night. We fought hard and it was a monumental struggle just to maintain contact with our opponents. The Devils made a miraculous last-minute rally and then the game came down to one possession and a time-out. We had the ball and national television picked up the Devils' coach, probably at this stage the most recognizable personality in all of Tasmania, giving his (my) team instructions and drawing up a game winning play. I had mixed emotions at the time. I was shocked that we were that close to victory and fearful that I was not going to be able to find the right move or words. The scene, a timeout on the Hobart bench, was similar to the scene from Hoosiers and the "picket fence play" call by the panicked, stand-in (alcoholic) coach named Shooter. Like Shooter, I stuttered, mumbled and finally said, "Clear the right side. Get the hell out of his way. Steve (Carfino) take them off the dribble…And WIN IT - WIN IT!"

The play unfolded perfectly and Carfino hit a fall-away 20 footer on the baseline over a triple-team. His defender and two Bullet inside players who didn't go with their man-to-man assignments on the clear-out were all over Carfino. He drilled a very tough, off-balance, eighteen-foot baseline jumper released slightly behind the edge of the backboard. He made that shot under extreme defensive pressure. Brisbane, after Carfino's clutch jumper, made a long, desperate pass which Carfino himself deflected. The ball rolled harmlessly out of bounds in the Bullet front court, as the Australian hooter sounded. The Devils had defeated the Brisbane Bullets for the first time ever, 91-90. Naturally, pandemonium and celebration followed.

The game was described by the national media "as the shot heard round Australia" and one of the great moments in Hobart's painful history. The next day the Devils' supporters were still rejoicing. In Hobart, people either loved the team or hated them, but this was obviously a day for the backers. Coach Kerle and the Bullets vacated Kingborough and traveled back to their Hobart hotel in record time. I, too, knew it was cause for some celebration. The truth was that those wins against teams with the stature of the Brisbane Bullets never came easily, nor often. Kerle had been the NBL's most successful coach and had put together a potent crew, but we had managed a huge upset and had become the major attraction in Tasmanian sport. It was the night of the Devils, and the poppy was growing.

After the Brisbane game, as I was making my way through the throngs of stunned fans to our locker room, a nice lady forced her way up to my side and delivered to me a rather hostile message spoken in the Tasmanian language, "Why don't you play the local players more? I don't understand why you don't play the locals more." Then she insisted, "You promised that you would build this team around the locals." In the locker room I told my assistant coach Pat Whalen, an ex-patriot New Yorker and a math teacher in the Hobart schools, of the incident. Pat said, "I wonder if anyone said that to Red Holzman after the Willis Reed game and the Knicks' 1972 NBA title? Red, you gotta play more New Yorkers."

I was aware that - seriously - it could have happened to Holzman too. Parochialism can be found anywhere. Some very small thinkers can inhabit the world's largest cities and also some very small thinkers can reside in the world's smaller cities. I have yet to meet a parent who would trade a team victory for his or her son's playing time or personal glory - the Little League Syndrome.

We finished the 1986 NBL with nine wins, a benchmark, and 17 losses in NBL play. The nine victories eclipsed the cumulative eight-win mark of the previous three years by Devils teams in league games. We won an additional 11 pre-season games. However, unlike NCAA competition in the U.S., the Australians don't count "friendlies" - non-league games, as in U.S. college pre-season mismatches - on official records. That policy, if implemented in the U.S., would have removed hundreds of coaching victories from the NCAA record books and would have given a more valid picture of coaching achievement. Nowhere else in the world did pre-season gimmies count as authentic wins as they did in U.S. college hoops. Even in the National Basketball Association, pre-season games have never appeared as official games worthy of preserving the results. Thus, with pre-season games included, we would have recorded a 20 win season, the mark of respectability in American college ball.

At the end of the 1986 season there was some minor drama around the attempt at a *coup d'etat* by some former Hobart Devils committee members. With a successful season recorded, things looked easy and they wanted back in the spotlight. Wayne Monaghan called me and said he was concerned about his position as club president and that I had some power in this matter on the basis of the progress shown in the 1986 season. I called the blokes who were causing the problems. I emphasized that Monaghan was the only guy who had ever taken financial responsibility to see that NBL fees were paid and that I received my meager salary. That, in itself, was a good enough reason to keep him in the president's job. Also, I mentioned that if Monaghan wasn't running the show, I wouldn't be coaching. There was silence and a moment of uncertainty on the other end. It worked and the coup was over, as Monaghan and I began to plan to improve the team for the next season. The first thing we did was to re-sign American Steve Carfino and naturalized Australian Jerry Dennard. Former teammates at the University of Iowa, these two were the key ingredients to continuing progress.

I thought that it was important to make incremental progress each season. After only one year, expectations remained reasonable, and I felt that wholesale change in personnel could have been disastrous. Given a certain talent level on the team, the rest was up to the coach's ability to define roles, sell the roles, and thus promote team chemistry. Then it was up to the players to do their jobs within their roles. Bodies alone can't get the job done, nor can coaching alone.

Mr. Magic

The city of Hobart was very happy to hear that Steve Carfino, named Mr. Magic for his first year NBL heroics, had been retained with a substantial salary and benefit increase. Actually, any salary would have been an increase because Carfino had received no payments from the club in 1986. In the first season, Steve had worked full-time in sales for the Canterbury Store in Hobart selling labeled New Zealand sportswear. I recall on his first day at the office with Canterbury that Carfino parked his twenty-year old, 4-door sedan in a public lot which had an escalating hourly charge. At the end of the day, he had just about broken even. A new parking plan was implemented the next work day. Carfino became an asset to the Canterbury business and was a cornerstone in the Devils resurgence years.

Steve Carfino was a solidly built 6'2 195 lb. combination guard-point or shooting guard. His real strengths offensively were pushing the ball on the fast-break and taking his man off the dribble in the half-court set. He had excellent elevation on his jump shot, went up strong maintaining nearly perfect balance and released the ball flawlessly. Originally from Bellflower, California, Carfino had played at the University of Iowa for four years, three years under Lute Olson and his senior season under Coach George Raveling. Even though his older brother, Don, had been a star player at the University of California, Steve Carfino had gone to Iowa to play for Lute Olson - no one else.

Carfino was recruited by Olson and prospered as a player at the point-guard position in Lute's disciplined system. Steve recalled, with obvious respect for Olson and the Iowa program, his first official practice with the Hawkeyes as a freshman. Four hours later he returned exhausted to his dorm room to collapse into bed at 7:00 p.m. Carfino grimaced as he recalled hearing the news that Lute was leaving Iowa for Arizona. Then he described the first practice under George Raveling in which the coach playfully wrestled on the floor with 6'10 Greg Stokes at the end of the session. Although George Raveling was a proven recruiter, Carfino described his new coach as Lute's opposite in regard to philosophy, discipline, and program organization. Carfino saw Lute Olson as a perfectionist like himself, and Raveling with more of a seat-of-the-pants coaching style.

Twenty-win seasons were routine for Lute Olson and Carfino loved the winning, the structure, and the challenge of playing the point. Olson brought his Iowa teams along fast each year and believed in the virtues of a strong non-conference schedule. However, Lute left the Iowa winters to rebuild the University of Arizona program and George Raveling from Washington State was hired. Raveling moved Carfino to the shooting guard. Carfino questioned the change of position. The new coach did not meet Carfino's expectations, nor those of many Iowa supporters, in his tenure at Iowa. Nobody doubted Raveling's ability to recruit, but his style - warm-up suit in lieu of coat and tie on the bench - and coaching prowess were always controversial in Iowa City. Olson's last Iowa team had been 21-10 and 10-8 in the Big Ten in 1982-83. Raveling had inherited three starters from that Olson team including twin towers 6'11 Greg Stokes and 6'10 Michael Payne. Carfino and seven-footer Brad Lohaus, a future NBA player, also returned along with other experienced bench players. The cupboard was far from bare. Wearing his black and gold sweat suit on the sidelines, Raveling posted a 13-15 overall and 6-12 in the Big 10. Like Ken Trickey at Iowa State and Tom Abatemarco and Rudy Washington at Drake, Coach Raveling was a poor fit in Iowa City. His legacy was that he had recruited the talent which enabled successor Tom Davis to win a school-record thirty games in 1987 when the Hawkeyes reached the NCAA regional title game.

Drafted by the Boston Celtics in 1984, Carfino attended a Celtic camp in Massachusetts when Red Auerbach was still active. Carfino had two memories of that camp: outdoor basketball courts with Red riding around from court-to-court on a golf cart, and Auerbach addressing Carfino as "boy." After completing his eligibility and graduating from Iowa, Carfino worked in Cedar Rapids during the 1984-85 season in a sporting goods store. This job was a tough adjustment after his glory days in Big Ten Conference basketball - no cheerleaders and standing ovations in the retail business.

I was at the Hobart airport to welcome Carfino to Tasmania in December 1985. He wanted to go directly from the airport to the gym ala Cal Bruton, and Steve lit up the old Warrane stadium with his smile, his lively body, and his enthusiasm. It was nice to see club directors happy and it was already clear that Carfino would become a huge asset to the Devils team, and he was, for two memorable seasons in 1986 and 1987.

While Steve Carfino had been a great choice as the team's number one import player, we had a real struggle to get the second foreign-player spot right for the 1987 NBL season. We tried Melvin Mathis and Kevin Lewis for a couple of weeks in that spot. Mathis, who had been a good offensive player at Drake under Gary Garner, reported to a trial contract in Hobart weighing 270 lbs., 50 pounds over reasonable playing weight. We implemented a Weight Watcher's program with Mathis. He weighed in daily with the team doctor and did extra conditioning work with a football club, but he never showed much in three weeks of practice or in exhibition games. Mathis was replaced by Kevin Lewis, an 18-point per-game scorer for Dave Bliss at SMU. He also was not the answer as he did not produce in the second import spot.

Spike Stanley

Eventually we picked up Paul Stanley from the Melbourne Tigers. Stanley was a 6'5 lefty shooter supreme from an obscure NAIA school, Waynesburg, in Pennsylvania. He had great range, a confident left-handed perimeter stroke, and a nasty temper which at times was an asset to the team's competitiveness. In a well-defined role as shooter and with Carfino always looking for him, Stanley led the league in scoring at 35-points per game. We signed Stanley two days before the season openers on the road at Geelong and North Melbourne. We lost both games, but I was optimistic that it would come together. In the second game on that season opening trip, Stanley went nose to nose with, and was even accused of expectorating in the direction of, opponent Scott Fisher of North Melbourne.

Known as "Spike," Stanley was always on the edge emotionally, but a great shooter. Also, I understood, Spike was an effective and willing street fighter in Hobart, a place where it was not difficult to find an opponent. I found also that our lefty gunner had unusual sleeping patterns. I stopped by his apartment one afternoon about 2:00 p.m. to discuss "a special deal" with Spike. Paul answered my knock and felt that he needed to explain why he was still in his pajamas at 2:00 o'clock in the afternoon. He said that he liked to watch videos into the early morning hours, then sleep until early afternoon, but arise in ample time to make the 6:00 p.m. team practice sessions. It was a unique schedule, but the purpose of my visit was to confirm our agreement. I said that I would give Stanley permission to stay two extra days in Melbourne to visit friends after the Devils weekend road trip, providing that we won both games with Southeast Melbourne and the Melbourne Tigers. The arrangement worked out well. Stanley was a key in leading Hobart to a sweep of the Melbourne teams on that road trip. He spent extra time in Melbourne, as agreed, and showed up in Hobart on Tuesday after the Sunday game. Everybody was happy.

Eventually, as I got a better feel for Stanley's game, I clearly defined roles and challenged each player to excel within that role. For example, Jerry Dennard: sixteen foot maximum on jump shot; post-up; fill lane and finish on break; rebounder; gambler on defense; per game expectation - 15 points, 55% field goals, 8 rebounds, and 3 steals. Each player's role was different and played to his particular strength and away from his weaknesses.

The role assigned to Paul Stanley was to take reasonably good shots, rebound on the defensive board, and bare down on defense on critical possessions, as determined by a signal from the bench by Assistant Coach Pat Whalen waving a red, cardboard "Stop" sign. When Stanley would get out of control during a game, usually in regard to a referee's call or a mid-game shouting match with an opposing coach, I would motion him over to the bench. Eventually, he would heed my signal and I would tell him to settle down or come out of the game. Paul "born to score" Stanley knew that on the bench his point totals would suffer. He would, therefore, grudgingly accept my settle-down order. I wanted him hungry and point conscious; scoring was his strength and it was also my wedge in keeping him under some control. In spite of his rocky disposition, he was a great player for Hobart.

Because of the team's dramatic improvement, the Devils were truly embraced by most of the community and by the press. The 1987 team broke all club records in regard to winning with media attention, and public support was at an all-time high. The Hobart Devils were clearly the biggest story in the State of Tasmania. Naysayers again were temporarily silenced, as the Devils poppy had become prominent in the local Tasmanian field and even across Bass Strait on the Australian mainland.

□*10*□

PERTH AND ADELAIDE:
DOOMSDAY DOUBLE

The Doomsday Double was the name given to the road trip to Perth and Adelaide. We played Perth on Friday and then caught a Saturday morning plane, flying against the clock, back to Adelaide just in time to check into the Adelaide Hilton. The players dressed to play in their rooms and then headed for Apollo Stadium. The Hobart-Perth trip was similar in distance and flying time to an NBA Atlanta-Seattle trek and then back to Minneapolis for a game the next night. Only in the NBL, teams flew commercial economy class, not by charter, and we were at the mercy of the normal flight schedules, a big problem for Hobart on the Perth-Adelaide trip.

Cal Bruton was player-coach of the Wildcats, but on this occasion was away in Melbourne with the Boomers on a National Team engagement and put his assistant, Jim Markey, in charge. The two formed an effective tandem and made the best of the situation in employing a player-coach system, an outdated arrangement by 1987 in NBL play. We had anticipated a very tough night. I was concerned about the game because I did not feel that we had any edge to get us going on a special mission. However, all of that changed when we walked into the visitors' dressing room. The host team had provided game programs for our players. A clever Perth writer had decided to select an All-NBL Ugly Team with detailed remarks and explanations on why each player qualified, replete with photographs. In his wisdom, this writer had selected our own Jerry "Deno" Dennard as an All-Ugly team member. Naturally, everyone was giving it to Deno, especially Steve Carfino. Deno was embarrassed and angry; his face was red with disgust as we took the floor. Deno's competitive juices were flowing in warm-up and continued into game action. I took along a copy of the article to our bench just in case.

We whacked the Wildcats that night and the difference was, of course, Jerry Dennard. Deno finally missed a shot on his 9th attempt of the game early in the second half and had twelve huge rebounds. Dennard loved to gamble on defense. He would trail the play and follow an opponent dribbling the ball up the court. He would track down the dribbler and swat the ball free for a teammate to complete the steal or do it himself. He was a 6'9 guy who ran very well and had long arms. On this occasion at Perth, he added six steals to his evening's performance. Everyone did his job that night, but Dennard was the key and dedicated this one to the enterprising *journo*.

After the game there were two little kids running around our dressing room. Even though Cal Bruton had been (fortunately) out of town, C.J. Bruton, 11, and Austin David Bruton, 5, were present and not taking the Perth loss too hard. After the game and back at the Parmelia Hilton - the NBL was moving up with a sponsorship deal with the Hilton chain - Paul Stanley summoned a doctor in the middle of night because of nausea. His roommate, veteran Rick Hodges, a valuable acquisition from Adelaide, told some other players the next day about Stanley and his previous night's illness. A nurse actually came to their room at 3:00 a.m. to give Stanley a shot. He screamed when she started to put the needle in his left arm, his shooter, and deferred the injector and injection to the right arm.

Jay "Buddy" Brehmer

The road win at Perth was the first ever for the Hobart Devils and a memorable evening in their troubled history. I had had a flashback to the previous year in Perth when the Wildcat team was coached by Jay Brehmer, known as Buddy Brehmer when he took the 1964 Rockhurst College team to the NAIA title in Kansas City versus Luke Jackson and Pan-American in the final game. Jay was promoted to the St. Louis Billiken job on the impetus of the NAIA success, but in three seasons he was never able to turn the corner in Division I college basketball. Brehmer then headed for Florida, but I lost track of him until 1984 when Geneva and I were in Kansas City for a weekend. *The Sunday Kansas City Star* newspaper had printed a full back-page story on the twenty-year reunion of Rockhurst's 1964 NAIA title team (That Championship Season). One haunting part of the story probed the whereabouts of their coach, Buddy Brehmer. Nobody knew where the head man was; he had seemed to disappear. I was aware that Brehmer was in Melbourne, Australia, making a name for himself for his basketball knowledge, his coaching ability, his staccato voice, his taste for whiskey, and his unpredictability.

With a new moniker and known as Jay, Brehmer had made his way west from Melbourne, Australia, and was coaching the Perth Wildcats in 1985 and 1986, my first season with the Devils. He did a respectable job in 1985, going 13-13; however, the record dropped to 8-18 in 1986. He was probably in his sixties then and the Wildcat administration was looking for some new blood. I wrote a letter at his request on his behalf to Perth management to retain him. However, the nod went to Cal Bruton, who had the ability to create excitement with the public, sponsors, owner Bob Williams, and the Perth administration.

I had several extended basketball conversations with the loquacious Brehmer in Australia. All discussions with him turned out to be extended. I recall one particular story which he told me about a coaching experience against the legendary Adolph Rupp. At the time Brehmer was at St. Louis University and his team was playing the fast-breaking Kentucky Wildcats in Lexington, Kentucky. Coach Brehmer knew that he was in for a tough night and wanted to slow down the game. He attempted to take advantage of a rule which allowed a substitute to enter the game after a successful foul shot. Thus, when his team was at the foul line, he would send a substitute to the scorer's table to prepare to report into the game. If the shot was good, the horn would sound and the substitute would enter the game, thus delaying the action and taking away an opportunity for Kentucky to fastbreak after the successful foul shot. However, the scorekeeper refused to sound the horn and allow the St. Louis player to enter the game. He explained to Brehmer, "Coach Rupp thinks that this is a stupid rule and therefore we do not allow the substitution after foul shots at Kentucky home games." Brehmer was livid and speechless - in itself notable.

After our loss to Perth and Coach Brehmer in 1986, I took advantage of some free time in the morning after the game and before our noon flight to Adelaide to include Brehmer in a walk-through practice session. He was a good defensive coach and was especially clever in his use of the 3-2 zone defense. I asked him to explain individual defensive positions on ball shifts out of the 3-2 zone set. We were pressed for time and I figured that he could cover this nicely in about 15-20 minutes, but that was not to be. Brehmer, with his Mr. Magoo-like appearance, explained and re-explained and pontificated and roared, but never got further than the defensive shifts on the initial pass from the point guard to the wing.

Our players, tired from the previous night's loss, were as baffled as I was. I took advantage of a slight delay when Coach Brehmer was clearing his throat, thanked him, and hustled everyone off the court, as the explanation was going to take much longer than we had available. I learned that this situation was an example of one side of a complicated man, but very knowledgeable basketball coach.

Black for Bruton for Black

Cal Bruton, who replaced Brehmer as the Perth coach, had led the Wildcats to a 19-7 record and to the Grand Final, losing best-of-three to Brisbane in 1987. The next logical step was, in the eyes of the Wildcat administration, to win it all in 1988. Perth's league record dropped to 13-11, but the team made a run in the playoffs before losing to North Melbourne in the 1988 semi-finals. Cal Bruton was replaced as coach by Alan Black, Australian born and a former Nunawading and Wildcat player.

The 1989 Wildcats showed an improved record under Black, going 16-8 but falling in the best of three series to nemesis North Melbourne in the semis. However, in the final game of that series the Giants unloaded and scored a 165-110 massacre of the Wildcats - not a good sign for first-year coach Alan Black in a program financed by high-roller millionaires with huge expectations of everything they touched, including the Perth Wildcats basketball team.

The 1990 Wildcats got under way with Alan Black still at the coaching helm and Cal Bruton, NBL legend as a player and an aspiring coach, as General Manager. The Wildcats were off to a rocky start under Black. In a surprise move by management, Cal Bruton was reinstated as head coach with Alan Black bitterly stepping down. A huge public outcry and backlash followed the announcement of the Bruton for Alan Black coaching change. The press, talk shows, and general public reaction to the sacking of Black, the native Australian, and replacing him with Bruton, the American-born Aussie, was explosive, insidious, and unrelenting. Bruton detractors screamed, "Black Stabber." That event - *Bruton for Black as Perth coach* - had remained one of the most controversial events in Australian sporting history and continued to be an issue in Perth.

Bruton had attempted to mend fences with Black, but the Aussie was having no part of it. Bad feelings between the two have persisted far too long. Black apparently still carried a grudge in spite of the fact that he had held three NBL head coaching jobs since being sacked at Perth in 1990 - the Illawarra Hawks, Sydney Kings, and Perth Wildcats again. In contrast, Bruton had had one brief stint with the Hobart Devils and ironically was replaced by his assistant coach, Australian Bill Tomlinson, under similar cir-cumstances to the Bruton-Black change-of-the-guard at Perth. In compari-son, the fact remained that NBL records showed Bruton with superior play-ing and coaching achievements compared to those of his two Aussie adver-saries, Black and Tomlinson, the latter of whom was never an NBL player. I believed the matter was still a factor, or the source, of Cal Bruton's employ-ment outside of the NBL coaching fraternity. The continuing controversy was, in part, responsible for Calvin Bruton Jr. selecting the Brisbane Bullets, or anyone else for that matter, over the Perth Wildcats to resume his profes-sional career in 1997.

To Calvin Bruton's credit, he dodged the Bullets, both on the local scene and also in the 1990 NBL Grand Final. He was under maximum pres-sure created by an unrelenting media blitz and public criticism of the sack-ing of Alan Black. The Wildcats under Coach Bruton finished fifth in league play with a 17-9 record, but became only the second team in league history to win a title from outside the positions of one or two in the regular season standings. Bruton's team whipped Brian Kerle's Brisbane Bullets, who had the home-court advantage in the best-of-three series, to take out Perth's first-ever NBL Championship.

Like Jim McGregor many years before, Bruton had returned home with the trophy for well-deserved glory and affirmation of a job well done. Also, like McGregor, he received instead his coaching pink slip from the boss. One Perth director said that the club had been "Brutanized" for the last time. Brian Kerle, the Brisbane coach was named Coach of the Year. The Black Pearl was replaced by American college coach, Murray Arnold, who gained a repeat title for Perth in 1991. At the end of that season Arnold was named Coach of the Year, an honor which had eluded Cal Bruton in his title season as Perth coach. However, Coach Arnold was not able to sustain the pace in 1992, finishing 12-12 and going out in the quarter-finals at the hands of the Melbourne Tigers. Murray Arnold was then replaced by Dr. Adrian Hurley, who led the Wildcats to two Grand Finals, capturing the 1995 NBL championship over the North Melbourne Giants. Cal Bruton took one more shot at an NBL job in Hobart, but that was short-lived. He was edged aside by the Devils' assistant coach, Victorian Bill Tomlinson, who coached the Devils to a seemingly non-controversial 17-71 NBL record with a team and club that called it quits at the end of the 1996 season because of irresolvable financial problems.

Fellow Victorian Tom Maher, my successor as Hobart coach, went 17-37 on the Devils' bench prior to the abbreviated Bruton era in Hobart. Tomlinson, like Maher, found the going in the National Women's Basketball League (NWBL) more agreeable. Maher, who was later named the Australian Women's National Team Coach, had won NWBL championships in Victoria. Likewise Tomlinson bounced back from the Hobart experience and coached the Sydney Flames to the 1997 Women's League title and an undefeated season. Apparently on the momentum of his work with the Flames, Bill Tomlinson was named head coach with the Sydney Kings, as Alan Black resigned and returned to Perth in 1998 for his second tour of the Perth Wildcats head coaching job.

The past history of coaches - Brehmer, Bruton, Black, Bruton again, Arnold, Hurley, and Black again - at Perth had been a game of coaching musical chairs and thought provoking, but I had to get back to the present and focus on Adelaide. With the road game at Perth miraculously in the 1987 Devils' win column, we worked out at 9:00 a.m. in Perth on the way to the airport, this time without Coach Brehmer. We caught the 11:00 a.m. Queensland and Northern Territory Air Service flight (Qantas) to Adelaide to complete the Doomsday Double. At that point in NBL history, no team had ever won both games on that trip. Yet we had one down and one to go, and I thought that we had a chance, slim, but a chance. We checked into the Adelaide Hilton at 6:00 p.m., hastily dressed for the game, and took the short drive from the hotel over to Apollo Stadium in the suburb of Findon for the 8:30 p.m. tip-off. In addition to the full day of travel, flying against the clock, we had a formidable opponent in the Adelaide 36ers, who were the defending NBL champs by virtue of a win over Brisbane in the 1986 Grand Final.

Al Green-Cal Bruton: A Classic Feud

As we entered the creaky old Apollo Stadium in Adelaide, I stopped to recall the 1986, 36er-Bullet Final Series from the previous year. Adelaide won at Brisbane in the opener in the three-game series. I had flown over to Adelaide from Hobart and saw Cal Bruton come off the bench to give Brisbane a win in game two. He scored an immaculate 38 with Al Green scratching, gouging, and slugging - anything to stop The Pearl. Bruton and Green had a savage rivalry on the court for a decade, but somehow maintained a friendship otherwise. The action between the two great NBL athletes went far beyond spirited and Green was one of the champion NBL trash-talkers of all time. Bruton was a stocky, muscular 5'7 and Green was a strongly built 6'1 and 200 lbs., also a great athlete.

Al Green had run a 9.5 hundred-yard dash at Louisiana State University in addition to high-level production on the basketball court as an All-Southeastern Conference guard. He had also averaged 18-points per-game in the Continental League in the U.S. prior to his arrival in Australia. His NBL game was to post-up, destroy opposing guards on the block, and to intimidate and pound opponents at the defensive end. His defensive transition was amazing with his natural foot speed and desire. It was one thing to have your average, aggressive, motivated defender in your face and quite another to have an athlete of Al Green's strength, stature, and nastiness at work. Bruton's ability to score consistently, and at times at will, on Green was truly an amazing fete. I have seen Bruton make shots with Al Green's hand cupped over the Pearl's eyes. I hoped that this great rivalry would not be forgotten by NBL historians. It was probably the fiercest one-on-one dual in National Basketball League history.

Ken Cole

The Green-Bruton feud continued the next afternoon in the third and final game in the 1986 NBL Playoffs. In a key match-up, Adelaide's Peter Ali was literally all over LeRoy Loggins, and Brisbane was slow to get Bruton into the game. The contest was a "10" in intensity as the super-physical game favored the 36ers, who had reached down and called on the mongrel in their competitive makeup. That style of play spelled victory for the home team and an Adelaide title.

In addition to the competitive, elevated level of play in the 1986 series between the 36ers and Bullets, another drama was simultaneously playing out. Adelaide Coach Ken Cole, one of Australia's most flamboyant basketball personalities, had been suspended by 36er President Malcom Simpson for the last three league games of the 1986 season, but was reinstated to coach in the playoffs. Cole was a 6'7, former Australian National Team player who, as a coach, wore western clothes on the bench, including cowboy boots and matching garb.

But it wasn't on the bench that was the issue with Mal Simpson and the 36er administration; it was the after-game activities. Cole had apparently thought that his conversation and post-game socializing with *Adelaide Advertiser* journalist Andrew Both were off the record. However, Both reported that Cole had been smoking marijuana on the Canberra-Brisbane road trip that season. Later, Cole went on a national TV interview with reporter Mike Willesee on his show, *A Current Affair.* Cole openly discussed his use of marijuana for purposes of relaxation and relief from the stress of coaching. Ken explained that he was diabetic and could not drink alcohol; therefore, he smoked marijuana instead. I understood that the 36ers had been willing to go along with Cole, until he went public with his statements.

Subsequently, Ken Cole was suspended by the 36ers but came back to the bench and summarily went out with the 1986 NBL title at Adelaide. Emotions in the 36er camp regarding the suspension were hot and there was no love lost between club President Simpson and Coach Cole. In retrospect, it worked out perfectly for Adelaide - winning solved most of the problems - but the 36ers removed Cole as coach right after the playoffs. After the 36ers' championship season, Ken Cole had two other NBL coaching stints, with Sydney and Newcastle, but with limited success.

The Business at Hand

Past events at Apollo Stadium had been dramatic, but sweeping the 1987 Doomsday Double would have been historic. Back to the Hobart Devils and the Perth-Adelaide road trip, we clearly had our hands full. It was the same Al Green, who chose Steve Carfino as his defensive assignment instead of Cal Bruton, and essentially the same 36ers' title team from the previous year which the Devils faced that evening. We slowed it down and did a good job of getting the ball to our shooters, until the 36ers got Paul Stanley upset and Green increased the pressure on Carfino. We were right there for a run, down only seven points with six minutes remaining. But the run came from our opponent and we limped back to Hobart with a respectable split on the weekend with nonproductive dreams of what could have been.

One other memorable road trip that year was the West Sydney-Westside

Melbourne weekend. We defeated West Sydney on a Friday and then faced a three-hour fog delay the next morning in making the 45-minute flight to Melbourne. I was concerned about the game. Our opponent, Westside Melbourne, was the old St. Kilda Club, the team which we had humiliated in Hobart the year before, to the consternation of its entire organization. Andy Blicavs, a former National Team player, was under orders from management to settle the score. Blicavs had no love for Yanks in general, or for me in particular. They had added incentive because American Kevin Lewis, whom I had cut in the pre-season, had been picked up by Westside Melbourne. Lewis, like his coach, was not kindly disposed toward me. Lute Olson was in the country as a guest of the Australian Basketball Federation, and he and his wife, Bobbi, were present at the game. Two of our players, Carfino and Dennard, had played for Lute at Iowa.

Westside came out in a triangle-and-two defense, playing man-to-man on Carfino and Stanley. Actually, we were vulnerable to that defense, as those two players did the majority of our ball-handling and scoring, and both were perimeter players. Wayne Larkin, still remembering from the year before the punches which he received on his trip into the Hobart stands, was fired up to disrupt Carfino's game. In fact, Larkin with good quickness and aggression was all over Carfino, until we called a timeout.

I instructed Jerry Dennard to set at the high post on offense and for Carfino to run our rub-screen play with Carfino taking his man off the dribble and Dennard stepping out to pick the defender at the top of the circle. I further suggested that Dennard set a physical screen on Larkin to discourage his continued enthusiasm for harassing Carfino. I believe that I asked Deno "to rattle his teeth." We ran the rub-screen, Deno stepped out and nailed Larkin, Carfino penetrated off the dribble and hit Stanley for a wide-open three-pointer. We won the game handily, and afterwards I talked with Lute Olson. He said that he liked the way that we had attacked Westside's triangle-and-two defense, which ironically was to be his nemesis in the 1998 NCAA Tourney loss to Utah.

The 1987 Devils proved to be record breakers, finishing 14-12 for the club's first and only winning season in the NBL record book. We actually went into the final week of the season at 14-10 and were alive in the six-team playoff picture. But the final road trip to Illawarra and Canberra ended in two decisive losses; apparently we couldn't stand the prosperity. At Canberra we just were not ready to play and the Cannons took a commanding 20-4 lead. At that point I told Patrick Whalen, the Devils assistant coach, "Pat, you have done a great job and deserve a chance. You take over from here - I am going back to the hotel." However, I stayed on the bench for the final whack from the Cannons which concluded the record-setting Hobart season on a low note.

The Yank Public Servant

When I took the Hobart job in 1985, I worked it a day at a time. I had no plan to stay a certain amount of time. Two years had passed rapidly and with the season behind us, Geneva and I pondered a third year in Hobart. The $6,000 coaching salary in the first year had been raised to $15,000. Also, the club had arranged additional income for me through a job with the Tasmanian State Department of Sport and Recreation. Although I was well-qualified for the job with a doctorate and my background in teaching and basketball, there had been some resistance to my employment within the department. David Williams, the Sport and Recreation director, supported my job application and I finally was hired. I spent most of the 1987 season in that job, and I was, therefore, in touch on a daily basis with the Australian public servant. I found the Devils to be a popular topic of discussion at work and noted that the tall poppy was alive and well in the Tasmanian Department of Sport.

I worked at a desk from 8:00-4:30 p.m. Monday through Friday in an office with two Tasmanian career public servants. I heard that one of them was taking some time off starting at the end of the work week. On a Friday at 4:30 p.m, John cleaned up his desk and said, "See you in six months, mate." Six months paid leave - socialism at work - out of my paycheck.

I occasionally felt quiet satisfaction from a couple of the Department of Sport boys when I returned to the desk job after a weekend NBL loss. Of course, that year we won more than we lost, so I had a little extra status around the place. The Department of Sport had refused to provide any subsidies to the Devils program - a sore point with Devils administration - yet jumped on the band wagon to support the local women's team in the NWBL competition. Although David Williams, the Department director, was cordial and gave me some temporary work, it was a difficult situation. I didn't mind the work responsibilities, but I could not hide the fact that my main priority was coaching and that my routine duties at the desk were of secondary importance. I sensed that this didn't go down particularly well with my colleagues.

Greg Norman

Australians loved their sports, especially Australian Rules football, cricket, horse racing, tennis, swimming, and golf. Australian athletes competing overseas carried a special responsibility. Because of the country's geographical isolation and small population, the Australian public and the press were always anxiously waiting for the results. When an Australian managed a victory overseas, especially in the U.S., the country celebrated and the newspapers carried banner headlines.

One morning, I arrived at work at 9:00 a.m. at the Department of Sport and several men, including the boss, David Williams, were huddled intently around the television set in the board room. I walked in and took a position behind the group, which was cheering every shot by Australian Greg Norman in his bid to win the Masters Championship on April 12, 1987, in Augusta, Georgia. I was an interested observer, as I had followed Norman for eighteen holes and had observed his every stroke from the gallery at the John Ruan Celebrity Tournament at Des Moines' Wakonda Country Club. That day in Iowa I had been very impressed with Norman and his powerful, athletic build, similar to an NFL defensive back, and his strength in crushing the ball off the tees. I made no comment nor showed any favoritism, but a part of me was pulling for Norman and a part of me was pulling for Larry Mize and against the wishes of my cheering co-workers.

The 1987 Masters was a live telecast. Tasmania was sixteen hours ahead of Georgia time, and Norman was head-to-head with American Larry Mize and Seve Ballesteros of Spain in a sudden-death playoff. As the three players approached the second hole, Norman was on the green and appeared to be in a position to close-out his opponents and win the tournament, all Australia was preparing to celebrate. Then Mize hit a chip shot from off the green and the ball, as if directed by radar, went right into the hole.

I shall never forget the reaction of my fellow employees. It was as if an arrow had collectively pierced their hearts. They let out a deep groan in unison, followed by complete silence, a moment's hesitation for reflection. Then Williams abruptly snapped off the television set, as if to stop the pain, and everyone returned quietly to his desk for another day of Tasmanian public service. The reaction underscored the fact that golfer Greg Norman carried the hopes of all Australians for victory and international recognition, but on this occasion he came up short. All of Australia and the Tassie public servants, in particular, had been denied the afterglow of victory. The aborted celebration was replaced by an unofficial day of national mourning.

Although the full-time, off-court work provided a financial lift, it was also time consuming and detracted from my coaching duties. Overall I met some good people and enjoyed the experience at the Department of Sport and gained insight into the Tasmanian cultural value system. After the surprise success of the 1986 Devil season followed by improvement and a winning record in 1987, the marketing responsibilities as Devil coach were increasing. Wayne Monaghan proposed a contract with a salary of $40,000 for 1988 with full-time coaching and marketing duties. Wayne and I agreed on the terms, as we made plans for one more season in Hobart a day at a time, our third year.

Preparations for the 1988 NBL

We had retained Jerry Dennard and Wayne Burden, a naturalized Australian from Chico State. Burden had played a key role in the 1987 success as the starting two-guard and back-up point to rest Carfino. Burden had been an asset offensively and also provided consistent defense with veteran leadership. In college and in his first few years in Australia, Wayne Burden had been a good leaper and athlete. However, he had to have some knee repair. After the surgery, he was forced to change his style and learn to play with both feet on the floor. Nevertheless Burden was a valuable player.

There was quite a stir in the press when the club announced that Paul Stanley would not be retained. Stanley had been a great scorer in 1987 and author of the "impact 3 pointer" which carried the team at the end of tight games. However, he had an irascible personality and was one dimensional as a player. We felt that we could bring in a better athlete and a more versatile player in the second-import spot. The Melbourne press reported that Stanley had talked himself out of the NBL, and a concerned lady stopped me on the street in downtown Hobart. She chided me for cutting Stanley, but it was too late. Stanley was gone and Joe Hurst was in as his replacement.

Hurst, an athletic 6'5 small forward, came from St. Louis and had played his college basketball at Northwest Missouri State in a strong Division II conference, the MIAA. I had seen Hurst at the Quad City Thunder's veterans camp. He had played briefly in the CBA for Mauro Panaggio. Although not Stanley's equal - few were - as a perimeter shooter, Joe Hurst was a superior athlete with a good attitude. He was named league Most Valuable Player at the end of that 1988 season.

Also, on that final road trip of the 1987 season with the NBL Playoffs at stake, Steve Carfino did not play at his normal level. In fact, Phil Smyth turned the tables and outplayed Carfino at Canberra. The club discussed Steve's situation at the end of the season and it was decided to send him a letter to challenge him for the 1988 season. Unfortunately, the letter did not come across as intended and Carfino took offense. He called me in Des Moines in December of 1987 and said he was disappointed with the club position and wanted to play elsewhere. He eventually signed at Sydney and was later named to that club's All-Decade Team.

Tim Boyd

Seeking a replacement for Carfino, I contacted Greg Giddings, who had previously played well at Geelong. Greg was a combination guard from Midwestern University in Texas. He was signed primarily on the basis of his Australian NBL experience and his reputation as solid on and off the court. Giddings teamed with Joe Hurst to fill the two import jobs. When we started pre-season conditioning for the 1988 season, everything in the Hobart camp was upbeat. We looked better on paper with veterans Wayne Burden, Peter Mann, and Jerry Dennard available and imports Joe Hurst and Greg Giddings in good shape.

A particularly bright spot in our preparation was Tim Boyd, a blonde, 6'7 power-forward from Sydney. Just 21 years old, he made rapid progress, fit in well with the other players, and was a reason for optimism. Jerry Dennard told me after an early season practice that he thought Boyd was already one of the better young players in the league, and we hadn't even played a game yet. The kid had long arms with a wing span, good body, and excellent anticipation in chasing down rebounds. He ran well and looked like a real find. Tim and his father, Peter Boyd, had seen the Devils come-from-behind win over West Sydney in 1987 and decided that night that Hobart would be a good place for Tim.

Raised in Sydney near the ocean, Tim Boyd loved the beach and surfing. On a Monday afternoon in late January after a training session, he drove out to Clifton Beach near Hobart with some friends to spend a couple of hours in the rolling surf. Tragically, so tragically, he was involved in a head-on auto accident while returning to Hobart. The driver in the other car apparently veered across into Tim's lane and they met head-on.

I got a call at home on that Monday evening from Peter Boyd, Tim's father, in Sydney asking, "How is Tim doing?" I had not yet heard the news of the accident and replied that he was a breath of fresh air in our team and that he was doing very well. Peter said that he had received a call earlier from the hospital in Hobart and that Tim had been in a serious accident that evening. I said that I would go immediately to the hospital and call him later.

Geneva and I rushed to the hospital in downtown Hobart and entered the turmoil of the emergency room with hospital personnel attending to another serious accident which had also occurred that same evening. One of the nurses recognized me and said that Tim was in serious, but stable condition. I asked, "Is his life in danger - will he live?" She replied that he would recover, but that the doctors were concerned that he had possibly sustained a spinal injury and was going to be transported by helicopter to Melbourne for specialized treatment. He had been experiencing localized, severe pain in his lower back. I called his father, Peter, from the hospital with that report.

I had no more hung up the phone than the same nurse returned with a revealing look on her face. She said that things had changed suddenly and that Tim was fighting for his life. Fifteen minutes later she returned and told us that he didn't make it. The back pain had apparently to do with a ruptured aorta, caused by the impact in the collision and which proved fatal. I had rung Wayne Burden, who had just arrived at the hospital, and the two of us went up to the operating room to identify Tim. What a difficult, senseless end to such a promising young man's life. Just a few hours before, I had been watching with joy at the Devils practice, as Tim was showing daily improvement on the basketball court.

Peter and Bev Boyd came to Hobart for a special memorial service for their only child with the other players and club members in attendance. Several players spoke at the service for Tim. The sad occasion was punctuated by the reality that we had a game the next day in the pre-season NBL tournament in Melbourne. Tim Boyd was buried in Hobart and I believe with him the hopes of improvement over the previous year's performance. His loss was a huge setback to the entire Hobart Devils NBL program. It was never the same.

Coach of the Year- Almost

Geneva and I had returned to Hobart in December prior to January 1988 pre-season drills. We had taken a trip back to Des Moines to settle the sale of our condominium and to attend to the recruiting of Greg Giddings. Back on the job in Hobart, I had a meeting with club president Wayne Monaghan. Among other things, Monaghan confided that he had received a call right after the 1987 season from Bill Palmer, NBL General Manager. Palmer apparently said that I was the leading candidate for 1987 NBL Coach of the Year Award on the basis of the team's first winning season and overall improvement. He wanted to know if I would be in Melbourne for the league's post-season awards banquet, a black-tie affair in a downtown hotel.

Monaghan told Palmer that I had returned to the U.S. for a few weeks and would not be present at the banquet. That was the last that we heard of the Coach of the Year Award except that I had finished second behind David Lindstrom of Illawarra, who had guided the Hawks' 20-6 regular season record backed up by a first-round playoff victory over North Melbourne. Lindstrom's selection was well deserved, but the Palmer call to Monaghan was a puzzling sidelight.

A few years later I was able to help David Lindstrom by recommending him for the assistant coaching job at Townsville. He became a valuable basketball mentor to Coach Mark Bragg. The two worked well together and had the savvy to run an offense to get Cameron Dickinson open enough to have back-to-back 20-point per-game seasons with the Suns. David Lindstrom, "the blonde assassin," as Brian Kerle called him, moved from the Townsville Suns to the head coaching job with Mitsubishi in Japan in 1998.

In spite of the loss of Tim Boyd, we were off to a 6-2 league start which featured good defense and a balanced offense. Giddings fit in well although it was clear early that he did not have the talents of Carfino. I foolishly pondered bringing in a more talented, explosive player to replace Giddings. In retrospect that player change was a bad decision for everyone concerned - the team, the club, and me as a coach. With Giddings in the lineup, we would have been likely to finish, at worst, 13-13, very respectable at Hobart. If the team had continued to improve, we would have probably knocked on the playoff door. In this case, my best coaching strategy would have been no move at all. In retrospect, Greg Giddings had been the right player for the job.

A Bad Decision

However, I decided to bring in Kelvin Scarborough from New Mexico to replace Giddings. The move was a disaster, as we lost seven consecutive games with Scarborough in the line-up. Although reputedly a great point guard at New Mexico with impressive scoring and assist numbers, Scarborough was not in game condition and spent most of the season trying to catch up. I had scheduled two practices on a Saturday open-date and had arranged referees to work a game-condition, inter-squad workout, organized mainly to bring Scarborough along. Unfortunately, he showed up that morning with a bad hang-over and was too sick to play. To the consternation of our veteran players, they were forced to adapt from the reliable Giddings to the unpredictable Scarborough. I met with Kelvin three mornings a week at 7 a.m. for sprint work. His fitness improved, but he was never consistent on the court.

My credibility was damaged as a result of this disastrous decision. The Giddings-Scarborough situation taught me a huge lesson: don't tamper with good team chemistry, a rare and valuable commodity in basketball, for dreams of something better. After my recruiting transgression, I knew we needed a lift and that I had to figure out a way to get the team back together. I considered bringing in an American coach as a consultant for two weeks.

Back in Kansas City, Ron Waggener, the advertising executive who helped me with the recruitment of Cal Bruton, had a good athletic background and had shown interest in my previous work at Brisbane. He had recommended players from time to time and had good judgment regarding basketball talent. He had told me on a couple of previous occasions that Lynn Nance, who had coached Central Missouri State to the Division-II National Title in 1984, had shown consistent interest in doing some basketball work overseas.

Lynn Nance in Tasmania

I remembered Nance from his days as head coach at Iowa State University, and I had mixed emotions about the possibility of working with him. He had inherited a 3-24 team from Ken Trickey in 1976 and made some progress with the ISU program. Hopes were lifting at Iowa State in Nance's second season in charge of the Cyclones, as the team finished runners-up in Big Eight play with an impressive 9-5 conference record and 14-13 overall. His continuing feud with ISU athletic director Lou McCullough reportedly led to Nance's mid-season resignation on January 26,

1980. He abruptly left Ames in his fourth year having compiled an overall 44-64 record. I recall that an Iowa State player, Bob Fowler, ripped off his game jersey and threw it into the stands when he heard of Nance's departure. Ironically, Chuck Harmison and Dean Uthoff, later Australian NBL stars, were seniors on the last Lynn Nance team at Iowa State.

Nance had worked as an assistant for Joe B. Hall at Kentucky during a controversial era. Kentucky was one of the most penalized schools in NCAA history. The local newspaper, *The Lexington Herald-Leader*, won Pulitzer Prize recognition for a series of stories discussing the details of payments to Kentucky players during Joe B. Hall's 13 years as head coach. Nance got some national press for his disagreement and exchange of words with Bobby Knight during a Kentucky-Indiana game. He had done stints with the FBI and the NCAA as an investigator before his work as head coach at Iowa State. However, he resurrected his coaching fortunes after his Big Eight shot fell short and delivered the 1984 D-II NCAA title at Central Missouri. From there he had planned to assist Frank Arnold at Hawaii, but that relationship ended before it got started and Nance landed at Fresno State as an assistant under Boyd Grant. When I talked with Lynn Nance in 1988, he was at St. Mary's College in Moraga, California, building a strong mid-Division I team. I told him that if he still was interested in an overseas trip that I could accommodate him for two weeks in Tasmania working in a consulting capacity. He accepted and flew to Hobart.

I appreciated Nance's interest and suggestions in regard to our half-court sets and also our defensive transition. He attended the training sessions and also the league games. At the end of the stay, I felt that he had given me a boost in some areas and that we had established a positive relationship. In fact, at the end of the season, I was planning to return to the U.S. to spend some time with a college program between NBL seasons and Lynn offered me a spot at St. Mary's as a guest coach.

We finished the 1988 season 10-14 and I talked publicly of our two consecutive double-digit victory marks in NBL play, a first and only in Devils history. Nevertheless, I was disappointed and I sensed some problems with the press, as the "tall poppy" crowd began to gather some momentum. I had pushed the team very hard down the stretch and we had managed some impressive, but inconsistent performances. It had been a controversial year and the action continued in the Tasmanian press long after the season had ended.

John Briggs, born and raised Tasmanian basketball *journo*, started a post-season barrage through an interview with Peter Blight. He had exited Van Dieman's Land (Tasmania) for Victoria and had played with the Coburg Club in 1986 and at Eastside Melbourne in 1987. Although Blight had spent his most productive years in Melbourne, due to a shortage of local players, the Devils administration was keen to bring a native Tassie son home. He had joined the Devils brigade in 1988 and contributed off the bench at the offensive end. Blight had been a key in the early season victory over the Melbourne Tigers as he posted Andrew Gaze and scored on three consecutive back-to-basket moves in the final minutes of the game.

Blight apparently disagreed with my perception of his game and talent level and unloaded on me in the Brigg's article. Just what we needed: a disgruntled player who had left his home state to play against Tasmanian teams in his prime. He then had returned in the twilight of his career to contribute marginally in his only season with the Devils. Briggs and Blight, the two Tasmanians, had teamed up to Tall Poppy the Yank coach. Blight told Briggs that I, as coach, thought that only Americans, naturalized and imported, could play and that I had ignored his abilities. He felt he had been slighted.

Blight's comments revealed not only his attitude toward me, but also his sensitivity about American players in general, even those who had become Australian citizens. The impact of Blight's interview was due more to his local boy status than the substance of his comments. Nevertheless, it did not set well with me; I considered it negative and I took the first serious step in my plans to leave Hobart. It was a controversial interview and, therefore, a good story for the local press. It was also a signal to me to begin to think about making other plans.

Blight's decision to take his frustrations to the press and make the matter public was unusual in my experiences in dealing with Australian players. However, a similar situation did develop in Adelaide after the 1996 NBL season. Mike Dunlap had built a strong program at Cal Lutheran before going to Australia. He won the Adelaide contract over former NBA head coach Stan Albeck and Kevin McKenna, seven-year NBA player and head coach at Sioux Falls in the CBA. Albeck later became assistant to Lenny Wilkens on the Atlanta Hawks' bench and McKenna returned to his alma mater, Creighton University, to work on Dana Altman's coaching staff.

Mike Dunlap at Adelaide

Adelaide club president Malcom Simpson and administrator Barry Richardson had flown to the U.S. to interview their top three candidates, Albeck, McKenna, and Dunlap. They eventually selected Dunlap, who had the inside track because of some previous consulting work with Melbourne clubs. As head coach, Mike Dunlap had taken the 36ers to three consecutive finishes among the top four teams in the league. He had established a 59-36 record at Adelaide, was making plans for the 1997 season, had another year on his contract, and the 36er administration was planning to honor it. Mal Simpson, the club president, was firmly behind Dunlap.

I had seen the 36ers soundly beat Iowa State, 86-66, in Ames, Iowa, on

November 19, 1996, in spite of the Cyclones' 21-4 scoring advantage at the foul line. Kelvin Cato, the ISU shot-blocker, was being disciplined and didn't play, and leading-scorer Dedrick Willoughby saw limited minutes. Adelaide was also short-handed and had only three starters on the trip. The referees extended their welcome to the visiting Australians by awarding the home team 28 foul shots and the visitors only four. One of the fouls was a technical called against 36er Leon Trimmingham, one of my players, for decking Cyclone Paul Shirley with an elbow. The ISU crowd booed Trimmingham's every move the rest of the evening en route to his 24-point performance.

I had received no indication from Dunlap that night in Ames that he would not be coaching another NBL season. However, while the team was on its U.S. tour, Adelaide writer Boti Nagy wrote a very critical article regarding Dunlap's performance as a coach with the 36ers. Nagy particularly questioned his player management in regard to handling veterans and also honed in on one of the favorite topics of the Australian press - the development of young local players, in this case South Australians. Another criticism of Dunlap in Adelaide was his decision to bring his own assistant coaches from the U.S., rather than developing qualified Australians in that position. However, he had somewhat remedied that particular situation with the hiring of David Claxton of the Gold Coast as his top assistant for the 1997 season.

Like the Briggs article in Hobart, Nagy's public statement created an uncomfortable atmosphere for the American coach. Dunlap's decision to resign put the Adelaide administration in a tight spot with the 1997 season set to open three weeks hence. David Claxton, veteran NBL coach at the Gold Coast, was in a favorable position as Dunlap's assistant and was named interim head coach for the 1997 season. Subsequently, the team finished below .500 and failed to qualify for the playoffs for the first time since 1992. Claxton was dismissed after one season. Phil Smyth, former Olympian and NBL All-Star, was named head coach and in his first season in that position won the 1998 NBL Championship. Ironically, while criticized by the Adelaide press for not developing young South Australian players, Coach Mike Dunlap returned to the U.S., became the head coach at Metropolitan State in Denver, and immediately recruited three Australians as building blocks for a strong Division II program. Although Smyth was on the bench and directed the 36ers to the '98 title, Dunlap had set a disciplined tone and had established a sound base in Adelaide for the future. Smyth gave the players a freer rein and they responded with high-level play.

In addition to the Briggs article, a number of other off-court developments occurred after the 1988 season and in the build-up to the 1989 NBL at Hobart. As a result of the surge of support for the Devils due to the team's improvement during the previous three years, club president Wayne Monaghan had taken advantage of the momentum and worked hard to pro-

mote interest in a new arena. Monaghan had recruited prominent business-
men as new board members, whom he felt would boost the Devils' financial
position.

Finally, the Derwent Center, the new arena, had been approved and
work had started on the 4,000 seat entertainment center built on the banks of
the scenic Derwent River in suburban Hobart. The Derwent Center was a
great physical improvement over the old Kingborough Stadium. Yet I knew
immediately, with the new place, that we had lost our homecourt advantage
and that the Derwent would be a much more neutral setting, and therefore a
negative for the future of our hard-earned wins. Competing with half the
budget of many opponents, the home court had been the Devils' trump card
and was critical to continued success. When everyone was saying, "How
beautiful. How nice," I was thinking that the loss of a home court edge was
another reason to turn this headache over to someone else.

The 1988 season had ended with the 10 win 14 loss record posted; Joe
Hurst was named the league's MVP on a disputed vote. Hurst had played
well and was a bright spot in an otherwise difficult season. Wayne Burden,
Peter Mann, Jerry Dennard, and Murray Shiels had also made valuable contributions. But overall it had been a tough year in Hobart; I needed a change
of scene. I was relieved to arrive in San Francisco for a few days rest before
heading out to Moraga to work as a guest coach between Australian seasons
with Lynn Nance at St. Mary's College.

□*11*□

THE BELLS OF ST. MARY'S
AND THE LAST HOORAY AT HOBART

St. Mary's College was a private, Catholic school situated in the beautiful foothills of upmarket Moraga, California, a 45-minute drive to downtown San Francisco. Although the school had never had a consensus All-American basketball player, Tom Meschery was the local legend. Meschery had recorded a successful ten-year NBA career, principally with the San Francisco Warriors, from 1961-1971. The St. Mary's home court reminded me of the Ohio Valley Conference gyms of the early 1970s. It seated about 3,500 with a good playing surface, and the school competed in the mid-level Division I West Coast Conference with Pepperdine, University of San Francisco, Gonzaga, San Diego University, Santa Clara, University of Portland, and Loyola Marymount. Paul Westhead at Marymount had developed a nationally ranked team and was the media focal point in the conference, while Jim Harrick had used his work at Pepperdine as a springboard to the UCLA head job.

The St. Mary's basketball headquarters were located in a far corner of the gym with one larger office for the head coach, Lynn Nance. It was joined by a shower and a bathroom to a second, very small office inhabited by two full-time assistants, one part-time assistant, and me. The second office was about 15 feet square and crowded, at best. I decided immediately after seeing the set-up that I would need a desk in our apartment and that I would not plan to do any serious paper or telephone work at the gym because of the lack of space and privacy. Also, the gym parking situation was cramped with a few spaces marked and reserved by campus police for the coaching staff on the back side of the building. There were three spaces reserved for men's basketball. I never did see all three occupied, but I noticed on occasion that Nance's car was parked cross-wise over two of the spaces.

I immediately sensed competition between the two full-time assistant coaches, Russ Crutchfield and Darryl Winston. Crutchfield had been a star player at the University of California-Berkeley and Winston had also been a good college player at Kansas State of the Big Eight Conference. Each considered himself to be the top assistant and it seemed that Nance let them compete to figure it out for themselves, although Crutchfield had the seniority. When Nance was absent from practice, like many college situations when the head man was gone, it was close to chaos. In authoritarian leadership situations, when the boss is gone, normal production usually stops.

I learned rapidly that Lynn Nance had developed an efficient system of play from knowledge gained through his years as an assistant at Kentucky and other stops. He had his system packaged and organized superbly for the U.S. college game. His defensive philosophy interfaced perfectly with the offense and he had an answer for every game situation. I recalled a 6:00 a.m. practice where I was taking some notes on a new warm-up drill, which the staff had just installed. Coach Nance approached me warily and asked what was I doing. I was surprised at the question. I had arranged a trip to Australia for this guy and I had come from Australia to California at his invitation. I replied that I was taking notes on the drill. He queried, "You aren't writing a book, are you?"

The pre-season schedule at St. Mary's in 1988-89 included the Brisbane Bullets of the Australian NBL. Brisbane, like other Australian NBL teams, came to the U.S. on a college tour, only three weeks after the nine-month NBL grind, to tryout new players. The tour was of little value to veteran NBL players and it was always difficult to convince them to make the trip. In fact, in many cases the trip was more for the benefit of the coach than the players. Both American and Australian-born NBL coaches used the tour to satisfy their own curiosity about U.S. college basketball, possibly to act out some unfulfilled dreams about Division I coaching, and to develop contacts. Nevertheless, Australian clubs have persisted with the U.S. trip and used the opportunity to develop younger squad members and to look at new import prospects in game conditions.

In the Hobart situation, I saw no value in such competition. A U.S. tour extended the Australian season, which was already the world's longest basketball season running from January through October. There had been discussions among NBL administrators and the league office regarding the image of the Australian league in the U.S. on these post-season tours, as NBL teams were never at full strength, were worn down from the regular season's tenmonth grind, and usually played inconsistently at best. LeRoy Loggins and Robert Sibley were the only starters present with the Bullets at St. Mary's with three 1988 Brisbane starters absent. The missing veteran players included Shane Heal, John Dorge, and Larry Sengstock, all three Australian National Team players. Also, the Bullets were without their two regular American import players. They were at about 50% strength.

· Radio Moraga

St. Mary's was primed and well prepared. They had a double digit, halftime lead over Brisbane, which was lethargic and relatively disinterested. I was sitting at the end of the St. Mary's bench and the radio announcer asked me to chat with him during the halftime break. I sat down and was greeted by a very aggressive statement from the announcer. Essentially he was questioning the NBL as a professional league with a Division I college team, St. Mary's, leading the Bullets at halftime. I said something to the effect that St. Mary's was a well-coached, veteran team, but to speak honestly, that Brisbane had starters missing. Further, this was not the same Brisbane team that had just finished 18-6 in the 1988 NBL league race.

Maybe I had annoyed the announcer when I had inquired if the interview was going world wide (it went county-wide at best), for there was little cordiality in our exchange of comments. The interview lasted about five minutes and I didn't think anything more about it. I felt that I had been honest and reasonably tactful. I could have told the harsh truth that St. Mary's didn't have one player capable of winning an NBL import contract and that the full-strength Bullets would have destroyed them, but I didn't. The interview had been a typical half-time filler with nothing important said, in my opinion.

St. Mary's won the game and the next day at an afternoon practice I was greeted by Assistant Coach Darryl Winston, who seemed to be awaiting my arrival. Winston said that he had heard about the radio interview. At that same time Lynn Nance strode out of the office onto the floor and joined us at midcourt. I was shocked when both started a verbal attack on me regarding the interview. I could feel paranoia in the air. My concluding comment was that the truth was the truth, and St. Mary's had beaten the Brisbane bench plus two starters. It was not a matter of opinion; it was fact. It was clear that I was no longer welcome around the St. Mary's program, nor did I want to be there. I left the gym in disbelief that this had actually taken place. Apparently Nance and Winston felt that they were defending their turf against foreign invasion.

St. Mary's finished the 1988-89 season with an outstanding 25-5 record, losing to Eldon Campbell and Clemson in the NCAA tournament. Lynn Nance returned to his alma mater at the University of Washington as head coach on the impetus of the success at St. Mary's in 1989, but was not able to turn the Washington Husky program around in his four-year tenure. Charges by a Washington player against Nance regarding a racial issue drew national media attention, not the kind of publicity that coaches and university officials wanted - in fact, the kind they dreaded.

Lynn Nance teams were 22-50 in Pac-10 Conference play over four years and he left the University of Washington amid controversy after the 1993 season to later take the head coaching job at a Division II school, Southwest Baptist University in Bolivar, Missouri. Nance had played at Southwest Baptist when the school was a junior college; thus he was coaching at his second and last alma mater. I understood from Australian club officials that he had pursued both the Sydney and Adelaide jobs, but to no avail. Lynn Nance had gone full-circle in his coaching career and found himself back in Bolivar, Missouri, in Missouri Intercollegiate Athletic Association (MIAA) competition.

After the blow-up over the Moraga radio interview, I continued to work on preparations for the upcoming Australian season, but not with Coach Nance's basketball program. Geneva was taking a couple of courses at St. Mary's, while I attended local college and Golden State Warrior games in Oakland. We stayed in Moraga until the semester ended in December, then moved into the St. Francis Hotel in San Francisco for a week of relaxation before heading back to Tasmania for another year.

I had stayed at the St. Francis, not knowing that it was world famous, on my way to Okinawa in 1968. I had paid $16.00 for a room in the old section of the hotel. In that era, the city was in turmoil because of Vietnam War protesters who had established a campground in the heart of San Francisco in Union Square, directly across the street from the St. Francis Hotel. I had gone to see a performance of *Hair,* the Broadway protest musical which depicted societal upheaval in the war years. It had been playing at the American Conservatory Theatre. Twenty years later, in 1988, the city had returned to normalcy, a Neil Simon play had replaced *Hair*, and San Francisco was doing business as usual, with no seamy encampment in Union Square, only a few left-over hippies, now street people. The Age of Aquarius had passed.

After the week's break in San Francisco, we took a late-evening, Qantas flight to Melbourne with the 45-minute connecting flight to Tasmania. The Hobart Devils basketball scene in 1989 had changed dramatically since my arrival three years before. We were no longer a two-man operation with Mr. Monaghan handling the money and me the team. A new executive board had been recruited by the enterprising Wayne Monaghan with promising sponsorship contracts and other revenue generating opportunities in the works. Also, the new Derwent Center was a reality and the first home game of the 1989 season was set to be played there. I drove out to the new building in the final days of construction work. The floor had been installed and the goals had been hung. I went back to my car to grab a ball out of the trunk. I returned to the building, walked onto the court and shot a lay-up off the glass through the virgin basket, presumably the first two points registered in the Derwent Center. I likened the experience to carving one's initials in a desk on the last day on a job, for the sake of posterity.

There had been much progress made in Hobart basketball since our arrival in 1985. The building of the new arena was a monument to the Devils team's competitiveness and respectability in the Australian National Basketball League. My salary had increased nearly ten-fold in four years with a new car, instead of a 1962 model, also at my disposal. We had recruited Gordie McLeod, a former National Team point guard, from the Illawarra Hawks, and Wayne McDaniel, a naturalized Aussie from Newcastle. I had placed McDaniel out of Cal-State Bakersfield with Adelaide in his first job in Australia. He had since become an Australian citizen and established a name for himself as a scorer and rebounder in NBL competition. We retained Dennard, Hurst, Shiels, and Cameron Dickinson from 1988. This team looked okay on paper, but upheaval followed and the '89 Devils were never able to develop focus nor find effective chemistry.

Dicko

Cameron Dickinson was 18-years old when he flew over from Melbourne to attend a Devils training session during the latter stages of the 1988 season. He was a strong, 6'5 lefty shooter with considerable energy and athletic ability. Jay Brehmer had coached him as a junior and had called me to recommend Dickinson as a player with NBL talent. Jay said that he was a kid who had been ignored by Melbourne clubs because he had been in a little trouble, but that he had good athletic ability. I figured that Dickinson must have had something serious in his background, because the Melbourne clubs were thorough in their recruiting of local talent.

Brehmer gave me Cameron's number and I arranged to fly him over for a few days. Then I received another call from Brehmer, apparently in his cups from a pub, and he really chewed me out for "poaching" his player. I was a little confused, as Brehmer himself had initiated the idea of the player coming to Hobart. I wasn't sure what was going on, but I didn't contact Dickinson for a few more weeks. Finally we were able to bring him to Hobart, with Brehmer's blessing again.

I vividly recall the day that Cameron Dickinson arrived in Tasmania. I looked up from a drill at Warrane Stadium and saw this tall, sinewy-built, red-headed kid stride onto the floor with Wayne Monaghan. Two redheads side-by-side, Monaghan, the club president, and Dicko, the rookie. However, Dickinson's red hair was the more distinctive, as he had somehow applied a blonde strip down the sides. This brash young street kid immediately called me "Dave" and "mate" and made himself at home. Amidst his chatter, he sat down to pull on his boots, as the Aussies call basketball shoes. I noticed that he had huge holes in his socks but he paid no attention, talking away in a non-stop sales pitch about his game. Also I noted that his eyes were bloodshot and he acted a little hyper. During the practice, he showed that he was very raw, but talented. That day he ran harder, faster, and longer than anyone in the gym. I liked him, but the veteran players didn't.

We signed Dicko to a contract, which included only board and room, with a job at a commercial laundry, not easy work. Dickinson complained of the hours, the pay, and the bloodied sheets from hospital accounts which he had to handle. He was with the Devils while Lynn Nance was visiting in Hobart. Nance liked him, and at my request contacted Coach Dan Johnson at Southeastern Community College in Beatrice, Nebraska. On the basis of Nance's recommendation to Dan Johnson, Dicko was offered a scholarship there for the 1988-89 U.S. college season.

While we were on a road trip over that weekend in Melbourne, Dickinson wanted to visit his old neighborhood in Broadmeadows, a rough Melbourne suburb. Somehow, he convinced Coach Nance to go along with him. They got a lift out to Broadmeadows, but had to take the 45-minute taxi ride back to the hotel in downtown Melbourne. The fare came to $30.20 and Dickinson volunteered to pay his part; he said, "Here's the twenty, Lynn." He handed the .20 coin to Nance and then disappeared into the hotel - vintage Dicko at that stage of his life.

Cameron Dickinson completed the season with Hobart and was primed to leave for Nebraska when Coach Dan Johnson, who had been Lynn Nance's student basketball manager at Iowa State, called me. Coach Johnson was concerned and said that he had not received Dickinson's high school transcript, which was necessary for admission to school. I replied that it would be impossible to provide the transcript as Dicko had not gone past his freshman year at a Melbourne area high school. Johnson then explained that the only alternative to the high school transcript and diploma, which were out of the question, was a satisfactory score on the American GED high school equivalency test. The test was not available in Australia, but Cathy Lincoln, an administrator from Senator Michael Tate's office in Hobart, said that she could organize the shipment of the GED to the University of Tasmania.

Ms. Lincoln made special arrangements to have it sent via diplomatic pouch from Washington, D.C. The GED arrived and Dickinson took the test supervised by Tasmanian University officials. I knew that Cameron Dickinson was street smart and had some charisma, but I was amazed that he was able to score in the 80th percentile overall on the test. He was particularly strong in English and math, without having attended high school.

With the GED requirement behind him, a U.S. visa was the only hurdle to his departure to Beatrice, Nebraska. I took Dicko back to Cathy Lincoln to expedite the visa application. As Dickinson was filling out the application, he stopped dead, his face redder than usual, and I asked him what was the problem. There was a section on the application regarding a police clearance. He said that he had been arrested a "couple of times" as a juvenile, but was never convicted. I spoke with Cathy Lincoln about this and she said that he would probably be okay as the arrests had occurred before Dicko had turned 18. She also mentioned that the U.S. Consulate owed her a couple of favors. So Dicko was granted his visa, thanks to the work of Lincoln, and he departed in August 1988 for two years at the Nebraska junior college.

I knew that Cameron Dickinson was a raw kid and had had some problems with the law, but I also sensed that he had some drug and alcohol problems. When I asked him about this, he, of course, denied it. Two weeks after his arrival at school in Nebraska, I received a call from his new coach, Dan Johnson, saying he thought Dickinson was an alcoholic. Johnson said that he had smelled alcohol on the Aussie on several occasions, during the school day. Further he said that Dicko was on his way out at Southeastern for visiting the girls dorm in the wee hours without invitation. The coach confirmed that this Australian guy was out of control and something had to be done immediately.

I was in California at St. Mary's College at the time and told Cameron, "It is back to Melbourne to live like a rat or enter a drug and alcohol outpatient rehab in Beatrice." Without hesitation, he chose the rehab and miraculously stayed clean and sober for 18 consecutive months. However, he wasn't really distancing himself from the chemical problem through a twelve-step program; he simply stayed busy and didn't use drugs or drink. He went to school, played ball, and developed a dependent relationship with a local girl as a substitute for his chemicals. He was struggling to survive in what he perceived as stark, sober reality. Dickinson was staying clean temporarily, but not laying the foundation for long-term recovery. As in all such cases, the use of chemicals was only a symptom; he had yet to address the source of the conflict in his life and it was impossible for him to get comfortable in his own skin without a thorough accounting of his past bizarre and anti-social behavior.

Temporarily out of trouble on the drug and alcohol scene, Dickinson averaged 20-points per-game at Southeastern and was recruited by a few mid-Division I colleges. However, at my urging he signed with Coach Brad Dunn at Quincy College, a good Division-II basketball program in a manageable small school environment. Dickinson returned home to Melbourne after graduating from Southeastern for a visit but decided to stay in Australia to play in the NBL, rather than return to the Quincy scholarship. He signed with the Brisbane Bullets and blazed a very ominous trail there during the 1991 league season. Eventually he was drug-tested off the team in October and called me with the news, which I already had received from Bullet GM Ted Seymour. I advised Dicko to admit himself to drug rehab in Brisbane and to stay in Australia. He did spend two weeks in rehab, but he did not stay in Australia. He showed up at our home in Des Moines in December after his release from the Brisbane hospital.

Athletically and academically, Cameron Dickinson was a mid-Division I prospect all the way, but emotionally and behaviorally he needed some firm guidance and special attention to succeed in a four-year American school. His recovery had to take precedence over basketball, and, of course, no one was looking for a high-risk player of his background, especially in December. That is, except the 24-year-old Nick Nurse. He was the new coach at Grand View College, a private, liberal arts NAIA school in Des Moines.

Nick Nurse and Mr. V

As a player, Nick Nurse had been a walk-on, non-scholarship athlete at the University of Northern Iowa for Coach Jim Berry. He broke into the starting lineup early and held the job for four years. He had played his last three years in college under Eldon Miller, who came to Northern Iowa directly from his NIT title team at Ohio State University. Nurse, the youngest of nine children from Carroll, Iowa, had done a good job as player-coach in Derby, England, right out of college. He had then returned from England to take the head job at Grand View College.

I was, at first, skeptical regarding the Dickinson situation and Grand View because Nick Nurse was very young, only one year out of college, with little coaching experience. I learned that Nurse was a good coach and as tough as he needed to be with his players. He left Grand View after two years for an assistant job at the University of South Dakota, but returned later to England and coached Birmingham to the 1996 English championship. On the basis of his success in England, Nurse, at 31, was promoted to head coach at Sunair in Belgium, one of Europe's most challenging coaching jobs.

Nick Nurse learned some things at Grand View. He also gained experience in working with problem personalities in his relationship with Cameron Dickinson. He continued to grow as a coach through his work in England and then at Sunair Basketball Club, in Oostende, Belgium. Sunair was one of Europe's best known upper-level basketball organizations. Family owned since 1958, patriarch Mr. Rudolf Vanmoerkere, close to seventy at the time, still attended all Sunair home games and called the shots. He occupied a place among season ticket holders; however, Mr. V. had removed the seat formerly located directly in front of his own for extra leg room.

Walking through that section of the Oostende arena, I had noticed that the space in front of the V-man's seat was dented and damaged, signs that the floor had taken a beating through the years. The scarred floor indicated that Mr. Vanmoerkerke had vicariously stomped many Sunair opponents into submission from his special seat. I actually witnessed a new floor scar being added at a Sunair league game, as Mr. V. was very upset with one of Mr. Nurse's under-the-basket plays. I imagined that from this special seat, the

Sunair boss had also made decisions and wielded the power to seal the fate of a string of U.S. import players and coaches trying to meet management's lofty expectations in the Sunair program, which proved nearly an impossible task to those brave enough to try.

Rudolf Vanmoerkerke, known as one of Europe's wealthiest men, had developed his fortune through Sunair Travel, which he purchased in 1958. The basketball team had carried the company name through the years. When I visited Coach Nick Nurse in Oostende in January 1998, Mr. V. had recently sold his travel company for a reported U.S.$400,000,000. However, he remained in control of the basketball team along with son, Mark, and frequently attended practices and all games. His chauffeur-driven Mercedes, tracking to and from the Mr. V. Arena, had been a familiar sight in Oostende, Belgium, for over four decades.

Oostende was a smaller city of 80,000, located on the North Sea and a very breezy place in the winter time. The gym, Mr. V. Arena, was a renovated tennis club and had a seating capacity of 2,500 with a nice wooden floor and playing surface. The facility served as a commercial fitness club and also included tennis and squash courts with two secondary basketball floors. The facility included a full-service bar on the top level of the building. The bar was always a profitable enterprise and a staple at most overseas basketball arenas, providing a pre-game and post-game meeting place.

Nick Nurse definitely took a step up in his career when he earned the Sunair job on the basis of his achievements with the Birmingham Bullets in England. I had recommended him to Sunair and had convinced Mr. V. that Nurse had the maturity to handle the challenge. Rudolf Vanmoerkerke, the hard-driving businessman, expected to win the championship of Belgium every year. As he said to me in the stadium named after him,

"We spend a lot of money on this team. Gate receipts cover about 20% of expenses in the million-dollar annual budget, so we rely on local sponsors for the balance. They expect success and I do, too. Mr. Nurse has a big responsibility."

Bruce Chubick

Mr. V. and Sunair have had numerous coaches through the years and have accepted and rejected U.S. import players right and left. A few years earlier, I had sent Jeff Warren, the 6'7 University of Missouri forward, to Sunair for a tryout. He was awakened early one morning by a club official with his airline arrangements home that very morning. Prior to Nurse taking the job in August 1997, veteran coach Tom Boot of the Netherlands held the Sunair head job for three years. Boot, a rigid disciplinarian in his fifties, and Nurse, more of a player's coach and only 32, were opposites.

Boot made life miserable for American import Bruce Chubick in the 1996-

97 season. Chubick was a talented 6'8 power forward, a good athlete, skilled, and an 'A' in work ethic. He had been a four-year starter at the University of Nebraska of the prestigious Big Eight Conference and a productive CBA player with the Omaha Racers in 1995-96, where he averaged 11.3 points, 8.3 rebounds, 53% field goals, and shot 47% from the three-point arc. I had watched him carefully during the 1995-96 CBA season at Omaha, and we agreed to work as player-agent in the overseas market after the Racers' season.

While on an NBA scouting trip to Europe in 1997, Ron Adams observed that Chubick had become Coach Boot's whipping boy at Sunair, confirming other reports which I had received. I knew that very, very few players would have stayed with the task and maintained the positive attitude that Bruce Chubick did. At the end of the season, Sunair released him but I received calls from four other Belgian clubs with firm offers for Chubick. It was apparently the consensus of Sunair opponents that Bruce Chubick was one of the best players in the league and it was common knowledge that Boot had done little to maximize this player's abilities. Chubick further enhanced his reputation with productive play at Wevelgem in the 1997-98 Belgian season. Sunair again showed interest in him as a player, as his productivity had increased in a more favorable player-coach situation.

One particularly distressing experience, which Bruce Chubick had to endure in Oostende, was an anti-doping test administered to the Sunair team. Chubick revealed in the drug testing materials that "yes" he was taking an expectorant which contained eferine and norefedrine - banned substances in Europe - in Bronchaid, an over-the-counter decongestant product. Of course, when the blood analysis was run, it was found that these two banned substances were in fact present (surprise).

I guessed that Sunair wanted to unload Chubick's guaranteed contract, but apparently that wasn't the case or they had reconsidered. Bruce had to put considerable time, effort, and worry into resolving this mess. Eventually he was cleared at a hearing with a Belgian sports tribunal in Brussells and finished the year, without penalty, with Sunair before moving on to Wevelgem.

I had worked as an agent with both Nick Nurse and Bruce Chubick, and I felt that they would have been a solid coach-player tandem in high-level European basketball. Nurse's *laissez-faire* coaching style would have enhanced Chubick's talent and work ethic. However, it would have been a long-shot for this to come together at Sunair, given the volatility of the coaching job and the player's past problems with that club.

Nick Nurse and Dicko at Grand View

Back at Grand View College and before his adventures in Birmingham and Oostende, Nick Nurse had planned to use this NAIA job as a career launching pad. But his first team there was off to a disappointing 2-11 start at Christmas break and Cameron Dickinson was 0-9 in Australia, counting his eight juvenile arrests and sacking after one season at Brisbane. So Nurse and Dicko were a perfect match at this time in their basketball lives - both needed a lift. I warned Nick of Cameron's potential to disrupt the team, the school, and the city of Des Moines, but Coach Nurse figured what could he lose. Maybe he could help the kid, and Dicko couldn't hurt a 2-11 team. Also, it was a good situation for Dickinson as Coach Nurse had three former Division I college players working as volunteer assistants, Mike Born (Iowa State), Pat Springer (Iowa), and Brian David (Arizona). This was a solid group of people who had the personalities and athletic backgrounds to get Dickinson's attention and to influence him in a positive manner.

Cameron Dickinson had been a strong "B" student at Southeastern Community College and had graduated on time; therefore, he was eligible immediately at Grand View as a junior college transfer. Overnight, he had become a U.S. college student. He did a good job at Grand View that season. The team went 11-8 after Christmas with the Aussie in the lineup and finished 13-19. Dickinson was the leading scorer with 19-point per-game production.

Every day was a challenge that first year at Grand View, as Dicko, though not using, was still in drug and alcohol withdrawal. His adjustment to reality was a slow, confusing process. However, he was making progress. He had a positive routine with school, basketball, and AA meetings, which he willingly attended. He made a few friends at school and in various recovery groups and slowly, ever so slowly, showed signs of a possible turnaround in his life. Then in the summer between his junior and senior years, though still clean and sober, he began to slip back into dishonesty and negative thinking. He demonstrated hostile behavior toward other students, especially teammates. This behavior continued periodically after the summer and into his senior year. Just before Christmas, he experienced dramatic mood swings and showed some exceptionally aggressive, angry, unsociable behavior on the court and on campus.

The Australian was kicked out of a couple of games and was responsible for a mid-game fight on a road trip. He remained drug and alcohol free, but went through "a stark raving sober period," and his negative behavior began to wear on Coach Nick Nurse. He gave Dicko every opportunity to come around, but finally dropped him from the Grand View team at the Christmas break. Nick called to inform me of Dicko's suspension and I fully agreed with the decision. At about the same time as his dismissal from the basketball team, I told Dicko that he was no longer welcome at our house because of a situation in which he had lied to me. Also, his girl friend in Nebraska had finally had enough of a fruitless relationship and had broken up with him. Thus Dicko's three sources of security in sobriety - basketball, our home, and his girl friend - had been removed from his life, and his fourth, drugs and alcohol, fortunately, did not seem to appeal to him. These events jolted Dicko and forced him to take a hard look at himself and to accept more responsibility for his bizarre, self-centered behavior.

Coach Nurse told me that Dickinson might be able to return if he apologized and admitted his drug and alcohol problems to the team. He had actually been a hard-core user since age 13 and had lived with other addicts in Melbourne, surviving through theft and by selling drugs on the street. Somehow he had made his way back to basketball. Fate had steered him to Hobart, and eventually to this opportunity in Des Moines. Nick Nurse called me to report that Cameron had, in fact, met with the Grand View team and had told his story honestly and sincerely to his teammates. Not all of the Grand View players were convinced, but the players had voted 12-yes and 3-no for Dicko's return to the squad for the rest of the 1992-93 season.

After he had been reinstated to the team, Dickinson had some severe problems with wisdom teeth. Because of his previous life-style in Melbourne during his early teen years, he had neglected dental health and was experiencing painful wisdom tooth flare-ups. He went to a dentist who had worked on Grand View players through the years, and had the two wisdom teeth removed at 1:00 p.m. on a week day. The dentist had called Coach Nurse and said that Dicko would have to miss two days of practice, as the wisdom teeth had abscessed and were going to cause considerable pain. However, at 3:00 p.m. that same day, 30 minutes out of the dental chair, the Aussie was back on the court warming up for the practice session, in which he participated. He missed no time from his regular basketball, school, and work schedule because of the teeth.

Cameron Dickinson finished that season without further serious incident and left Grand View with six semester hours of incompletes on his transcript and a promise that he would finish his degree. He returned to Australia to the NBL and put together back-to-back seasons of 20-point per-game scoring with the Townsville Suns. After the Australian season in 1996, he called me and said that he was coming to the U.S. to play on a tour against Division I colleges and that he would like to spend a few days in Des Moines in our home. I replied that he was welcome, but only if he brought with him the two completed term papers which he needed for graduation from Grand View. In other words my agreeing to his stay in Des Moines was conditional upon his keeping his promise to complete his degree. I felt that the time had come for him to make that promise good. When I picked up Dickinson at the Des Moines Airport, he walked through the arrival lounge with a small travel bag in his right hand and a folder, which he held up for me to see even before I had greeted him in his left, his shooting hand. The folder contained the two term papers, completed and ready to be exchanged for his college diploma.

That trip was one of the most rewarding periods in Cameron Dickinson's life. His hard work in basketball, school, and recovery had come together at this time. On the basketball tour with an Australian team, Dicko scored 39 points and 38 points on consecutive nights at the University of Georgia and University of Pittsburgh. In the Georgia game he was 14-22 from the field and he went 14-24 at Pitt. In the two games, he hit on 17 of 30 three-point field goals - spectacular shooting. More importantly, he had kept his word and arrived in Des Moines with his college assignments completed. He took his term papers to the Grand View College campus and spent the entire day meeting with his teachers. He returned to my house in the evening with a diploma in hand confirming his earned Bachelor of Arts Degree in Human Services and Psychology. He had kept his promise and had even graduated with a "B" average. On that same visit he received his medallion at a Des Moines AA meeting, which marked six consecutive years of clean and sober living. All things considered, he was living a miracle. Cameron Dickinson played the 1997 NBL season with the Sydney Kings and later signed a contract with the Illawarra Hawks for 1998-99. And most importantly, he had shown a continued commitment to his ongoing recovery and personal growth.

Final Days in Hobart

Looking back to 1989 in Australia, as the Hobart Devils started preparations for the NBL season, Cameron Dickinson was a long way from the person which he was on course to become. He had returned briefly to Hobart between his first and second years in junior college but returned to Beatrice, Nebraska, to summer school. I told him that I was planning to resign from the Hobart job and that he should go back to the U.S. and focus on recovery and school. On paper, the Devils team looked pretty good, but the exhibition season showed that veteran point-guard Gordie McLeod was carrying an old injury and that team chemistry was lacking.

I coached the Devils through an exhibition schedule and then after the first two league games, resigned to return to the U.S. Wayne Monaghan, still at the Devils helm as president, wanted me to finish the season; but it was clear, after a week of meetings with him, that I was making the right decision in leaving Hobart. I had fought the battle of Van Dieman's Land long enough and was ready for civilian life in the U.S. The Devils hired Tom Maher, a successful National Women's Basketball League coach from Melbourne, who confidently stated in his initial press conference, "I am not here to talk about victories, I am about titles." I knew that he had buried himself with that comment before ever coaching a game.

There was strong media reaction to my resignation. Some writers gave me credit for resurrecting the NBL game and the franchise in Hobart and others felt that I was deserting the program. None could deny that my work with the Devils had lifted public interest in the game to an all-time high. *The Mercury* ran the story as a banner headline on the front page of the May 5, 1989, edition of the Tasmanian paper.

We lived in a townhouse in a rather isolated Hobart suburb, so I had some privacy during this turbulent period. I had to adjust to the quieter times, as I experienced a period of emotional disengagement from over three years of non-stop participation in what had become a high-profile Australian coaching job. There were times during that period in which I questioned my own recovery from alcoholism, as I felt that I could have been replacing the drink with the "high" of coaching and public recognition. I knew that I would not miss the emotional roller-coaster which I experienced in the Hobart coaching job. I was also aware that I would have to find a way to fill the holes of my ego which had been fortified by the demands of the job and by the constant media attention. I either felt "too good" or "too bad," determined by the outcome of the last game. However, I trusted my own judgment. The timing of my resignation was inconvenient to the club, but I knew that it was important to move on with my life. Hobart had been a good stop. It was sound thinking and a good decision to resign. Just after my decision to leave Hobart was announced publicly, I received a call from a Des Moines friend in Sydney at a convention. He flew over to Hobart and we spent the day together taking in the local sights. He seemed troubled. Several months later, Steve Blank took his life back in Des Moines.

The most significant comment on my resignation came from the National Basketball League's general manager, Bill Palmer, who stated in the *NBL Official Press Release* of May 8, 1989, the following:

"When Adkins came to Hobart they were teetering on the edge of financial collapse and the Devils were the League's whipping boys. Adkins gave the Devils a respectability on the court around the nation which galvanized the pride in the team on the Apple Isle. He, with Hobart's new administration, put the Devils amongst the leading teams in the NBL and, for that, the League is indebted to the 'Doc'. We wish him well."

The Devils played the 1989 and 1990 seasons with players left over and some resurrected from my coaching days. Their scorer was Wayne McDaniel, the veteran naturalized forward, with return appearances in Hobart by Paul Stanley and Wayne Burden. The club and new coach were trying desperately to recapture some of the juice that had given the 1987 team the winning NBL record. But it was not to be. The 1987 Devils team had developed a special chemistry through well-defined, on-court roles combined with a genuine camaraderie among the players off-court. The team chemistry and the occasional "magic" of the past could not be haphazardly re-created. Some of the names were the same, but they were connected by different team dynamics. Hobart won eight games in both the 1989 (8-16) and 1990 (8-18) league seasons.

Prior to the 1991 season, with Maher still in command as coach, Wayne Monaghan contacted me in Des Moines and asked me to recruit two new imports. I sent the Devils Jason Reese, a talented 6'7 post player from Northern Iowa and Wayne Engelstad from Cal-Irvine with an NBA call-up on his resume. The Devils started slowly. Maher was sacked after picking up only one victory in the early going of the 1991 NBL campaign. He returned to Melbourne after going 17-37 in his stint as the Devils coach. He was replaced by Cal Bruton, who had appeared to be making some progress with the Devils and probably would have turned things around eventually. In terms of coaching record, Bruton was by far the best qualified for NBL duty of any of the coaches in Devils history, including me. I was instrumental in Bruton being hired at Hobart through my long-time relationship with Wayne Monaghan, who was still wielding some power in Hobart. I thought that I was doing both Bruton and the Devils a favor, but it was a gamble, especially given Hobart's history in the NBL.

Cal Bruton, including the Hobart job, had achieved a 138-83 National Basketball League coaching mark punctuated by a league championship at Perth in 1990. He had been a great U.S. college player at Wichita State, an NBL All-Star, an Australian National Team player, and had earned a championship ring as a point guard on the Brisbane Bullet 1985 title team. Cal naturally favored the use of a quick, creative point guard in one of the import slots.

I had sent Donald Whiteside from Northern Illinois University to Kalgoorlie in the goldfields of Western Australia to play for the Goldfield Giants. Kalgoorlie was a desert community of about 20,000 located in a region so arid that water needed to be piped in from Mundaring Weir, near the city of Perth, 300 miles away. Donald Whiteside was doing very well in the Western Australia State League when Coach Cal Bruton in Hobart decided to tap his services. I arranged a replacement at Kalgoorlie and Donald Whiteside jumped from the state league to the NBL five games into the 1992 season.

Ironically, Whiteside was eventually cut by Hobart to return to the U.S. to stick with the Toronto Raptors during the first months of the 1996-97 NBA season and was with the Atlanta Hawks briefly in 1997-98. Whiteside, a sub-six foot point guard, became, quite remarkably, the second Kalgoorlie Giant player to return to the U.S to an NBA job. The other, Snoop Graham, had played with the Atlanta Hawks after his goldfield stint. Also, Whiteside joined Winston Crite and Ronnie Cavenall as American players cut by their Australian clubs only to come back to the U.S. and draw NBA paychecks.

Crite was dropped by Brisbane and went to the Phoenix Suns, and Ronnie Cavenall, sacked by Sydney, stuck with the New York Knicks. Donald Whiteside has used his Australian start and NBA time to propel himself into high-paying European pro jobs.

At this time there were some major changes and hints of scandal in the Hobart program. The new Devils administration was finally able to unseat the club's president, Wayne Monaghan, Cal Bruton's only link to a fair shot in bringing the Hobart team back. Bill Tomlinson, Bruton's assistant, had his hand raised to take the reins. He coached the Devils to a 17-71 record, as the Devils franchise ceased operations in 1996.

My modest 33-45 coaching record in Hobart was, by far, the most productive in Hobart's history. The 1987 team achieved the club's only winning record in the NBL books. The 1988 and 1986 Devils teams, respectively, remained the second and third most successful in club history. Tom Maher, my successor, chose to bag me in an interview in *The Mercury* after I had returned to the U.S. However, I received a copy of the article from some friends in Hobart and responded. I accurately explained in a letter to Maher that I had blazed the trail at Hobart so that it was possible for coaching successors to build on my work (when were they going to start?) and enjoy a decent salary with full-time coaching responsibilities, with no side jobs to survive financially. Unfortunately, no one else as yet had been able to equal or exceed the production of 1986, 1987, and 1988. The groundwork of the program, established in that era, had remained the standard for future achievement, should Hobart ever field another NBL team.

The city of Hobart had shown interest and demonstrated support of NBL basketball during my tenure as coach. This support, though sporadic, continued into the leaner years in the nineties. Hopefully, the Devils can reorganize, field a successful team, and again utilize the modern Derwent Center. As former baseballer Mickey Mantle reportedly said to teammates in describing the hitting of a home run in an afternoon game, after a night on the town, no one really knew how difficult that home run was under the circumstances. I felt the same way about those achievements in coaching the Hobart Devils, but not because of a hangover. The Hobart NBL franchise became defunct after the 1996 season due to lack of achievement, both on and off the basketball court.

I had returned to Des Moines in June, 1989, while Geneva stayed four additional weeks in Hobart to complete her B.A. in Psychology from the University of Tasmania. When she graduated from high school years before in Grand Rapids, Michigan, her father had told his four daughters that he would pay for their college education if they became teachers or nurses. She declined his offer and moved to San Diego, California, where she worked in the savings and loan business for twelve years before entering the Foreign

Service. She had FS assignments in Washington D.C., the Netherlands, and Mozambique, where we met. She was a capable, motivated adult student and had an excellent experience at the University of Tasmania. I marveled at how much more she had learned as an undergraduate than I. She had made some good friends in the city of Hobart and at the university. Dace Shugg, a nurse, who came to Australia with her family during WWII as a Latvian immigrant, was Geneva's close friend and classmate. Plans were set for her return to the U.S. to assume a research assistant job in a gerontology project and complete a Masters Degree at Iowa State University. (Geneva completed the M.S. Degree in 1993 and was awarded the university's Research Excellence Award for the work in her thesis.)

My plans were also clear: to reactivate Overseas Basketball Services and to expand the scope of my overseas player recruitment business. I also considered writing a book about my overseas basketball experiences, outside of the loop of U.S. college and pro hoops. I was satisfied with my work in Hobart, but also pleased that it was now behind me. I was glad to be back in the U.S. and felt that we needed a period of stability in our lives, with no more moves for a while. I was also looking forward to regular scouting work at college games and in the Continental Basketball Association (the CBA), the official minor league of American professional basketball. It was good to be back in the U.S.

□*12*□

COCKROACH BASKETBALL LEAGUE, NBA, CBA, IBA

In 1989 there were three CBA franchises within easy-driving distance from my home in Des Moines - in Cedar Rapids, the Quad Cities, and Omaha. The teams were coached respectively by George Whittaker, Mauro Panaggio, and Mike Thibault. Omaha was only a two-hour drive and the most convenient trip for me. I was a regular at Racer games and I am certain that I was there more than most NBA scouts who appeared from time to time. I sat on the scouting bench at a Racer game one evening beside a scout from the Minnesota Timberwolves. He said to me at halftime, "I don't see anyone here who can play in the league." I was shocked. In that particular game there were six players with Omaha who had already played with NBA teams, including Tim Legler, Jim Thomas, Steve Colter, Alex Stivrins, Mike Higgins, and Bart Kofoed.

The CBA franchises have had a number of obstacles to overcome including cash flow, fan appeal, player recruitment and retention, and stability in general. College coaches in CBA towns have been known to resent the minor league team's presence and the threat to their schools' fan bases, as well as their own egos. Also, college stars, who have been cut in the CBA, have returned to their alma maters with horror stories of not getting a fair shot. Although the CBA has been tabbed as "developmental," it was common knowledge that winning took precedence over the priority for player development, which has occurred, incidentally, in many cases. Chris Monter, the NBA draft expert, commented on the developmental aspect of the league as follows, "CBA teams are more concerned with winning than with developing players. Many times the (young) players get the short end of the stick."

I did some research, supportive of Monter's statements about development, on the CBA when C.J. Bruton was considering an offer from the Quad City Thunder, which had drafted him in 1997. I felt that most CBA coaches did not like to use rookies at the point-guard position and was concerned about Bruton getting enough minutes to improve. I could find only four rookies who had played at the point guard position in the CBA during the 1996-97 season - Drew Barry (34 minutes in 6 games), Moochie Norris (11 minutes per game in 20 appearances), Eric Strickland (8 games at 12 minutes per game), and Chucky Atkins.

I found that Atkins of the University of South Florida was the only rookie who played more than 225 minutes. I concluded that Bruton, rookie point guard, would probably play more in his native Australia in the NBL competing against former CBA and NBA players at that position. However, I did not rule out the CBA after he had matured and gained professional experience in Australia. I came up with the following list of point guards logging more than 225 minutes of CBA playing time - note asterisk(*) indicates the *only rookie*.

Re: Point Guard Minutes - 1996-97 CBA Unofficial Numbers

CBA Team	Primary Pt. Guard	Age	Minutes per Game
Connecticut	Kevin Ollie	24	43.64
Florida	Terrence Rencher	24	37.57
Fort Wayne	Myron Brown	27	30.45
Grand Rapids	Melvin Booker	24	36.79
LaCrosse	Chucky Atkins*	22	38.14
Oklahoma City	Elmer Bennett	27	35.96
Omaha	Kelsey Weems	29	32.50
Quad City	Rick Brunson	24	34.87
Rockford	Michael Hawkins	24	40.48
Sioux Falls	Stevin Smith	25	35.50
Yakima	Duane Cooper	28	32.16

In addition to criticism leveled at the league for limited playing time for rookies, the CBA had even taken an indirect hit in fiction literature. Charlie Rosen, former CBA coach-turned-novelist, wrote a clever parody using fictional characters, but many feel based on real CBA counterparts and situations. Phil Jackson wrote the Foreword to Rosen's satirical book, called *Cockroach Basketball League*, a humorous account of a season with Coach Rob Lassiter and the Savannah Stars of the C.B.L.(Cockroach Basketball League). Rosen also provided insight into realities of the minor league coaching routine including living alone in a motel for a season, players' egos, coaches' egos, the press, and the mentality of management. People close to the CBA scene could put real names on some of the quasi-fictitious characters in the book and could match many of the humorous dramas with actual events, some close to incriminating.

Sound and the Fury

Charlie Rosen was well-qualified to provide accurate insight on the minor league playing and coaching experience, as he had been a CBA assistant coach under Phil Jackson at Albany for three years including the 1984 title season. He later served as a head coach at Savannah and Rockford, taking the latter to the CBA Finals in 1989. *The CBA Media Guide* stated that Rosen's favorite read was *The Sound and the Fury*.

Although Faulkner's famous book was not about basketball, the title was an apt description of Charley Rosen's volatility on the CBA bench, especially in Cedar Rapids, Iowa, on December 30, 1989. *The Cedar Rapids Gazette* reported that Rosen charged George Whittaker, the Cedar Rapids coach, on the sidelines and later went after him again. Rosen was arrested for assault and spent the evening in jail. I talked with Whittaker about that evening. He told me that Coach Rosen apparently felt that Whittaker was "pouring it on" by employing a full-court press after the Cedar Rapids victory had been assured. However, Whittaker said that was not the case and that some miscommunication with CR player John Starks had triggered the press and ensuing controversy. Prior to the Cedar Rapids incident, Rosen had received some national publicity and had been suspended in the 1988 season. Coach Rosen was assessed with several technical fouls and then accused the referees of fixing a Rapid City-Rockford game.

Charlie Rosen, an adept writer, retired from CBA coaching in 1990 and has had several successful books - fictional accounts of various basketball dramas. In *The House of Moses All-Stars*, a story of a touring all-Jewish basketball team set in the depression years, Rosen got even with Cedar Rapids. He described a scene in which the team of Jews was refused rooms at a restricted hotel - gentiles only - with Cedar Rapids the villain city where the discrimination occurred. The police were summoned by the hotel manager to settle the ensuing confusion - reminiscent of Mr. Rosen's CBA experience in this same Iowa community. However, unlike the real basketball scene in December of 1989, no one went to jail.

Colorful characters like Charlie Rosen made life interesting in the CBA. I myself considered the CBA a great, no-frill basketball league - no cheerleaders, no school songs, just high-level playing and coaching, and unpredictable, or predictable, annual franchise turnover. I enjoyed the unpretentious minor-league scene and learned to respect the efforts of the players, the coaches, and the owners. I considered the CBA to be the least understood and the most under-rated basketball competition in America, possibly in the world, in spite of its billing as "The Official Development League of the NBA." The fact was, of course, that these franchises fought to make it financially with survival being tied directly to marketing and winning. It would seem that the CBA could serve itself, the game, and the NBA better if the baseball system of farm teams were implemented with a formal relationship between NBA teams and a minor league CBA farm team.

Ironically, one of the impediments to this type of common sense has been resistance from the National Basketball Players' Association, the NBA players' union, and its paranoia about NBA owners. The players' union has expressed concern that owners could use a CBA farm system concept as a means of getting rid of non-productive NBA players, as can happen in baseball. While sending a player down from the NBA to the CBA might not disturb the player's contract guarantee, it would disturb his ego and the NBPA feared that owners would use the CBA as a veteran-player purgatory.

Shortage of Big Men

The CBA has always been a guard's league with quality paint players at a premium. For example, in the 1998 CBA Championship Series, the post position at both the Quad Cities and Sioux Falls was occupied by ex-NBA veterans: Stacy King at age 31; Bob McCann at 38; Barry Sumpter, 32, and Doug Smith at 29 with knees making him seem 39. All were still productive at the CBA level, dominant at times in short spurts. McCann, in fact, was consistent and nearly unstoppable.

They were better choices than in past years when the likes of Pat Cummings and Darryl Dawkins, both in their late thirties at the time, had made cameo CBA playoff appearances after their productive NBA playing days. My point was that a veteran like Bob McCann, who became a solid producer in the 1997-98 season for Sioux Falls, hardly fell into the category of a developing player. He was actually a developed player in the developmental league; same with King, Smith, Sumpter, Dawkins, and Cummings.

In fact, quality paint players, no matter which league or where, NBA or overseas, were always at a premium. The NBA has looked overseas for 7-footers, as many of the young American-born and bred athletes have developed oversized bodies and undersized skills and work ethic. But hiring an authentic pro talent from Europe can be a daunting task, even for NBA teams. The fact was that the money in Europe was in some cases better, more playing time available, with less travel and fewer games, and much more recognition.

The primary motivation to be an athlete can be, in many cases, in the overlooked area of personal recognition - ego. That recognition can come only with scoring, rebounding, and assist production, which in turn were tied to playing time. For example, let's say there was a Commissar of World Professional Basketball with the unilateral power to make policy, and he gave notice that starting next season no player in the world could make more than $250,000 per season for the next ten years. Would these seven-figure NBA and European players quit playing? Of course not, and for three reasons: 1) their egos are intertwined with basketball recognition; 2) they love and need to play the game; and 3) where else could they (legally) make $250,000 a year?

Foreign to Most

Opening day's roster listed thirty foreign players on NBA teams at the start of the 1997-98 season. The largest percentage, two-thirds of these players, had had previous experience in this country on the hard courts of U.S. college basketball. These itinerant athletes were graduates of the overseas club system of basketball. They were definitely top-drawer players in their respective foreign clubs and it would be interesting to know their salary histories before, and during, their participation in NCAA competition (re: C.J. Burton case - Chapter 16). Regardless of their participation in U.S. college ball, it was seldom a smooth road for foreign players in the NBA. Prior to the 1997-98 NBA season, *Dino Radja* of the Celtics, *Sasha Djordjevic* of the Blazers, and *Sasha Danilovic* of the Dallas Mavericks decided to draw European paychecks in lieu of continuing NBA careers.

I was particularly interested in the situation with *Stojko Vrankovic* as I had seen him in the 1994 World Championships and recalled hearing that he was then considering a return to the NBA. Seven-footer Vrankovic was a Croatian with MVP credentials and seven-figure contracts to his credit with the *Panathianaikos Club* in Athens. However, I understood that Vrankovic was having some doubts about leaving his home in Europe and returning to the NBA. He had been able to separate the perceived glamour from the realities during his previous, uneventful, two-year stint with the Celtics. The 82-game schedule, constant travel during the season, and separation from friends and family in Europe were always an issue with foreign players in the U.S. pro league. Ron Adams, who had been responsible for Portland's European scouting, commented on the foreign players in the NBA;

> "My opinion of foreign big guys is a very positive one. The best young centers in the world, at this time, are all foreigners. They all seem to do quite well in the NBA, as contrasted to the smaller foreigners who try to make it."

I saw Vrankovic in the hotel restaurant in Toronto and thought by his appearance and demeanor off the court that there was an "old-line European player," smoking a cigarette, sipping a coffee, and leisurely talking with Croatian teammates. He looked natural and comfortable in that setting. Not known as particularly industrious on the court among some NBA people, big Stojko had been raised on the European two-game per-week schedule and I knew that the NBA hurry-up lifestyle and U.S. culture would have caused him some concern. Europe was in his genes and his game fit so well there - why bother with the NBA?

From that Toronto hotel scene in 1994, Vrankovic delayed his decision to come back to the U.S. paycheck and played two more seasons with his Greek club, Panathinaikos A.O., returned to the NBA with Minnesota in 1996-97 and then went to the Clippers for the next season. Clipper Coach Bill

Fitch commented further on the big post player:
> "Stojko is a player that I wish I could have coached when he was 24 instead of 34. His timing in regards to what teams and when he was in and out of the league was not to his benefit. He had his best years in Europe. His forte was blocking shots and rebounding and I think he was labeled foul prone by too many officials and it hurt him emotionally as well as limited his playing time...This will be his most important season (1999) if he is to continue in the NBA."

(Note: he was expected to surface with a top Croatian team in 1998-99, but had not done so).

Two factors have made NBA contracts more appealing to qualified Australians than to Europeans: the NBA money and the U.S. culture. The money in Europe has been competitive with the NBA in lower and mid-salary jobs, while Australian league salaries were not close to being competitive with either upper-level Europe or the NBA. Also, the adjustment to life in the U.S., with no language barrier either on the street or on the tube, was much easier for a Sydney-born athlete as opposed to someone like Vrankovic with roots in Croatia.

Even though European players may speak English as an acquired language, spoken from the mouth, with Australians it was mother tongue and spoken from the heart. Also, the salary cap issue explained, in part, the appeal of the Australian player to NBA teams in the draft. By Australian basketball salary standards, the NBA "minimum wage" of $270,000 was big money to the Aussie player and a pittance to the NBA club, perfect conditions for expedience in contractual negotiations. Of the four Australians taken in the 1997 NBA draft, three - Chris Anstey, Ben Pepper, and Paul Rodgers - were 6'11 paint players - and the fourth, C.J. Bruton, a point guard.

Australia has had the "catch 22" situation in its National Basketball League: good basketball but with lower pay than in comparable levels of competition in Europe. The Australian NBL champion would be competitive with the top teams in Italy, Spain, and France, and the Boomers, the Aussie National Team, can be considered in the top five in the world. Yet NBL salaries can be classed no better than "lower to mid" level by European standards. Government programs down-under have demanded high taxes, which all players felt in their paychecks. The taxes, coupled with an unfavorable U.S. dollar exchange rate, can make the NBA minimum-salary contracts very attractive to all Australians with big-time aspirations and the game to back it up.

NBA - A Delicate Balance

With NBA salary caps consumed by about a dozen mega-star players, the lower six-figure deals have not satisfied the quality European post players. Actually, if a couple of key players were taken out of the NBA today, or just Michael Jordan, what would happen to the market appeal of professional basketball and the league's product lines? The league did survive and regrouped after the departure of Julius Irving, Larry Bird and Magic Johnson, great players who earned their money and established the credibility of the NBA. These players, who were the drawcards when the NBA made its resurgence in the American marketplace in the 1980s, have retired, as in the cases of Irving, Bird, and Magic or have approached retirement, as with Michael Jordan, Karl Malone, John Stockton, and Charles Barkley. But in today's league, there are many around the world who consider Michael Jordan "to be the NBA." Without him, general public interest could drop dramatically.

Also the balance of on-court power in the world could change with this deletion of key name players. Although NBA players in general held a decided edge over most good European players, especially in the area of athleticism and competitiveness, the possibility of a European team upsetting an NBA team existed. There had already been a couple of close calls in the McDonald's Cup, a pre-season international tournament with NBA and foreign club champion representation.

In the 1991 "Mac Cup," the Los Angeles Lakers slid past *Joventut Badlona* of Spain, 116-114, in Paris; and in 1990 *Scavolini Pesaro* took the New York Knicks to overtime, 119-115, in Barcelona. Without Jordan in the lineup at the 1997 MacDonald's Cup in Paris, the possibility of a European team upsetting the NBA champions was a reality, even though the European clubs could use only two foreign players in the McDonald's Cup competition. The Spanish ACB rules allowed for three foreigners per team in league play, but the McDonald's Cup representative from Spain had to delete one of its foreigners for the event in which the NBA and European champions participated. In fact, in the 1997 Mac Cup from Paris, I saw one of my former players, Troy Truvillion, playing for a Pro A French club.

Another dark cloud which has formed on the horizon of NBA basketball has been the constant threat and then the reality of work stoppage in the form of a lockout by owners. The source of this issue can be traced to a handful of big-time agents who have key NBA players under representation contracts. In a worst-case scenario, in combat with club owners, these agents for the mega-star players could force an NBA shut-down by convincing their clients to stay off the court as leverage in negotiation, or could even use their players to form a new league. The lockout of 1998 killed the NBA summer competition, so critical to free agents and second-round draft choices.

In such a climate, everything would go - training camps, the season, or even the league itself. From my perspective, that type of mentality clearly spelled "the rich getting dumber." Did anyone remember the baseball strike and its impact on the credibility of the game? Also, did the average American really care what happened to the NBA and its millionaire players and owners? I didn't think so. NBA work stoppage had nothing to do with the loss of critical goods and services, like gasoline, electricity, food, or water. For most Americans, losing NBA basketball would mean finding something else to watch on the tube for a couple of hours a week in the winter.

The CBA Dilemma

In spite of the fact that the NBA has been a billion dollar business, there has been little trickle-down to the minors. All CBA teams have had real problems in making ends meet financially and the marketing of minor league basketball has remained a complex, unsolved problem. At the end of 1997, three teams called it quits, leaving only nine to compete for the 1998 title. Ironically, Oklahoma City won the 1997 CBA Championship in a final series with runner-up Florida, and both went under financially. The Omaha Racers, CBA champ in 1993 and finalist in 1994 under Coach Mike Thibault, also closed their doors. Minor league hockey continued to thrive in Omaha, but the Racers struggled in spite of on-court success. Rumors persisted that Omaha, a respected CBA club, had lost up to $800,000 per season in the last few years of the franchise.

Teams in the CBA, the Official Developmental League of the NBA, needed more than the prestige of "NBA" in their promotions materials. They desperately needed direct financial assistance from NBA teams, ala major league-minor league baseball. The NBA has thrown a few bones to the CBA for the development of referees, but the big league had not stepped in, as the CBA membership continued its volatility and shrinkage. The minor league has apparently lacked negotiating posture to secure meaningful financial support from the big league. In fact, the NBA looked as if it had taken advantage of the CBA. It seemed that the CBA lacked the leverage to negotiate a win-win deal and that the NBA had invested little hard cash in the development of minor league call-up players.

Another problem in the CBA has been fan appeal, due in part to the constant turnover and disappearance of key players. Therefore, it has been difficult for fans to follow a particular player over an entire season - here today and gone tomorrow. The NBA can grab a minor leaguer on a ten-day call-up at any time. However, players leaving for higher-paying overseas jobs have also plagued roster solidarity.

The Marty Blake Rule

Marty Blake, the often-quoted NBA scouting director, told me emphatically a couple of years ago in Portsmouth that the CBA had to stop the player drain to foreign shores. Although Blake, who has served as a consultant to the CBA, later said that he had nothing to do with the CBA's overseas transfer fee policy, it was ironic that this very rule was implemented shortly thereafter. Initially the transfer fee was U.S.$5,000 and increased as the season progressed. In 1997 the first increment on the transfer fee schedule was U.S.$17,500, which was increased as the season progressed to $25,000. The transfer fee payments can be expected to increase each year. As Jim Sleeper, the CBA player-personnel wizard, stated:

"The transfer fee has probably helped stabilize our (CBA) rosters - foreign clubs that pay it are definitely serious about wanting the player. It discourages contracted players to jump and just take any overseas job. Overall it's probably been positive from the CBA club's point of view."

The CBA player contract has also been controversial. While attending a seminar in Los Angeles organized by the National Sports Law Institute at Marquette University, I spoke with several sports lawyers, including James Gray, the assistant director of that organization. I showed them the CBA contract, and the informal consensus of this group was that it contained similarities to the old major league "reserve clause" which automatically renewed itself each year without the player's approval and was thrown out in baseball's free agency decisions years ago.

Ray Owes

Regarding CBA contract issues, I was involved in a situation in December 1997 involving Ray Owes, whom I have placed in the Australian NBL on two separate occasions. Owes, a talented 6'9 forward out of the University of Arizona, signed with the Florida Beachdogs of the CBA in September 1995, although was never enthused about playing in the CBA. I was advised by Arizona assistant coach Jim Rosborough that Owes was hoping to play overseas.

Acting on the information from Rosborough, I called Owes four days before the opening of the 1995 CBA training camps. He expressed strong interest in going to Australia, as he had visited there with the Arizona team on tour. I then contacted Ian Stacker, the coach at Geelong in the Australian NBL, David Claxton at the Gold Coast, and Brendan Joyce at Illawarra. I needed an answer on Owes in 24 hours and under those rush circumstances, only Geelong was able to make an official offer the next day. Owes signed the contract immediately and I informed the CBA V.P. for Basketball Operations, Clay Mosher, what had transpired. Mosher grudgingly agreed that Owes should be cleared to play overseas but had no other choice as the player had never reported to the Florida Beachdog camp and the overseas contract was signed in advance of the opening day of CBA training camps. On this occasion, Ray Owes was subsequently cleared by the CBA via USA Basketball and he played the 1996 season in the Australian NBL, being named to the first all-league team.

Returning to the U.S. from Australia in September 1996, Owes was invited to Golden State's vets' camp. He impressed them, and stuck the entire season, playing in 57 NBA games. Owes was disappointed that he had not received guaranteed money from Golden State in a 1997-98 contract offer. He therefore turned down the Warrior "make good" contract proposal and did not go the NBA training camp in October 1997. In July, prior to his decision to pass up the NBA offer, I had presented him with a firm $250,000 one-season offer from a Japanese club. He also turned down that opportunity which required less than seven months of work. In the meantime, the new CBA franchise in Boise, Idaho, had obtained Owes' CBA rights from the defunct Florida Beachdogs.

Ray Owes then went through a period of further uncertainty, as many players do. He finally called me in October 1997 to confirm his possible interest in playing in Australia in the 1998 NBL season, which ran January through July. He also was considering a $150,000 offer from a club in the professional Spanish ACB, but instead he signed a contract with the Townsville Suns on October 26 for much less. The CBA's Idaho Stampede had given a strong pitch for Ray to come to its camp starting on October 30, but he did not report.

As Ray Owes' NBL Australia agent, I made application on the player's behalf to USA Basketball and FIBA, the process required for players asking clearance from an NBA team. I received notice of the clearance, which was granted on November 7. However, a couple of days later I received a call from Eric Chapman, the player personnel director with the Stampede, informing me that his club would block the clearance and demand a transfer fee from the Australian club. I replied that I did not see that the CBA had anything to do with this transaction, as Owes had been previously cleared by Florida in 1995.

On November 17, I received a fax from USA Basketball stating that Ray Owes' original Letter of Clearance had been rescinded, based on information from Wade Morehead of the CBA office in Denver. I called USA Basketball and was referred to the FIBA Eligibility Committee in Germany. I then faxed a letter to FIBA with a copy to Townsville, the Australian club in waiting, and Basketball Australia. I stated the facts of the case as follows:

1. Ray Owes signed a CBA contract with Florida in 1995, but did not report to camp as he had signed, prior to the opening day of CBA camps, a contract with Geelong in Australia.

2. The CBA cleared Ray Owes and USA Basketball issued the official clearance from Florida on December 1, 1995.

3. Idaho obtained the player's rights from defunct Florida in the summer of 1997.

4. Owes signed a contract with the Townsville Suns of the Australian NBL on October 26, 1997, and did not report to the CBA training camp on October 30.

5. USA Basketball issued the Letter of Clearance on November 7, rescinded it on November 17 as a result of the CBA intervention. (Note: it was reissued on November 19 after my [agent] appeal to FIBA representative Christel Lindow-Dodmeier in Germany.)

The overseas transfer fees have apparently become an important source of cash flow to the CBA office and to league teams. I understood that it was the CBA policy that these two parties - the league and the club - split the revenues from the international transfers. The above situation with Ray Owes was an example of a CBA team attempting to secure the fee without any reasonable position, as the player had been cleared from the same contract two years before, had never reported to a CBA training camp, and had never played in the CBA.

The Transfer Fee and CBA Cash Flow

The CBA has had many marketing and logistical challenges and I have always been an advocate of basketball in that league, even though I did not agree with all aspects of the overseas transfer fee system. I could see that the CBA had every right to seek transfer fees during the course of the season, from training camp to the end of the playoffs. The fact was that, even though a team may have been eliminated early in the playoffs or may not even have made the playoffs, all players - whether involved in the playoffs or not, were still bound to the transfer fee until the end of playoff series.

I imagine that the logic of this was based on the possibility of a player unconsciously letting down in the playoffs to get overseas as soon as possible and not giving his all at the end of the season. Or maybe it was just good business on the part of the CBA, as European teams were also in championship modes at this point in their season and wanted players urgently and immediately; thus some have agreed to pay the CBA fee.

I can also understand the CBA's thinking behind the transfer fee, which was intended to be a deterrent to players packing their bags and leaving their CBA contracts for better paying overseas jobs. I have seen teams devastated, virtually overnight, by players defecting. I recall driving to the Quad-Cities in February of 1993 to see the Thunder defend its home turf at the old Wharton Fieldhouse in Moline against Eric Musselman's Rapid City

Thrillers, who went into the Quad game with a 29-4 record. Musselman, known for his player personnel expertise, obtained a league record 28 draft choices in the 1993 CBA draft and always had a roster full of ex-NBA players in Thriller uniforms. That day was no exception. Fennis Dembo, Wes Mathrews, John Morton, Shelton Jones, George Ackles, and Stanley Brundy had all played in the NBA and were at the time drawing CBA paychecks from Rapid City. Quad held on to win, 104-101, behind the amazing athleticism of Harold Ellis, but four starters abandoned Rapid City the next day to accept overseas contracts.

The transfer fee has slowed the slippage from CBA contract obligations to foreign shores. But also, I can see the possibility of some major snags in player movement, should European clubs decide to employ the CBA contract model and transfer fee policy in clearing American players back to the CBA. For example, the CBA could charge an Italian club a $20,000 transfer fee on a player who left his CBA club and played in Italy. However, if the Italian club refused to release the player back to the CBA or NBA without at least reimbursement of the initial $20,000 transfer fee, it could get more confusing and bureaucratic than ever. In fact, the National Basketball League in Australia has implemented a new transfer-fee policy for NBL players wishing to break their Australian contract for NBA opportunities. The NBL has followed the CBA's lead on this matter.

The IBA - International Basketball Association

Because of the financial difficulties in most CBA franchises and with only nine teams having competed in the 1997-98 season, a newcomer known as the IBA has been finding a niche. The "International" Basketball Association, may be stretching reality with a lone Canadian team, Winnipeg, in the competition. Nevertheless the presence of Winnipeg justified the ceremonial playing of the Canadian National Anthem prior to IBA games. The league standard of play has been shown to be a couple of notches below the CBA in terms of talent, especially among bigger players. While the CBA has attracted a large number of ex-NBA players to its rosters each year, the IBA was fielding teams composed of rookies with solid college backgrounds, but casualties at CBA veterans' camps.

Des Moines, one of this country's very best supporters of minor league professional sports, had an IBA team in the 1997-98 and 1998-99 seasons and led the eight-team league in attendance with a reported average of 3,300 fans per game. The Dragons, the Des Moines IBA franchise, had successive home gates with over 5,500 in attendance. In IBA language, that is huge. Glen Duhon, a veteran ex-college coach from McNeese State, was named head coach of the Dragons. He used his 30 years of experience effectively. He combined solid coaching with savvy player management and took the Dragons to the playoffs.

Owners Dick Giesen and Paul Miller along with Tim Kelly, Dragons' general manager, had exercised sound judgment in hiring both Duhon, who had coached Joe Dumars at McNeese State, and Mike Born, as a playing assistant coach. Born was a popular local athlete who had played at Iowa State with a career highlight of back-to-back games of 26 points vs. Kansas and Oklahoma State in 1989. He also had a brief overseas playing experience in France and Germany. One of Mike Born's most unique achievements as a player was his 17 for 17 shooting night - 46 total points - while playing for Marathon Oil at the University of Massachusetts in 1990. Born was never able to duplicate that game performance in the IBA. He was, however, a double-figure scorer and combined effectively as a player-assistant with Duhon. The Des Moines franchise was a first year success, actually a (minor) sensation in the world of minor league sports.

The Des Moines Dragons were slaying opponents on a consistent basis in 1997-98 until Rosell Ellis, the team's most productive scorer and leading rebounder, lost his temper at a home game and grabbed an unsuspecting referee in a head lock. Ellis was subsequently suspended from league play for the balance of the season. His loss spelled the end of any Dragons title hopes. It was a disastrous situation, as Ellis and the Dragons were dominating opponents and on course to win the league in their first year as an IBA franchise.

While the Ellis situation in the IBA was unfortunate, the Kenny Pratt incident was bizarre. Pratt, a 6'3 power forward and no stranger to problems, had been an outstanding player for Tim Floyd at Iowa State in 1995-96 and 1996-97, as a double-figure scorer and consistent all-around player. He played much bigger than his 6'3 stature, with great heart, and had no trouble scoring on players 5-6 inches taller in the Big Eight Conference. He had been previously arrested and jailed in Ames for a few days on a disputed case involving drinking and driving. Pratt returned to Iowa as a member of the IBA's Fargo Bees for a play-off game in Des Moines in February 1998.

I arrived at the game just before tip-off, played at Dowling High School as the regular 10,000 seat Vets Auditorium was not available that night. I noticed police officers stationed at the two exits near the court and asked Jay Goodman, former Utah State standout and Dragons official, what was going on. He said that Kenny Pratt was to be taken back to Ames after the game by the police to pay a past-due fine from the previous arrest. Apparently the police had conferred with Pratt before the game and had agreed to let him play and then take care of the fine business afterwards. But when the game ended, Pratt sprinted out of the gym and jumped into a van. The van driver sped away but later denied that he knew that Pratt was running from the police. However, an O.J. Simpson-like chase developed on a local freeway. Finally, Pratt turned himself in and apparently served some jail time after the season. The Ellis suspension and the Pratt chase were not the norm in the Dragons season, but a memorable part of it.

In addition to the Ellis and Pratt adventures in the IBA, and in spite of Darryl Dawkins' presence as head coach of the Winnipeg Cyclones, the team that made the league name accurate, Coach Kevin Mackey has to be considered the most colorful of all the IBA participants. Mackey got his start as a high school coach in Boston and then became an assistant to Tom Davis at Boston College in 1977. He taught at a junior high school as he was not earning enough at BC to make ends meet. Mackey worked for Dr. Tom for 6 years, all 20-win seasons, and recruited future NBA players Michael Adams and John Bagley. He later built a 144-67 record at Cleveland State but was fired in August of 1990 after a drunk-driving arrest. Mackey entered drug-alcohol rehab and received some very damaging publicity about his life style.

Since the days at Cleveland State, Coach Mackey went to Korea for a while and has kept busy in the minor leagues. He took the reins of the Mansfield Hawks for the 1998-99 IBA season. I saw him and his team in action at Des Moines and he looked about the same: city guy with black suit, thick around the middle, shuffle-strut, cocky and in-charge, but doing a good job in the Greyhound league. His team played hard, moved the ball, and were pulling in the same direction. Mackey looked to be a good fit and at home on a pro basketball sideline. He also looked to be the type of guy who would question why he's not in the bigs.

The keys to success in the International Basketball Association, to date, have been low budget (total player salary cap at $27,000 in 1997-98), short season (December-February), and hungry players. However, minor league hoops have proven to be a tough sell anywhere. Once that survival formula has been tampered with and egos have prevailed, current CBA financial issues (too much money going out, not enough coming in) could sink the IBA - an honorable attempt at a minor professional basketball league.

The IBA, with humility and fiscal sense as its critical ingredients, seemed to be on track for league expansion and another year of competition. Des Moines, Iowa, could be the best minor league sports market in the U.S. Area fans have made triple-A baseball, minor-league hockey, and arena football winners in this relatively small market. The encouraging first year response to the Dragons and IBA basketball was yet another example. It was surprising that the CBA had not previously tested the potential for success in the Des Moines market.

Finding the Right Player - The Overseas Tryout

I have always considered (some) CBA and IBA players as ideal candidates for overseas jobs. In fact, I thought that Rosell Ellis had a good future overseas, even though the suspension was publicized worldwide (in the *FIBA Magazine* in Europe) and had become an obstacle, probably temporary, to his future. I was always looking for overseas prospects in CBA camps and on team rosters. These pros were more mature than most players right off a college campus.

Sam Johnson, 6'8 out of San Diego State and with minor league pro experience, was one such player and I had recommended him for a job with Japan Energy Basketball Club in July, 1995. I flew out to Stanford University for the three-day tryout, in which ten players competed for one or two six-figure job(s). The club was requiring that the two incumbents try out and compete to retain their contracts with the Japanese team. Richard Lucas and Trevor Wilson had been in the two U.S. import spots in the previous season. Lucas, a 6'7 paint player from the University of Oregon, survived the tryout and was offered a new contract, while UCLA's Wilson was replaced by NBA journeyman Alex Stivrins.

My player, Sam Johnson, was the most versatile player and possibly the best athlete of the group, but he did not play well until the last workout, which was too late. Sam had been a solid contributor with Omaha in the CBA, but I was concerned that his game was too team oriented and his value too subtle to win the job. He knew how and when to step out and screen to clear a shooter for an open shot; he was a solid inside-outside defender; and he was unselfish and passed intelligently out of double teams. Although not a great scorer, Sam Johnson was an effective paint player with range to fifteen feet on the jump shot. He was also capable of getting to the ball quickly on the glass, and he did other things as well as, or better, than score and I feared that this could hurt his chances in the tryout. I was right. Japan Energy selected Alex Stivrins, a reliable left-handed jump shooter, to team with incumbent Richard Lucas with Sam Johnson as alternate, which was of no value to the player, or his agent.

Ron Adams had introduced me to Masao Montonaga, who was accompanied by Tadashi Ota and Akira Takagi at the Stanford tryout. These three gentlemen were in town to pick the right players to strengthen their team back in Tokyo. Also, Al Klein, who was the head coach at Menlo College, was working in a consulting capacity to the Japanese club in the player-selection process. The next year, in 1997, Klein was appointed head coach at Japan Energy and returned to California in the off-season on recruiting business. However, the job was short-lived as Japan Energy overspent and dropped its basketball team at the end of the 1998 season.

Finding the right U.S. talent, who can adjust and produce at the overseas site, not just in the tryout for the job, has been a never-ending process for the overseas club. The American athlete who can play at the same level in the uncertainty of a foreign environment as he has in the security of familiar surroundings is a valuable and rare commodity to an agent and to overseas teams. I have heard on many occasions the complaints of foreign coaches: "He is not the same player here. He was much better when we scouted him in the U.S."

The selection of the American player can make or break the coach and his team. I can speak from personal experience on the importance of selecting the right import player, especially with a team that has limited local talent. My choice of Steve Carfino in Hobart in 1986 was a "make" decision, while only two years later my decision to bring in Kelvin Scarborough turned out to be a "break" decision.

Brian Kerle, the Brisbane Bullet coach, was in a recruiting mode, as he faced such a decision in selecting an American point guard for Australian NBL play in 1990. A veteran NBL coach, Kerle knew that the decision made on the import player would determine the fate of his Bullet team.

□*13*□

NATIONAL TEAMS, CLUB TEAMS, AND JOHN LUCAS

In November 1989, the Brisbane Bullets of the Australian National Basketball League were playing a pre-season game in Ames, Iowa, against Johnny Orr's Iowa State Cyclones. Orr's team featured the bulky, yet skilled Victor Alexander. After his college eligibility, big Victor immediately became a rich man, but also an unrecognizable name in NBA box scores, so unrecognizable that after four low, double-figure scoring seasons as his NBA bench mark, Alexander moved on to Europe, where he has had questionable impact.

I was especially interested in the Brisbane-Iowa State game because of the presence of Derek Rucker in the Bullet line-up. In the spring of 1989 Ron Righter, former Iowa assistant and head coach at Clarion University in Pennsylvania, had recommended Rucker to me. Coach Righter said that Iowa had recruited Rucker, the six-foot scoring point guard, but that he had eventually played at Division I Davidson College, a private school, respected for its academic standards. Derek Rucker, the son of former NFL player Reggie Rucker, had been an Academic All-American selection at Davidson in Economics and was a potent Division I backcourt player. He also spent some time in the Cavaliers camp system. Rucker was at home in Cleveland when I contacted him to participate with Brisbane in a tryout situation on the Australian club's 1989 U.S. college tour. Brisbane Coach Brian Kerle had also included Andre LaFleur, former NCAA assist king and feeder-to-scorer Reggie Lewis at Northeastern University, on the tour to compete for the point guard job. Thus Derek Rucker and Andre LaFleur, both talented players, were going head-to-head, but as teammates, for the same job with the Bullets.

Kerle left me tickets for the game with seats behind the Bullets bench. I was most interested in seeing Rucker and LaFleur compete. In the pre-game announcements, the Iowa State public address man announced the Australian visitors as "The Australian National Team." I was shocked, then amused, and later became disgusted with the team introduction. I knew that the normal patriotic refereeing job was to follow, a fact that foreign touring teams have come to expect on U.S. college tours, with the favor returned when American teams travel abroad.

The Brisbane Bullets was a club team which participated in the "professional" National Basketball League of Australia. I have qualified the word professional because salaries were (and always will be) much lower than what Americans term professional, as in the NBA. Average player salaries in Australia were about 60,000 Australian dollars per season. The highest pay in the Aussie league goes to Australian-born National Team players. These select few make A$100-A$160,000 per season, while U.S. import players earned from A$60,000-$135,000. The final measure for the exact amount was always determined by proven or perceived worth to their respective teams. First-year Americans start at the low end. If they happen to have NBA experience, CBA all-star status, or a strong European record of achievement, the U.S. player could attract a higher first-year wage.

If the Brisbane Bullets were, as introduced, The National Team of Australia, then it would have been permissible to call Iowa State University the National Team of the United States, i.e., Dream Team. I doubted that Iowa State in its entire basketball history had a player make the U.S. National Team, with the exception of Jeff Grayer in the 1988 Olympics and Pan-American Games representative Gary Thompson back in 1959. U.S. colleges and the media from coast-to-coast have through the years used the National Team label incorrectly on printed schedules, in pre-game introductions, in post-game reports, and in publishing scores.

The National Team terminology error could be connected to the fact that back in the 1970s foreign countries did send their National Teams to compete against U.S. colleges. However, as foreign basketball became stronger and U.S. college squads were over-matched by overseas national teams, club teams replaced the nationals as tour opponents. The host-college public relations people have been slow - some have yet to make the adjustment - to acknowledge the change in name and degree of competition. Foreign teams have impressed American college coaches with two things for certain: in addition to athleticism and the inside game (trademarks of college basketball), maturity and the 3-point field goal (trademarks of foreign teams) were critical factors in winning consistently in highly competitive basketball. I would not have identified the "National Team" terminology mistake as arrogance, but more parochialism and professional carelessness by U.S. basketball offices, athletic directors, sports information directors, and the press.

Basketball Outside the School System

The club system, as opposed to the school system of competitive junior basketball (junior high-high school age), has been used for decades in foreign countries. Basketball clubs have been organized outside of the scope of the school systems in Europe, Asia, Australia, and South America. It has been, in many cases, the norm to subsidize, i.e., to pay junior players who have signed contracts and have committed to their respective clubs, even at age 14, 15, or 16. The young player there has competed for that particular club and progressed through the system of Under-14, Under-16, Under-18, and Under-20 competition. However, at any point a talented player could be moved up to the higher-paying Senior Team. He then competed in the country's strongest competition, often a professional league, which may not pay players more than $25,000 per season. However, player salaries in Greece, Spain, Italy, and France can, in special cases, be competitive with some NBA financial packages. In the Spanish pro league, the ACB, six-figure player salaries have been common and at the high end could equal the NBA buck.

Real Madrid, the most prestigious of Spanish clubs, maintains a junior development structure starting with 12-year-olds and fielding under-14, under-16, and under-18 teams that compete locally and in other countries. At the top of the basketball section at Real Madrid is the professional team, which pays its players very well. Even though the basketball team is always one of the best in Europe, the Real Madrid *futbol* (soccer) team is the organization's top priority and provides most of the financial support for basketball. In fact, when I visited Madrid in January of 1998, the RM soccer team was down and club officials were concerned about meeting basketball budget needs. Spanish ACB teams can use three foreign players and occasionally import a coach. George Karl, the American NBA coach, spent time in the Spanish ACB as Real Madrid's head coach.

I had a good talk about the club system of basketball in November 1997 with Neil Gliddon, the veteran Director of Coaching with the South Australia Institute of Sport in Adelaide. I have scheduled games in the Midwest for several years for this organization's junior teams. Gliddon had just returned from a trip to Europe and was coaching an under-20 women's team on a six-game tour with Iowa college teams. We discussed at length the club system in Croatia, home country for NBA players Dino Radja, Toni Kukoc and Stojan Vrankovic.

Gliddon said that in talking with Croatian basketball officials he found that Croatian basketball clubs followed the normal routine of signing players at age 13 and 14, similar to Real Madrid in Spain. The clubs also made it a practice to re-sign the top talents again at age eighteen to a five- or six-year contract. The process assured that the top prospects not be lost to another club or to a higher-paying job in another country.

The re-signing at age eighteen was a clever tactic. Most eighteen-year-olds have just begun to develop as players and would have had little knowledge of opportunities elsewhere, unless they had already established a reputation through junior international competition or had been moved up to the men's professional team. The re-signing process was a particularly effective business move to keep talent at home in that the Bosman Rule, which allowed players with passports from Western European countries to compete as local players in other countries in Europe, created an "open-season" atmosphere in recruiting young players. Before the Bosman Rule was implemented, a player with an Italian passport was considered a foreign player in France or any other European country and had to compete against American players for the limited two-player import slot. However, the Bosman Rule made all players with European passports, known as Europlayers or EC players (the 15-member European Community), eligible to compete in other countries as local players, a huge advantage in terms of European player job security and salary.

Paul Rogers - An International Experience

Paul Rogers knew about the Bosman Rule and took full advantage of his dual citizenship status. He was born in Adelaide, Australia, played junior basketball down-under and college basketball in the U.S., and used the NBA draft along with an English passport as his ticket to a high-paying job in Spain. An interesting case of the Bosman Rule in action involved the seven-foot Aussie Rogers. He played three years at Gonzaga University in Spokane, Washington, and then passed on remaining college eligibility to enter the 1997 NBA draft.

Selected by the Los Angeles Lakers in the second round as their 54th pick, he went to camp but needed some more seasoning. Rogers had family ties in the United Kingdom and had been issued both an Australian passport and later a "golden" English passport, golden because the English passport made Rogers a Euro-player and thus able to take full advantage of the Bosman Rule. He signed in 1997 with *Real Madrid* in Spain, one of Europe's premier clubs, for a reported $500,000 per season, double the value of a minimum-salary NBA contract. But without that English passport, Rogers would have been, at best, a $100,000 per-year player in the Australian NBL or a $1,200 per week CBA player, with NBA call-up potential, in the United States.

I saw Rogers play limited minutes in the *Real Madrid-Estudiantes* game in Madrid in January of 1998. When I spoke with him briefly after his team's loss to the other Madrid team in a Euro-game, Estudiantes, he seemed upset with his limited minutes and confused over his role on the team. Nevertheless, with his substantial contract, he could probably learn to endure the adjustment to European coaching and refereeing, and sort out his playing role on the way to the bank. Rogers might be tempted to return to Australia to play in the Olympics in spite of the big money in Spain. Big Paul played for the Boomers in the 1998 World Championships in Athens, and the Sydney Olympics in 2000 could serve as strong motivation for Rogers to take a huge pay cut and sign with an Australian team for the 1998-99 and 1999-2000 seasons to assure selection to the Australian National Team.

I attended the Spanish game with Javier Artime, a public relations consultant working with professional basketball agent Arturo Ortega, in Madrid. Ron Adams, then of the Trailblazers, knew I was going to Spain and introduced us in advance of my trip. While we were watching the game, I mentioned George Karl to Javier, who frowned. He said that Spanish club officials did not understand, nor necessarily agree with, Karl's coaching techniques when he was at Real Madrid. I was not surprised by the comment, as most American coaches (I have been there) have never fully convinced their foreign hosts that they, the Americans, actually knew what they were doing. There are exceptions, of course, but precious few.

George Karl - *Habla Español*?

George Karl took his great basketball background as a player and coach to the Real Madrid job for the 1989-90 and 1991-1992 Spanish professional seasons. Having played for Dean Smith at North Carolina and also three years as a pro in the American Basketball Association, Karl sandwiched a 50 win 6 loss Continental Basketball League (CBA) coaching record between his two seasons in Spain. Winning 50 of 56 games was a miraculous achievement in professional coaching at any level, IBA, CBA, or NBA. Prior to signing with Real Madrid in 1989, Karl had four years of NBA head coaching experience with Cleveland and Golden State.

Since the Real Madrid job, Karl had taken the Seattle Supersonics to seven consecutive playoff appearances before being fired after the 1998 season - the fate of all NBA coaches who don't get over the hump and win a championship. His Seattle teams won more games during that stretch than any NBA team except the Chicago Bulls. In other words, George Karl was a very good American professional coach by any standard when he took the Real Madrid job. Still, the Spanish were reluctant to concede that Karl was doing a good job with the Real Madrid team.

That evening in Madrid as I watched Real Madrid and Estudiantes play a slow, half-court game, I could only imagine what George Karl had been through in attempting any fast-breaking tactics. I can recall the controversy that I had caused with Sporting of Lourenço Marques in 1973 when I put in a half-court trapping defense for a particular opponent. Headlines in the Portuguese paper the next day, after our victory, read simply: "PRESS-ING?" In spite of the success of the tactic, the local paper was critical of "risky, revolutionary coaching techniques" by the American, Dave Adkins.

Another common practice in the club basketball system in Europe has been to assign the outstanding teen-aged player to a lesser men's league and/or to a U.S. college for further development. For example 6'10 Ricky Peral, who finished his NCAA eligibility at Wake Forest in 1997, developed his game as a junior in the Spanish club system. Although clearly a prospect for the ACB, Spain's highly competitive Division I professional league, Peral needed time to mature. He played in the less financial EBA, the Spanish second division, before moving on to Wake Forest. However, George Karl (*This Game's the Best*) mentioned that Ricky Peral at age 16 had also been with Real Madrid, the first division Spanish power, prior to his NCAA experience at Wake Forest.

Innocence Abroad

Ricky Peral played junior basketball in Spain, a country which had one of the most highly developed pro leagues in Europe. *Julius Michalik*, who played for four years at Iowa State, hailed from Slovakia. Whereas top players in the Spanish ACB could draw salaries of $150,000 - $500,000 per season, and more, Michalik came from Slovakia where the better players were making around $30,000 per season, or less.

Michalik, a skilled 6'9 forward, was a precocious teen-ager and a valuable senior-league player at a younger age. His talents were outstanding relative to the level of senior competition in Slovakia and reliable sources have reported that he played for a club in his country's top league prior to his four years at Iowa State. It was, of course, not unusual in such a situation for a talented young guy to pick up respectable pay checks from his club's senior team before entering a U.S. college.

Another former Big Eight Conference player who had developed in the European club system was *Pekka Markkanen* of Finland. He gave the Kansas Jayhawks an inside target in the 30-5 season in 1989-90. Markannen played only one season at Kansas before returning to his club in Finland. Markkanen, like Michalik in Slovakia, was an unusual commodity as a junior player in his home country of Finland, which played very average basketball. With his size and mobility, Pekka Markkanen was able to play in senior men's leagues in Finland as a teen-ager. While playing at Kansas, rumors persisted that Markkanen was receiving regular paychecks from his club in Finland, expedited through an agent in Kansas City. (The agent himself told me of the payment system).

I asked *Petri Rosenquist*, a European agent based in Stockholm, if that rumor was true about Markkanen. Rosenquist replied that he could not confirm it, but he didn't doubt it and it would not have been unusual. However, he did qualify his statement by saying that Markkanen never made a great deal of money in Finland - "probably less than $30,000 for the year." (Note: a figure more than three times the salary paid C.J. Bruton at Perth in 1994.)

Would a club, player or parent in Spain or Italy or France, or even Australia, have advised a young player that he should not participate in his country's basketball system and refuse these normal club payments because of (college) competition rules in another country? In other words, would a European player at age sixteen receiving, for example, U.S.$1,000-$3,000 a month to play club senior ball, have refused this contract because of his fear of disturbing his U.S. college eligibility? The answer was, of course, "no." How would a teen-aged European know what the NCAA rules were, when most of the American member schools can't figure them out?

Has the NCAA put its 500+ pages of rules on the internet translated in Greek, Italian, Spanish, French, Portuguese, etc., or in English? Even if the Overland Park gang had gone to cyberspace, who would have bothered to read this 100% culturally biased set of rules certainly bizarre for players raised in the European club system. It was a long shot that the foreign kid would even know that such rules existed, and even if he did, what was the big deal? Hundreds of foreigners from the European (overseas) club system, which routinely contracted and paid young players, have played in U.S. colleges through the years. *The World Basketball Club Almanac* archives showed a steady, annual increase in the number of non-American players on Division I rosters over the past decade with 262 *estrangeiros* (from foreign shores) in pre-season 1997-98, while *Sports Illustrated* reported yet a higher figure. Regardless of the exact number, it was clear that hundreds of foreign players had taken advantage of the opportunity to play NCAA Division I basketball and that this trend was continuing.

The highest player salaries, outside of the NBA, are paid in the top competition in Greece, Italy, Spain, France, Turkey, Japan, etc. It is only common sense to assume that a junior player, good enough to play U.S. Division I college ball, would take advantage of the everyday business of his country's basketball system and would have accepted his own market value in his country's club system. Why wouldn't he? Further, if a player came through the club system in Italy or Spain, it was safe to assume that he would have received more money earlier in his career than in a country such as Luxembourg, near the bottom of European club system in player salaries.

Australian Amateur Junior Development

The Australian NBL has never been in the top ten countries in the world in terms of player salaries outside of the NBA. They do not have a typically European club system, in that its junior basketball has remained totally amateur. Under-12-year-old through under-20-year-old competition, and other junior teams, are not tied contractually to NBL professional teams, as they could be in Europe. The only exception was that if a junior player, as in the case of Andrew Gaze, or Tony Ronaldson, or David Stiff, or Michael

Pennisi, or Craig McAndrews, or C.J. Bruton, showed unusual promise and signed with an NBL team as a teen-ager. Of these six players, who had virtually the same backgrounds in Australian basketball, only C.J. Bruton ran afoul of the NCAA and was declared ineligible **before** he was able to compete at a U.S. college. C.J. Bruton, like many under-aged Australian players, had accepted a contract in the NBL less than the value of many Division I college scholarships in the U.S.

Foreign National Teams - Elite Players

While club teams form the core of competitive overseas basketball leagues, National Teams consist of the best players from the clubs selected to represent their respective countries in international competition. Using the Australian system as an example, the National Team program has a system of talent identification throughout Australia including the AIS (Australian Institute of Sport) where full-time coaches work for twelve months of the year with talented young players on AIS scholarships. National Teams throughout the world pay their players, of course, and many have been composed of players with NBA experience.

The Nationals are thus the best, strongest, most mature, professional players in that particular country's system of basketball competition. However, National Team selection can be very political, and usually is, so on occasion, a country's best might never have worn his country's colors. Thus, the Iowa State announcer, and many of his compatriots around the country, have totally missed the mark in regard to objectivity and accuracy in the classifying of the visiting foreign club teams as National Teams through the years.

As the 1989 Brisbane-Iowa State game progressed and the local referees, with an eye to future Big Eight refereeing contracts, did their patriotic best, Iowa State got the expected win. I was impressed with both Rucker and LaFleur. They were scoring point guards who could get their teammates involved, but still could take over in critical possessions. LaFleur was stronger and Rucker quicker; both were potent perimeter shooters. However, I was representing Rucker, not Andre LaFleur, and put in a plug for Derek with Brisbane Coach Kerle after the game. I also suggested to Derek that he look particularly hard for Simon Kerle, the son of coach and selector Brian Kerle, filling the lanes on the break.

Derek Rucker was eventually awarded the Brisbane contract and has gone on to an outstanding Australian career, a first-team all-league selection currently on a long-term contract with the West Sydney Razorbacks. After the Brisbane tour, I received a call from Andre LaFleur who asked if I could help him land an NBL job. He had labored in the obscurity of the Australian CBA, National II, and wanted to move up. I agreed and felt that Andre had proven himself as a player in Australia and deserved an NBL contract. Although it was unusual for an American playing in the second-division in Australia to move up to the NBL, I finally convinced David Claxton to sign LaFleur, who became a consistent producer at the Gold Coast and with the Illawarra Hawks. He produced for seven years at 20 points per game, 9.5 assists, 80% free throws, 43%-3 point shooting, and 50% field goals as career stats.

Quad-City Thunder Camp

With Derek Rucker and Andre LaFleur fully employed in the Australian NBL, I continued to work from my Des Moines office on new overseas prospects. In August 1993 I took Leon Trimmingham, Cameron Dickinson, and Ron Bayless to a free-agent camp with the Quad City Thunder of the CBA. The workouts were held at Marycrest College in Davenport, Iowa, and at The Mark, a 9,500 seat arena in Moline, Illinois, and home base for the Thunder. Dan Panaggio, son of legendary CBA coach Mauro Panaggio, was the head coach and Mike Mashak, later named head man at Rockford, was Dan's assistant along with ex-NBA great Mo Cheeks.

When we arrived for the weekend camp, I talked with Mo Cheeks about Ron Bayless, the quick six-foot point guard from Iowa State. I thought that Cheeks, as a former point guard of similar size, might like Bayless. But that weekend Ron appeared to lack game fitness and struggled at the offensive end. At the end of the weekend, Panaggio invited all three - Dickinson, Trimmingham, and Bayless - to Quad's veterans' camp, and especially liked Dickinson's perimeter game and his ability to run the court as a 6'5 off-guard. In the first practice session, Dicko was running offense with one of the less talented groups (unconscious phenotype error by Coach Panaggio- "red-headed dude, can't be a player") and was getting frustrated. But Dickinson himself fixed that, as I saw him in a conference at midcourt with Panaggio. Soon after, and regardless of the color of his hair, he was working with the good players. Dicko had learned at an early age, running loose on the streets of Melbourne, that he had to look out for himself.

Sir Leon

The sensation of the Thunder camp was Leon Trimmingham, the 6'7 athlete from St. Croix in the Virgin Islands. I had seen Leon play in Des Moines against Dickinson's team at Grand View College and was very impressed with his natural talent. However, Briar Cliff College used him as a post player and he showed very limited footwork at both ends of the court. But Leon was an athlete: he jumped very high and very quickly, had a nice frame with great muscular definition. He was a great looking physical speci-

men. In recruiting Trimmingham, I had invited him to my home in the summer after his senior year to discuss his career plans. We were in a serious
discussion, with Leon seated on the couch in the living room with his well-
formed, shaved head glistening. My German shorthair pointer could not
resist. She edged up behind Leon and gave his bald pate a thorough, enthusiastic lick. I wondered if that had ever happened in the board room of
David Falk discussing contract terms with Michael Jordan.

At one point in the Quad camp, all 50 players stopped in their tracks
and watched Trimmingham. He had just slammed an offensive rebound
from a flat footed start and word got around. He had previously drawn my
attention in a post-season senior all-star game in Iowa a couple of months
before, when he scored 38 with future NBA player Acey Earle as the opposition. Trimmingham had signed right out of college with an agent in
Chicago, but was disappointed in the arrangement. Nick Nurse invited him
to our Overseas Basketball Services tryout camp at Grand View College earlier that year.

Leon had requested to play the off-guard and small-forward positions at
the camp in a series of full-court, scored, refereed games. At the end, I suggested that he could make a living overseas as a quick 4, a power-forward,
not as a 2-3, a swing-guard, but that he could develop his range and his
face-up game from the wing on his own time. At that stage, Leon was very
impressive physically, but raw in the skill and savvy area. He had only
played basketball since age 16 and was just beginning to learn some important lessons in footwork and offensive technique off the dribble.

The Quad City Thunder later called me about Trimmingham, who asked
me what I thought he should do, even though he had not as yet signed with
me to represent him. He was cautious about the player-agent contract
because of his first experience with the Chicago-based player rep.
Trimmingham told me, "Dave, you get me a job and I know I will move up.
But I don't want to sign until you find me something." I agreed that he
needed a job more than an agent and that I would find him a good place to
start his career.

I felt that he would play very limited minutes as a rookie, if at all, in the
CBA. Also, I left the final decision to the player, but posed the question,
"Which do you prefer - Sydney or Moline?" But I wasn't certain that I could
deliver on the Sydney job because of Leon's lack of pro experience, so I
suggested that he go back home to the Virgin Islands for a while and be
patient until something definite developed.

Dicko Goes Public

Mark Bragg, the Townsville Suns coach in the Australian NBL, was
also present at the Quad camp to look at Cameron Dickinson. He was fully

aware of Dickinson's drug and behavioral problems. I felt confident in recommending Dicko to Townsville as he had shown great progress at Grand View, both on and off the basketball court. It seemed that he had fully committed to his recovery through AA. Coach Mark Bragg agreed to sign Dickinson to a two-year playing contract with the Townsville club under one special condition. Bragg required Dickinson to go public on his past problems upon arrival in Townsville and Dicko agreed to lay it all out in a comprehensive article in the *Townsville Bulletin* newspaper. It was a good move by Bragg, as Cameron had established his identity as a recovering alcoholic-addict on arrival in Townsville and built on that position. There were no secrets about who he was or why he was there, and Dickinson from this experience had begun to learn the value and power of honest, up-front behavior.

I was confident that the Dickinson-Townsville liaison would work for both parties, even though the player was high risk because of his past drug problems. The fact that Coach Mark Bragg was willing to address the issue head-on, in requiring Dickinson to tell his story publicly through the newspaper interview, showed me that the club was going to do its best to work with Dicko. I also liked the business and administrative side of the Townsville operation.

Townsville Sun Basketball Club chairman David Carmichael, a wealthy, self-made businessman, controlled the purse strings. He had appeared on the cover of Australia's *Time Magazine* and was recognized in that publication for his effort and expertise in guiding three automobile dealerships to profitabilty in North Queensland, the source of his fortune. Cut from similar cloth as Rudolf Vanmoerkerke, the Sunair owner from Belgium, and the Wrublewskis from Sydney, each of these unique people had the ability to start a negotiation by putting little on the table and asking much in return, yet at the same time appearing generous. Each was a master intimidator in his own way, and I had learned from every conversation and transaction with them. Thus there had never been a question about the financial leadership in Townsville with David Carmichael in charge.

Called "Boss" by the players, I knew that Dickinson could not con Carmichael and would benefit from his boss's firm position. You always knew where you stood with D.C. and he never minced words with Dickinson - exactly what the player needed. In Dickinson's first year in Townsville, I traveled there to check his progress. I was talking business with David Carmichael at the Suns' Strand Marina office near the arena when we heard car tires squeal in front of the building. Carmichael smiled slightly, looked me in the eye, and said, "Dicko."

In addition to Mark Bragg of the Suns, Bobby Turner, head coach of the Sydney Kings, came to Des Moines in September 1993 to look at Leon

Trimmingham and Mario Donaldson, a former Drake and CBA player. Trimmingham had arrived in Iowa from St. Croix and was working out in preparation for an overseas opportunity. He had been renting a room from Greg Lansing, the Roosevelt High School coach, since departed to Indiana State as an assistant coach. Lansing opened up the Roosevelt gym on a Saturday, and we invited ten local players for a workout, along with Trimmingham and Donaldson. Turner liked what he saw and signed both Trimmingham and Mario Donaldson to play for the Sydney Kings in the 1994 NBL season.

Trimmingham on the Move

To Coach Bob Turner's credit, he was willing to gamble on Leon Trimmingham's athletic ability and overlooked his lack of pro experience. It paid off for Turner and the Kings. The team improved from 11-15 in the previous year to 16-10. Trimmingham had a huge first year in the NBL at 27 points and 12 rebounds per game, and progressed with his skills through liberal playing time and individual workouts. Between the 1995 and 1996 NBL seasons, I was able to arrange through club General Manager Terry Schofield, a job in Braunshweig, Germany. Chet Kammerer, a veteran U.S. college coach and NBA scout, brought Trimmingham's game along further in the German league and played him at the wing position in preparation for future NBA trials.

Also during that period, Trimmingham got an opportunity to show his abilities to an NBA team. At the end of the 1994 season in Australia, John Lucas, on the recommendation of Ron Adams, had decided to take a look at Trimmingham in the Philadelphia 76ers' vets' camp at Franklin and Marshall College in Pennsylvania. I flew out to Philadelphia to the camp. I was greeted at the Franklin and Marshall gymnasium door at the Friday night practice by Coach John Lucas and Assistant Coach Ron Adams. They were enthusiastic about Trimmingham and said that he had created a stir on the first night with a couple of exclamation-point dunks over Shawn Bradley. However, as the camp continued, it was apparent that Leon needed more polish on his wing position skills, even though he had left a definite impression with his natural athletic talent. He returned to the Australian NBL with Sydney in 1995, after the 76er camp appearance, with a better idea of what he needed to work on to become a small forward in the NBA or in a high-level European job.

Leon Trimmingham came from St. Croix, U.S. Virgin Islands, to Briar Cliff College in Sioux City, Iowa. Coach Ray Nacke at Briar Cliff, an NAIA school, had a history of recruiting foreign players, especially from Panama and the Virgin Islands. Trimmingham experienced some severe cultural shock coming from tropical St. Croix to the four seasons and harsh winters in the Midwest.

When the weather started to get cold and the snow fell in the fall of Trimmingham's freshman year, he called home and said he wanted to quit school and come back to St. Croix. LeRoy Trimmingham, his father, confirmed that Leon would in fact stick with his plans, stay in school, adjust, and under no circumstances quit. This was some strong parenting and the firmness has paid off many times over. Leon Trimmingham finished his degree at Briar Cliff, earned NAIA 1st Team All-America honors in basketball there, and has since in his overseas professional career demonstrated the ability to adjust quickly in different countries. He has been able to adapt to the environments of Australia, Germany, the Philippines, Venezuela, and Japan and become immediately productive in the critical first two weeks on the job, a trial period during which clubs make daily checks on new players to determine their value to the team. The disciplined "no" from his father has given Leon Trimmingham the foundation for the "yes" in building a profitable overseas pro career.

Iowa - Fly-over Country, But More

Besides Trimmingham's alma mater, Briar Cliff College, there are 33 other four-year colleges in the state of Iowa, with four of these playing Division I basketball - the University of Iowa, Iowa State, Drake, and Northern Iowa. In addition to opportunities in higher education and an occasional nationally ranked college football and/or basketball team, the state is known for corn, beef, pork, insurance, and high scores by high school students on Scholastic Aptitude Tests (SATs). In fact, in competition with the other 49 states, Iowa students have ranked number one in the country in SAT scores on several occasions. Performing arts are also alive and well in Iowa. Des Moines, the capital, has an excellent symphony orchestra, and Drake University, Grand View College, Grinnell College, Iowa State University, and Simpson College provide a well-rounded area calendar of professional and student plays, operas, and concerts.

While the state of Iowa has had just one native son elected president, several have made names for himself in the NBA. Herbert Hoover of West Branch was the only native Iowan to be elected president of the United States and served from 1929-1933. As Gene Shallit once quipped on the Today Show, "Where are all the Washingtons, Jacksons, and Jeffersons now that this country needs them? Why, of course, they're playing in the NBA." Bob Hanson, Matt Bullard, Larry Creger, Fred Hoiberg, and Loren Meyer, along with Bill Fitch, are some of the state's NBA representatives.

Des Moines was the home of two players who have drawn consistent paychecks in the NBA, Bob Hansen of the Bulls and Matt Bullard of the Rockets. Hanson attended Dowling High School and Bullard went to Valley with both playing collegiately at the University of Iowa. Hansen averaged

15.4 points in 1982-83, his senior year, and was drafted in the third round as the 53rd pick by the Utah Jazz. He played in 575 regular season games over a nine-year span in the NBA. Bob Hansen played an important role in hitting an impact three-pointer in Chicago's game-six victory over Portland en route to the 1992 title. While Matt Bullard ended his college career as an Iowa Hawkeye, he actually started at the University of Colorado. He was off to a fast start in his senior year in 1989-90, but was plagued by injury. Undrafted, Bullard has been skillfully managed by agent Herb Rudoy of Chicago and had been signed as an NBA free agent on several occasions. He has sustained a career as a reliable NBA bench player with Atlanta and the Houston Rockets.

Fred Hoiberg, known as "The Mayor" in his hometown of Ames, averaged 15.8 ppg for his 4-year career at Iowa State and was an all-conference selection. A second-round pick by the Indiana Pacers in 1995, Hoiberg has continued to show NBA promise and stuck with the team for three consecutive seasons. Loren Meyer hails from Ruthven, Iowa, was Hoiberg's teammate at ISU, and was a first-round pick by Dallas in 1995. Meyer was later signed by Denver as a free agent. Still another University of Iowa player, Chris Street, was headed to first-round NBA selection and a pro career. The 6'8 Indianola, Iowa, native was tragically killed in 1993 in a two-vehicle accident three games into the Big Ten season.

One of the most unique single-game performances in major college basketball history in the state of Iowa was recorded by Lafester Rhodes, a 6'8 lefty from Iowa State. Rhodes was rangy and had exceptionally long arms. He released the ball once his body parts were in sync from far behind his head. Lafester raised his scoring average by nearly 20 points per game as he scored 2.8 ppg as a junior and 22.5 ppg as a senior. In the Iowa-Iowa State game in December of 1987, Rhodes led ISU to a 102-100 overtime victory and scored 54 points in converting 21 of 30 field goal attempts. He showed up in Australia at Geelong in 1988 but was cut after two weeks and returned to the U.S. for some part-time work in the CBA and other overseas assignments. The 54-point burst has remained this player's benchmark and only real claim to basketball fame.

Another Iowan with a unique basketball background was Larry Creger. He got an unlikely start to a coaching career in the pros back in the 1950s at Franklin Community High School serving the two tiny Iowa communities of Latimer and Coulter, population unknown. Creger moved to California in 1961, became friends with ex-Boston Celtic Bill Sharman, and was named as Sharman's assistant at both Los Angeles and Utah in the American Basketball Association. Creger, as the Lakers' director of player personnel, engineered the trade which brought Kareem Abdul-Jabbar to L.A. from Milwaukee.

The ex-Iowa high school coach was also remembered as the man who drafted high schooler Moses Malone at Utah in 1974. Larry Creger spent ten years in the big leagues as an assistant coach with four different teams - L.A., Utah, Detroit, and Cleveland. Creger said, "Those are the things that I am known for - the Jabbar trade and the drafting of Malone. Had Bill Sharman's wife not passed away, we still might be on an NBA bench." Larry Creger later worked for 13 years as director of the famous Los Angeles Summer League, the proving ground for many free-agent pros with NBA aspirations. In addition to Larry Creger, Bob Hansen and Matt Bullard, all native Iowans, Rodney "Pop" Wright, originally from Baltimore, also had NBA potential, but had other obstacles in his life. He has settled in Des Moines via his playing career at Drake University.

Jerry Crawford, a lawyer and friend of Pop Wright, had told me, when I returned from Australia in 1989, that Wright was back in Des Moines and was living a productive life, clean and sober. After my previous experiences with him in the Newcastle job, I replied that I doubted it and would have to see it over a period of time to believe it.

I eventually did become a believer and did see Pop Wright start to use his charisma and talents in a positive manner. He had through the past ten years become an asset to the city and a good friend who never ceased to amaze me with his energy and ingenuity. Wright has developed a unique drug and alcohol education lecture program. He was delivering a strong anti-drug message to schools in a four-state area, with his program being sponsored by Hy-Vee Supermarkets. Rodney Wright has turned his life around through his commitment to sobriety, church attendance, and participation in AA and NA support groups in Des Moines.

As college players in the Missouri Valley Conference, Pop Wright and Lewis Lloyd, who averaged 30.2 points in 1979-80 and went on to an NBA career, finished their eligibility at Drake University in 1980. Drake is located in Des Moines about three miles from my Overseas Basketball Services office. A member of the Missouri Valley Conference, Drake established a basketball history having appeared in three-consecutive NCAA tournaments in 1969, 1970, and 1971 under Coach Maury John.

In the NCAA Final Four in 1969, the Drake Bulldogs challenged Lew Alcindor and UCLA in a 85-82 game that went down to the final seconds. I recall walking around the Kubasaki school grounds on the island of Okinawa in a steady rain with a radio pressed to my ear on the day of the Drake-UCLA game in 1969. I was simultaneously supervising physical education classes and listening to the game, which was broadcast live on Armed Forces Radio on Okinawa, and pulling for a miracle upset.

Ron Adams

Those were the glory days, but recent Drake teams have more than struggled. Ron Adams, the defensive consultant for Jerry Tarkanian at UNLV, had been hired to upgrade Coach Rudy Washington's defense in the 1991-92 Drake season. Adams put in his match-up zone defense and it clearly stymied opponents, changed game tempo, and impacted several games. However, the Washington era at Drake was dismal (53-102).

Ron Adams left Drake to join Jerry Tarkanian with the San Antonio Spurs. When Tark was fired at San Antonio, Adams stayed as an assistant to John Lucas with the Spurs and in Philadelphia before joining Portland as East Coast and European scout for the Blazer organization. Adams had previously been the head coach at both Fresno State and at Sunair Basketball Club in Belgium. He had shown insight and interest in the European game and was clearly one of the most respected American coaches on the international scene. Adams has the rare ability to combine a strong background with a low-key teaching approach, along with ethics and humility, rare commodities anywhere - especially in the cut-throat world of top-level professional basketball.

Orv Salmon's Basketball Theories

Orv Salmon, former Missouri player and Drake assistant coach in the Gary Garner years, introduced me to Ron Adams when he first arrived in Des Moines. Salmon did the commentary at Drake games on radio after his coaching days, along with work in his insurance business. He was fond of the term "young players"; listeners could hardly expect "old players" in the college game. Orv had two theories, which he developed with other coaches through the years, and which I think of often in my day-to-day basketball business.

Theory 1: "One Step Back": Many college coaches are most effective at one level below their career objective. Salmon's old boss at Drake, Gary Garner, was a good example. Garner struggled at Drake, but in retrospect was one of the school's most productive coaches. He was, however, fired. Gary Garner came back strong and established a solid program in NCAA II, winning the National Championship at Fort Hayes State in 1996. Lynn Nance was another example. He won the Division II NCAA title at Central Missouri State in 1984 and did a masterful job at St. Mary's College, a mid-Division I. But he was not able to win consistently at either Iowa State of the Big Eight Conference or at the University of Washington in the Pac Ten.

Salmon's Theory 2: "Best of the Worst": Statistics can be deceptive, as a poor team usually has a 20-point scorer. They play 40 minutes and somebody has to score. Thus, Salmon contended that just because the individual stats look good doesn't necessarily mean that the guy was a player. Statistics have been important criteria in assessing a player for overseas jobs. However, the level of competition, where the statistics were produced, had to be factored in also. All overseas clubs are looking for ex-Division I college players with reasonable statistics. The level of competition and individual production within that competition can determine the player's starting point overseas, along with his attitude, athleticism, size, competitiveness, and position.

My "Over There Theory" can come into play in considering the application of the player's game in the U.S. to an overseas setting. I have seen great performances during a tryout for an overseas job in the United States, followed by abject failure on the job in the foreign country. He did it "over here" (U.S.); now can he do it as well or better "over there" (on foreign shores) on a consistent basis? Career U.S. minor-league careers were born from the inability of players to adjust to life in a foreign country. These CBA and IBA lifers have preferred lower-paying familiarity to higher-paying new surroundings.

Orv Salmon's second bit of wisdom, the Best of the Worst Theory, tied in with my "Big Fish Theory." If a player has not thoroughly dominated the competition at a smaller school, then he was suspect. Just because he did dominate weaker competition made that player only less of a suspect, but at times, worthy of further evaluation. In spite of the fact that Leon Trimmingham played at a very small school, he clearly had the physical tools and attitude to go with his college scoring and rebound production. The same had applied to LeRoy Loggins and James Crawford, both NBL Australian legends from obscure U.S. NAIA schools.

Another similar case was Tony Dorsey. He was a two-time MVP in England, who hailed from Southern Tech, also an NAIA school, in Georgia. These small college players were "big-fish" and had the talent and competitiveness to lift their games as the competition improved, and thus became employable pro players in spite of the smaller school background. On numerous occasions in their overseas travels, Loggins, Crawford, and Dorsey have outplayed American players from big-name Division I college programs, CBA stars, and ex-NBA players. A player with a Division I background always had an easier time breaking into a job than the NAIA and Division II athletes. For example, although not from a name school, Melvin Thomas, by virtue of his D-I play at Texas-Pan-American, was easier to place. Also, it helped that Thomas was a great player and carried a 20-point per-game at Pan-American and built on those numbers as an overseas pro in the NBL.

I have done most of my business travel alone, so it was a pleasant change when Orv Salmon or Ron Adams went along. Both were, of course, experienced coaches with basketball insight. Salmon and I discussed our theories and player evaluation on trips to games in Omaha and the Quad-Cities, and would apply them as we watched overseas prospects in CBA uniforms. I traveled to Continental Basketball League (CBA) games frequently. When Ron Adams was at Drake in 1990-91, he went with me a few times to Omaha, the nearest CBA franchise. It was a two-and-a-half-hour drive and we talked basketball non-stop. Never did I hear Adams bag Rudy Washington, who at the end of his tenure had worn out his welcome at Drake, and that would clearly have distinguished Adams from the Des Moines population in general.

I felt that Drake University had given Washington more than a fair chance with plenty of time to get the job done - six long years and a painful, cumulative record of 53-102. Unfortunately, Rudy never really unpacked his bags while in Des Moines at a time when many authentic college coaches would have walked, or crawled, to Des Moines for the Drake job. It was the opinion of many Drake supporters that Washington was more interested in his work with the Black Coaches Association than in winning games at Drake, a legacy which had followed him from his previous job at the University of Iowa, but had been reconfirmed at Drake.

The Drake Dilemma

Washington's successor, Kurt Kanaskie, could dispute my claim regarding the positive nature of the Drake situation. A former LaSalle player and successful Division II head coach at Lock Haven and Indiana of Pennsylvania, Kanaskie had established a 207-107 record over 11 years and had twice won *Basketball Times* Division II Co-Coach of the Year Award. However, his Drake teams won just five games (5-50) in his first two seasons at the helm, including thirty-nine consecutive Missouri Valley Conference losses spanning the 1996-97 and 1997-98 seasons.

While Drake was losing consistently, Division I basketball supporters in the Des Moines area had continued to think that just possibly Kanaskie could turn the corner in his third year (1998-99) as coach. Others felt that the hole was already too deep. Kurt Kanaskie had won other places, knew the game, and appeared to have the patience and character to lift the floundering Drake men's basketball program. He showed unusual poise in the face of the adversity of loss after loss and, overall, had retained credibility among fans. But the losing cannot continue; neither the coach nor the Drake program can endure much more.

I had an experience in the summer of 1996 with Drake when Coach Kanaskie and his coaching staff had just arrived in Des Moines. I had talked with Kanaskie about Travis Lindstrom, an all-state player with a 25 ACT from the state of Washington. I was friends with David Lindstrom, his father, who had been a great player and assistant coach at Puget Sound University with Coach Don Zech. David Lindstrom had been coaching in the Australian NBL for about ten years and was with the Townsville Suns when his son, Travis, graduated from high school. The younger Lindstrom was living in Townsville with his family, as he had decided to wait for a year after high school graduation to enter college. At 6'5 and 200 pounds, Travis was a good athlete and versatile basketball player. I recommended him to Kanaskie, who referred me to assistant coach, Lenny Parham.

I delivered a game tape from Australia to Parham and discussed Travis Lindstrom as a prospect for Drake. About a week later, Parham rang, thanked me, and said that he didn't think that Lindstrom could help them. I retrieved the tape from Drake and had planned to look at it myself; however, when I ran the video, I found that it was on the Australian VHS System and therefore impossible to watch. I went to a local company which converted the tape to the U.S. system. Then, and only then, was I able to view the tape and look at the play of Travis Lindstrom, who I knew could have helped Drake. He accepted a scholarship to Hawaii-Hilo where he was a freshman starter, recorded several double-figure point and rebound games (double-doubles), and was named the team's outstanding newcomer. After one year at Hilo, he used his dual-citizenship to win a contract with the Townsville Suns in the Australian NBL. Drake had gone into Missouri Valley Conference play in 1996-97 and 1997-98 with lesser players than Travis Lindstrom in its starting lineup.

A footnote on Drake basketball: some supporters thought that Drake's on-court problems could be traced directly to school President Michael Ferrari. He departed to a new position at Texas Christian University, a school which had invested in big-time basketball and in a name coach, Billy Tubbs, a high profile coach and an aggressive recruiter, an empire builder. In contrast to the five victories in Ferrari's last two years at Drake, T.C.U., under Tubbs, lost just five times in recording a 27-5 season including a 14-0 mark in the Western Athletic Conference in the 1997-98 regular season. Tubbs was hired at T.C.U. on the basis of his 439-200 record. Always controversial and color-ful, he had won games and influenced gate receipts in previous stops at LaMar and Oklahoma, while Dr. Ferrari's Drake teams had posted an eight-year record of 58-152. Ferrari also was given "credit" for firing Gary Garner, the second-winningest coach in Drake basketball history. Tom Abatemarco was Drake's choice to replace the popular Garner. Abatemarco was a bad fit and was remembered for a player strike and a mid-season dismissal as coach in his second season.

Can the reader visualize a meeting on the T.C.U. campus between Tubbs and Ferrari to debate the role of a big-time basketball program in a higher education setting? On the basis of won-loss record, I would have to favor Tubbs in the debate. What if Tubbs had already been the head coach at Drake when Ferrari was hired there as president - would Drake have had a winning team? That would have been interesting. Both had been successful and were empire builders in their own areas of expertise, Ferrari in academe and Tubbs in basketball. I still would have had to favor Tubbs, again on the basis of record. And I would say "yes," Drake would have won under Tubbs, with or without a Ferrari driving the academic program as president.

Dr. Michael Ferrari had established a reputation as a progressive educational leader, as well as an effective fund raiser at Drake. Yet, he seemed to show little interest in capitalizing on a Division I men's team as a source of alumni pride and as a resource in the fund-raising effort, life blood of the private school. Also, during Ferrari's tenure, wrestling was dropped and football was de-emphasized. Some saw Ferrari, whose leadership philosophy obviously did not include strong support for men's basketball, as co-author of Drake's 39 consecutive conference losses. That ominous string was intact on his day of departure to Texas and has remained in Des Moines as a part of his legacy as Drake's president.

Ferrari was reportedly mildly enthusiastic (initially) and was involved directly with the hiring of Rudy Washington. Reliable word was that Washington, hired at Drake before A.D. Lynn King arrived on the scene, could by-pass King and answered directly to President Ferrari.

In discussing Michael Ferrari at Drake, I was reminded of Robert Maynard Hutchins, a college president of another era who led the University of Chicago out of the Division I college football arena. Hutchins had been the Dean of the Yale Law School, had then assumed the University of Chicago presidency in 1929, and did not relinquish that position until 1945. The University of Chicago became a charter member of the Western Conference (later called the Big Ten) in 1895 along with Illinois, Michigan, Minnesota, Northwestern, Purdue, and Wisconsin. Iowa and Indiana joined in 1899, Ohio State in 1912, Michigan State in 1950, and Penn State in 1992.

When Chicago left the conference in 1939, the nine teams which remained were joined by Michigan State eleven years later to form today's Big Ten. Penn State has since been included which brought Big Ten membership to eleven teams. But President Hutchins was the key figure in moving Chicago out of major college football into the elitist academic arena. He had introduced the Great Books - from the Bible to Nietzsche (Friedrich the philosopher, not Ray the Packer). The Great Books program was the heart of Hutchins' educational philosophy, and the football program, from tackle to tackle, was de-emphasized.

Hutchins had set out to kill major college football. I don't know if Ferrari actually set out to de-emphasize Drake basketball, or whether he just became discouraged with the headache and the constant losing. I can understand what could have been his well-justified point of view that

"I am doing my job as university president; why aren't these men's coaches doing theirs? They have scholarships, a new on-campus arena, and membership in a decent, but not great, top to

bottom league. There were opportunities of which they did not take advantage. Why can't they go .500?"
(The coaches thought Ferrari was a major part of the problem by imposing higher academic standards for admission.)

Possibly the Rudy Washington era at Drake coupled with the Kanaskie losing streak had soured Ferrari completely on the basketball program. Even college presidents, with other priorities, get tired of hearing about their school losing, but academic leaders don't usually know how to stop the losing. That has to be in the athletic director's court, but ultimately, it was the coach's area of responsibility. I agree that a cooperative president can be a great benefit in building a winner; however, most basketball programs have grown and prospered on the fire and effectiveness of the head coach himself. If Ferrari was actually a roadblock to basketball success, which many Drake fans agreed that he was, I maintain that it was the job of the coach to sell the school president, as well as top recruits, on the virtues of ending up in the left-hand column of the lists of scores read across the world by the school's alumni. The best way to convince Ferrari would have been to win a few at first and then sell from a stronger position. Winning, like losing, can be hard to head off once it has started.

Empire Builders

I would have thought that the dream of a college president with a low priority for athletics, men's basketball in this case, would have been a coach who would not rock the academic boat, would quietly go to the gym each day, and would win occasionally. In contrast, the actual prototype for the highly successful coach is the "empire builder," the creator of a basketball tradition through his own efforts and enthusiasm. Basketball empire builders, always get more ink than college presidents. And at times, college basketball empires can be built and a winning tradition established in spite of the president and without the school itself actually realizing it. Winning can be contagious and can translate into institutional pride and expedite alumni gifts, the dream of all private college presidents.

I have previously mentioned two empire builders, Dolph Stanley at Beloit and Billy Tubbs at Texas Christian. Other names that come to mind in this category were Jack Hartman at Coffeyville Jr. College, Southern Illinois, and Kansas State; Norm Stewart at State College of Iowa and Missouri; Lute Olson at Long Beach State, Iowa, and Arizona; Bill Musselman at Ashland and Minnesota; Charlie Spoonhour at Moberly and Burlington Jr. Colleges, Southwest Missouri State University, and St. Louis; and Bo Ryan at Wisconsin-Platteville. I can also add three other prominent names to the list - Terry Carroll at Indian Hills Community College; Bruce Stewart at West Virginia Wesleyan, Middle Tennessee, and the Grand Rapids Hoops; and Rod Popp at Viterbo College and Cairns, Australia.

Terry Carroll, Bruce Stewart, and Rod Popp were three exceptional coaches (empire builders) whom I have seen in action and have known well through some of the successes in their careers. Like the others, they shared the common trait of having the ability to win basketball games consistently wherever they worked. Terry Carroll, twice National Junior College Coach of the Year, had won 72 consecutive games including back-to-back national championships in 1997 and 1998. He had established a 269-50 record over nine seasons at Indian Hills Community College in Ottumwa, Iowa.

Ironically, after that amazing achievement, he was rejected by two Division I schools in his (own) home state of Iowa - Drake and Northern Iowa, Carroll's alma mater. Terry Carroll was passed over without an interview in 1996, as Drake selected Kurt Kanaskie from Indiana University of Pennsylvania, and Northern Iowa in 1998 picked Sam Weaver, a competent Tim Floyd assistant at Iowa State. I was certain that Carroll, with 72 consecutive victories and back-to-back national titles, would not get the Northern Iowa job; it made too much sense. Besides, Floyd, although a friend of Terry Carroll's, pushed Weaver hard for the job and apparently dazzled Northern Iowa athletic director Chris Ritrievi, who came from a wrestling background. I heard stories of a three-hour Floyd conversation with Ritrievi in support of Sam Weaver. Tim Floyd had credibility at UNI and it was hard to refuse him, yet the NCAA found it easy to say "no" to Floyd in the Bruton case.

Empire builders Bruce Stewart and Rod Popp were two other coaches who have done their work well and whom I was able to assist in their transition from college coaching to professional jobs, Bruce Stewart from Middle Tennessee to the CBA, and Popp from Viterbo College to Australia. Alabama-born Bruce Stewart became head coach at West Virginia Wesleyan, with a 14-13 record in 1981-82, and ran 64 wins against 9 losses in a two-year period. Impetus from that work propelled him to Middle Tennessee State University of the Ohio Valley Conference. At MTSU Stewart's teams won 21 or more games in five of his seven seasons, made five post-season tournament appearances, and established an overall record of 141-76. The year before Stewart's arrival in Murfreesboro, Tennessee, MTSU had gone 11-15.

Having run into problems with the NCAA, Stewart called me seeking a pro job and I put him in touch with Mike Thibault at Omaha who, in turn, introduced him to the president of the CBA's Grand Rapids Hoops. Bruce Stewart was hired and didn't waste any time there, winning the team's first ever CBA Eastern Division title in 1992-93 followed by an appearance in the CBA Championship Series in 1993-94.

Another guy in that same category, but from a little-known NAIA school, was Rod Popp, who blazed a trail of consecutive 20+ win seasons over a 12-year period at tiny Viterbo College in LaCrosse, Wisconsin. Popp became discouraged with the academic side of the college game and contacted me in

1992. He was desperate to get into an overseas job and because of his great record I was able to assist him in Australia.

I actually thought that Popp might better learn the Australian system first as an administrator and later as a coach. I recommended him for the State Director of Coaching job in Queensland, a position that I had held for two years. But he saw the empire potential in sleepy Cairns, a tropical North Queensland town. He picked up in Cairns immediately where he had left-off at Viterbo and has done a miraculous job of taking that Australian team from Division III (state league) up to Division II (CBA-Australia). Cairns and Popp have committed to another huge step up, as the club was awarded a National Basketball League (NBL) franchise for the 1999 season.

Popp's work in Cairns was clearly an example of an empire builder at work. He knew what he had to have out of his coaching work and he went after those objectives knowing that he understood much better than others, including college presidents, what those basketball jobs should become. Incidentally, the cost of the NBL franchise fee for Cairns was $1,000,000 along with the obligation to double the capacity of their current gymnasium within a five-year period. Like the guy or not, I believed that he would build a winner wherever he went, providing that he did not violate, and he hasn't yet, the "One Step Back" principle. He had stayed within his level of expertise, but had single-mindedly built winners; however, the Australian NBL could be a different story. It is not all glory for empire builders.

Ironically, in spite of his consistent victory pace, Popp had not been able to win the Australian CBA, National II, even though the Cairns Marlins qualified for the Grand Final on two occasions. In the 1997 season, his Marlins team was defeated by the Sunshine Coast Sea Eagles on a last second, three-point field goal by one of his former players, Billy Ross, an American who had played for Cairns. He had tired of Popp's coaching style and signed with the opposition.

Ross was recommended to me by George Morrow, an assistant coach at Appalachian State and former NBL All-Star. I sent Ross, a 24-point per-game producer at Appalachian State, to Cairns, where he played for three seasons. Billy Ross, a strongly built 6'5 off-guard had a quick release with great range. His shooting stroke reminded me of that of former Celtic Jo Jo White. Ross averaged 37 points in leading the CBA in scoring each year, including a 50-point performance against a visiting University of West Virginia team in 1996. Obviously a prolific scorer, Ross played the last half of the 1996-97 season with Birmingham in England. I saw him score 26 and 18 in league games in the UK, but he returned to Queensland immediately after the English season. Upon his return, he delivered the game and CBA title winner to the Sunshine Coast in the Finals vs. Rod Popp's Marlins.

Winning a Day at a Time

Ron Adams had left Drake after one season and was named to Jerry Tarkanian's staff with the San Antonio Spurs in 1992, the same year that Rod Popp went off to Australia. Tark's NBA career was short-lived, as Spur Owner Red McCombs made an abrupt change after the Spurs' 9-11 start in the 1992-93 season and John Lucas assumed the Spurs head job. Lucas had been a great point guard at the University of Maryland and was the first player selected in the 1976 NBA Draft. His 14-year pro playing career was somewhat overshadowed by his recurrent problems with drugs and alcohol. However, he did finally commit to clean and sober living and has provided a rare, positive example for other athletes struggling with addiction.

I kept in touch with Ron Adams in San Antonio and was enthused about the opportunity to see him again and also to meet John Lucas. I drove up to Minneapolis to touch base with Adams when he was with the Spurs and also the 76ers later. He introduced me to John Lucas in 1994 at the Minneapolis Marriott Hotel after an afternoon Spur victory punctuated by a 50-point job by David Robinson. Lucas impressed me as a man with his personal priorities in order. He was keeping his drug and alcohol recovery first, and with that firmly in place, he was able to use his NBA playing background to do his work as a head coach. In a *Sports Illustrated* interview, after taking the San Antonio job, Lucas had the character to affirm that his recovery took precedence over all other areas of his life, including coaching. That statement might have sounded like sacrilege to the fans, but Lucas knew exactly what he had to do in order to continue on a positive course with his life.

After meeting John Lucas, I kept in touch with him from time to time. In the summer of 1995, Pat Springer, who was the director of the Kansas City Midnight Basketball League program, and who later became the head coach at College of the Desert in California, asked me to assist in arranging an appearance by Lucas in Kansas City. The Mayor's office in Kansas City, Missouri, was supporting the National Midnight Hoops Tourney and wanted Lucas to appear to discuss his recovery and also to attract media attention to the event.

I called John Lucas in Houston; he agreed to do the seminar and I met him and Dirk Minniefield, former Kentucky and NBA guard, in Kansas City at the Midnight Basketball League function. Lucas was an excellent speaker and a positive presence at the conference. I had a good opportunity to talk with him again about recovering athletes, whom each of us had known, and about our own programs of recovery. We agreed that addiction was an insidious infirmity which "told" the addict-alcoholic that he was okay. Although the guy in trouble with chemicals, drugs and/or alcohol continued to behave in an irresponsible and at times bizarre manner, he also continued to listen to the "you're okay message," and the biggest egos were the most likely to deny and repeat addictive behavior. We also talked about the symptoms, progression, and predictable outcome of the addictive cycle, and the inability of many to grasp this progression, even when they were in its midst. (In his book, *Winning a Day at a Time*, John Lucas told his gut-wrenching story.)

John Lucas had helped many people find their way to recovery in the maze of chemical dependency, in addition to his achievements at the University of Maryland and in the NBA as a player and head coach. Lucas had used his name, his personality, and his playing experience to develop an effective pro coaching style. He had had no previous head coaching experience when he took over the San Antonio job from Jerry Tarkanian, but was able to adapt and survive as a coach for several years in the league. He gave players with histories of drug and alcohol abuse more than an opportunity to become NBA players, including Lloyd Daniels, B.J. Tyler, and Richard Dumas. They really never contributed much to team objectives at either San Antonio or Philadelphia, but Lucas had to give them a chance, or a second chance. John Lucas kept recovery as the first priority in his life and was therefore able to work in the NBA as a coach. These players put basketball first and were not able to sustain pro careers at the highest level. While John Lucas was trying to win with NBA players, Lute Olson had his own unique challenge: winning without NBA players.

□*14*□

LUTE OLSON - HIS SECOND GREATEST MOMENT; MARTY BLAKE, AND A CUBAN DEFECTOR IN TORONTO

The year was 1994 and the event was the World Championships, the most important event in international basketball in the eyes of every country participating, with the exception of the U.S.A. The first World Championship Tournament (WCT) was played in Buenos Aires, Argentina, in 1950, and has been repeated every four even-numbered calendar years between Olympic events.

Since the inception of this great world tournament and before the decision to include NBA players in 1994, the United States had won just two gold medals, in 1954 and in 1986. The U.S. basketball bureaucracy had never agreed, for some reason, on the importance of winning or losing the World Basketball Championship. They were perhaps not aware of the international prestige at stake in this competition. Parochialism, or even arrogance, must have distorted the decision-making process. Nevertheless, for whatever reason, the United States' meager record of accomplishment in this great international event was official.

I flew up to Toronto for the week to attend the 12th World Championship Tournament in July 1994, caught up with the Australian National Team, and also renewed acquaintances with basketball contacts from Europe and South America. I enjoyed the great cosmopolitan city of Toronto which I would characterize as the Sydney of the Northern Hemisphere. Fourteen countries participated in the event. When the final curtain had fallen on the 1994 Toronto World Championships, the U.S. pro crew, humbly named Dream Team II, had methodically done its job on the court. They had played and defeated the world's top national teams, whose rosters also included some NBA players. The United States won the Gold Medal with Russia, Croatia, Greece, and Australia finishing in the top five.

Heavy Artillery - Marty Blake and David Stern

I walked into the weather-beaten, aging Maple Leaf Gardens in downtown Toronto to attend the Russia-Angola, Canada-Argentina double header in the first round of the ten-day event. I had no passes nor special seats. However, I heard someone yell at me from the vast press section cordoned off with ropes from the rest of the arena. Marty Blake, the NBA's scouting director, was waving at me with his program and pointed to an empty seat at the press table next to him. He met me at the entrance to Press Row and told the security guard to let me in, which I, of course, appreciated. I was somewhat surprised to see Blake, as I am never quite sure what to expect from him. He can be cordial, as he was on this occasion, or not so cordial. He had asked me to bring back from Australia the official Sydney 2000 Olympic pin for his wife, who collects these. I did that; maybe this cordiality was a payback. Blake was an NBA original. He started working for owner Ben Kerner with the Milwaukee Hawks in the league in 1954, the year the 24-second clock was introduced. He later gained fame as general manager of the St. Louis club in the late 50s and during that time the Hawks won four consecutive divisional titles and an NBA Championship behind Bob Pettit in 1958.

I first met Marty Blake at the Portsmouth Tournament several years before. He knew that I sent players to the NBL and always had a comment about Australian basketball. I usually had a similar preliminary conversation with him. It went like this:

Blake: "Some of those players (referring to my recruits in Australia) can't play and are over-paid."

I would respond, "Do you mean NBA players can't play and are overpaid?"

Blake: "No, in Australia."

Me: "There aren't any overpaid players in the Australian league. The overpaid players are in the NBA, here in the U.S."

On this occasion in Toronto, between the first game, in which Russia beat Angola, and the second game, which featured Canada vs. Argentina, there was a press conference in an enclosed area at the back of Press Row. Marty invited me to go along and we listened to interviews with the winning Russian coach, *Sergej Belov*, and the loser's mentor, *Victorino Cunha*. Cunha was a wiry, light-skinned African, or possibly Cuban; and Belov was an impressive looking, grayed-haired, mustachioed 6'7 former Olympic star from the Soviet Union's glory days in international hoops. I had previously talked with Coach Cunha, who had been on a U.S. tour with the Angolan team in Des Moines the previous winter. I sat directly behind the Angolans' bench in an exhibition game against an Iowa AAU team and recalled the coach's most frequent instruction - which he periodically yelled in Portuguese from the bench: "*Joga . . .Joga . . .Joga.*" It was a clear, simplistic and reasonable command to his players: "Play . . . play . . . play."

The two coaches with translators at their sides were standing at a lectern on an elevated stage and fielded questions from the international press corps with whom Blake and I were sitting. I was able to understand the Portuguese spoken between Victorino Cunha and his translator, and I would describe the Angola coach's position as negative and defensive, like most coaches who have just been soundly whipped by an opponent. He was berating the referees for allowing the game to have been played in a rough, physical manner. He further said that his players were smaller than the Russians and therefore were at a distinct disadvantage in a physical game. However, the English translation to the press was measured and did not include much of the moaning and groaning.

After a few routine questions, Marty Blake, a natural entertainer, couldn't take it any longer; he had to participate. He raised his hand, and first addressed Coach Cunha of Angola, "I have watched your team play before and you have the reputation in the U.S. as playing hard-nosed defense and always getting the most out of your players." Mr. Cunha didn't need a translator for that one. He was beaming at the patronizing comments. Blake then directed comments to Sergej Belov,

"Sergej, I was in Moscow a couple of months ago at a tournament and I lost my bag at the airport. You didn't see a large, black NBA carry-on laying around there anywhere in the Moscow airport, did you? If you see it on the way back, let me know."

I found Marty Blake's sense of humor most entertaining, but no one else seemed to know who he was or what was going on. He didn't stop there, of course, but the message had been presented in a non-stop, stacatto delivery and, in context, was hilarious. The press conference ended and we walked out with the incredulous sports writers still casting glances our way.

The NBA had its heavy artillery ready for the World Championships. In addition to Marty Blake, David Stern, the NBA Commissioner, was there and was quoted in the Toronto press as proclaiming, "We are going to take back our game." When I read the articles, I thought at first that Stern was referring to a U.S. victory in the World Championships. However, as I read on I found that he was talking about the League's resolve to control the on-court, and off-court, violence involving players in National Basketball Association competition. In the Toronto setting, the statement sounded patriotic, but he was not referring to the World Title; it was the league's image problems, caused by player misbehavior. Although the work was well done by DTII and its millionaires in short pants, there was little drama in Toronto as the outcome was obvious from the outset and did not compare to the 1986 U.S. title year.

In Madrid in 1986, U.S. Coach Lute Olson built a team, and a great defense, with limited preparation time and with only college players at his disposal, yet defeated a similar field which DTII had destroyed. Olson's title was a tribute to a superior coach maximizing the talents of willing players, and thus won the respect of basketball people around the world.

BUT IT WAS IRONIC THAT THE BEST COACHING JOB AND THE GREATEST ACHIEVEMENT IN U.S. BASKETBALL HISTORY IN MAJOR INTERNATIONAL COMPETITION HAS GONE VIRTUALLY UNNOTICED AND UNRECOGNIZED. Lute Olson coached the U.S. to the Gold Medal in the 1986 World Championship of Basketball in Madrid, Spain, using college players. This marked the period between "the gimmies" for the U.S. It happened after foreign teams had started their surge in development, and at the time when international competition results were underscored by the fact that U.S. college all-star teams could no longer win major overseas events. It was, of course, before the use of the NBA All-Stars, called Dream Teams.

The Road to NBA Participation in International Events

Nineteen eighty-seven was not a good year for U.S. basketball prestige in the international arena. That year the U.S. staggered badly, losing to Yugoslavia in both the 1987 World University Games and in the World Junior Championships, and then fell to Brazil with shooter supreme Oskar Schmidt in the Pan-American Games. The Pan-Am Games result was a shocker, as the American team faltered on its home turf, Indianapolis, blowing a 20-point lead in a devastating 120-115 loss.

The Brazilian victory provided strong impetus for U.S. basketball officials to seek a solution to the sobering losses to the foreign teams and to seriously consider using NBA players in future major international tournaments. However, they did not act quickly enough as the John Thompson-coached Olympians fell hard in the key game with the Soviets, and the U.S. picked up only third place and the bronze medal in the 1988 Seoul Games. That finish was a bleak and humbling moment in American basketball history, especially for those of us who were employed in the game overseas. The loss in Seoul confirmed what most foreigners had known for a decade: the U.S. could not take major international competition lightly and expect to win with college players.

At this point it had become painfully clear that foreign basketball had methodically been catching up to the United States, and now overseas national teams, once pushovers, were able to consistently defeat U.S. college players in international competition. The time frame of these events has put in better perspective the huge accomplishment by Coach Lute Olson, his coaching staff, and the 1986 U.S. World Championship Gold Medal Winners.

Madrid-1986

The 1986 U.S. National Team had received little fanfare as Coach Lute Olson and his assistants, Scott Thompson, Jerry Pimm, and Bobby Cremins, put the players through summer workouts in Tucson in preparation for the World Championships in Madrid, Spain. Actually, the coaching staff was cautious and realistic, as several top college players declined invitations, including Pervis Ellison, Fennis Dembo, David Rivers, Steve Alford, and the injured Danny Manning. Yugoslavia was paced by Drazen Petrovic, who led Croatia to a Silver Medal in the 1992 Barcelona Olympics. He later died in an automobile accident on June 7, 1993, to cut short his outstanding start in the NBA.

Thus, Yugoslavia and the Soviet Union with Arvidas Sabonis were the favorites to capture the Gold Medal. The caliber of competition against mature players, limited preparation, missing names, and lack of international experience on the part of the young players and the coaching staff all made U.S. expectations bleak.

Scott Thompson, former Arizona assistant, did the pre-world tournament scouting for the 1986 U.S. team. He spoke to Marc Hansen, who was doing a special interview for this book, in January 1998 from his office at Cornell University, where he was in his second year as head coach. Thompson commented as follows:

"There was a terrorism scare from Libya. A lot of U.S. State Department releases warned that Americans shouldn't travel over there. With Libya right across the Mediterranean, everywhere that we went there were people with machine guns and helicopters. There were soldiers protecting us in the hallways at all times. In the team bus nobody was allowed to sit in the back two or three rows. It was a very scary time. My wife and I scouted another pool (tournament bracket) in the Canary Islands. As soon as we arrived we had body guards. We would sit scouting games with people around us protecting us . . . and the odds of us winning, considering the history of U.S. performance in that competition, were not good. There was concern whether we could put our best competitors on the floor against the best players in the rest of the world."

With consistent defense and unity, the team led by David Robinson, Charles Smith, Kenny Smith, and Tyrone Bogues took home the first U.S. World Championship title since 1954. However, it was not easy and the outcome was uncertain until the waning seconds of the final game against the Soviet Union.

Lute Olson, whose Arizona team won the 1997 NCAA Tournament, recalled flying with the 1986 American team and delegation to Paris for some warm-up games, prior to the start of the official World Championship competition in Madrid. Olson discussed this experience with me from the basketball office at Arizona in January 1998 and commented as follows:

"We had only ten days of workouts in Tucson and lost to the French National Team by 20 points in our first game in Europe prior to the tournament, and the French had been defeated in the qualifying rounds and were not a participant in the WCT. And then we traveled by train for some opening round games in Malaga, Spain, and we seemed to improve each quarter that we played. Rony Seikaly translated the French newspapers. They said that we didn't have a chance to win. That was extra motivation for this team."

In preliminary pool play, the U.S. team came together and did handily beat the Ivory Coast, China, and West Germany. However, Puerto Rico was a different story as Lute's crew needed a buzzer-beater from The Admiral - David Robinson - to seal a 73-72 victory, followed by a 22-point win over Italy. The American team was not to go unbeaten in Barcelona, as Argentina nailed them in a 74-70 upset. Then the U.S. summarily disposed of Canada, Yugoslavia, and Brazil before meeting the USSR and the 7'2 Sabonis in the Final. Ironically, a key in the surprising 69-60 U.S. win over Yugoslavia had been the match-up of the 5'3 Tyrone Bogues defending 6'6 perimeter star Drazen Petrovic.

Coach Lute Olson continued:

"The U.S. Selection Committee was against the selection of Tyrone 'Mugsy' Bogues as they felt that we needed big guards to beat the Soviets. I was actually concerned about winning enough games to earn the right to play them. I felt we needed his quickness in spite of his lack of size."

Standing 5'3 and weighing one-hundred-forty pounds, Bogues did not fit the phenotype profile (the idealized picture) of a point guard in international competition, which was a big guard, 6'4-6'5, who could match up with the Soviet's backcourt. But Olson knew how critical quickness would be, and he was proven right, as the presence of Bogues was a key to U.S. successes.

Petrovic was being held scoreless for eight minutes while trying to adjust to Tyrone's defensive pressure, during which the U.S. built an insurmountable 19-2 lead and never were overtaken. Coach Olson gave Bogues instructions to "put your nose in his (Petrovic) belly and take away his game off the dribble." The unusual size and quickness of Bogues completely disrupted Drazen's rhythm and that was the difference in the American victory. Olson said that Petrovic had become so frustrated with Bogues' tenacity that on one occasion he had dropped the ball over Tyrone's head, Globetrotter style, and tried to run around him to recover possession and get open for a shot.

In the Gold Medal game, the U.S. was in control, leading by ten at halftime, and building the lead to 78-60 with less than eight minutes remaining.

However, the Soviets rallied behind the powerful, skilled Sabonis, and it took a Kenny Smith drive with 15 seconds remaining to seal an 87-85 U.S. World Title. Savoring that magic moment of victory, Coach Scott Thompson vividly recalled Lute Olson's measured reaction to the outcome:

"I remember Lute walking down to shake the Soviet Union coach's hand. I can still see Lute walking down, shaking hands in his usual way, acting like he knew it was going to happen all along. No big deal, just winning The World Championship. How many times do you win a conference championship or a national championship? How many times do you win a world's championship?"

Never again were we likely to see an American amateur team win Gold in an Olympic or World Championship event. In retrospect, Coach Olson summed it up by stating: "The use of pros has taken a lot from international competition - it is hardly worth watching."

Toronto 1994 - What a Difference

The humility of the 1986 World Championship Tournament (WCT) victors stood in stark contrast to the events involving the U.S. team at the 1992 Barcelona Olympic Games. Dream Team I, the first time that NBA players had represented the United States in Olympic competition, was the big story at Barcelona. The world press asked, "How can the U.S. lose? Look at that list of players - Michael Jordan, Magic, Bird, Barkley, Ewing, Robinson, Pippen, Malone, Stockton, Drexler, Mullin, and Laettner."

DTI was obviously the most talented group to ever represent the U.S. However, since the competition itself was somewhat of a farce in regard to final outcome, the story most compelling in Barcelona to foreign writers was the decision by the U.S. men's basketball team to give "thumbs down" to the spartan Olympic Village accommodation and move into a $900 per night hotel. Charles Barkley left no doubt regarding his position on the matter when he reportedly told veteran U.S. Olympic official LeRoy Walker that he was a millionaire and could afford to live where he wanted. . . etc. Barkley also got international media attention when he tried to brush off criticism for elbowing an Angolan player. He was quoted around the world as saying, "He might have pulled a spear on me." (What if Laettner had made such a comment?)

The 1994 Dream Team II effect was different, entertaining many, selling t-shirts and caps, and proving that "We are number 1." The qualifier was, of course, when we used NBA players. Coach Don Nelson's biggest job with this group was keeping them interested and together on and off the court. He seemed to achieve both with reasonable efficiency. Neither cordial nor humble, the NBA players barely passed the sportsmanship test in an aloof display of grudging tolerance for lesser talented players, making much less money. However, the Dream Team's big-time demeanor did not meet the expectations of several Canadian journalists, who saw the U.S. players as unnecessarily arrogant and abusive. I figured that those writers just didn't understand NBA Properties and the international t-shirt and cap business; sportsmanship, like amateurism, had become a moot point in the U.S. camp.

Nevertheless, on court the 1994 Toronto event demonstrated the large gap that still existed between the best overseas internationals and the NBA Dream Team in regard to pure basketball talent. Putting NBA product-marketing strategy in Canada aside, it would have been a much more interesting (and a further barometer of foreign progress versus the U.S. standard of play) to have seen the 1994 Dallas Mavericks, rather than DTII, in the World Championships. The Mavs could have used the work at the time, but also had some excellent young players in Jackson, Mashburn, and Kidd, and their inside people would definitely have been challenged by the Russians, Spanish, and Croatians. Participation of a lower-end NBA team in this event, or even a CBA all-star team in place of the Dream Team, would have made the event more interesting and would have inserted the element of doubt in the outcome. In fact, the European soccer technique could have been employed with the last place team in the NBA playing in the World Championships, requiring a title to justify its continuing as a member of the league (NBA) and a loss meaning relegation to the CBA.

Defensive transition was a big problem for the overseas teams, and little effort was made to contain U.S. ball handlers in the back-court after the fast-break-outlet pass. Also no pressure was put on the first pass out from the rebounder. The lethargic retreat to the paint proved fatal, but there was more to this issue than defensive transition by the foreign teams. There was a lack of depth, lack of big-time, consistent competitiveness, and a shortage of NBA standard athletic ability. I saw no NBA impact players carrying foreign passports in Canada outside of Tony Kukoc; yet, I felt that Croatia with Kukoc, Dino Radja, and Stojan Vrankovic or Russia with Bazarevich, Babkov, Mikhailov, and Kissourin would have made it tough for Dallas, or other bottom-of-the-ladder NBA teams.

Wonderful World of International Hoops - Almost

After one evening of games, I caught the Australian delegation bus back from Copps Coliseum in Hamilton, a 45-minute ride to the hotel in Toronto. The bus trip gave me an opportunity to talk with Pat Hunt, veteran administrator and coach at the Australian Institute of Sport in Canberra. Our discussion was about the city of Toronto, Australia's close call in the opener with Korea, and, in general, the positive direction international basketball had taken in the past ten years, with emphasis on the game in Australia.

Australian Pat Hunt worked full-time in junior-basketball player development and has had vast experience in regard to the various opportunities provided for Australian junior players in American colleges. With Aussie juniors coming through a sound secondary school system of education, coupled with their basketball talent developed outside of the schools in clubs, study at an American university has been a unique educational and athletic experience. Therefore the U.S. college alternative was of value to many young Australian players, and others, from all over the world. Also, Hunt and I agreed that many of the young Australian players had fit perfectly the mold of the NCAA's dream and their over-worked "student-athlete" terminology. Although the student-athlete buzz words were often meaningless and oxymoronic when applied to many U.S. college players, young Aussies were, for the most part, better prepared academically than their American counterparts. They were perfect candidates for NCAA scholarships in the classroom and on the basketball court.

Pat Hunt and I further agreed, especially with the U.S. now using NBA players in the World Championships and Olympic Games, that the old standards and definitions of amateurism had become outmoded in today's world. We discussed how even FIBA, the world basketball federation, in 1989 had removed the word "Amateur" from its name after the distinction between amateurs and professionals was dropped. We concluded that even the NCAA had apparently come to terms with obsolete attitudes and outdated rules regarding amateurism. It appeared that they had begun to cut slack in regard to eligibility requirements with junior players from foreign country club systems. As proof, about 250-300 overseas players had been wearing U.S. Division I college team colors annually.

Everyone involved in overseas basketball knew that most foreign junior players could not meet the strict interpretation of NCAA rules in regard to amateurism, and I naively gave the NCAA credit for coming to terms with the reality of the differences between the foreign junior club system, which regularly paid players, and the U.S. high school system. Apparently this new insight and "modern-world view" regarding rule interpretation on amateurism by the NCAA was working well for U.S. colleges. For example, Seton Hall had benefited greatly from the services of the great Australian player Andrew Gaze in 1988-89. Further evidence of this "new approach" by the NCAA was the hundreds of foreign players, past and present, who had played in NCAA Division I, NCAA II and NCAA III programs. In fact, I estimated to Hunt that there were probably about 700-800 foreign players participating at all levels of U.S. men's college basketball annually. He smiled and shook his head approvingly.

After all, the exchange of basketball talent flowed in both directions, as hundreds of U.S. players, through the years, had had the opportunity to play in

Australia at different levels, as well as in other countries around the world. Some American players had even married and still lived down-under; thus it was only right that Aussie youngsters could have an opportunity to study and play in the U.S. It was a two-way street of opportunity made possible by the NCAA's willingness to junk its outdated views of amateurism. What better setting than World Championships for Australian Pat Hunt and me, an American, both of whom had spent close to a lifetime in basketball with special interest in the Australian game, to discuss and celebrate the shrinking world of international basketball and the new opportunities available to players of all nationalities. (Little did I know, at the time, how wrong I was about the NCAA and its "worldly view" of amateurism. Dead wrong.)

Lindsay and Andrew Gaze

The next morning in Toronto, I was still feeling good about my chat with Pat Hunt. I walked across the street from the hotel to the train station to get a cup of hot espresso. My thoughts about the previous evening's talk with Hunt were underscored when I ran into Lindsay Gaze with Phil Lynch, Australian TV man and former player, back in the lobby of the Royal York Hotel, the World Championship Tournament headquarters. The former National Team coach and long-standing Melbourne Tiger Club leader, Gaze, was rushing off to Maple Leaf Gardens to catch the Australia-Cuba game.

As I spoke with Lindsay, I also thought of Andrew Gaze, the greatest of all Australian players, and his rich background - Melbourne Tigers, Seton Hall, NBA, Greece, and Italy. While unquestionably the greatest player down-under in the minds of most Australians, American basketball fans would recognize ahead of Andrew Gaze the name of Aussie Luc Longley, the veteran NBA post player and teammate of Jordan and Pippen with the Chicago Bulls. Longley, as an NBA player, had definitely achieved more at a higher level of professional competition - the world does concede the NBA as the best - than any other Australian. Yet Gaze had gained his fame in Australia, had performed in front of Australians, and had represented his country in numerous major international events, including the Olympics and World Championships. Longley had not.

Andrew Gaze was clearly Australia's favorite son, a consensus choice as that country's greatest player, and a respected competitor worldwide. Gaze was Mr. Basketball in the land down-under. Had Luc Longley played for the Australia Nationals, the Boomers, in the 1994 Toronto World Championships, I felt that Australia would have been a medal winner. Further, it made sense that the Year 2000 Sydney Olympics could be an ideal time for the 7'2, 300-pound Longley to make the Australian cause his top priority. He couldn't possibly need any more NBA money.

It could be a lift for all parties in Australia - the Boomer team, the Sydney Games, the sport of basketball itself, and for Longley himself. He would have planned, no doubt, to go back to Perth to live after his NBA career, in the not-too-distant future. The Sydney Olympics could be the perfect opportunity for the Favorite Son, Andrew Gaze, to team with the Prodigal Son, Luc Longley, to lead their country to its first-ever Olympic Medal. Skeptics in Australia contend that Longley has let them down before and he would probably do the same in 2000.

As usual, a major international basketball event meant that Andrew Gaze was present in the Australian Green and Gold, and the 1994 World titles in Toronto were no exception. Andrew Gaze, the player and son, had played exclusively for Lindsay, the coach and father, with the Melbourne Tigers' Basketball Club in NBL competition. This combination had netted two league titles, 1993 and 1997, and I felt some genuine pleasure again in reflecting on the great world of international basketball and my own experiences. I even recalled with a smile Andrew's Monday night April 3 appearance in the Seton-Hall-Michigan 1989 NCAA title game in Seattle.

After the 80-79 loss to Michigan and his MVP work in the Western Regionals, Gaze called it a day in American higher education and on Friday, April 21, returned home to lead his Melbourne Tigers to victory over my Hobart Devils in the NBL season opener. That marked Hobart's first loss to the Melbourne Tigers in six previous NBL games over my three-year span as Devils coach, and it was Andrew Gaze with his perimeter-driven 35 points that made the difference.

Back in Toronto, I took the short cab ride with Lindsay Gaze and Phil Lynch from the Royal York Hotel to Maple Leaf Gardens to see the Australia-Cuba game. Lindsay was pumped, as if he were still a player or the coach of the Australian team. The Cuban team was quick and athletic, but lacked the execution to defeat the Australians. Arriving early, I watched the Cubans in warm-up and was impressed with their trim, lithe bodies and their athleticism. I especially recalled, one *Cubano* looking good in warm-up, but a bench player, *Augusto Duquense*. He was a particularly impressive 6'8 athlete with a nice lefty jump shot; however, he got little playing time and I wondered why. Little did I know at the time that Augusto was planning to defect from Cuba, seek political asylum in Toronto, and eventually become one of my Overseas Basketball Services clients.

Augusto Duquense

After I had returned home from the World Championships in late August of 1994, I received an interesting call from Kerry Vinson, the head coach at Durham College near Toronto. Coach Vinson asked if I had remembered the Cuban team from World Championships, and if I would be interested in representing one of the Cuban players, Augusto Duquense, who had chosen to defect and stay in Canada. After his defection, Augusto had enrolled at Durham College, a two-year school near Toronto, and was playing basketball there. Vinson explained that the Cuban player was being bombarded by calls from U.S. colleges and was confused about what to do.

In talking with Kerry Vinson, I initially thought the young Cuban might be better off going to a U.S. college, but as I discussed the situation further, I saw some obstacles in his path. Augusto was already 26-years old and spoke very little English; further, his progress in the learning of English had proven to be very slow. At the time, he could not read or write close to a level required to stay eligible in an American college, or even be admitted. Also, Augusto had some major hurdles to clear with Canadian immigration officials. He had no passport and needed about a year to establish residency in Canada; otherwise he was truly a man without a country.

It had already been agreed between Coach Vinson, the player, the player's Cuban advisor, and Canadian immigration officials that it was in the young man's best interest to stay in Canada to gain his residency status. I met with Duquense, coach Vinson, and *Alfredo Jordan*, a former defector and leader in the 12,000 strong Cuban community in Toronto, who acted as the player's confidante and advisor. The three of them convinced me that it was best for Augusto to commit to an agent agreement, even though I emphasized that I saw only limited possibilities for him in overseas professional basketball competing against American players for import jobs.

Also, I was concerned about his eligibility in Canada if he signed with an agent. Vinson confirmed that this was not the case in Canadian college basketball, and further that it was perfectly legal to sign with a professional agent as long as the player was not paid by the agent when the player was competing collegiately. Thus, the signing of the agent contract would get the U.S. colleges out of the picture, as he would then be ineligible in U.S. college ball, and he would be in a position to achieve his first priority, Canadian residency. Further, it would provide some hope and motivation for the player to work hard to improve his game with the objective of attracting overseas offers in the spring of 1995, after the Durham season.

Subsequently, I flew back to Toronto to meet Coach Vinson and Augusto Duquense and to see the Cuban in action. I did sign him to an agent contract at that point and eventually placed him in his first job in the Western Australia State League after the Canadian college season. He scored well in Australia, but was suspended by the league in the playoffs for aggressively disputing a referee's call. Although Augusto had shown some definite talent and achievement in a lower-level Australian competition, the suspension had temporarily put a halt to his progress in overseas professional basketball.

I tried to move him from the job in Australia to the National League in New Zealand, a step up professionally. He was given strong consideration by a New Zealand team, but the Western Australian suspension issue became a factor in the Kiwi club selecting another player. As I had suspected and had forewarned against, Augusto's options professionally were limited from the beginning, and the suspension had become an added obstacle.

In addition to the call from Kerry Vinson from Toronto, I had also received another call from overseas at about the same time. A message on my office voice mail said, "Message for Dave Adkins. This is Trish Bruton; please call me back in Perth as soon as possible. C.J. is having some problems."

"□*75*□

NOT READY, PRO CAMPS, AND THE LEGENDARY BILL FITCH

I had maintained contact with the Brutons through the years, but had not seen C.J. Bruton since 1989 at a pre-season tournament in Perth when I was coaching at Hobart. I was concerned about the message from his mother and hoped that nothing serious had happened. I returned the call to Perth, Western Australia, and connected with Trish Bruton. She told me that C.J., at age 18, had signed a contract to play with the Perth Wildcats of the NBL for the 1994 season. He had been with the team eight months - since January - and was having some problems. He was unhappy and not ready to handle the full-time responsibility with the Wildcats.

She explained that, in addition to training and games, he had to work about 20 hours a week for the club in promoting basketball through school clinics; so he was working on and off the court 40-50 hours a week but still making very little money. He was still living at home and paying rent, but once he put gasoline in his car, he had nothing left of his meager paycheck from the Wildcats. In general, he was not having fun and had taken on far too much at the tender age of 18. Could I help C.J. get into a U.S. college? I told Trish that I was coming to Sydney in a couple of weeks and that I had already planned to catch up with her middle son at the Perth-Sydney game. I said I would give the college idea some thought and better evaluate where he might fit in as a player after I had seen the kid play.

Sydney

On September 10, 1994, I walked into the Sydney Entertainment Center, saw the Wildcats warming up, and immediately caught "the smile," the Bruton trademark. C.J. was used sparingly that evening in a high-level, hotly-contested road win by the Wildcats in front of 9,500 King fans. Even though young Bruton played only seven minutes, he nailed a three-pointer, set up teammates through penetration, and pushed the ball with confidence. Yes, he certainly showed the ability to play Division I college basketball.

I talked with C.J. for about ten minutes after the game, but we really didn't get much accomplished as we were constantly interrupted. I finally gave up and told him that I would see him in California in November when the Wildcats were scheduled to play a U.S. college tour. I left the dressing room and went upstairs to a huge bar area at the Entertainment Center for the post-game bash. While talking with Steve Carfino there, I noticed a group of about 100 teen-agers mob someone just entering the bar. It was C.J. and he was the center of attention. I froze for a moment and thought what a horrible situation. This 18-year-old kid was getting NBA-like, super-star attention, yet playing only sparingly, and developing neither his fragile personality nor his game. I felt that he was getting many unhealthy signals through the adulation and that he definitely needed to get out of the NBL and into a college. It occurred to me that C.J. Bruton, who should have been a college freshman, had been exploited through bad career advice accompanied by meagre financial reward.

Between my Sydney trip in September and the Wildcat-U.S. tour in November, I had talked with C.J. Bruton's divorced parents, Trish Bruton and Calvin Sr., I found that C.J. had reacted strongly when, at age 16, he had heard of his parents' separation and eventual divorce. He had been detained by the police for shop-lifting in Perth on the day that the divorce was final. In fact, he was still showing some instability in regard to acting responsibly to his basketball job and to his mother at home. Trish felt that C.J. needed to get out on his own, away from Perth, and into an educational and athletic structure with players more his own age.

Los Angeles

In November I met C.J. Bruton in Los Angeles at an airport hotel, where he was staying with the Perth team on an eight-game tour with American college teams. I talked to him briefly that afternoon and then met with Adrian Hurley, the veteran coach, and Vern Reid, the general manger. I knew Adrian from the first year of the NBL, 1979, when he was the coach at Illawarra and I was in Brisbane as director of coaching. However, I had never met Vern Reid, but I did recall receiving a fax from him objecting to my participating as the Bruton family's advisor in the U.S. college decision process. Also, Vern Reid had negotiated the infamous Perth playing contract, which eventually spelled NCAA ineligibility for C.J. Perth told C.J. that the contract was to have been structured like a scholarship, but that didn't happen. It was a straight-forward, NBL player-club contract.

In my opinion, Reid and the Wildcats had given C.J. Bruton some bad advice and had taken advantage of his youth and inexperience in convincing him to commit to a low-paying NBL contract far too soon for his own good. In addition to his potential as a player, Perth was interested in capitalizing on the Bruton name for marketing purposes. C.J. had no representation in dealing with the club, so it was basically a situation of an 18-year-old and his mother negotiating with the general manager of an Australian professional basketball club. Vern Reid, the Perth Wildcats, and C.J. Bruton knew little of the NCAA rules, which were the farthest thing from everyone's mind at the time. However, the results of signing that contract proved to be disastrous in regard to C.J.'s educational plans, NCAA eligibility, and exposure to NBA scouts. Along with that, the chance of being selected in the first round of the NBA draft disappeared with the NCAA's subsequent ruling on Bruton's eligibility based on the Perth contract.

However, I listened carefully, as both Hurley and Reid stated that C.J. was showing promise as an NBL player, but was still immature and, therefore, used sparingly. I told them Bruton wanted to go to college in the U.S. and would not be playing with the Wildcats the next season. There was little resistance. Adrian Hurley, who had attended graduate school at the University of Oregon, knew the American college scene and agreed that it would probably be a good move. When I said that I saw C.J. Bruton as a Big Eight or Big Ten player, Hurley said that he was skeptical.

After my meeting with the Perth people, I jumped in a cab and rode over to Pauley Pavilion for the Perth Wildcat-UCLA match-up that evening. I was curious to see C.J. compete against the quickness of UCLA guards Cameron Dollar and Tyus Edney. Before the start of the game, I ran into Jim Kelley, Toronto Raptor scout, and he invited me to sit with him courtside at the scouting table. Kelley and I were impressed by the level of talent on the UCLA roster; four of the five UCLA starters on that team were to be drafted by the NBA. Only six months later, that same UCLA group went 31-2 to win the 1995 NCAA Title, under Coach Jim Harrick, with Ed O'Bannon and George Zidek going in the first round of the NBA draft, and Tyus Edney and Charles O'Bannon in the second round. Also, both Bruin point guards who played in the Perth game, Edney and Dollar, were formidable opponents and an excellent gauge in assessing Bruton's abilities. He played about 14 minutes against the Bruins and held his own in regard to quickness and also in ball handling in the face of full-court pressure. Young Bruton was tentative at the offensive end and spent most of the evening reversing the ball and trying not to make mistakes; but he was only 18. He was just getting started in his basketball career, yet he showed streaks of exceptional talent.

Afterwards Jim Kelley and I rehashed the game and discussed Bruton's situation. We agreed that he needed to leave the Perth Wildcats to go to school where he could play and mature. I said I felt C.J. had shown in competing with the UCLA guards Edney and Dollar that he had the talent and skills to be a factor at that level of college basketball, Division I in the Pac-Ten Conference. Kelley smiled and said, "I think so, too."

I could not help but make comparisons between C.J. Bruton and his dad, although I didn't see Cal Sr. play until he was 24-years old. At that stage of development, Cal Sr. did very little reversing of the ball. He could score on anybody and usually did. Cal Sr. was the prototype scoring point and Jr. had yet to assert himself offensively, but the younger player had all the other tools to stand out at the point-guard position at a high level of competition. In comparing the two, father and son, it seemed as if the younger Bruton had consciously, or unconsciously, set out to develop his own style of play, different from that of his father. C.J. had a tendency to hold back offensively and over-pass, while Cal Sr. saw few scoring opportunities that he didn't take advantage of. However, both Brutons were the complete package at the point-guard position; it would have been an interesting head-to-head match-up.

I saw C.J. Bruton play one more time on that tour, at St. Mary's College in Moraga, California. The last time I had been on that floor I had been asked to leave by Coach Lynn Nance for mutinous acts to the St. Mary's program, via the local radio waves, the voice of Moraga. Bruton was used sparingly against the weaker competition at St. Mary's; I thought that he had played better at UCLA. We huddled after the game and confirmed the plan for C.J. to come to Des Moines for a few days after the tour. Perth cooperated and changed his airline ticket so that the Des Moines trip would work without added expense.

When I returned from the California trip, I immediately called Kevin McKenna at Creighton. The former Creighton great had played seven years in the NBA and had returned to his alma mater to assist head coach Dana Altman in working to rebuild the Bluejay program. McKenna was a low-key coach with successful experience at every level of American basketball - NBA, CBA, and college - and someone whom I thought would be a positive influence in a college setting on C.J. Bruton. Creighton was interested in talking to Bruton, so when he arrived in Des Moines we made plans to drive over to Omaha to visit the campus.

I myself had been recruited by Creighton's coach, Tommy Thomsen, many years before. He had come to our home in Grinnell to discuss the school. I recall that Coach Thomsen said it was a short train ride from Grinnell to Omaha, but as an immature 18-year-old even that sounded way over my head. On the two-hour drive from Des Moines to Omaha, young Bruton was having second thoughts about leaving his home in Australia. He suggested that he wanted to wait another year before making a decision on college. I carefully selected my words and replied,

"C.J., you have the talent and abilities to play Division I and to finish a degree. You naturally feel uncertain, but you can do it. Geneva and I will be here when you need us. The clock is running and it is time to make some changes in your life. You can do it."

It was quiet the rest of the way to Omaha that day. C.J. was probably thinking about the future with some apprehension and I was thinking back to my own situation nearly 30 years before at a similar juncture in my life. I felt, because of my experience as an unstable 18-year-old who left Drake University, that I was better able to give C.J. Bruton the words and support which I had needed. My own disappointment regarding the Drake situation had finally shown its positive side; I knew exactly how C.J. Bruton felt that day and I was there to offer some support.

Although located in the city of Omaha with a metro area of 500,000, the Creighton campus was small and compact, and it was easy to walk from building to building. Coach Dana Altman was concerned about C.J.'s modest high school academic achievement, as there were now few academic short-cuts for athletes at Creighton. Both the player and the school were interested, but C.J. later took the ACT in Perth and the results printed out "JUCO," a 4-year school would have to wait.

Indian Hills Community College in Ottumwa, Iowa, had the strongest junior college basketball in the area and competed in a national schedule. Terry Carroll, who had played at Northern Iowa and worked as an assistant under Gary Garner at Drake, was the head coach. He had much energy and was building Indian Hills into a national junior college power. I was impressed with Carroll's intensity, commitment, and his track record as a coach, both on the court and in the classroom, with a history of high-graduation rates for his players at the junior college level. He was ably assist-ed by Mike Cappacio, who spearheaded the academic counseling program for the Indian Hills' players.

Carroll started his college playing career at Oklahoma State and then transferred to the University of Northern Iowa. I had heard that in his junior year at Northern Iowa, Carroll had been used as a part-time starter by Coach Jim Berry, and that player and coach agreed to disagree after a particular road game in which Carroll thought Barry had conceded victory at Morningside College without playing the game to the wire. After the player-coach disagree-ment, Carroll left the basketball team at the end of his junior season and played only baseball in his final year. Coach Jim Berry, who had been a solid point-guard at Creighton University as a player, was credited with leading the University of Northern Iowa from Division II to NCAA Division I competi-tion.

I contacted Indian Hills and told them about Bruton; Coach Carroll then called Australia and talked with C.J. and his mother. I later spoke with the Brutons and suggested that Indian Hills would be a wise move for C.J. and a good place to build some academic skills and further develop his basketball. The Indian Hills decision was made in December 1994, but C.J. had to stay in Australia until school started in August of 1995 before coming to Iowa. His plan was to work in Perth, save for the expensive airline ticket, stay in shape, and sever all ties with the Wildcats, which he did.

Portsmouth

During the months that followed, while C.J. was working at a sporting goods shop in Perth and preparing for his college experience at Indian Hills Community College, I was involved in my normal basketball placement business work and attended NBA pre-draft camps. I went to the PIT, Portsmouth Invitational Tournament, in Virginia in April 1995, which was billed as the 43rd year of that event. The PIT Committee invited 64 seniors from across the country, but mainly from the eastern seaboard and south, to play in front of professional scouts from around the world.

The NBA was well-represented at Portsmouth with scouts and general managers who were seated in a special NBA section courtside. Marty Blake was a prominent figure in the gym and engrossed in the task of keeping the VIP (NBA) section clear of intruders. I noted that Blake was busy checking the credentials of CBA coach George Whittaker when I arrived at the gym. When I first started going to Portsmouth, I used to make every effort to secure an NBA identification badge, but I had decided that it was now not worth the effort. I was there to see some people and look at players. I didn't need an NBA badge to accomplish this. Looking around the Portsmouth high school gym, the PIT game site, I could see "who's who in the NBA": Jerry West, Willis Reed, Kevin McHale, Billy Cunningham, etc.

The participating players were projected as hypothetical third, fourth, and fifth round draft choices. They were trying to play their way up via the PIT in front of NBA people into the second round, with a few possible late first rounders present also. The PIT had a distinguished alumni list, guys who had played there and then gone on to NBA guaranteed money. For example, PIT graduates included Scotty Pippen, Dennis Rodman, Jerome Kersey, and Terry Porter, Division II and NAIA college stars who benefited greatly from the exposure. The previous year's tournament included 13 players who were taken in the 1994 NBA draft; ten of the thirteen were second rounders and three were first rounders, including Greg Minor of Louisville, Brooks Thompson of Oklahoma State, and Dickey Simpkins of Providence.

The positive side of the Portsmouth tournament was the opportunity for exposure for the players, the community spirit and enthusiasm for the event, and the non-stop games showcasing basketball talent for the four consecutive days. The event was always well-organized and the 64 players, divided into eight teams, were directed by ex-college coaches from the area. I liked the Portsmouth trip, the games, the faces, and the Virginia springtime weather.

Another aspect of the PIT was the proliferation of agents, would-be and real, who combed the hotel, clubs, and gym for potential clients. As in all fields of endeavor, quality control in the business of player representation was defined by the background, ethics, and character of the people involved. And also, as in all businesses, the quality of the participants ranged from honorable to despicable. There were always some very "needy" characters present. I had never actually seen an overzealous agent arrange a *monican* favor, as an inducement, in the recruitment of a potential client in Portsmouth, but I sensed that it could have happened. The Portsmouth Invitational was truly open season for player-agent signings, which were a major part of the attraction. Players thinking NBA contract, with little idea of their own real market value, were looking for jobs. Agents, many of whom were oblivious as to where the players fit into a professional structure, were looking for clients.

The whole scene at Portsmouth reminded me of the force that drove the industry: "the Bubba Factor." In Spike Lee's *He Got Game* everyone was trying to cash in on his/her relationship with Jesus, the nation's top high school player. The kid's girlfriend was using sex to direct him to an agent; Jesus's father was given a week-long release from prison to secure a commitment from his son to go to the Governor's old school, Big State; Jesus' high school coach was trying to influence the kid's college decision with under-the-table cash; and Uncle Bubba explained his own blatant attempts to use Jesus for financial gain as just wanting to wet his beak. Surprisingly, real-life, big-name U.S. college coaches got into the Spike Lee production and Jesus act. At the top of their profession, big-time college coaches have evolved into "men for all seasons" - coaches, shoe salesmen, and actors.

I was sitting on the far end in the back row of the bleachers at the Churchlands High School Gym, the playing site of the PIT, with Bruce Stewart, then a CBA coach, and Sharm Scheuerman of Athletes in Action. Looking around the gym at the crowd gathering for the next game, I spotted a familiar face. I recognized the French agent *Paco*, who lived in Phoenix but spent considerable time in Europe. I recalled that I had an unfinished transaction to discuss with him. I had placed Troy Truvillion, a D-II All-American guard from Eastern Montana, in a state league job in Western Australia. He had played well there, and at mid-season I was able to arrange a promotion to the Newcastle Falcons of the NBL. The Newcastle coach, Ken Cole, had cut guard Jerry Everett and signed Truvillion for the balance of the season. After the NBL replacement job, Troy returned to the U.S. and stayed in touch with me about future employment. I found him a job in New Zealand, but he didn't pick up his ticket at the airport and disappeared. A few months later, he surfaced. Troy called me from France and said that his French agent, Paco, wanted to talk with me.

Paco had done his homework. He found that Troy had been born in France and therefore could qualify to play as a local French player and did not count against the two-foreign-player per club limit. When Paco rang me, he was trying to further confirm Troy's identity as a Frenchman and prove that the player had applied for his USA Basketball Clearance as a French player. I had arranged Truvillion's first USA clearance and Paco asked me to write a letter to the French Federation confirming that Troy Truvillion had applied for that USA clearance as French. I agreed to confirm the player's employment in Australia as a foreign player, but I could not speak to the issue of his nationality. I faxed the letter to Paco, who said that he would send me a cheque for my assistance. I imagined that it was still in the mail.

A few months after my contact with Paco, Kenny Grant, an American agent living in France and former confidant of Jim McGregor, updated me. Apparently Troy Truvillion had done well by Paco, who placed him in a French Pro A job through the recently attained French player status. In fact, Grant told me that *L'Equipe*, the French language sports publication, featured an amusing headline (in English) proclaiming, "TROY TRUVILLION IS FRENCH." I looked up again and the ubiquitous Paco had disappeared into the PIT crowd. (While watching the 1997 McDonald's Cup from Paris, I suddenly noticed a familiar face appear on the TV screen. It was Troy Truvillion at the foul line for the French club, Racing Basket PSG. Yes, he *was* French - a job well done by agent and player.)

The PIT schedule included games starting at noon and ending at 11:00 p.m. I took a short break from basketball on Saturday morning and rode the ferry from Portsmouth to downtown Norfolk. There were several coaches and agents on board, and I noticed Dave Fredman, assistant coach with the Utah Jazz. I introduced myself and said that I had placed Marcus Timmons, a talented 6'8 forward from Southern Illinois, in Australia. I mentioned that Marcus had played well in the NBL and might be worth a look at a Jazz camp. Timmons had participated in a previous Utah free-agent camp and I thought they might be receptive to giving the player another look. However, in no uncertain terms, I was informed that Timmons had worn out his welcome with Utah. Fredman told me that Marcus had allegedly conned a Jazz summer intern out of extra meal money and the club saw this as a bad sign, especially in a lowly free-agent.

While the Portsmouth Tournament attracted both NBA and overseas agents, an official, standard agent-certification process in overseas basketball did not exist. However, the National Basketball Players Association (NBA Players' Union) required agent application and registration through its office in New York. Once it was determined that the agent-applicant met the NBPA standards, the prospective player representative paid a $1,500 annual fee, an important hurdle for certification. He was then required to attend one seminar per year in New York or Los Angeles. The seminar lasted about two hours with NBPA representatives in charge. They were normally dressed in their three-piece, home-court uniforms and occasionally cast supercilious glances down from the meeting room lectern at the fifty or so agents present, each of whom, I am certain, was asking himself why he was required to be there.

Of the four hundred or so registered agents, I imagined that maybe 25% of those actually had clients with NBA playing contracts. I had none at the time. However, NBPA agent certification did provide a screening process for applicants and was an organized effort to assure some control over who could be involved with NBA players. Also, the registration fee provided annual cash flow for the players' union New York office.

My priority has always been overseas player placement and representation; thus I associated mainly with overseas agents, CBA coaches, and a few NBA assistants at Portsmouth and the other pre-draft camps. I had been registered as a professional sports agent with the State of Iowa and with the NBL in Australia, and from time-to-time with the NBPA.

Agents and Player Blind Spots

A stereotype of the NBA agent was big city, big cigar, big diamond ring, tasseled footwear, earring, sun tan in December. However, there were refreshing exceptions, in both the U.S. and overseas markets. Most were lawyers, a few ex-NBA players who had attended law school, but the majority had never drawn a paycheck anywhere from the game itself as a player, a coach, or a scout. Yet I got the impression that most considered themselves knowledgeable in all phases of player evaluation. Another movie, *Jerry McGuire*, provided a believable account of a large, player representation office. The character, Sugars, was the typical snake in the business, humorously portraying the agent image at its worst. The scene in which Sugars in a telephone conversation tried to lure the star quarterback prospect, Cush, away from McGuire was classic and realistic.

The PIT was the worst possible time for me to talk to players about mid-level overseas jobs, where many would end up. These guys, right out of college competition, had no idea of their pro market value and they all seemed to think, of course, that they were going to play in the NBA. In fact, I believed that most college players have entertained serious thoughts of playing some form of pro ball after college competition, not knowing "when to go home when the party was over." The reality was that few had the physical, mental, and emotional tools to make a living as a basketball player, even at the lower levels, and a very small percentage could qualify for a mid-level $50,000 per season overseas job.

Seduced by the monotony of the shoe company TV advertisements, the idea to just do it seemed to impact and encourage the young player to dream on. The message: identify with the NBA player in the ad, buy the shoes, and play in The League. Regarding an actual pro basketball career, this subliminal cue precluded reality for about 90% of the undergraduate players, whose message should be "use your talents to get on with your life."

In contrast, I saw the commercial messages saying that the player could buy the shoes and could wear them in recreation or amateur sport participation, not in the NBA, after he completed a legitimate day's work in a real job. And, further, if a young basketball player today really wanted to be unique and distinguish himself, he could try living drug and alcohol free, finishing his degree, using his abilities in a full-time job, becoming a reader, and learning to be a responsible husband and father. With that type of behavior, he would clearly be in a class of his own - "All World" - and doing things much more important than dreaming of playing basketball. For the vast majority of ex-college players, the dream of a pro career was just that - fantasy.

These former college players and aspiring pros had a large blind spot in regard to assessing their own abilities. Most had ignored the active screening which had already taken place in their athletic careers. College recruiting was a thorough process of basketball talent evaluation. Players had received information early regarding their talent level, by whomever recruited them, out of high school and/or from junior college. Further, degree of success along with difficulty of college competition were key indicators in taking the next step to the NBA, CBA, or overseas.

Only the very best college players (achievers) have made CBA teams or played overseas at lower-mid ($30,000-45,000); mid ($45,000-60,000); or upper-mid ($60-90,000). Overseas jobs that paid $90,000 to $150,000 and from $150,00-$1,000,000 were reserved for ex-NBA players, CBA all-star level achievers, talented improvers, and the exceptional big-name rookies. The requirements for each level have been well-defined and clear-cut, and it was the overseas club which made the ultimate decision on whom it thought could do the job and who deserved the contract.

Many players mistakenly thought that they determined their own market value. It was my job to get the player a job in an appropriate level of overseas competition. His progress then became a matter of his own achievement reflected in contract renewals or offers from other clubs. Too often I hear a player tell me, "I am playing in a league where other Americans are making a lot more than I am." My answer to that complaint was simply, "That is because the clubs in that league, based on their observations of your game, feel that other players are worth more." (Or taking a little less allowed the player to get the job in the first place.)

There were some overseas jobs that paid only $1,000-1,500 per month, but it has not been cost-effective for most agents to devote time in securing jobs for players at this level. It was as much trouble to place a player in a

$1,500 per month job as to put a better qualified player in one at $60,000 per season. I usually have attempted to find the club a player or the player a job regardless of the salary level. All agents with overseas reputations have received numerous calls from unemployed players with distorted perceptions of their own market value.

College vs. NBA, CBA - It's Never Easy

Players have found that the U.S. pro game (NBA/CBA) was much different from college hoops. Most college teams placed strong emphasis on team balance, roles, motion offense, pressure defenses, and zone defenses. Perimeter players in the pro game have had to score and pass off the dribble in the open court and also had to make plays off the screen and roll. One-on-one penetration, power, athleticism, and transition have comprised the heart of the pro offense. A good college team could have two or three good athletes and occasionally a great one, while NBA teams can have many great ones. Some college systems have been more suited to NBA player development than others.

When Andre Woolridge came out of Iowa in 1997, NBA scouts liked his strength and body, but questioned his defense. As one scout said, "How can you tell about his defense the way that Iowa plays?" He was referring to zone pressing and falling back into a 3-2 and 2-3 zone set. It should be noted that Woolridge improved dramatically under Coach Tom Davis at Iowa. As a junior, he was a so-so 13ppg point guard, but as a senior he became the first player in Big Ten history to lead the league in scoring and assists. Andre averaged 20.2pppg and 6.0apg in leading the Hawks to 22-10 overall and 12-6 in league. The scout's comment was overly critical and irrelevant, as all college teams have used some zone and Tom Davis' pressing style has made playing the Hawkeyes a nightmare. The Iowa press has worn down many opponents, kept the Hawks in virtually all games, and provided consistent victories. In addition, the Davis Press has given his teams a potent weapon on the road and a better than normal chance for victory in hostile arenas. If an opponent was not prepared, even at home, the Hawk press prevailed. Through the years, I have watched the Iowa defensive system break open close games, but more importantly, the press also rapidly erased double-digit leads by opponents.

Nevertheless, the development of NBA players has always taken a back seat to winning in college programs, where the coach gets more publicity than the players. However, "NBA" has become an often-used term in recruiting dialogue and college coaches do not expect to keep a great player more than a year or two with the millions from the pros within his reach. College basketball, with the coach as star, and the NBA, with the fallible players as gods, are truly different worlds. However, I can understand why

NBA people know more of college basketball than college coaches know of the realities of the NBA, CBA, and overseas competition. NBA personnel have had experience in college basketball, playing, coaching, or assessing talent. College basketball has remained an end in itself - rightfully so - and in a world of its own, aloof, and somewhat naive about the pro game.

Pro scouting has developed into an ongoing process. The NBA and the CBA require exceptional athletes with size and either pro skills or demonstrated "upside" talent to develop those skills, as judged by NBA scouting staffs. There have been as few rookies in the CBA as in the NBA; the road to the top (the CBA) was found to be as inaccessible to the college player as the top itself (the NBA.) Many so-called "good college players" have been cut in three days, or less, at CBA camps, beaten out by experienced pros. I was at the Omaha Racers CBA veterans camp in November of 1994. Competition at point guard included Duane Cooper (USC, Phoenix Suns and LA Lakers), Corey Williams (Oklahoma State, Chicago Bulls), Melvin Booker (Player of Year in the Big Eight Conference at Missouri), Darryl Johnson (Michigan State, CBA vet, NBL Australia) and Sean Gay (Texas Tech, CBA vet). Exit Williams and Booker, who had since become an NBA player.

Another example of a very good college player with little success in the CBA was Curt Smith, Missouri Valley Player of the Year at Drake, who had been cut on multiple CBA tryouts, yet has recorded strong seasons in the IBA and was MVP in the United States Basketball League in 1998. Also Randy Blocker, an all-Missouri Valley Conference forward with great college numbers, was cut after five days in Hartford (CBA) and has done little since as an overseas player. Good college players don't just walk into a CBA camp, make the team, and then put up notable numbers. Adjustment from college to the CBA has proven to be a big step, a move from one comfort zone in search of another. Those players were a small sample. It has been routine for Division I college achievers to get cut in large numbers in the CBA. It was pro basketball business as usual: many were called, few were contracted.

Also, there have been many cases of the player from the name schools who had pro talent, but lacked the patience and humility to develop it in the CBA or overseas, both perceived as a step down in glamour from the college game atmosphere. Thomas Hill of Duke was cut in the CBA, but came back briefly to that league to record a productive year. However, he has since disappeared from the U.S. pro scene and played briefly for the Perth Wildcats in the 1998 NBL season. In order to survive and progress, an aspiring pro must improve as much, or more, in the four years after college ball as he did in the four years in college after high school competition.

First rounders don't automatically stick - in the NBA or the CBA - even though they have received guaranteed money. Bo Kimball, a 1990 NBA lottery pick, played a full-rookie season with the Clippers and has struggled since to find his place in the U.S. professional game. Willie Burton of Minnesota and Rumeal Robinson, Michigan, both first-rounders, have had similar problems in stabilizing their careers. Les Jepsen, the Iowa seven-footer, drew some large paychecks with Golden State, but later had trouble producing at the CBA level. He has since surfaced in lower and mid-level European competition. The list could go on ad infinitum.

I can believe that there have been cases of talented players with overseas employability who have preferred to live in the past. I picture them walking through the business district of their college basketball town, looking at their own image in the store windows, dreaming of yesterday's glory, and waiting to be recognized by a booster club member. To some players, this was preferable to accepting the challenge of the facts of their professional basketball level and then working to improve on it.

The NBA has made a very clear statement regarding college players with pro potential in their invitations to the pre-draft competitions each spring at Portsmouth, Phoenix, and Chicago. They have invited the players who have been thoroughly scouted and who were considered to be the best pro prospects. The draft itself along with summer free agent tournaments was the final assessment of talent regarding invitations to NBA vet camps. At the actual NBA veterans' camps, players have found that the level of play elevated dramatically from the summer leagues and other preliminary camps. They have learned the difference between the prestige of being drafted and the reality of making an NBA team, or being cut. Most second rounders have required at least two years of steady improvement in the CBA or in a good overseas league before they can draw a consistent NBA paycheck - and many never do.

After the Portsmouth tournament, I normally headed to the Desert Classic in Phoenix, the next step in the pre-draft process. The forty or so players invited to Phoenix were projected late first round or early second rounders, like Portsmouth, trying to play good enough to improve their positions in the draft. NBA registered agents with proof of their current credentials were allowed entry to the Desert Classic practice sessions. Practices and the games were played at America West Arena, one of the NBA palaces where it would not have surprised me to see helmeted security guards on horseback checking agent credentials and ticket stubs. I particularly valued the opportunity to watch the practices at Phoenix, as I usually wrote a player report on both the PIT and the Desert Classic for my own purposes. I also provided this information to CBA coaches who were unable to attend because of playoff responsibilities.

Coe College to the NBA

At the 1995 Desert Classic, I ran into Clipper coach Bill Fitch, a man who clearly understood the odds of making it in professional basketball and who came from an obscure college background to the NBA as a head coach. He had been in Phoenix at the Desert Classic the year before coaching one of the four teams of draft candidates along with other ex-NBA coaches Bob Bass, K.C. Jones, and Al Attles. I knew that Fitch loved the game and that he wanted another NBA head job. He had used the Phoenix event for professional exposure and to advertise his availability, as he had last coached in the NBA at New Jersey in the 1991-92 season. I hadn't talked with him for probably 20 years. It was good to see him again. He was cordial and was agreeable to discuss some of the players at the camp.

Fitch had graduated from Coe College in 1954. After having worked at Creighton for two years as an assistant in basketball and as head baseball coach, he came back to his alma mater as head basketball coach in 1958. He has also been erroneously identified as an ex-Marine by other writers. He did try to join the Marine Corps at age 16, just out of Wilson High School in Cedar Rapids, Iowa.

Young Bill Fitch and two of his Cedar Rapids high school buddies traveled to San Diego and were waiting for induction into the Marines. Fitch said, "We had our heads shaved and were ready to go when my Dad showed up. He was an ex-Marine D.I. and he took me back home. My two friends did go into the Marines, and neither came back. Both were killed in Korea." In addition to his brief experience with the Marines, Fitch was in the Air Force ROTC Program at Coe and then was drafted into the U.S. Army after college graduation.

I was a player at Cornell College during Fitch's four-year span at Coe. He then left Coe in 1962, my senior year at Cornell, and took the University of North Dakota job where he went to the Division II Final Four with his star player, Phil Jackson. In the 1965 Division II-NCAA Final Four, Jerry Sloan led Evansville to the title; Walt Frazier took Southern Illinois to the runner-up spot; and Jackson was with Bill Fitch's North Dakota team in third place. Fitch recalled a big win when North Dakota knocked off Loyola of Chicago, the 1963 NCAA Division I Champion:

"We ended Loyola of Chicago's winning streak after their 1963 NCAA Title, ten games into the 1963-64 season. The headlines in the Chicago paper read 'Loyola Scalped by Sioux, 73-71.' I called back-to-back timeouts to ice the shooter. He missed both shots, and the next year the Loyola coach, George Ircland, lobbied to have the rule changed. After that year, it was illegal to call consecutive deadball timeouts."

Fitch had further college stops at Bowling Green and the University of

Minnesota before becoming the first head coach in the history of the Cleveland Cavalier NBA franchise. In his first year at Cleveland, where the Cavs played their games in a rough area of town, Fitch quipped, "We led the NBA in stolen cars." Coach Bill Fitch has been criticized by some short-sighted journalists as being "the losingest coach in NBA history." Losses outnumbering wins in his NBA dossier were a result of his first four years in Cleveland where the Cavs dropped 67, 59, 50, and 53 games. It was doubtful that a Phil Jackson (Fitch's former college player) or a Pat Riley, or anyone else, could have done better under the circumstances, as normal loss numbers in these years would have netted a winning NBA record for Fitch today. A rebuttal for Fitch naysayers: in his four seasons as head coach of the Boston Celtics, Bill Fitch's teams won over 60 games on three occasions. In Red Auerbach's 20 years in the same job, his teams reached the 60-win mark twice. Further, Tom Heinsohn like Auerbach, eclipsed the 60-win plateau twice also in his ten years on the Celtic bench.

After the foundation was set at Cleveland, the next five years were winning seasons and play-off appearances for Fitch's teams. He was twice named Coach of the Year in the NBA, at Cleveland in 1975-76 and in Boston in 1979-80. The Coe College graduate took over the Celtics after a franchise low 29 wins and established a 61-21 in his first year there, and the next season, 1980-81, his Celtics won the NBA title. He was hired by the Celtics in 1979 to restore consistent winning to the franchise and to develop the club's prize rookie, Larry Bird.

Boston gave Fitch, the first non-Celtic to have been put in charge of the team, full control over the basketball operation and he immediately cleaned house. Considered a perfect choice to coach Bird, who respected his new coach and his work ethic, Bill Fitch guided the Celtics to 61 wins, a 32-game improvement over the previous season. He commented as follows on his days in Boston:

> "Coaching Larry Bird wasn't difficult at all. He was a rookie at the time, but a student of the game and like a sponge - eager to learn and no nonsense. He worked very hard. At first, our veterans would come on the practice court and it was like Peggy Lee (regarding Bird) - 'Is that all there is?' - But he got better and better. He not only learned his position, but he knew the other four also. My coaching philosophy was 'prepare, practice, go at it, and create game situations in practice' - and Bird responded."

Fitch has been known for taking franchises in down cycles and turning them around, as in Cleveland, Boston, Houston, New Jersey, and the LA Clippers. Bill Fitch had coached more NBA games than any coach in league history: 32 games into the 1997-98 season he hit the 2,000 game mark.

Citing the importance of the club's ownership and the entire organization in building a winner in the NBA, in addition to the on-court talent, Fitch identified the Los Angeles Clipper job as his most difficult. Fired after the 1998 season, he said, "You would have had to be there to believe it with the Clippers." In contrast, he was complimentary about the Boston organization and further commented on his experience with the Celtics:

> "Harry Mangurian, the owner, deserved more credit than Red (Auerbach), Larry, or myself in regard to my success with Boston. He was a fantastic owner. He supported a disciplined approach to coaching the team. He made good decisions and wanted everything to be first class. And Red was a good friend. We were both living as bachelors in Boston and played racquet ball and ate Chinese four nights a week. He never put pressure on me nor told me how to do it."

I had exchanged several phone calls with Fitch after the Desert Classic and before the '94 draft, prior to his being named the Clipper coach. We discussed Vashon Lenard, the Minnesota perimeter shooter. Lenard declared for the draft, went back to Minnesota for his senior year and since has become a double-figure scorer with guaranteed money for Pat Riley in Miami. Shortly after, Bill Fitch was named head coach of the Los Angeles Clippers. He told me that he missed coaching and was looking forward to the Clipper job. He also said that he needed good players more than good luck.

I knew that he had a nice place near Houston and didn't have to work, but he wanted to get back into the NBA's hectic routine, and he did. I figured that Fitch was about sixty at the time and I wondered why he would want to take on this massive headache at this point in this life, but I also knew that he was a guy who loved the coaching end of the basketball business. He did what he had always done; he took the job offered and made the best of it.

While Bill Fitch had not only distinguished himself for his NBA rebuilding jobs, durability, and longevity, he was a guy from a small school, Coe College, who has achieved at the highest level of professional basketball. I recall seeing Bill Fitch, the player, in games at Darby Gymnasium with the Grinnell College Pioneers in the early fifties. He was an all-conference selection and good scorer, 15 ppg in his playing career at Coe. These two basketball figures with the same name, phonetically, met in Iowa. John Pfitsch, the Grinnell coach, did his best to recruit Bill Fitch out of high school. However, finances were a major issue and Fitch chose Coe as he was able to live at home to make ends meet while attending college.

Coe College to the NFL

Another well-known professional coach attended Coe at the same time that Fitch was there: Marv Levy, the retired Buffalo Bill head man. According to John Pfitsch, Levy played football in his freshman year at the University of Wyoming and then with the assistance of Grinnell College coaches John Pfitsch and Hank Brown, who came to Grinnell from Wyoming, transferred to Coe College.

Levy graduated from Coe as a Phi Beta Kappa, studied English literature at Harvard grad school and then returned to Coe to become an assistant to Dick Clausen at Coe in 1952-53 and 1953-54, Fitch's junior and senior years. I learned from Bill Fitch that Marv Levy was the assistant basketball coach those two seasons at Coe with Fitch as a player. After graduating from Coe College, as mentioned, Fitch spent two years at Creighton and then returned as head basketball coach at his alma mater in 1958. Levy was never a head football coach at Coe, but he did spend a season there in the head basketball job, as he took his first head football job at the University of New Mexico in 1958. He later held head coaching positions at the University of California and William and Mary College before his pro career.

Amazing that two guys who attended the same tiny school in the same time frame had distinguished themselves in their respective professions in careers spanning five decades in the cut-throat world of professional sports. They not only got there, but they excelled and endured. Fitch went to the top of the list in the NBA record book for the most games coached, while Levy established a 123-78 record at Buffalo, appeared in four Super Bowls, and gracefully retired at a young 70 years of age.

Summer Basketball

In August of 1995 I flew to Los Angeles to meet Nick Nurse, the Birmingham (England) Bullet coach. He had been an all-state point guard from Carroll High School in Iowa, a walk-on at Northern Iowa, and a precocious young basketball coach. From walk-on to four-year starter in Division I college basketball, Nurse went to Derby, England, as player-coach right out of college. He returned to the U.S. and spent five years in college coaching, two years in the head job at Grand View College and three years as an assistant at the University of South Dakota under Coach Dave Boot. He left South Dakota to take the reins for owner Harry Wrublewski at Birmingham in the under-rated English league.

I normally have preferred to travel alone on basketball business, but I enjoyed Nurse's company and he was an asset as a sounding board in my assessment of possible overseas prospects. Also, I found that he really loved the game, while I, at times, only tolerated it. We spent three days in Long Beach at the LA Summer League where I introduced Nick to Larry Creger, the transplanted Iowan, former NBA coach, and long-time summer league director. We then headed to Salt Lake City to take in the Rocky Mountain Review, a professional tournament featuring a mixture of free agents, rookies, and roster players representing various NBA teams.

From the player's perspective, these events, LA and Salt Lake, were further opportunity to show-case their games to NBA and overseas scouts, as the constant process of player evaluation in pre-draft tournaments, summer leagues, mini-camps, etc. has taken on a life of its own. I can imagine that some NBA scouts could go for years, or forever, without their employers actually acting on their draft reports, but the idea was to keep the process going and to continue to make the player information available to their bosses. The pro-scouting process was, of course, an end in itself.

While in Salt Lake City, I received a call from Cal Bruton Sr. in Perth, Western Australia. He was calling to update me on the progress of his son. He sounded concerned and said that C.J., in preparations to come to the U.S. for school, had had his ups and downs in the past few months. Yes, he did work and did save some money for his airline ticket, but also he became engaged to a young Australian girl and had used some of the hard-earned cash to buy a ring. Also, C.J. and his mother were at odds because of the engagement. Cal said that he was planning a fund-raiser game to help underwrite C.J.'s ticket to the U.S. I felt rather helpless as I would have bought the ticket immediately, but I felt that C.J. needed to take that responsibility. Also, I did not want to violate any NCAA rules.

However, I, too, was concerned about the irresponsibility of C.J.'s actions in becoming engaged at a time when he needed to focus on school in the U.S., a sign of the continuing pattern of instability in young Bruton's life. I wondered what was the source of his recurring problems, but I knew that I would find out when he came to the U.S.

□*16*□

THE C.J. BRUTON STORY
AND THE JIM THORPE RULE

In mid-August of 1995, I went to the Des Moines airport to meet C.J. Bruton en route from Perth, Australia, via Los Angeles. Terry Carroll, the Indian Hills coach, had driven the 80 miles from Ottumwa along with Pat Curran, a lawyer and Indian Hills supporter, to take C.J. back to campus. When the kid appeared, he was flashing that great smile genetically passed down from his dad. On the surface, he looked confident and self-assured, but I knew from his past behavior that the young guy was going to have a tough year. He had some huge academic, athletic, personal, and social adjustments to make, but also had a perfect opportunity in a college educational and basketball structure to work on himself, as well as his game. He had a chance to progress with his life and face issues which were holding him back and which he had never wanted to look at. I hoped he could do it.

C.J. Bruton traveled from the airport to Indian Hills College and Coach Carroll deposited him in his 10' x 10' dorm room in Wapello Hall. When the coach left the room, the door closed and C.J. was for the first time in his life alone with himself and his own thoughts. He told me that he panicked and was overwhelmed by feelings of self-doubt and fear. While in bed he heard doors slamming and the howl of dorm plumbing. He said that the dorm sounds reminded him of prison doors slamming shut as depicted in the book and movie of the same name, *Shawshank Redemption*. C.J. had traveled for thirty-six hours in flying from Perth to Des Moines. Perth was a beautiful, tropical city of a million people located on the West coast of Australia on the Indian Ocean. In contrast, Ottumwa, his college home, was a quiet, rather isolated Iowa town of about 40,000, and it snowed there. The physical setting was to be the easiest adjustment.

C.J. Bruton had always been in the basketball spotlight, as a child, because of his father's celebrity as a player, and as a teen-ager because of some of his own modest achievements. When I saw him in Sydney, he had been mobbed by a hundred autograph seekers. At that very moment I recognized that C.J. needed a life of his own. Now, even though he had made the logical decision to leave Perth and go to school in the U.S., he was faced with the harsh reality of being alone for the first time in his life and building his own identity, on and off the basketball court.

Even though he had been uncomfortable with whom he was becoming in Perth, he had to bring all of those negative feelings along to Iowa and face them in Ottumwa at Indian Hills College. He was just another unproven first-year player there, not Cal Bruton's kid nor C.J. Bruton, NBL child celebrity. In addition to the adjustment to a different environment and the challenge in basketball, he had to become accountable in his studies, an area which he had ignored in high school. It seemed overwhelming.

In September, I received three disturbing calls from Coach Terry Carroll. The first - C.J. had fallen asleep on a bus after a weekend trip to see family in Wichita and failed to get off in Ottumwa. The second - C.J. had been involved in a fracas with an Ottumwa policeman outside of a college bar. The third - C.J. had partied and had become disoriented and made several incoherent phone calls back to Australia and to me in Des Moines.

On each of these occasions, I drove down to Ottumwa to discuss these problems with Terry Carroll and C.J. I found that young Bruton had some holes in his personality and that there was little coping ability there between the beautiful smile and the quick feet. I knew that he had to endure some short term, but major discomfort, and take responsibility for his behavior and learn from his mistakes. His first response was to retreat, and C.J. insisted that he wanted to go home, and I always replied, "To what?" He had already tried the only available basketball to him in Australia with the Wildcats and that did not work. The fact was that he was in a corner; he had to change his behavior and to face his life at Indian Hills.

After receiving the news regarding his disoriented "around the world" telephone calls, I drove to Ottumwa and was just entering the Indian Hills campus when my car phone rang. It was Cal Sr. calling from far-away Perth; he was concerned and wanted to know what was going on with C.J. and what was going on at Indian Hills.

I explained to Cal that I thought that his son had some major conflicts between his values and his behavior and that he was finding it difficult to act responsibly academically, athletically, and socially. I added that the school itself was a pleasant cluster of newer buildings in a setting of green grass, hills, trees, and a pond. I said that I had complete confidence in the coach and the school in general and that the problem was of a personal nature, inside of C.J., not outside. I assured Cal that his son was in a great situation to mature and get his life in better order, but that we could not allow him to take the easy way out. I emphasized that it was critical that C.J. learn to face his life and take responsibility for his behavior with no excuses. Cal Bruton Sr., accepted my explanation and trusted the process which I had explained. He promised "no soft shoulder" for his struggling son.

The lunch that day at the Ottumwa Sirloin Stockade was a breakthrough. I talked very candidly, and C.J. eventually broke down and shed some tears in the restaurant. I assured him that he was safe and loved and that he would succeed, but also that he would be uncomfortable for a while. He had to accept that. He was to take his life a step at a time, go to class, study, practice, and have faith that his life would improve. I also suggested that since he had allergies to nearly 200 different compounds and chemical dependency and alcoholism were present on both sides of his family, that just maybe he himself had similar problems. It was in his genes. He listened intently.

Indian Hills finished the 1995-96 season rated number one in the U.S. in Division I junior college basketball, but was not able to win the National Tournament at Hutchinson. C.J. had played well and was tabbed as the top returning junior-college point guard in the country. However, when he came back to Indian Hills from the Nationals in Hutchinson in March 1996, he hit a bottom in his life. He had not kept up with his studies and now had to face papers, tests, reading, etc., and it was too much for him. He used alcohol again to escape and became severely depressed.

C.J. called me early one morning in April of 1996 on Drake Relays weekend in Des Moines. He said that he needed to talk to me in person. He sounded desperate. I asked what was the nature of this problem, and he replied that he was confused and worried about what was happening when he drank alcohol or smoked weed. He said, "I need to stop this and I need some help." Terry Carroll let C.J. out of the car in front of our house that day and my wife, Geneva, said that she could see the black cloud around the young Australian as he approached our front door. That weekend, he began to get honest and good things slowly began to happen.

In the fifteenth year of my own recovery from alcoholism and living sober, I understood C.J.'s dilemma. Although I was from a different generation, the problem was basically the same. I too had violated values learned at home and used alcohol to allow the out-of-sync "gears" to mesh and to avoid responsibility for parts of my life. Trish Bruton had taught her sons the importance of honesty and responsibility, as had my own parents. Yet, both C.J. and I - in a different era - had lived dishonestly and irresponsibly and in doing so had caused massive emotional conflict in our respective lives.

In the basketball world, young Bruton had seen self-centered, immature behavior from some older players whom he had admired on and off the basketball court. In imitating them, he had violated his own values, then had lied to explain his behavior and to interface with his mother's scrutiny. Add the fact that there had been serious alcohol problems in his family with a grandmother, a grandfather, an uncle, and others and it was pretty much a sure thing the kid would get unusual effects from a beer or a drink or a smoke. But he also had a finely tuned conscience and paid dearly, inside, for his aberrant behavior.

C.J. had not established a pattern of regular, heavy use and fortunately he had been able to take some positive action before that happened. However, he definitely had some changes to make in his life. That weekend in Des Moines, C.J. went to a couple of AA meetings and also decided to tackle the issue of the engagement back in Perth. He wrote the girl a letter and leveled with her that he had made a mistake and felt that it would be better for both sides to end the engagement. He also called his mother and began to make amends to her for several things on his mind including the issue of the engagement. Thus he had begun to clear some past wreckage and move on in a more positive direction.

I drove him back to Ottumwa that Sunday in a heavy rain along with a former Nebraska football player who was a recovering addict. C.J. agreed to check in with me by telephone at 8:00 a.m. each day, not use alcohol, and attend some AA meetings. His willingness to accept this responsibility and then actually live up to his promises were huge in his getting off to a good start. His behavior began to change. He rallied in his school work and achieved a "B" average that semester.

While attending summer school at Indian Hills between his freshman and sophomore years, C.J. called me about recruiting letters and telephone calls, which he was receiving from Division I coaches. He felt that they were becoming disruptive. It was safe to say that he would have received a scholarship anywhere he wanted to go in the world of NCAA basketball, but he decided early on Iowa State. I thought that it was important that he stay close to Geneva and me, given his turbulent first year in school, and he agreed.

I met Terry Carroll and C.J. at the Iowa State basketball office in July of 1996, and on that day he verbally committed to Coach Tim Floyd and Iowa State. I had previously discussed with Floyd and Gar Forman, an assistant, that C.J. had played one season with Perth in the Australian NBL and would need to inform the NCAA of that playing experience. However, everyone figured that he would lose at most seven or eight games, as had been the precedent with foreign players. No one dreamed what was to occur.

C.J. Bruton was really beginning to develop personally and he enjoyed Indian Hills academically and athletically in 1996-97. He became willing to do the school work, enjoyed learning new things, and received maximum encouragement and extra help from the faculty. He was showing signs of becoming a good student. He had dealt with many of the past conflicts in his life and had begun to live in harmony with his values; his new approach to life, based on honesty and responsibility, also showed in his basketball.

C.J. led his Indian Hills team to a 37-1 record and to the 1997 National Junior College Tournament Championship. He was named Most Valuable Player in the tournament. Orv Salmon told me that Gary Garner, who had coached Fort Hayes State to the D-II NCAA National Title, Eddie Sutton of Oklahoma State, and Norm Stewart of Missouri were very impressed with Bruton. Seated together at one game, Stewart asked, "Why don't we get kids like that?"

Thus, young Bruton had weathered a very difficult first year in the U.S., had faced his reality, changed his behavior, and adapted to college life at Indian Hills in his second year. He had become responsible academically and led his team to the National Championship. He was on schedule to graduate with a "B-" average. C.J. told me, "I know that I can make it at Iowa State. I know I can do it." I was impressed with his priorities. He was referring to college academics, not basketball. It was a given that he would star in Big 12 basketball. His future looked bright. He had followed up his verbal commitment to Iowa State by signing a National Letter of Intent.

Ineligible

On March 27, 1997, C.J. submitted a letter to ISU-NCAA Compliance official, Tim Bald. In addition to the letter, he was required to include the Perth Wildcat contract from the 1994 NBL season. The Iowa State coaching staff was naturally interested to find out C.J.'s eligibility status in order to make future recruiting plans accordingly.

On April 21, I was pulling in to have a cup of coffee at the Zanzibar Coffee House in Des Moines when Tim Floyd rang on the car phone. He said that he had bad news and was sick that the NCAA had denied C.J.'s college eligibility. He also said that it looked final and no appeal was planned. I was disgusted, but not shocked, as I was aware of the NCAA's track record in other matters. Also Gar Forman, the ISU assistant, had indicated to me earlier that ISU had become increasingly concerned after C.J. had presented his Perth contract. Prior to the NCAA decision, as C.J.'s appointed guardian, I had called Tim Bald, the NCAA compliance official on the Iowa State campus. I wanted to be certain that C.J. had provided all needed information. Bald told me that he could not talk to me. Actually Bald came across as blunt and rude. He made a definite impression. I was baffled, but knew something was up.

I called C.J. at Indian Hills and informed him of the eligibility decision. No one drawing ISU paychecks - the A.D., the coaches, the NCAA compliance official - nor the NCAA had contacted C.J. Bruton on this matter. He had received nothing from anyone in writing regarding this decision. But it had sounded final from my conversation with Tim Floyd, so I told C.J. that there were still many options - the NBA draft, the NBL in Australia, or possibly NAIA college basketball competition.

On April 29, Tim Floyd announced in *The Des Moines Register* that C.J. Bruton was declaring for the 1997 NBA draft and would not be playing at Iowa State. Terry Carroll at Indian Hills confirmed Floyd's announcement. At the time, Indian Hills was somewhat concerned about C.J.'s situation there. He had been cleared for eligibility by the National Junior College Association prior to his freshman year at Indian Hills and it appeared that there would be no problem. The worst scenario would have been that C.J. be declared ineligible and the National Title taken from Indian Hills. In contrast to Iowa State's passivity in this matter, we were pleased to hear that Dr. Lyle Hellyer, the Indian Hills College president, had told Coach Terry Carroll that "we will fight" any junior college eligibility problems. I knew that he meant it.

During the week of May 12, WHO television's Keith Murphy was all over the story and announced that Bruton had received money as a player with the Perth Wildcats in the Australian NBL. C.J. and I were working out at Oakmoor Health Center in Des Moines, side by side on treadmills, on a Saturday afternoon when we saw the story on TV. I said, "Let's finish up here; I have to make a phone call."

I felt that it was time to take some action, as C.J. had already been declared ineligible at Iowa State and the media was following up on the story. I called Portland scout Ron Adams at his home in suburban Philadelphia. Adams, an astute coach who understood player development as well as anyone in the NBA, was interested in Bruton's situation. I trusted Ron Adams and knew that he would consider C.J.'s welfare first. I told him the story and asked if there was any possibility that the Blazers would look at Bruton. Ron said that he would discuss it with Mark Warkentien, Portland's Director of Scouting. C.J. received good news two days later as he was invited to a mini-camp in Portland May 19-22, 1997. He was in decent shape, but we agreed that he needed some preparation for the Blazer camp, so I supervised his two-a-day workouts for five days at Oakmoor. He reported to Portland in good shape physically and with a plan: keep expectations down, give it his best, learn, listen, and improve each day.

I flew to Portland on the 20th to attend the camp sessions. C.J. improved each day and at the end had impressed the Portland organization including Mark Warkentien, Ron Adams, and Tates Locke, as well as Jim Paxson. Portland said that on the basis of his camp performance it would give serious consideration to drafting C.J. in the second round, and it preferred that he not play in the NBA pre-draft camp in Chicago. That was not a problem, as he had not received an invitation. However, in the meantime, six other NBA teams had called Terry Carroll at Indian Hills regarding tapes, stats, and possible mini-camp participation. Bruton did not respond to the other teams and participated in the Portland camp only, prior to the draft.

Tates Locke

While in Portland, I had some good conversations with Tates Locke, a Portland scout. Tates had been a controversial, but successful and respected head college coach at Army, Clemson, and Jacksonville. He also was a head man in the NBA with the Buffalo Braves. The NCAA put the Clemson program on probation (in 1975) for a series of violations and Locke left there amid national publicity and controversy. He later was an assistant at Indiana, head coach at Indiana State, and then went on to the NBA as a scout with Portland. When I was at Middle Tennessee in 1970-71, Coach Jimmy Earle spoke often of Tates and always made efforts to hear him at clinics. Tates Locke was the hottest coach in the South and when he spoke (about defense), everyone listened.

C.J. Bruton was the type of kid and point guard that Tates Locke loved - a talented scorer, but looking to make the extra pass to help the team play better. Tates even drew comparisons between Bruton and Isaiah Thomas in regard to skills, size, and quickness. However, I knew that Isaiah had a huge edge in the area of competitiveness, the one area which Tim Floyd would have addressed, and hopefully remedied, at Iowa State. Locke and Ron Adams spent considerable time with C.J. at the camp and gave him valuable coaching at this point in his transition from junior college to NBA training camps. When we discussed the Bruton eligibility situation, Tates Locke, through his past experience with the NCAA, made an interesting comment that "they (NCAA) stuck C.J. with the old Jim Thorpe Rule."

I knew a few things about Jim Thorpe and had seen a movie depicting his life. However, I was curious about more details on him, made some phone calls to his home state of Oklahoma, and found that Thorpe was considered by many sports historians to be the greatest athlete of all time. Jim Thorpe was born in Prague, Oklahoma, in 1888 of Sac and Fox tribal heritage. He became a student at Carlisle Indian Institute in 1907 and led the famous Carlisle Indians under Coach Glenn Warner to national prominence in football. In 1911, Thorpe played semi-pro baseball for the Fayetteville and Rocky Mount teams of the Eastern Carolina League for a reported $15 a week. And in 1911-12 he was named to the Walter Camp All-American football teams. In 1912, Jim Thorpe earned Gold Medals at the Stockholm, Sweden, Olympics winning both the decathlon and the pentathlon events. Upon returning to the U.S. after the Olympics, he signed a professional baseball contract for $4,500 with the New York Giants. However, an investigation revealed Thorpe's prior semi-pro baseball experience in the summer of 1911 and the $15 per week, and his medals and Olympic records were wiped out. Only in 1983 did the International Olympic Committee resurrect his achievements. His family was later given duplicates of the Gold Medals and Thorpe was posthumously restored to amateur status for the years of

1909-1912. Thus his Olympic titles of 1912 were placed back in the official record book.

I told C.J. Bruton about Jim Thorpe, and I am sure that he immediately felt better. Just think, the NCAA might someday in its wisdom in the next 50-60 years restore his college eligibility. Like the appeal process in C.J.'s case, all too little and too late.

Sports Illustrated Article

On June 12, I received a call from Mike McKenzie, a freelance journalist and former sports writer, in Kansas City. He inquired about C.J.'s situation in regard to a story for *Sports Illustrated*. McKenzie followed through with the story and it was published the week of June 23, 1997. In the meantime, Tim Floyd, who was aware of the article, called and asked me if C.J. was still interested in Iowa State. I said that had not changed - yes, he wanted to go to ISU. Floyd then rang me back and said that he had talked with Gene Smith and that ISU was going to appeal. He said that Smith was flying to Kansas City the next day to confront the issue with the NCAA. Further, Floyd said to bring C.J. to Des Moines immediately, as he might be required at the meeting with the NCAA also.

The next morning I drove the fifty minutes to Knoxville to pick up C.J., as a friend had dropped him off there at a McDonald's after driving up from the Indian Hills campus at Ottumwa. We were riding to Des Moines when Tim Floyd called on the car phone and asked if I had seen the SI article; I had not and he read it over the phone. I remarked that it sounded accurate. However, Floyd also said that the Smith trip to the NCAA was called off and that the matter would be addressed next week as the NCAA staff was having an important meeting in Las Vegas. C.J. looked at me, shook his head, and frowned.

Taped Interview and Meeting with ISU

On Friday of that week, with the NCAA still hard at work in Las Vegas, I called Tim Floyd. In that conversation I heard for the first time that my own name was involved in the eligibility issue. He said that he had a recent meeting with Gene Smith. Floyd asked Smith why he had not returned any calls to Dave Adkins. Smith told Floyd that he had not returned the phone calls because he himself had listened to the NCAA-Bruton interview tape and in that tape Bruton had said that Dave Adkins was his agent. Floyd was shocked, because if this was true it would have reflected badly on his judgment and, of course, it would have reflected badly on me. This taped interview had been conducted by NCAA rep Kevin Fite, on the Indian Hills campus during the 1996-97 basketball season.

I was amazed that I had been called C.J.'s agent and told Tim Floyd that

1) I was not C.J.'s agent, 2) I seriously doubted that C.J. had said such a thing, and, 3) Terry Carroll had been present during the interview and could help clarify this matter. I immediately called C.J. and Terry Carroll and both vehemently denied that C.J. had made such a comment. Carroll said, "I was with C.J. during the entire interview and he said nothing about having an agent. Fite asked him how he got to Iowa from Australia and he said that he knew you (Dave Adkins) through his dad. But he said nothing about having an agent." When I spoke with C.J., he also denied having said anything about having an agent.

After speaking with Carroll and Bruton, I called Tim Floyd right back and said that it was urgent that I straighten this matter out and that Floyd, Smith, and I needed to meet. Floyd arranged the meeting and confirmed it with me that day. On Monday, June 23, I drove up to Ames for this meeting in Gene Smith's office on the Iowa State campus. Over the weekend prior to the meeting, I became aware that the C.J. Bruton case was one huge mess and I was dealing with people who appeared to know little or nothing about overseas club basketball, including both the NCAA and Iowa State.

I had formed a positive impression of Tim Floyd in Iowa State's recruitment of C.J. He was an effective recruiter and backed up his salesmanship with sound coaching. However, I had had one other experience with Coach Floyd which left some questions in my mind. At the end of the 1997 season, I had run into Floyd in the lobby of the Crown Center Hotel in Kansas City. I took that opportunity to arrange an appointment to talk with his senior players on campus about their professional basketball aspirations. Floyd told me to come to his office at Hilton Colosseum at 2:00 p.m. on a Monday in April, 1997.

When I arrived, no one seemed to know why I was there. I noted that Herb Rudoy, a successful NBA and overseas agent from Chicago, was also present. Coach Floyd was preparing to leave town and was obviously preoccupied with several different matters. Floyd finally directed me into an office with Kenny Pratt and Shawn Bankhead, and steered Kelvin Cato and Dedrick Willoughby into another office with Herb Rudoy. Pratt had been a problem athlete at ISU, and Bankhead was a lower-end overseas prospect. Cato and Willoughby were NBA prospects or high-end, Italy or Spain, European players.

That day I saw Tim Floyd, the busy man, not the patient, focused coach. On this occasion, I noticed that Floyd, like many top-level coaches, operated at high speed, was preoccupied with self, and appeared to be steered by his own adrenaline. Although I was okay in talking with Pratt and Bankhead, I was disappointed in those events. Herb Rudoy and I went to downtown Ames later that afternoon, had a coffee and exchanged some stories about our experiences in the overseas business. Rudoy and I had both had some dealings with Shelly Clark, the ex-Indian Hills and University of Illinois post player. I had sent Shelly, a massive 6'9 inside player, to France. He did a good job there for three months and then called me, said that he wanted to come back to the U.S. and that he was considering attending law school. However, he passed up the bar and continued on a path in overseas basketball. The last time I spoke with Clark, he turned down a $100,000 contract in Poland which I had arranged through European agent Petri Rosenquist. I heard that he had subsequently accepted work in Turkey. The coffee break with Herb Rudoy concluded the Ames trip on a positive note.

Even though I was not impressed with the treatment which I had received that particular day, I wanted to trust Tim Floyd and felt that I could. However, I had never met Gene Smith and was not encouraged by the rumors that Smith hoped to use the A.D. job at Iowa State to launch a career as an NCAA executive. Nevertheless, I went into the meeting with an open mind, doing my best to remain objective and to work with these two ISU athletic officials to resolve the Bruton eligibility case.

Just before our meeting on that morning, June 23, Smith received a fax from Trish Bruton in Australia. She wanted to clarify again, once and for all, that Dave Adkins was not C.J.'s agent. The verbatim text of the letter is as follows:

Iowa State University   June 23, 1997
Athletic Director
Attention: Mr. Gene Smith

Dear Mr. Smith:

This letter is to confirm that my son C.J. Bruton has never signed a contract with an agent. Specifically, he has never signed an agent contract with Mr. David Adkins.

C.J. would undoubtedly seek our permission before he took such an action. I will reiterate emphatically that the relationship between David and Geneva Adkins and my son, C.J. Bruton, is exactly as stated in my letter of March 27, 1997.

David Adkins is C.J.'s friend, confidant and a close family friend of many years. We, Cal, my husband and I, have asked Dave and Geneva to assume a parental role with C.J. since he has been residing in the United States since 1995 and we are residing on the other side of the world in Perth, Western Australia.

I hope this letter now settles the matter of this relationship once and for all.

Sincerely,

Patricia Newman-Bruton
Scarborough, Western Australia

Smith's secretary brought the fax into the meeting room where Floyd and I were seated. Gene Smith acknowledged that C.J.'s mother had sent him a fax. I knew what was going on and I received a copy of the fax from Trish later that day. I felt that Smith was satisfied at this point that I was not Bruton's agent and we were able to move forward with the meeting in a reasonably cooperative manner. Also, I discussed with Smith and Floyd the fact that overseas professional basketball in Australia was, at best, in the lower-mid to mid-category regarding overseas player salaries. I pointed out that C.J. had earned no more than the value of most one-year, NCAA Division I basketball scholarships. Further, I emphasized the numerous cases of "real pros" from foreign countries who had later played in NCAA competition without controversy. I commented that if each case of foreign-player eligibility were scrutinized carefully and judged by the letter of the rules of amateurism, as in the case of Bruton, the NCAA would probably have to cancel the results of the last ten years of Division I competition.

I found Gene Smith to be personable in the June 23 meeting at Iowa State; I was somewhat impressed with him and at this juncture I thought he seemed interested, even mildly enthused, and said that he would present this new information immediately to the NCAA. I provided Smith with a memo regarding overseas player salaries. However, I was concerned that Smith was not taking notes during the meeting and we were going over a great deal of detailed material, as it pertained to the Bruton case.

Smith also commented that he would offer a payback of Bruton's earnings and suggest some reduced eligibility. I immediately said that I did not agree with the payback plan. I thought a payback would have been unfair to C.J., as I was sitting at a table with a coach making $500,000+ and an Athletic Director on a six-figure salary. Also, down in Kansas City the NCAA bureaucracy was being underwritten from the sweat of "amateur players" who generated millions of dollars through their TV game appearances. C.J. had worked his tail off as one of the very lowest paid players in the NBL to earn that money and to give it back sounded hypocritical in the context of the financial realities of the ISU officials and the NCAA.

I left the meeting at Gene Smith's office and walked to the parking lot with Tim Floyd, who was leaving on vacation that day. Floyd told me that he and Smith were having problems and had some serious differences of opinions on the matter of the terms of (Floyd's) new contract. I sensed from this conversation that the Smith-Floyd relationship (at that time) would make it impossible to expect a unified front from Iowa State University in C.J.'s advocacy. I understood that Gene Smith and Tim Floyd had had a good working relationship until the contract problem had occurred and unfortunately that coincided at a critical juncture in the Bruton eligibility case.

As I drove back to Des Moines on a beautiful June day, I thought that this whole eligibility controversy was a farce and no one really knew what the hell he was doing in judging overseas player eligibility. There had been a couple hundred foreign players on Division I school rosters every year for a decade, but C.J. Bruton was declared ineligible; I found that to be grossly unfair. I was doubtful that anything positive would come from that morning's meeting at Iowa State, but at least I had the opportunity to talk with Smith and Floyd face-to-face, and it was clear to them that I was not C.J. Bruton's agent. That was progress.

Drafted

On June 25, C.J. Bruton was selected by Vancouver as the 53rd pick in the second round of the 1997 NBA draft. Bruton's rights were immediately traded to the Portland Trailblazers. We thought that C.J. would be taken by Portland in the 48th spot, but when Alvin Williams was announced, I received a call from a despondent C.J. Bruton. I told him that it didn't matter that much and that his future was bright regardless of the draft. About that same time, I heard yelling in the background both at my end and his: he had been selected 53rd by Vancouver. When we hung up, Portland's Jim Paxson rang me asking for C.J. and explaining, "He is our pick - tell C.J. that he is our pick. We have purchased his rights from Vancouver."

I found out later that in a meeting on draft day, Tates Locke, the Portland scout, was concerned that someone might take C.J. ahead of the Blazers. I understood that Portland had tried unsuccessfully to protect Bruton and to trade for one of Philadelphia's picks - 34th, 36th, or 37th. Nevertheless, Bruton was drafted, and projected late-first/early-second round choices from the state of Iowa, guards Dedrick Willoughby of Iowa State and Andre Woolridge of the University of Iowa, had completed strong senior seasons yet were, surprisingly, passed over. Being selected by Portland was a great break for C.J., as the Blazers persisted with his instruction and development in various camp settings. Mark Warkentien, Ron Adams, Tates Locke, and Jim Paxson had been strong Bruton backers from the beginning of the draft process. However, even after the draft, C.J. wanted to continue the Iowa State eligibility quest; he really wanted to go to school and to Portland's credit, it was fully supportive. The Blazers felt that they had grabbed a future first-rounder as a 53rd pick and knew that C.J. would need further experience, either in college or overseas. C.J. himself much preferred the college possibility. He wanted to play under Tim Floyd and develop his game. He wanted an education.

"The Appeal Process"

After the draft, business on the college eligibility issue seemed to grind to a halt. The rest of the week passed with no word from Iowa State - no update, no contact, no nothing. On June 29, I talked with C.J. and said that I thought the whole Iowa State appeal business was just more talk, a knee-jerk reaction to the *Sports Illustrated* article, and not to expect any good news. I suggested that he request an answer in writing from Iowa State by July 3rd or move on to other options. He did that. He faxed a letter to Gene Smith asking for an answer on his eligibility by July 3rd. On June 30, Gene Smith called me and said that he had received C.J.'s letter and would have an answer for him as requested. On July 1, Gar Forman caught me on the car phone and said that he had talked to Gene Smith that day and that it looked good for an answer and some possible progress in C.J.'s case. I also had a message on my voice mail from Rick Brown of *The Des Moines Register*, who said the same thing.

However, I received conflicting news from John Walters of Channel Five-TV, as he informed me that he had called Kerry Doyle in Legislative Services at the NCAA and she told Walters that ISU had yet to file papers previously requested by the NCAA. She said that a letter from Smith at ISU had been received on July 1, but that he had not as yet addressed the issue of the requested information. Doyle further stated that no appeal could be started without that information and that the July 3rd deadline would not be possible. Walters reported this story on Channel Five sports that evening. Fortunately Walters was able to locate Smith, on the golf course, and he said between holes that "everything was in order" on the paper work. (Fore)

On July 2nd I called Brenton Benowksi at the Big Twelve Conference office, and he checked the rules and confirmed that Iowa State could pay the legal bills on this appeal process. We discussed the matter further and Benowski mentioned Mike Glazier as a possible attorney to handle the appeal on C.J.'s behalf. It was clear that an appeal would be necessary, as Gene Smith informed me on July 3rd that the new information on the case had been rejected at the NCAA staff level. When I told him that C.J. wanted to pursue this matter still further, Smith resisted and asked, "Why?" Gene Smith was reluctant to continue the process but eventually agreed to talk with Mike Glazier, the attorney. I had a rather heated conversation with Gene Smith from my car phone and I was convinced that he (Smith) at this juncture just wanted the whole Bruton headache to go away.

I had the mistaken idea that Glazier would become an aggressive advocate for Bruton and push the NCAA to re-think the entire situation. That did not happen. I talked with Glazier again and told him that Gene Smith was expecting his call and that he (Glazier) should be the point man and "carry the ball" on C.J.'s behalf. I also reiterated that the Big Twelve office had confirmed that ISU could, in fact, pay the legal fees for C.J. I understood from Glazier that the appeal process would take 10-14 days.

In another conversation, Smith informed me that the NCAA had refuted my statements from the June 23 meeting including my contention that the basketball salaries in Greece, Italy, Spain, and France were more than in the Australian NBL. Smith told me that the NCAA maintained that the NBL was a highly professional basketball league. Thus the NCAA apparently ignored my point that C.J. had received a small salary in a league that paid much less than the home countries of other NCAA approved players and had also rejected the other points of my conversation with Smith and Floyd.

This was frustrating news to me. I had been involved in overseas basketball for 30 years and worked with foreign clubs on a daily basis, yet the NCAA refused to listen to the facts which I had provided in good faith. At that point, I wondered what international basketball experience did these NCAA experts have - Kevin Fite, Carrie Doyle, Lisa Dehon - Cedric Dempsey for that matter. These people were passing judgment on a critical phase of C.J. Bruton's young life. Did they have in-depth knowledge and experience in basketball played in foreign countries?

When I had my initial conversation with Mike Glazier, I mentioned the matter of the Kevin Fite interview on the Indian Hills campus with C.J. Bruton and Terry Carroll. I told him that Bruton and Carroll had both denied that any mention was made of me as C.J.'s agent in the interview. With some persistence and a few calls, I was able to finally obtain a copy of the infamous tape. When I received the tape, I sat in my car in front of the West Des Moines post office and listened carefully; I later played the tape again. I heard no such comments by Bruton identifying me as C.J.'s agent, nothing like that at all.

I sensed that the agent issue in the taped interview could have been one of the initial impediments in NCAA-ISU discussions, a "red flag" to the progress of eligibility procedures. However, I felt that later in the meeting with Gene Smith and Tim Floyd, it had become clear to all parties that I was, in fact, not working as C.J. Bruton's agent. Yet, I still wasn't sure about the agent issue and the delays further convinced me that Iowa State University was not going to make an all-out effort to save C.J. Bruton's eligibility.

What the hell was going on? Did Fite actually tell ISU, possibly Tim Bald, that Bruton had identified me as his agent? Did Bald pass this on to Smith? Did Smith use the tape as a reason to discourage Tim Floyd from pressing for an immediate appeal? Why would Tim Floyd tell me, and reconfirm, that Smith had said that he himself (Smith) had listened to the tape and that I had been identified by C.J. as his agent, and then have Smith deny to me that he said this?

I spoke about a year later with Tim Floyd regarding the tape issue at a Future Stars Camp at Drake University on April 10, 1998. I specifically asked Floyd for clarification and confirmation on this matter. He *again* emphatically confirmed that, yes, Gene Smith had told him that the tape contained statements by Bruton that Dave Adkins was his agent. I reminded Floyd that I had obtained a copy of the tape and there was nothing on the tape to support Smith's statements. Floyd was furious again. I concluded that I had delivered an NBA draft choice to the steps of Hilton and had done my best to see that C.J. got a chance at Iowa State. Floyd replied, "We didn't do our best." I had to agree.

Between July 3 and July 16, Mike Glazier did some work on the Bruton case and said that he had submitted a letter of appeal for C.J. to ISU and that ISU was to present this letter to the NCAA. In the meantime I had heard nothing from Gene Smith. I called him on July 22. He was out of town on vacation, but returned my call from Shreveport, Louisiana. I asked what was happening on the appeal and he actually said that *he did not realize that this was an urgent matter*. That comment made me think. Was this man really working hard to represent C.J. Bruton's case to the NCAA? I had my doubts. I sensed in Smith's statement regarding *urgency* a lack of commitment and a certain arrogance, or maybe he had actually failed to grasp the urgency of the entire eligibility issue. I was truly shocked and disappointed at Smith's attitude, which revealed more clearly to me the low priority for Bruton's eligibility with the ISU Athletic Department.

I could see that Gene Smith wanted nothing to do with challenging the NCAA. Was it not urgent to the player, the player's family back in Australia, the Iowa State coaching staff, Iowa State fans, and to the Portland Trailblazers? I replied to Smith that I had emphasized from the start of the initial appeal discussion, i.e., after the *Sports Illustrated* wake-up call, that the matter was clearly urgent. C.J. Bruton had already missed the opportunity to play with Portland in the LA Summer League and the next Portland obligations were July 26 at the Rocky Mountain Review in Salt Lake City. He could not afford to miss that event.

At this time I also asked Smith about the Kevin Fite tape. I said that I was irate that statements were reportedly made about my being C.J. Bruton's agent. I told him that I understood from Tim Floyd that he (Smith) had confirmed the information on the tape. Smith denied to me that he had said this. I also confided to Athletic Director Smith that I was confused about the degree of Iowa State's commitment to the advocacy of Bruton. Further I stated that I thought in general Iowa State had done a poor job from day one on the C.J. Bruton eligibility case. Smith brushed off my comment, mumbled disagreement with my statements and the conversation ended.

On July 25, I heard from Assistant Iowa State A.D. Elaine Hieber that the NCAA had decided that there had been no new compelling information presented, therefore request for appeal was rejected. I later received a call from Gene Smith confirming that the issue was dead with the NCAA.

Essentially, nothing had changed and I felt that Iowa State had taken little effective action in the player's defense since C.J. Bruton was initially declared ineligible back in April. The entire matter was a huge disappointment to C.J. Bruton. He felt all along that Iowa State, both the basketball program and the athletic director, had showed limited interest in working to save his eligibility. I had on several occasions attempted to keep him on ISU's side and encouraged him to have faith in their effort, even though I had strong doubts also. However, I felt now that C.J.'s instincts had been correct from the beginning. We were both disappointed and confused regarding the final outcome, but we did fully agree on the extent of ISU's effort in the matter.

College Doors Closed

The case was officially closed. At 11:00 a.m. on Saturday the 26th of July, 1997, I reluctantly agreed to work as C.J. Bruton's NBA and overseas basketball agent, as he waited to depart for Salt Lake City and his first action in a Portland Trailblazer uniform. I would have much preferred to watch him register for college classes than to sign that agent contract. I would have much preferred to have met with him at the Iowa State University Library in Ames rather than at the NBA's Rocky Mountain Review in Salt Lake City. My reluctance was associated with my own frustration in knowing that C.J. Bruton had just missed out on a very important experience in his life. But there was no turning back now, as the NCAA had closed the doors tight on C.J.'s college career. The NCAA had successfully defended the "purity" of Division I basketball from a foreign invasion. However, C.J. was not foreign; he was born in Wichita, Kansas, and was a dual citizen of the United States and Australia. His mother and father were both American born.

The Rocky Mountain Review was played at the Delta Center in Salt Lake City, Utah, home of the Utah Jazz. Twelve NBA teams participated with player rosters which included a mixture of veterans, free agents, and rookies. Portland had planned to use C.J. for extended minutes in the LA Summer League played at Long Beach State two weeks before; the Blazers had played six games in Long Beach in the week of July 13-20. They had brought the team together to practice for LA the previous week. And after the LA competition, the team returned to Portland for another week's build up to the Rocky Mountain Review. C.J. missed these critical three weeks because of the NCAA-ISU delays prior to the Rocky Mountain Review and arrived not knowing the players, the new coaches, or the system.

In retrospect, he waited from June 3 to July 25 for Iowa State and the NCAA to advance his eligibility issues and nothing happened. Absolutely nothing new happened. His situation apparently did not progress past the original ineligibility decision of April 29. In my opinion the only reason that the matter was resurrected was the force of the prominent June 23, 1997, *Sports Illustrated* article (Scorecard) which explained that Iowa State did not want to "buck" the NCAA and therefore chose not to appeal Bruton's case, to the displeasure of Coach Tim Floyd. The article concluded that Gene Smith, ISU athletic director, had not returned calls on this matter to *Sports Illustrated*. (See Appendix F, pages 355-356 for reprint of SI story)

I would classify Smith and ISU's advocacy of C.J. Bruton, a young man who wanted desperately to attend ISU, as disappointing. The SI article put heat and national focus on the matter and Iowa State had no choice but to take some action. To my knowledge, ISU never did take the trouble to go to Kansas City to confront the issue. Tim Floyd, known as an aggressive coach, was uncharacteristically passive in the defense of Bruton. Smith was a reluctant participant during the entire process. He persistently maintained the position that C.J. was drafted by an NBA team and that there were so many players that would give anything to be in his position.

In September, after he had returned from the Rocky Mountain Review, C.J. went to the Des Moines Public Library to look up an article on Chris Childs, the New York Knick point guard who was doing well after treatment for chemical dependency. Bruton told me that he had inadvertently run into Gene Smith on the streets of Des Moines a couple of blocks from the library. C.J. said that Mr. Smith had told him the same thing that day that he had told me on a couple of occasions, that he (C.J.) was fortunate to have been drafted and to have opportunities to continue playing. C.J. was perplexed. I suggested that Smith was at least consistent on this point.

During this period, Floyd and Smith were apparently at odds over Floyd's new contract and there was (therefore) never a unified front from Iowa State University on C.J.'s behalf. Neither seemed to be able to fully commit to defend Bruton. Tim Bald, the NCAA on-campus compliance official, provided little instruction, no advice, and no support to Bruton. Essentially all he did for the player was forward mail to the NCAA. The Kevin Fite on-campus interview, ISU's apparent reluctance to challenge the NCAA, the NCAA's approach to foreign player assessment, communication with the player, ISU's limited advocacy of the player's position, the appeal process - the whole deal was a mystery from start to finish.

What was actually at stake here for C.J. Bruton? He lost the opportunity to continue his personal development and his education at a respected American university. He lost the opportunity to play Division I basketball for the fun of the experience. He also lost the opportunity to develop his obvious NBA talents under Tim Floyd, whom we considered ideal to bring out Bruton's best. C.J. needed to work on his offensive consistency, his competitiveness, and his intensity, and I was certain that Floyd could have developed C.J. Bruton into a great major-college point guard and a first-round NBA draft choice. Also, I respected Floyd and saw him as a coach with the unique ability to drive his team - very hard at times - to improvement, yet still treat the players decently and in a manner which maintained their respect. Not playing under Floyd at Iowa State was a huge penalty for Bruton to pay, and he lost the very real opportunity to be drafted in the first round with guaranteed NBA money in seven figures. He was cheated. He was treated unfairly.

There was a huge difference between C.J.'s position as a 53rd choice at age 21 with only two years of junior college experience (and no Division I participation) and coming out of school at age 23 with two additional years of major college experience, coaching and exposure. A first-round draft pick could be assured of a guaranteed contract and was in a strong position to make a team and to have special opportunities to progress in the NBA. Eric Monter, *Monter Draft News*, confirmed, "All of the 1997 first-round picks signed guaranteed NBA contracts." As a 53rd pick, nothing had been guaranteed except financial uncertainty.

Portland encouraged C.J. to play overseas in the 1997-98 season and Bruton signed a contract with the Brisbane Bullets for the 1998 Australian NBL season. He had a good year with Brisbane, averaging 15.0 points and started to show increases in strength and body bulk. He then planned to give it a shot via the Portland summer camp system, as the Blazers had retained his NBA rights. If he had shown progress and the Blazer coaches felt that he could help them to win, he would go to the 1998 Veterans' camp, most likely with a "make good deal" - no guaranteed money. However, the NBA labor dispute disrupted this plan and put everything on hold for twelve months.

C.J. agreed to play the 1998-99 season with the Wollongong Hawks in Australia and then return to Portland in the summer of 1999. He was also named to the Australian National Team Training Squad, but was not selected for the 1998 World Championship Australian team. However, he was retained on the training squad and has a good shot at a position on the Australian team for the 2000 Sydney Olympics. With continued improvement, the Olympics could be the launching point of C.J. Bruton's NBA career. He would still be only twenty-four years old then. I saw C.J. play in Brisbane in May of 1998 and was impressed with his progress. However, I add that the Australian league was Plan B, and I do not doubt that Tim Floyd's system would have been more beneficial in his development.

Others Can Play

Then there was the matter related to other Australians who were *allowed to play* in NCAA competition. P.J. Carlesimo, while head coach at Seton Hall, coached a Big East All-Star team on an Australian tour in the summer of 1987. As I recall, the American team did not win a game competing against the Australian National Team in a test series of seven games. In the Aussie press, Carlesimo called the Australians "a top 20 team in the U.S." (an understatement). I saw the Big East team lose to the Australians at Hobart during that tour. Ironically, Calvin Bruton Sr. was a member of the National Team and played in that game against Carlesimo and the Big East team.

Coach Carlesimo got a first-hand look at Andrew Gaze, who was a star player in the NBL and also on the Australian National Team. It apparently occurred to the creative Big East Conference coach - P.J. - that Gaze might enjoy a change of scene from beautiful, tropical Melbourne to drab, frigid South Orange, New Jersey, as an American college student. The next year, the 1988-89 college season, the 23-year-old Gaze enrolled at Seton Hall and led the team to the NCAA Final Four with a one-point loss in the championship game to Michigan.

Prior to his college days, Andrew Gaze had been named to the first all-NBL team in 1986, 1987, and 1988. The year that he enrolled at Seton Hall he led the NBL in scoring with a 36.9 point average in 24 league games. His team, the Melbourne Tigers, did not qualify for the six-team league play-offs and he was able to go directly from the last regular season game in the Australian pro league to Seton Hall. And he left Seattle immediately after the NCAA Finals the next year to begin preparations for the 1989 Australian National Basketball League season.

Rumors were rampant in Australia that representatives of Seton Hall had deposited U.S.$25,000 in a trust fund in Australia for Gaze as a recruiting incentive. (Dick Butler, Basketball Australia executive, later mentioned this "trust" to Marc Hansen in a November 11, 1997 *Des Moines Register* article). National Team players were the highest-paid players in the Australian NBL, and Andrew Gaze was the leading scorer on the Australian National Team when he played for P.J. Carlesimo at Seton Hall. With Gaze clearly recruited by P.J. Carlesimo as a "hired gun" and to be used only for the short-haul, one season, it proved to be a great move as the Australian was named Most Valuable Player in the NCAA Western Regionals preceding the Final Four. It was, of course, unlikely that Seton Hall would have been in the Final Four without the globetrotting Andrew. Where was the NCAA when this was going on, in courtside chairs at the King-Dome, the site of the Final Four, or in Las Vegas?

Although Andrew Gaze came to the U.S., played a season with Seton Hall in the Big East Conference on national television, and then quietly and immediately returned after the college season to his old job with the Melbourne Tigers, other former Australian NBL pro players have also competed in NCAA-I basketball. Tony Ronaldson, a 6'7 wing player, played the 1990 season (26 games, 15 minutes per game, 8.0 point avg.) and 1991 season

(20 games, 21 minutes per game, 10 point avg.) in the NBL with the Eastside Melbourne Spectres BEFORE enrolling at Arizona State and playing the 1991-92 season (7.4 points and 2.5 rebounds avg.) in Pac-Ten Conference competition. Ronaldson, like Andrew Gaze before him, stayed only one season and returned to his pro job in the Australian NBL in 1992 playing 31 games.

David Stiff, like Ronaldson, a lesser known as compared to Gaze, nevertheless applied his 6'10 frame to the task at Boston University in the 1992-93 season (12.4 points avg.) and 1993-94 (10.5 points avg.) AFTER playing the 1992 season with Hobart in the NBL, the pro league, where he had appeared in 18 games, averaging 15 minutes and 7.0 points. Craig McAndrew, another big Australian, played three games with the Perth Wildcats, Bruton's former Australian team, in 1995 before enrolling at the University of Virginia.

It was noted in the discussion of Australian players - Gaze, Ronaldson, and Stiff that two, Gaze and Ronaldson, had superior playing records and Stiff had achievement in the NBL comparable to C.J. Bruton before playing in NCAA-I competition. Of the three, only David Stiff was penalized by the NCAA, which took six games away from him at Boston University in the 1993-94 college pre-conference season. A fourth Aussie, Craig McAndrews, was penalized eight games by the NCAA but was granted a full four years of NCAA eligibility. Thus Gaze and Ronaldson received NO NCAA penalties, McAndrews and Stiff lost a few pre-season games, and C.J. Bruton had his ONLY TWO YEARS of Division I college eligibility COMPLETELY WIPED OUT by the wisdom of the Overland Park bureaucrats. The listing below summarizes NCAA action in regard to Australians who have played in the NBL, the Australian pro league, before playing in U.S. college competition in the U.S.:

****

Andrew Gaze (Seton Hall) - no NCAA penalty
Tony Ronaldson (Arizona State)- no NCAA penalty
David Stiff (Boston University) - penalized 6 games
Craig McAndrews (Virginia) - penalized 8 games -
　　　　　　　　　　　granted 4 full years of college eligibility
C.J. Bruton (Iowa State) - penalized 2 full years -
　　　　　　　　　　　declared ineligible to play NCAA basketball
****

In addition to the above, in my business travels to Australia, I noticed a unique situation. Mick Penissi, a 6'9 Aussie, played with the Townsville Suns in the NBL season during the U.S. summer and then returned to Eastern Michigan University to assume his NCAA competition. I saw Penissi in Australia in the summer and in an Eastern Michigan University uniform in Des Moines (at Drake) a few months later. In other words, Penissi not only played Division I NCAA basketball and like many American players needed a summer job, however, Penissi's summer work was playing in the Australian pro league between U.S. college seasons.

There have been large numbers of foreign players participating in U.S. college basketball for several years. Although most of the attention focuses on Division I, I would estimate that, including Division I, II, III, and NAIA Division I and II, there could have been 800 non-Americans in men's basketball in 1997-98. *Sports Illustrated* reported 268 foreigners in Division I alone that year.

ANYONE WITH ANY KNOWLEDGE AND EXPERIENCE IN THE OVERSEAS BASKETBALL BUSINESS KNEW THAT IF A YOUNG FOREIGN PLAYER WAS GOOD ENOUGH TO IMPACT A DIVISION I, U.S. COLLEGE PROGRAM, HE WAS GOOD ENOUGH TO DRAW A PAYCHECK IN HIS HOME COUNTRY BEFORE HE CAME TO THAT U.S. COLLEGE. In the 1997-98 college season, George Washington University had ten foreign players on its roster. There are few U.S. college teams that have not used foreign players in their lineups. Nevertheless, regardless of the hundreds of other foreign players who had played at U.S. colleges, Bruton's case was closed; he was ineligible for life. (See Appendix C for George Washington University roster and Appendix D for list of foreigners in NCAA-I competition. See Appendix E for list declared ineligible by NCAA.)

I have discussed the backgrounds of five Australian players because they played in the same professional league as did Bruton, the Australian NBL, prior to their NCAA competition. The fact was that the Australian NBL rated far down the list among overseas professional leagues in terms of player salaries, as I had stated previously to Gene Smith at Iowa State and which was reportedly refuted by the NCAA experts. The Australian NBL had an annual salary cap of about A$600,000 (U.S.$ at December 1998 exchange rates of .60 = U.S.$360,000 per team per season.) Individual players, not teams, in some other countries, outside the NBA, can make that amount and even as much as two and three times more than that amount. These higher-paying countries included Greece, Italy, and Spain. And France, Japan, Belgium, Israel, Germany, Argentina, Venezuela, and the Philippines, to name a few, pay significantly higher salaries to players than the Australian NBL.

Marc Hansen - Another Perspective

I spent many hours in the fall of 1997 meeting weekly with Marc Hansen, columnist for *The Des Moines Register*, who was interested in doing a major story on the C.J. Bruton case. After getting to know and learning to trust Hansen, I discussed the matter with C.J. and arranged for the Bruton-Hansen interview to take place in my home. I provided Marc Hansen with background information, insights, and the names of key people in the overseas professional basketball business to assist him in the writing of his comprehensive, three-part series in *The Des Moines Register*, November 9-11, 1997, on the C.J. Bruton-Iowa State-NCAA case.

In order to put Bruton's salary issue in perspective, I suggested Guy Zucker, Dick Butler and Walt Szczerbiak as reliable sources of information regarding basketball in Israel, Australia, and Spain respectively. Hansen did a thorough job of research, contacted these people, and wrote his November 11, 1997, column on Bruton titled "Honesty Does Not Pay."

Hansen reported that in talking with Guy Zucker, who was an Israeli basketball agent based in Boston, it was confirmed that Doron Sheffer had led Galeal Elyon (basketball club) to the professional league championship in Israel in 1993. Sheffer racked up 40 points in the semis and was the tournament MVP. He played three years at the University of Connecticut averaging 16.0 ppg, 4.8 rpg, 6.1 apg and shot 41% from the arc and 85% from the line in his senior year in 1996. Sheffer had previously played in the Division One, professional league in Israel, *before* he played three full seasons at U-Conn. Incidentally, salaries in the Israeli League were significantly higher than in the Australian NBL and it was noted that Scheffer was the league MVP *in advance* of his U.S. college competition. Zucker did his best to provide an explanation, as reported by Hansen:

> "Sheffer played in a professional league, but not everyone in the league is considered a professional. Anyone in the army isn't considered a professional."

Continuing his globetrotting interview process, Marc Hansen next focused on Spain and reported that Ricardo Peral, i.e. Ricky Peral, played for Guadalajara, Spain, a farm team to Real Madrid, one of Europe's very best professional teams. Hansen was told that Peral was paid about "the value of a scholarship to Duke." This was, of course, before his three seasons at Wake Forest.

In speaking with Walter Szcerbiak, a former star in the Spanish ACB and father of All-American Wally Szcerbiak, Hansen was informed that "it would not be uncommon for a player of Peral's ability to be handsomely compensated." Szcerbiak declined to go into specifics.

Note: Ricky Peral, 6'10 starter and three-point specialist, played three full years at Wake Forest leaving there after the 1996-97 Atlantic Coast Conference season. A comment in the above quotations on Spain mentioned that Peral was probably making "the value of a scholarship to Duke" prior to his U.S. college play. College admissions' information showed that basic student costs at Duke in 1998 exceeded $27,500 for tuition, room, and board. Thus, a full scholarship at Duke including tuition, room board, books, and fees would have been very close to $30,000 per year or well over $100,000 for four years. Further, I pointed out earlier in discussing the Spanish league that Coach George Karl had mentioned in his book that Ricky Peral, at age 16, was on the Real Madrid team. Did anyone from the NCAA brush up on his Spanish and interview Real Madrid officials regarding Peral? Habla Español?

Dick Butler, who headed Basketball Australia, was next on Marc Hansen's list. Butler emphasized to Hansen that Australia and the United States have different systems of junior player development and that it was difficult to equate them. Also, Mr. Butler said that the U.S. college rules were complicated (and needed clarification) as he did not understand why Andrew Gaze and Tony Ronaldson could play, but C.J. Bruton could not. Butler even mentioned to Hansen that "he believes Gaze might have had a trust fund of some kind before leaving for the United States, but can't say for sure."

Following the original Bruton three-part newspaper story, Marc Hansen examined the case of Lester Earl, the new transfer player at Kansas. When Hansen's column on Earl was printed, Tim Floyd, still irate at having lost Bruton through the NCAA ruling, told me that he had faxed the story to Kevin Fite, NCAA rep and "key player" in the Bruton eligibility case, in Overland Park, Kansas. Hansen took a strong position on the Earl situation and wrote as follows:

"THE NCAA'S CREDIBILITY IS CRIMINAL - THE NCAA CUTS DEALS WITH SCOUNDRELS LIKE KANSAS' LESTER EARL BECAUSE THAT'S ABOUT THE ONLY WAY TO GET ATHLETES TO SING. TOO BAD THE NCAA COULDN'T HAVE WORKED OUT A DEAL WITH C.J. BRUTON."

On this occasion Marc Hansen blasted the NCAA in a strongly worded article appearing in *The Des Moines Register* on February 1, 1998. I was in Lisbon, Portugal, at the time and heard about the article in a call home; I rang Marc Hansen from my Lisbon hotel and congratulated him on the article.

Hansen disputed the logic of the eligibility of Lester Earl, believed to have received more than $10,000 in improper financial aid at Louisiana State and the ineligibility of C.J. Bruton, who earned about $9,400 in his 1994 playing contract with the Perth Wildcats in Australia. Although it was not clear how the NCAA judged these matters (an understatement), it was ironic that the Iowa State basketball scholarship would have been worth far more than the $9,400, which Bruton worked hard to earn.

Memo: Basic costs in 1997 for room, board and tuition for out-of-state students at Iowa State were just under $12,000. This figure included the cost of books which would have been a part of the scholarship. In other words, Bruton made LESS in Perth than he would have received at Iowa State through the value of a full athletic scholarship. Also in Perth, in addition to practice and games, Bruton worked twenty-hours a week off the court for the club or about 40 hours total per week.

Marc Hansen saw Lester Earl as "a deceitful opportunist" who accepted money knowing that it was against the rules and C.J. Bruton as "a well-intentioned young man who was honest and straightforward" in dealing with Iowa State University and the NCAA. Yet, Earl continued his college basketball career at the University of Kansas and Bruton was prohibited by the NCAA from participation in the Iowa State program.

The Clincher

However, the clincher on the Bruton eligibility issue came on March 24, 1998, when Kevin Fite of the NCAA contacted Nick Nurse who was back in Des Moines after coaching the 1997-98 season in Oostende, Belgium. Fite had called to discuss Nurse's comments of November 11, 1997, in the column written by Marc Hansen in *The Des Moines Register*. Hansen had quoted Nurse in that article as follows:

"When it comes to the eligibility thing, most foreign kids just write no, they haven't been paid. C.J. said yes. The NCAA didn't just figure this out. It knows what's going on: these kids have been getting paid forever."

However, Fite called Nurse (on March 24, 1998) who was in Cedar Falls informally discussing the Northern Iowa coaching job with Athletic Director Kevin Ritrievi. Fite contacted Nurse to refute this and said that his (Nurse's) statement was incorrect. Nurse commented on Fite's March 24 telephone call as follows:

"Fite said that in reality the NCAA does not know what is going on (with foreign player eligibility evaluation) and they would like for me to educate them on policy and procedures of different countries regarding level of salaries. He said it was not a big deal and we could meet over a couple of beers in San Antonio (at the Final Four). I agreed to meet him, but said no to the beers knowing the background of NCAA investigations. I was being hesitant to meet with him knowing I had zero to gain from a meeting."

Nick Nurse, a former Division I college player, experienced U.S. college and overseas professional coach in England and Belgium, and Mike Born, who played at Iowa State and also professionally in Europe, talked with Kevin Fite at the 1998 NCAA Tournament in San Antonio. The principals in the conversation were Fite of the NCAA and Nurse, but Born listened as Fite sat between them at the National Association of Basketball Coaches (NABC) international exhibition game. Nurse continued:

"Anyway we met at halftime of the NABC Nike Hoop Summit game which matched the top U.S.A. high schoolers versus the rest of the world. Fite said that he was there on a fact-finding mission. He had meetings set up with me and some guy who heads up the Australian Basketball Federation. He said also that he (Fite) got a nice trip to the Final Four because hotels in San Antonio required a four-night stay during the Final Four which worked out well for him."

In that conversation Nurse told Fite that foreign players, who had been paid prior, had been playing in U.S. colleges for 25 years. Nurse said that Fite replied that he knew nothing of this, nothing of the history of foreign player participation in college basketball. Drawing from his personal experience as a player with the Derby Basketball Club in England, as the head coach of the Birmingham Bullets (England) and Sunair Basketball Club in Belgium, Nurse said to Fite:

"I told him that I thought that 90% of the players playing from overseas in NCAA hoops had probably been paid at some point in their club career. That was my experience in England and Belgium. Even if it was $30 a week - players have to sign contracts to conform to league rules."

Nurse said that Fite attempted to justify his action on the C.J. Bruton case by claiming many times "I was just enforcing the rules - that's my job." Fite further stated that Tim Floyd had called him several times and that if Floyd didn't agree with the rules, then he needed to propose legislation to change them. I had talked with Nick Nurse both before and after the Final Four regarding his conversations with Kevin Fite. I asked Nurse what was his opinion of Fite's background and level of expertise in dealing with foreign player eligibility issues. Nurse replied:

"Kevin Fite seemed to be confused in the area of overseas basketball with a lack of knowledge and experience and sounded like he might be trying to improve his job status by following and finishing off the C.J. Bruton story."

I also talked with Mike Born in Des Moines after the NCAA Tournament. I posed the same question to Born: "What did you think of Fite's background and understanding in the area of overseas basketball and in evaluating foreign player eligibility?" Born replied:

"I was basically just listening to the conversation between Nick (Nurse) and Fite. As I listened to Fite I was thinking 'Get a clue.' He (Fite) said that if C.J. had made under $7,000, he might have been eligible; then he said that it depended on other things too. None of it made sense."

Thus Nick Nurse, the experienced overseas basketball professional with a solid reputation as a player at his alma mater of Northern Iowa and as a coach at Grand View College, the University of South Dakota, and in England, confirmed in his conversation with me on April 17, 1998, something that I had suspected. As the C.J. Bruton saga had unfolded, in my heart I knew all along that Kevin Fite and his Overland Park cronies lacked the in-depth experience and knowledge in overseas basketball necessary to make vital judgments on foreign-player eligibility issues.

I understood that Kevin Fite graduated from high school in Ottumwa, Iowa, and actually had attended both Indian Hills Community College and Iowa State University, as well as the University of Northern Iowa. He apparently played a little high school football, but not basketball. I heard in Ottumwa that he had worked at Oklahoma State University as an academic advisor before securing the job with the NCAA. He had to my knowledge never held a job in overseas basketball. He had apparently told Ottumwa friends that he was doing the Bruton on-campus interview while visiting his family (in Ottumwa) in January of 1997. In fact, he discussed some of the details of his interview with C.J. Bruton and Coach Terry Carroll with Ottumwa friends afterwards over a few beers at the Green Brier, a popular restaurant and bar in Ottumwa.

I called Joe Curran, an Ottumwa high school coach, who said that he knew Kevin Fite as he (Fite) had worked as a sophomore football coach at Ottumwa High School. Curran, whose brother Pat was an Ottumwa attorney and prominent Indian Hills booster, was among the group at the Green Brier listening to Fite discuss the Bruton interview. Curran said that Fite explained how he had "turned off the tape" at one point and had said to Bruton and Carroll that he was there only to get information about Australian basketball, not to rule on Bruton's eligibility. Curran said that Fite acted pleased with his own expertise in handling the interview. Curran said "He (Fite) is the kind of guy who is always right."

I was shocked when I talked to Joe Curran and found that Fite was discussing the C.J. Bruton interview at the local bar. Does the NCAA condone this type of behavior from its investigators, going back to the old home town, busting the local junior college All-American, and talking about it among friends at the local watering hole?

I called Mr. Fite at the NCAA on August 10, 1998, from the office of Steve Addington, a friend and Des Moines attorney. Fite came across in the conversation as personable, reasonably open, and as a company man. He did not come across as knowledgeable in the area of overseas basketball. He knew that the NCAA had rules and he concluded that C.J. Bruton had violated them. When I asked for a bottom line on Bruton's eligibility rule, Fite replied, "He signed a contract with a professional team for a certain amount of money - I can't remember the exact amount."

I replied that (1) foreign associations which I have dealt with required their junior and senior players to sign club and/or association contracts in order to be eligible to compete, and (2) If C.J. had saved every cent that he earned with the Perth Wildcats in 1994, he would not have had enough to pay room, board, tuition, fees, and books for one year at Iowa State. In regard to the signing of a contract, he also was required to sign a contract, an NCAA Letter of Intent, at Iowa State. He would have earned more from the ISU contract (in scholarship) than he did in salary as a 'pro' in Perth. Yet, he was declared ineligible.

Regardless of his lack of direct experience in overseas basketball, Kevin Fite was just doing his job. In fact, he overdid it, and *Iowa State did not aggressively challenge him*; they provided little resistance. Fite maintained the strict interpretation of the rule against professionalism, which does not allow foreign players - actually any player - to be paid for playing prior to NCAA competition. Bruton was paid; therefore, according to the NCAA, he was ineligible. Yet he was, of course, paid on a par with the value of a one-year NCAA Division I college scholarship and hundreds of other foreign players have competed without interference to their eligibility.

Bruton was up-front with the NCAA on this matter and as a result, two full years of Division I college eligibility were stripped from him by Kevin Fite and the NCAA. Fite explained the "bottom line" on Bruton's eligibility consistent with a letter from the NCAA to Gene Smith. Lisa DeHon, NCAA Eligibility Representative, in her letter of July 2, 1997, to Gene Smith, explained the NCAA's position, apparently its final position, based on information that the Australian NBL was a professional league, that Bruton averaged 16 minutes and 6 points a game in 26 games (Bruton refutes the number of games - Perth isn't sure), and that C.J. signed a contract and was paid.

The point of my disagreement with the NCAA is not the financial details. C.J. was paid, no one has ever contended differently. Therefore, regardless of the amount and according to the strict interpretation of the NCAA rules of "amateurism," he would be ineligible. However, do the NCAA overseas basketball specialists actually believe that C.J. Bruton is the only one of the 250-300 foreign players who pour into U.S. Division I schools each year who has signed a contract and been paid? I know of no overseas club in the world that does not require their players to sign a contract. That is truly amazing. It appears that the NCAA made a special effort to stop C.J. Bruton from playing college basketball, yet allows anyone else to participate freely.

What about the other 250+ foreign players in NCAA competition in the 1997-98 season - topped by 291 in 1998-99? How do these players, for example, George Washington University with ten foreign players, satisfy NCAA requirements? Do the players and the colleges tell the truth? Does the NCAA selectively choose its targets? What about Andrew Gaze, Tony

Ronaldson, David Stiff, Craig McAndrew, and Mick Penessi - all Australians from the same league where Bruton played? What about Doron Sheffer who led his team to the pro league championship in Israel before playing at the University of Connecticut? What about Ricky Peral, the Spanish player who had been with the powerful Real Madrid club, at age 16, and then went on to play three full seasons at Wake Forest? Why was C.J. Bruton given the NCAA death sentence for telling the truth? What about Lester Earl who left Louisiana State in a huge controversy regarding illegal payments, showed up at Kansas, and immediately became eligible for Big Twelve Conference play? How could Kevin Fite, with limited qualifications in overseas basketball, have made decisions which impacted the life of young C.J. Bruton and arbitrarily robbed him of the opportunities of an Iowa State education and basketball experience, as well the possibility of a guaranteed NBA contract? And what about the repercussions? Do the NCAA and Kevin Fite continue along the current path of "shooting from the hip" in regard to making calls on foreign player eligibility? I have asked these questions in earnest because it appears that C.J. Bruton, who was seriously pursuing an education and college basketball experience, was compromised in this process.

What is the solution for the issue of foreign players in NCAA competition? The NCAA could continue on its current course and policy of hit-and-miss enforcement of its rule on professionalism. *I contend that if, over the past ten years, the NCAA had enforced the literal interpretation of its rules on professionalism (just as they did with C.J. Bruton) and had used its normal penalties of wiping out games which included illegal participants, a very large percentage of the Division I games during this ten-year period would have to be thrown out.* For example, look at the 1997-98 season alone with 250+ foreign players competing in Division 1. How many of them actually had signed overseas contracts (*probably all of them*) and had received payments prior to competing in US colleges (*50% - 75% would be an estimate and a good starting point*) and how many college games would have been affected? Does the NCAA know?

Point of fact, amateurism has been a moot point in world basketball since USA Basketball, of which the NCAA was a member, decided to use professional, NBA players, in the 1992 Olympics. FIBA, the world basketball governing body, actually removed the word "Amateur" from its title in 1989 explaining that the distinction between amateur and professional no longer existed.

A simple solution to this huge problem could be for U.S. colleges to adopt the European club system with payments to players being routine from an early age. Actually, when one considers the millions and millions of dollars generated by "amateur" basketball players performing on television and the players themselves receiving only a scholarship, the club system has merit. Or the NCAA

could even take a practical approach and implement an eligibility rule based on something as simple and obvious as the player's age. The rule could read,
> "Any foreign player is eligible to participate in U.S. college basketball if he is under 20 years of age on the first official day of practice in his first year at the American college in which he has enrolled. Any foreign player past age 20 at this time is ineligible."

Thus, a passport would determine the matter.

The Australian National Basketball League has figured heavily in the C.J. Bruton controversy. Another NBL player, American Isaac Burton, had also been in the news. First Bruton and next Burton. What a deal. While the NCAA was all over C.J. Bruton's eligibility case apparently relying on the judgment of personnel with limited knowledge of the workings of overseas professional basketball, recent revelations in the news reported of point shaving which created further controversy in the college game with players from Arizona State and Northwestern involved.

Enterprising gamblers employed some U.S. college players looking for a little extra cash, which their scholarships did not provide, to control scores and point spreads of selected games. One of the key figures in this point shaving scandal was another guard, an American, playing in the Australian NBL, but note the spelling - *Burton*, not Bruton.

□*17*□

BURTON, NOT BRUTON
AND THIS ISN'T AMERICA

Isaac Burton was another talented backcourt player. He returned to Australia after being cut by Sydney in 1997 and was subsequently contracted by Newcastle in February 1998 after he was the center of recent controversy in the U.S. The Sydney Kings had signed Burton, who played at Arizona State and spent the 1996 and 1997 NBL seasons in Australia. Burton had been a 14.0 point per game scorer in college, as a versatile 6'3 guard for Coach Bill Frieder. I saw Isaac Burton play in the International Basketball Association, a minor league, in St. Cloud, Minnesota, in January 1996. I was impressed with his lively body, his athleticism, his scoring, and his court presence.

Isaac was entertaining, played with a *joie de vivre*, and celebrated his own good plays by shaking from head to toe. In spite of his obvious talent, I wasn't enthusiastic about his play in the NBL in Sydney, as I felt that he dominated the ball. I noticed at the 1996 Brisbane-Sydney game that he got his points, but his shot selection was poor and he was definitely thinking score before team. Actually, he was a strange choice in the first place at Sydney, as the two-guard position was normally filled by a local player whether in Australia, Europe, or South America. If a country wasn't producing the 6'2 to 6'5 quality players, it wasn't meeting minimum standards in local player development. Even though the shot selection was an issue, I saw Isaac Burton as a CBA (U.S.A.) playing rotation player with limited point-guard instincts - a small though talented off-guard. However, with development Burton showed the talent level to become an NBA call-up player.

In August 1996 I was walking in the King's Cross district in Sydney and took a seat at an outdoor cafe where the waiters were Brazilian and I could speak some Portuguese. I was leisurely browsing through the Sunday paper when I came across a startling basketball article. It was written by former player turned journalist, Damian Keogh. Although never a big booster of American participation in the NBL, Keogh had been an effective back-court player with the Australian National Team. His basketball credentials were impressive and included participation in the Seoul and Barcelona Olympiads as well as the World Championships in Argentina and Toronto.

The Keogh story in the Sydney paper came across to me as one of the standard mean-street, hard-luck stories which went down big in Australia and which apparently were intended to empathize with Isaac Burton's misfortunes and also take a shot at social issues in the U.S. When I read the Burton story, I thought of Tommy Brown, the Dean of Black Students at Middle Tennessee State. I had a two-hour interview with him one spring afternoon in 1971 and asked him his opinion and philosophy on coaching the black athlete. This was in the early 70s and a growth period in U.S. race relations on college campuses, in general, with some positive expansion occurring, especially in Tennessee. Even after the famous court case (Brown versus Board of Education) in which federal law made segregation illegal, Nashville, Tennessee, had maintained segregation in downtown department store lunch counters into the early 1960s, until forced by non-violent student demonstrators to integrate.

Tommy Brown

Tommy Brown had played at Pearle High School in Nashville, known for its strong teams, and was an outstanding point guard at Middle Tennessee before going on the road with the Harlem Magicians. He returned to Middle Tennessee State University, his alma mater, as a student advisor and was later named Dean of Black Students. In my conversation with him, he openly and emphatically advised me to never let a player, black or white, sell a coach on bad breaks and disadvantaged background as excuses for poor performance or unacceptable behavior.

Brown emphasized that too many players raised on these same city streets had succeeded at basketball and in their post-basketball lives and that allowing the player to use his background as an excuse for irresponsible behavior was a great disservice to the player himself and eventually to society. That day Brown challenged me with the (enormous) moral and professional obligation to hold players accountable for self-destructive behavior. I have been able through the years to respond selectively to this challenge; it was a two-way street and required a willing player. The Burton attitude in the hard-luck story, as it appeared in the Sydney paper, violated every rule in regard to the player taking responsibility for his actions and the article seemed to blame externals for Isaac Burton's difficulties.

Isaac Burton was released by the Sydney Kings after the team's disastrous 1997 season; he again got his numbers but failed to make the team better. Cut by Golden State, Burton reported to the CBA. Jim Sleeper, the savvy director of player personnel, called me from the Quad Cities prior to the team's signing of Burton. I discussed with Sleeper my impressions of Isaac Burton's talent and shortcomings in his game, but I recommended the player as a CBA prospect. The Quad City Thunder subsequently signed

Burton to a CBA contract. Then in November 1997, a story was published in newspapers across the country which implicated Isaac Burton in a point-shaving scandal in a 1994 Pac Ten Conference game, Arizona State versus University of Washington. On December 6, 1997, a news service release reported that Steve 'Hedake' Smith and Isaac Burton Jr., two former Arizona State basketball players, had pleaded guilty to charges of conspiring to commit sports bribery in a point-shaving scandal involving gamblers. Isaac Burton stated that he had made a deal with bookmaker Benny Silman to control point spreads in certain Arizona State games by missing free throws. "...I was to miss the free throws to make sure we won by that certain amount," Burton said.

When the charges became official, Isaac Burton was immediately released by the CBA's Quad Cities Thunder. He had appeared in eight games and averaged 6.9 ppg in the 1997-98 CBA season. Maybe this disturbing situation would get the attention of the two players, Smith and Burton, and head off more serious problems in the future for them and others - or maybe not. I also wondered about players at other schools and the pervasiveness of this problem in college basketball, past and present. Two things were certain: it was difficult to detect point shaving and most college players could use the cash. These facts created questions as to whether the point-shaving had spread across the country in college basketball.

American Division I college basketball was no stranger to point-shaving scandals. The 1950-51 season saw Kentucky capture the NCAA title, as Brigham Young won the NIT (National Invitational Tournament). However, the headline news that year was the developing story of players from big-name schools controlling the point spread in key games to benefit the winnings of gamblers and in turn to create income for themselves. The investigation implicated thirty-two players from seven different schools involved in a plan to fix eighty-six college games. Sherman White, former Long Island University star, spent eight months in prison on conspiracy charges and was banned from the NBA. The players of the University of Kentucky Wildcats, the most glamorous name in college basketball history, were heavily involved in the scandal. Kentucky was forced to cancel its 1952-53 season as other schools refused to schedule them.

In 1985, John "Hot Rod" Williams from Tulane University, who went on to an NBA career, was indicted on bribery and conspiracy charges in shaving points in two games. I saw Hot Rod Williams play for Tulane at Drake on December 17, 1984, at Veterans Auditorium in Des Moines. He was one of the most impressive looking, smoothest college players in my memory. In addition to his lean but strong 6'9 frame, Williams had an excellent sixteen-foot jump shot - impossible to block and fundamentally sound. Hot Rod's dilemma and the problems of other college players with limited funds were simply that everyone was making money - coaches, administrators, referees, sports writers, radio and television announcers, and the NCAA - except for the player himself, who probably thought that he needed it the most.

The player's side of the story in point shaving was not much different in past eras. Gene Melchiorre was the Bradley University star guard of fifty years ago. I can recall Melchiorre as a stocky-built, ball-handling point guard and also remember action shots of him scooting around the Madison Square Garden floor in the old black and white newsreels. He was involved in controlling the point spread in big games of that time and has carried the burden of his indiscrete action for a lifetime. Like Isaac Burton, he probably needed the cash and it looked easy.

The Isaac Burton story appeared in the Sydney newspaper a year before the point-shaving scandal in the United States was made public. Further, the Burton story was an example of Australian gullibility and naiveté regarding matters of race issues in the United States, while ignoring similar problems in their own country. For example, I had read little in the Australian press of why Aboriginals don't play in the National Basketball League or participate in mainstream Australian life. It was not a popular topic in the sporting press down-under.

The Burton story, as written by Damian Keogh, would have appealed to a broad base of readers in the United States in the 1960s and the 1970s. Many thinking Americans have tired of people of *all races* refusing to take responsibility for their own lives, making excuses, and turning their backs on opportunities presented in the United States. Isaac Burton and Hedake Smith made bad, short-term decisions for little money, jeopardized their professional careers, and will carry the "point shaver" stigma forever.

Population alone has made life in the U.S., a country of nearly 300 million, much more competitive in all fields than in Australia, a country of only about 16 million. People down-under are surprised when they apply for a job and aren't hired; in the U.S. it is the opposite. I recall seeing a classified advertisement announcing a government job in *The Mercury* in Hobart in 1986 which read: "Drug Counselor Needed. Must be 21 and have driver's license." In contrast, a drug counselor in Iowa, for example, must be state certified with a minimum eight months of intense, specialized training through a hospital's substance-abuse counselor-training program, with a Bachelor's Degree normally required.

Sportswriters with U.S. newspapers must have a minimum of a Bachelor's Degree in Journalism, which would guarantee them nothing without exceptional skills in the eyes of an employer. The Australian way of life emphasizes on-the-job training over formal education - the way it was in the U.S. in the 1940s and 1950s. An example of this era was Walter Byers, who headed the NCAA for nearly four decades. He had steadfastly defended the "educational aspect" of college athletics against all comers. However, Mr. Byers, I understood, was an ex-journalist who had never earned a college degree. His closest encounter with a sheepskin was apparently on his Kansas ranch. The Aussie position on experience over formal education is that "Yanks know how to talk about it" and "we know how to do it." In many cases, they are probably right.

Basketball journalism down-under gained its legs with the onset of the Australian *National Basketball League (NBL)* in 1979. Many first-generation NBL journalists had to learn the basketball writing business on the job without the formal academic preparation and also with little first-hand knowledge of the game. Australians grew up knowing something of their grass-roots sports - cricket, Aussie rules football, and horse racing; across the Pacific most Americans learn something of football (gridiron), basketball, and baseball. As time passed and in an attempt to hire people with a basketball background, newspapers in Australia sought out former NBL players, handed them a pencil and provided them space to write, giving birth to the second-generation of Aussie hoop writers. The early ones knew little of basketball and the later ones little of journalism. Ironically, the next generation of Aussie basketball writers could have both academic preparation in journalism and a feel for the game, but there is then the question of the material: the survival of the NBL has been in question.

The career sports' journalists at Australia's major national distribution newspapers, such as Bret Harris at *The Australian*, and Stephen Howell at *The Age*, learned the game on the job, maintained unusual interest, and in time developed coast-to-coast credibility. The same could be said for Boti Nagy in Adelaide and Dave Hughes in Perth, who have established themselves as savvy basketball writers down-under, but from papers with less exposure. Earlier attempts at a national basketball publication, one known as *The Basketballer*, did not survive, but in the 90s *One on One* has become the staple hoop source and appeared to be on solid financial footing.

In the U.S., converting ex-players to writers does not usually happen. Instead, ex-coaches and some players are handed a microphone, with mixed results. Bob Knight once said to a room of journalists something to the effect that most people had learned to write in second grade and then moved on to bigger and better things. In response, these chastised journalists could have made a case for the same principle applying to Knight's profession, as in learning how to dribble in the second grade and then moving on. Writers considered Knight to be good copy, but also confided among themselves about his thin skin. In deference to Knight, I have some experience as both a coach and a writer and I can attest that hind-sight was much easier than making on-the-spot decisions.

Damian Keogh

In using Damian Keogh's basketball career as a microcosm for comparisons between the differences in the realities of competition in American life and that of life down-under, it seemed clear to me that opportunities have developed for him in this country of 16 million which would never have occurred in the same way in the U.S., a country of 300 million.

Damian was a nice-looking, 6'4 guard who used all of his resources, physical and mental, as a player and also in planning his post-playing days. He has been able to capitalize on his celebrity as a former Sydney King and Australian International and has used that background to promote his sports writing career and other business and promotional interests in this city of about 4 million, Australia's "big apple."

To his credit, Keogh definitely took advantage of his Australian professional basketball career to propel his writing and business careers. I regarded Damian Keogh as an outstanding young point guard who eventually became more of a combination 1-2 guard. He was a skilled left-hander with a complete game, but had limitations with only average quickness and athleticism. Ironically, and in support of my assessment of his basketball ability, Keogh was never selected to the first All-NBL team. His highest ranking among NBL players was second-team all-league selection in 1990, in the days when all-star status was dominated by visiting American players. Yet, in spite of limited all-league recognition in the NBL, Olympic and World Championship honors came his way along with post-athletic career opportunities galore in Sydney.

How does this career translate in U.S. basketball? I would have rated Keogh in his younger days in the NBL as a (U.S.) Division 1 college backcourt player, mid-major to major and not an NBA draft choice. If that were the case, no doors would open for post-career celebrity in New York or Los Angeles or anywhere else in the U.S. *The New York Times* does not hire ex-college players, or even ex-New York Knicks, as writers on the force of their athletic reputation. The level of competition for jobs at the *NY Times*, as in all top American companies, would be unfathomable down-under. In that regard, this player was very lucky to have been born in Australia. However, I believe that Damian Keogh had personal qualities to be competitive in higher-level U.S. college ball and also in the American business world. He saw to it that he became educated. He was intelligent and competitive, and he was ambitious, very ambitious - characteristics which will take a focused young man up the ladder in the U.S. business world. Damian Keogh has always been focused and he has always had a nose for opportunity. In short, he would have succeeded in some competitive endeavor wherever he lived. However, in the United States, basketball would not have been his springboard. The path and destination would have been more conventional; much slower, more difficult, more treacherous, less secure.

However, in regard to the Burton story, I did not like the idea that an Australian journalist, with little insight into American life, had accepted at face value the perceptions of a 24-year-old American basketball player. The player, Isaac Burton, clearly had limited life experiences at the time and was to be implicated later in a point-shaving scam. That alone would make one question his judgment and credibility. Burton's comments had apparently been accepted as an unquestioned source of reliable information, yet the message came across as an attempt to bag the player's home country, the U.S.A. I suspected that the writer had no ulterior motives and the player only knew that it was an opportunity to get his name in the paper. However, I was sensitive to the implied criticism of the United States in this article on social issues far too complicated to be resolved on the sports page, or in books on basketball.

Tony Bennett - Short Stay in Sydney

Ironically, Isaac Burton had been selected to replace Tony Bennett with the Sydney Kings in the 1996 NBL pre-season. I made arrangements with Sydney coach Alan Black to send Bennett to the Kings to provide backcourt leadership in addition to scoring punch. Tony Bennett had been a great point guard under his dad, Coach Dick Bennett, at the University of Wisconsin-Green Bay, averaging 20.2 points and leading the team in assists in 1991-92. The Charlotte Hornets selected him in the second round of the 1992 NBL draft and Tony played three NBA seasons for guaranteed money. He was injured in the 1994-95 season and was rehabilitating a stress fracture when I first made contact with him in September of 1995.

We agreed that I would look around for a job in the overseas market, and I recommended Bennett to Sydney. In January 1996 the Sydney Kings signed Bennett, and Tony and his wife, Laurel, moved to Australia's Crescent City for the NBL season. Bennett was the point guard in the Sydney backcourt with Australian Olympian Shane Heal, a combination which seemed to be sound. Tony Bennett was a talented, unselfish ball-handler and scorer, and Heal, a great spot-up perimeter shooter.

The Sydney guard tandem looked to be the best in the NBL, as opponents would have felt the impact of the Bennett penetration leading to open looks at the basket for Heal. Also, the talented duo would have presented difficult match-ups for opponents. Bennett had been known for his ability to score a quiet 20 points at a high percentage and distribute the ball to open teammates, and Heal's trademark was the impact three-point shot and periodic explosion for high point totals in big games. It looked to be a perfect combination, essentially an NBA backcourt, with Bennett setting up Heal for the three-point bomb, as each player even had his own personality role - Heal as aggressive and flamboyant, and Bennett as quiet and reliable.

Bennett would have gladly given Heal top billing. I thought that the Kings would get 50 points and 15 assists a game from that Bennett-Heal guard tandem. Bennett's unselfishness would have made all of Sydney's players better, but it was short-lived.

I followed up on Sydney exhibition games at that time with telephone calls to NBL coaches, and all reports from reliable basketball people were that Tony Bennett was an unselfish player, exactly what the Kings needed, and had the head and game to make Sydney a winner. One interesting comment by an Australian coach was, "Maybe he's too good." So when I received an urgent trans-Pacific call from Michael Wrublewski, long-time Sydney owner, I knew it was serious.

Wrublewski apologized profusely but said that Coach Alan Black had decided that the team would be too small with Bennett in the lineup. I responded that Black was fully aware of Bennett's size in advance, but the die was cast. The Kings had thus taken the first step in sinking their own ship in the 1996 NBL season. I knew the dynamics, as I had made the same mistake in 1988 in moving Kelvin Scarborough into the Hobart lineup in place of Greg Giddings. I paid the price for the move, as did Sydney, as the team failed to meet club expectations and went down to Canberra in the first round of the 1996 playoffs.

Therefore, after a handful of pre-season exhibition games in a mid-level overseas league, ex-NBA player Tony Bennett was cut - an excellent player and a top-level young man. Other former NBA players had been riffed before by Aussie teams, but never had a player with Bennett's background and character been dropped. A solid man on and off the basketball court with a strong spiritual commitment, Bennett accepted the Sydney decision with maturity and understanding, far beyond that of any player which I had seen in similar circumstances. It was normal also to hear cries of protest from the player's family under such conditions, but not a word came from University of Wisconsin head coach Dick Bennett. Tony Bennett had a legitimate gripe, was disappointed and had been inconvenienced; but he showed no hostility toward Sydney, only disbelief, which I shared.

No other Australian NBL teams were in need of a point guard at the time, so I made a quick call to a club in Auckland, New Zealand, and to my surprise Tony accepted the offer and flew over to Auckland to play in the New Zealand NBL. This was the same position that ex-Iowa State player Hurl Beechum had vacated after two games (18 and 10 points) and three days on the job, claiming that it wasn't strong enough competition for a player of his background. But ex-Charlotte Hornet Tony Bennett accepted the Auckland job with enthusiasm and re-signed for a second season.

Shane Heal - Point Guard

I knew that Sydney owner Mike Wrublewski was perplexed by Alan Black's decision to cut Tony Bennett, but he left the player personnel business to the head coach in this situation. Although there was a code of silence from the Kings on the facts of the decision to ax Bennett, I believed that Shane Heal was probably the key. I heard that he was unhappy in the shooting-guard position and wanted to play the point. He was at the time working on his point-guard skills with an eye to a future NBA contract. Heal had later gained some worldwide recognition when he exchanged words with Charles Barkley in a 1996 pre-Olympic exhibition game with the U.S. Dream Team. Nationally televised in the U.S., Shane Heal stood up to Barkley and also nailed 28 points against the NBA players on Dream Team III.

The impression created in the Barkley incident and Heal's overall play in the 1996 Atlanta Olympic Games drew attention from NBA teams. The Australian press carried endless stories about Heal and an NBA contract. I called Ron Adams, the Portland scout, from Sydney, and he said that his team, the Blazers, was not interested in Heal. It seemed to be the opinion of most NBA teams that Heal was considered more of a shooting guard than a point. However, the Minnesota Timberwolves thought otherwise and signed the Sydney King player to a three-year guaranteed deal for a reported $1.2 million.

Shane Heal thus became the third Australian-born player to draw an NBA paycheck, along with Chicago Bull starter Luc Longley and Andrew Gaze, who had played on a temporary call-up with the Washington Bullets. Shane Heal was the second Australian, after Luc Longley, to earn a guaranteed contract from a National Basketball Association team. Chris Antsey, selected in the first round of the 1997 NBA draft by Dallas, became the third. Although Andrew Gaze did play with the Washington Bullets, he was on a ten-day call-up contract with no further guarantee. Australia has yet to produce an NBA impact player, a star, with Longley by far the most productive Aussie in American pro ball.

Eddie Palubinskas was the first Australian ever selected in a U.S. pro draft; he was taken by Utah of the ABA in the eighth round in 1974. "Fast Eddie" starred at Louisiana State and was the leading scorer in the 1976 Montreal Olympics. He had a high game of 48 points, missing only one shot, in Australia's historic 120-117 overtime win against Mexico.

The Shane Heal NBA career was short-lived. After one uneventful season (43 games, 1.7ppg) with Minnesota, Shane was back in the Australian league with the Sydney Kings. To his credit and with vintage Shane Heal brass and confidence, he had created a worldwide reputation for himself, played in the NBA for a team which paid him well, and returned home to

Australia to the Sydney Kings with an eye to the 1998 World Championships in Greece and the Year 2000 Olympics in Sydney. Shane Heal had truly demonstrated NBA super-star confidence and ego in his whirlwind tour of the Atlanta Olympics and in the abbreviated NBA showing. The story went that only four people thought Heel could play in the NBA; T-Wolves GM Kevin McHale, Coach Flip Saunders, Heal, and his agent. After the 1996-97 season, there were only two. He may return, who knows?

Shane Heal has persisted with his point-guard aspirations. The Kings, having used eleven different U.S. imports in 1998 trying to find the magic for Coach Bill Tomlinson, finally settled on Kelsey Weems, a guard, and Evers Burns, a post player. A former North Carolina State and CBA backcourt player, Weems was assigned to the point-guard position with Sydney with Shane Heal shifted to the two guard. However, I noticed in *The Australian* (June 3, 1998) in a Bret Harris basketball story that Heal had publicly informed the Kings that he would not play the shooting guard position in the future.

It was well known around the NBL that Heal wanted to play the lead guard and control the ball. Shane had consistently maintained that the point was his natural position as he had played that spot for the Boomers, the National Team, and also overseas with the Minnesota Timberwolves. But Sydney coach Bill Tomlinson was determined to re-sign Weems as the Kings' point guard. The Shane Heal-Kelsey Weems matter underscored my perceptions on the release of Tony Bennett in 1996. Shane Heal wanted to play the point and the Kings had caved and released ex-NBA player Bennett.

Mike Wrublewski - The Owner

Long-suffering Sydney owner Mike Wrublewski has led an exciting basketball life. The Isaac Burton-Tony Bennett-Shane Heal dramas were routine for Wrublewski, a hard-driving businessman and a registered pharmacist who became a self-made millionaire. Born in Frankfurt, Germany, in 1946 and the oldest of three children, Michael Wrublewski and his family immigrated to Australia in 1955. Sam Wrublewski, the father, did not speak English on his arrival in Australia but used his drive, brains, and personality to build a profitable business in the garment industry of Sydney.

Brothers Mike and Harry Wrublewski are both emotional men and I imagined that each has much of his father's passion. They worked for the elder Wrublewski, and through my conversations with them, I surmised that Mike and Harry learned from their father the business principles which have led to their financial success in various ventures including the Sydney Kings, one of the few consistently profitable NBL franchises. Michael Wrublewski, the chairman of the Sydney Kings, broadened his basketball business horizons when he dispatched his younger brother, Harry, to England. They committed to building the game of basketball, in general, and the Birmingham Bullets, in particular, in the English National League.

The Wrublewski's purchased the Birmingham, England, franchise. Ironically, Mike Wrublewski has reportedly turned a large profit with the Kings in Sydney, but he has never had an NBL championship team. Harry's Birmingham Bullets have captured the English title twice, the first in 1996 under American coach Nick Nurse, and behind the play of MVP Tony Dorsey. The second was in 1998 under Coach Mike Finger, also a Yank, with Dorsey MVP again.

The Birmingham franchise and English basketball, in general, have struggled financially. Admittedly, if a basketball franchise had the remotest potential to turn a profit, the Wrublewskis could find a way. I have had dealings with both Mike and Harry for 15 years, and I have learned lessons in business every time I talked to them. They, like their father, have demonstrated that they are unrelenting entrepreneurs with energy and endurance to match their savvy, which has been required to survive as the decision makers for the unpredictable Sydney Kings and the Birmingham Bullets, respectively.

Although I have enjoyed a good working relationship with both of the Wrublewskis, I did have a misunderstanding with Harry in England. I represented Tony Dorsey, the English League's two-time Most Valuable Player. Bruce Stewart, the Fort Wayne CBA coach, called me to recommend Dorsey after a free-agent camp in 1994. I flew to Atlanta to meet Tony and to watch him work out. I was impressed and placed him with Harry Wrublewski's Birmingham Bullets, coached at the time by Steve Tucker.

After the 1998 season, after his second MVP year, Dorsey called me and said that he was changing agents and would not be working with me anymore. He also said that he was leaving Birmingham and going to Manchester in the same league. I was disappointed, but agreed and thought that was the end of my relationship with Dorsey. However, he called me back a week later and said he had already made a deal with Manchester for the 1998-99 season, but felt that he had made a mistake in changing agents and wanted me to work with him again. I agreed and called Scott May, the Manchester general manager, and introduced myself as Tony Dorsey's new and also former agent. May, the former Indiana All-American and NBA player, runs the English team from his office in Bloomington, Indiana. In fact, he was also in the process of interviewing Nick Nurse for the Manchester Giant head coaching job.

Nick flew to Bloomington and was discussing the Giant job in Scott May's car when The General rang May on the car phone. Nurse said that Indiana Hoosier Coach Bob Knight told May, his former player, to "hire Bob Donewald, Jr. - he's a hell of a coach." To Scott May's credit, he listened to the words of his old coach but made his own decision and hired Nick Nurse. Back in Birmingham, Harry Wrublewski was irate that Tony Dorsey was leaving the Bullets and asked the league for a transfer fee of 15,000 pounds, which would have been a record amount.

The fee was finally set at 8,000 pounds and Dorsey was apparently on his way to Manchester. However Wrublewski, still smarting from the loss of his player, lobbied the league office to audit Manchester. Harry couldn't understand why Tony Dorsey would leave Birmingham and go to a club which was reportedly paying him the same salary. The situation was finally resolved after the audit and Dorsey was wearing a Giant uniform in 1998-99 and was once again playing for Coach Nick Nurse. I had nothing to do with Dorsey's decision to leave Birmingham, but Harry apparently thought that I was in on the plot.

Former Sydney King player Leon Trimmingham, who jumped as quick and high as anyone, was a key player for the Sydney franchise in the 1994 and 1995 NBL seasons under Coach Bob Turner. At a home game, with 10,500 packed into the Sydney Entertainment Center, there was a temporary silence as the two NBL teams lined up for a foul shot. Owner Mike Wrublewski, leaning forward from his front row box, took the opportunity to give Trimmingham some vocal encouragement. Mike shouted, "Rebound, Leon," and everyone in the place heard it. Sir Leon didn't miss a beat. He turned to the Wrublewski box and responded with his finger to his mouth and a "Shhhhh."

The Australian journalist Bret Harris in his book, *Boom*, a comprehensive discussion of the development of the Australian National Basketball League, described Mike Wrublewski's schoolboy scraps as a newly-arrived immigrant in Sydney. I was aware from my own experiences in Australia that Aussie school kids in general, but especially immigrant children different in appearance and speaking with an accent, had to defend themselves on the Sydney schoolgrounds on a regular basis. In fact, the reverse had occurred with native-born Australian Cameron Dickinson, who had been a school-yard target with his bright red hair. Dickinson recounted being chased all over Melbourne by a gang of school kids of Pakistani origins. In Aussie-speak, the wogs were after the Aussie. Wrublewski mentioned to Harris the prevalence of the "wog syndrome" in Australia during his youth.

Wog, Septic, Boy

"Wog," not a complimentary term, had been used to describe nearly anyone different from the 100% "fair dinkum" Anglo-Saxon Australian. Even a POM, an Englishman, can be referred to as a wog and, of course, anyone with a foreign accent or person of color was an automatic wog, excluding the American born. Australia is a vast melting pot of races and nationalities. A walk down a Sydney or Melbourne street always offers a fascinating glance at any and all types of people. But at a rather base level of cultural perception, there have been two main racial classifications in Australia - Aussie and Wog.

Americans have been grouped into another cultural sub-class as they make up a third group called Yank, or Septic. Septic came from the Cockney rhyme, as Yank rhymed with tank in septic tank; therefore, Yanks can be called Septics. Many Australians refer to American blacks as Negroes - not meant to be in any way disrespectful, just behind the times in current politically correct terminology. I have heard many times from shop owners in Australia, innocently spoken, "That American Negro basketballer was in yesterday - my he's a big bloke."

Also, whereas the word "boy" can have a negative racial connotation in the American culture, in Australian slang, boy can mean someone who likes to drink, womanize, and party. For example, Australians might say, "He's a good player, but also a bit of a boy." (Boy referring to social behavior, not race.)

Modern racial terminology aside, there was nothing more confusing to Australians involved in basketball than the American university system. I understood their dilemma. On the one hand, Australians have known American players with college degrees, or those who at least had attended college long enough to play basketball, but who lacked communication skills, even basic communication skills, and were obviously in no way intellectual. In the U.S., too many go to college, in Australia too few.

I have developed this explanation, which has met with limited success: "Yes, there are players who have competed at the highest level athletically in universities, yet have taken a less competitive academic path.(cough) If the player was enterprising enough to capitalize on his athletic reputation and combine it with persistence, progress, class attendance, and common sense, he could have gained the confidence of his teachers, developed the basic skills necessary to pass courses, and earned a degree."

Or, reality was that at some schools his basketball ability was a ticket to stay eligible and precluded the need to really learn anything in classes. On the other hand, at the same university where athletes can follow this academic path of least resistance, across the campus from the basketball field-house or the football field there could be scientists working on an aerospace program or students learning skills necessary to become brain surgeons. In discussing the American university system with Australians, I invariably have used one word to sum up my explanation: diverse.

Even though most Australians have known a few Americans and the United States has been a popular place for tourism from down-under and vice-versa, I can imagine that, like all tourists - Australian, American, or otherwise - they really understood little of the subtle aspects of the host country's cultural mentality. Yet, I found it interesting that many Australians, in general, seemed to consider their own country to be the ultimate in racial fairness, with prejudice and bias reserved more for the United States. I was reminded of that in a conversation with Brendan Joyce, the coach of the Illawarra Hawks in the NBL.

An Opportunity Down-Under

I had sent Elliot Hatcher, the former Kansas State point guard, to the Hawks for the 1998 NBL season. Elliot was an All-Big Eight selection at Kansas State in 1995-96 under Coach Tom Asbury. Prior to his 1998 NBL job, Hatcher had done little as a player since leaving K-State. I saw him score 26 points in a minor upset at Iowa State in February of 1996 and must have seen him at his very best. I was impressed with Hatcher in that game, but he played poorly at the pre-draft tournament in Portsmouth (the PIT) and later created no interest in the Quad City Thunder free agent camp.

I had called Coach Dan Panaggio, now with two CBA titles to his credit, about Elliot Hatcher. I told Panaggio that, in spite of the Portsmouth showing, Hatcher had some talent, and at his best, could play in the CBA. Panaggio reported back to me after the Quad camp and said he had seen none of that advertised talent from Hatcher and was not further interested. But I maintained my interest and thought Elliot Hatcher might someday wake up and use his talent in an overseas job.

Hatcher later got an opportunity in Belo Horizante, Brazil, but spent only two months there and again did little to enhance his value in the overseas market. Many players just don't understand that a basketball club is like any other conscientious employer: it wants consistent production and its money's worth in employee (player) investments. After the Brazil experience had ended in February of 1997, Hatcher had no offers. To his credit he continued to try and participated in the 1997 Los Angeles Summer League in the smorgasbord, usually about 80 teams, free agent division, but, at least, he was keeping his career alive by playing and staying in front of scouts.

Elliot had called me several times from Brazil *cobranca revertida* (reverse charges) and continued to stay in touch after the LA league. He said that he had learned his lesson. I believed his story and thought that he was sincere and hungry to prove himself in another overseas job. So I, somewhat reluctantly, because of his so-so performance in Brazil and his lack of production since college, recommended him to Illawarra.

I had flown Hatcher to Des Moines to work out for Illawarra Coach Brendan Joyce in September of 1996; thus Joyce had already met the player, had seen him work out in person, and had a good idea of his talent level and game. Corey Williams of Arizona and Julius Michalik of Iowa State also participated in that workout at Drake University. However, on that occasion, the Hawks did not make a contract offer to any of the three players. I didn't completely lose confidence in Hatcher, as I remembered clearly what he was capable of from the K-State -Iowa State game. I felt Elliot Hatcher had the talent to play in Australia and I recommended him again, a year later, to Brendan Joyce in August, 1998. On this occasion, we were successful in securing a contract offer.

Anyway, Coach Joyce called me a few days after Hatcher's arrival in Australia in January 1998, as the player's attitude and effort were early season issues and sources of concern for the club. Joyce also said that he felt that maybe Elliot didn't trust white people. I agreed that you can't trust all of them, but I had spent some time with Elliot and I did not look at Elliot's problems in that context. I felt he was immature and didn't want to accept responsibility for consistent, high-level play, which was required to keep his job. I also thought he was afraid that he was going to fail in Australia after his experience in Brazil and in the CBA camp. However, I found the player to be a decent young guy overall, struggling with personal issues and not yet able to fully utilize his talent to the end of consistent professional basketball employment. He played pretty well in the NBL, but his contract was not renewed.

Racial Issues in Australia

Brendan Joyce also echoed a comment which I have heard often in Australia - that this was Australia, not America. I interpreted it to mean that Australia was free of racial problems and that this type of societal problem existed only in the United States. Although not claiming to be any type of authority on the subject, I did have interest, personal experience, and some understanding about the history of racial strife in the United States and in Australia. Also, after leaving Middle Tennessee in 1971, I had lived three years in Mozambique (Africa) and during that period I spent considerable time in South Africa, Swaziland, Rhodesia, and Angola. Thus I had witnessed first-hand the racial atmosphere in both colonial and independent political settings in Africa, including *apartheid,* South Africa's policy of racial segregation. Ironically, I watched Mozambique as it thrived as a colonial possession of Portugal and starved as an independent Marxist state.

I knew historically both Australia and the United States had had an unsavory past regarding racism. However, I was also aware that black citizens and other minorities in the U.S. had risen to positions of prominence in medicine, research, law, education, literature, politics, and, of course, sports and entertainment in American life. And, while many American blacks also have been successful in Australia, the Aborginal, the indigenous native thought by historians to have arrived in Australia from Southeast Asia 40,000 years ago, was not a part of mainstream Australia.

Although probably more shadow than substance, the Australian government saw fit to "apologize" to the Aboriginals for past wrongs. In the U.S., there has been a similar plea by various interest groups. I doubt that will happen. In fairness, such an apology in the United States would need to be tempered by a response from all *lucid* Americans thanking the country for opportunities to improve their lives. I have noticed that in my 30 years of working with athletes, 90% black, that character was not determined nor defined by race. Responsible players have learned positive values from parents, coaches, mentors, and role models. Irresponsible ones had not learned these valuable lessons. The successful among these athletes have placed self-reliance, discipline and consistent effort at the heart of their career game plan. These winners have committed to use their gifts in order to achieve personal goals and ignored the whine of those who wanted to explain to them why they shouldn't succeed.

Opportunities for minorities are, of course, far greater in the U.S., like Australia, than those afforded in their countries of origin. However, those who speak the loudest about racism in the U.S. are often writers and politicians who live the good life. Their agenda resides in the editorial sections of those American newspapers which have chosen to sacrifice objectivity and integrity for political alignment. They are America's social issue vigilantes who have cashed in on opportunities provided by the country of which they can be so critical. They do not, by any means, represent the interests of the best and brightest of America's minorities, nor of the public in general.

Cal Bruton, a New Yorker and naturalized Australian, rang me in 1997. He was upset that he was not able to secure another NBL coaching job. He asked me if I thought that NBL clubs were discriminating against him because of his race. I said no, but we both knew that racial discrimination, practiced by individuals of all races, was a fact of life in Australia and also in the United States. However, I did not want to give Cal permission to use race as an excuse to do nothing and I felt that it was non-productive to focus on previous rejection, for whatever reason. I assured him that I had been rejected fifty times more often than I had been accepted in the coaching job application process, in some cases probably because I was white. I believed there was a spiritual force at work in my job applications, that I received opportunities which were God's will, and I was denied, or protected from those not in my best interest. I looked at Mr. Bruton's situation from the same perspective.

He had already held three NBL head coaching jobs - Geelong, Perth, and Hobart - and he apparently hadn't been discriminated against in attaining those positions. However, he also had been involved in a "hostile take-over" of native son Alan Black's job at Perth. That action had rubbed Australian basketball bureaucrats the wrong way and was definitely still a factor in Cal's inability to attract another NBL coaching contract. I could understand Cal Bruton's concern. While Alan Black had held three NBL head coaching jobs since 1990, Bruton had been successful in only one NBL application - at Hobart - which Wayne Monaghan and I had arranged. Also in looking at the two, Bruton was a great player, Black a good one. Bruton had two NBL titles, one as a coach and one as a player, Black none. Bruton also had the superior won-loss record in NBL coaching. Black had one huge edge: he was a native-born Australian. Even though he clearly had earned the opportunity to work as a head coach in the NBL again, (on this occasion) I had suggested that Cal put the NBL coaching objective aside and begin to use his considerable abilities in a good-paying sales position.

To Cal's credit, he demonstrated the humility to take a part-time job delivering mail until he was hired as a sales representative with Sands Print Group in Perth. It was my understanding that he has been doing some good work for Sands, even landing one of the largest accounts in the company's history. Also, Cal Bruton has continued work in Australian basketball at the association level and was awarded a contract to do the commentary on telecasts of some NBL games. I looked at the racial issue with Cal Bruton like a "double-team." He always had had the ability and brains to beat the double team and likewise he had the character to overcome temporary rejection, for whatever reason. He may coach again someday, but he learned through his own initiative that he can do other things to make a good living and that he has other options; that's valuable information. Also, with his achievements in business, Bruton can be more objective about the "glamour" of the NBL.

While in Australia I had lived in Tasmania for four years and was aware of the Aboriginal graves there and also had read about the history of Australia's treatment of Aboriginals, in general, through the years. I visited the Tasmanian Museum and Art Gallery in Hobart on several occasions to pursue my interest in prior Aboriginal life in Tasmania. I was particularly taken by the paintings of *Mathinna* and *Trucanini*, two prominent Aboriginal women in Tasmanian history. I also looked into the work of several credible writers, including N.S. Kirkman, Harry Gordon, and Edwin Hall Smith, who researched and discussed some of the unsavory events in Australian history involving Aboriginals. Another source for background reading was author John Pilger who was considered a serious, accomplished journalist in Australia and the U.K. Pilger took a hard look at this matter in his book, *The Secret Country* (Knopf, 1991), and referred to one particularly disturbing historical event in which 80-150 Aborigines were slaughtered (shot) by government officials and gold miners along the Palmer River on November 7, 1873. Apparently, no one was punished for the infamous

Caulfield Lagoon massacre, nor was the event confirmed until a graduate student turned up the records and new evidence in 1984, over 100 years later. Pilger implied in his writing that the jury was still out on other similar (uninvestigated) black marks in Australian history and that more atrocities would probably be revealed.

While the Palmer River killings were only one aspect of the Australia-Aboriginal issue, I was aware of similar types of racial brutality in American history. Having been at Middle Tennessee State University in 1970, just eight years after the integration of Nashville's downtown businesses, I learned from Tommy Brown and from my other black colleagues at the university about some of the harsh realities of racism. I updated and reinforced this personal experience in Tennessee with a reading of *The Children*, a riveting study by historian David Halberstam, who discussed the non-violent protest movement which led to integrating Nashville in the early 1960s.

I had also read of the matter of the Australian Royal Commission investigation in 1991 prompted by the inordinate number of Aboriginal deaths in Australian jails. In fact, John Pilger believed that rates of deaths (many unexplained) among those incarcerated in Australia to be much greater than in the Republic of South Africa. The Commission Report confirmed the serious problems in Australia revealed in tragic events and unexplained deaths of Aboriginals, while in police custody, and their economic and social plight as they remained positioned outside of the Australian mainstream. The fact was that Aboriginal life had been excluded from many accounts of Australian history, apparently the thinking among historians was that to ignore or forget Aboriginal issues was, in a sense, a way to resolve the problem.

In a recent trip from the Travelodge at Rushcutter's Bay in Sydney to the airport, a well-meaning cab driver asked me innocently and inoffensively about the "Negro problem" in the United States. I replied that I had not heard the term Negro since 1979 when Cal Bruton came to Brisbane and recalled the story headline in a Brisbane paper - "Star Negro Basketballer Arrives in Brisbane." I then suggested that the cabby first tell me about the "Abo problem" in Australia.

There could be no argument that Australia was a great country with agreeable climate, nice people, good basketball leagues, and interesting, melting pot, cosmopolitan cities. However, the reality was that Mother England herself in former colonies in Africa and India had set a bad example for The Commonwealth and had left an embarrassing trail in regard to the treatment of the non-white population and in the area of human rights issues, in general. Also, Australia, like the United States, had a sordid past as well as recurring racial controversies in the present. In fact, Australian governmental policy, *which prevented the immigration of non-white people*, existed down-under from the late 19th century to 1974. On the other hand, the United States and Australia have distinguished themselves as the most desirable of all destinations for ambitious immigrants seeking freedom and economic opportunity.

The Australian Royal Commission Report seemed to be an effort to address and hopefully to initiate action which would put to rest these haunting social (racial) issues. Yet, I have always been comfortable in sending American players to Australia and feel that the ones who did their job and were responsible were treated very well. Although there have been few racial problems for American players in Australia, some have occurred.

In 1980, while I was still in Brisbane as State Director of Coaching, I received a call from Cal Bruton, then playing in the VBA in Geelong. The call came early on a Monday morning and Cal was upset and shaken over a situation which had developed at the Geelong-Chelsea game that past weekend at the Chelsea gym. One of the Chelsea players, an American, had grabbed a pom-pom away from Elliot Bruton, Cal's eight-year-old son, and then exhorted the Chelsea backers, "We came over here to get away from these niggers." Shoving matches and tension continued throughout the game that day.

On the return match in Geelong, the stage was set for further conflict. Mark Wright ran under Cal Bruton on a lay-up attempt and a fracas ensued. John Revels, a black American from Wichita, punched Wright and the benches emptied. Wright, an Australian, Bill Runchey, an American from Chelsea, Bruton, a naturalized Australian, and Revels from Geelong were ordered by the league to appear before a basketball tribunal. During the procedures with the tribunal, there was another outburst in which the Aussie Wright called Bruton "a fucking black bastard." Bruton, Revels, and Wright were all given six-week suspensions. Mal Speed, VBA league administrator, asserted himself after this incident and made it clear to all teams that no racial name-calling nor racially based conflicts would be tolerated. Speed's decisive action seemed to quiet most of the blatant problems at the time in the VBA.

A more recent situation developed in the Townsville-Southeast Melbourne NBL game at The Furnace in Townsville during the 1998 season. Simon Kerle, a fiery Aussie, was guarding Clint McDaniel, former University of Arkansas guard. It was reported that McDaniel had spit at or on Kerle after an aggressive play between the two on the court. The Townsville crowd apparently saw the incident and began to taunt McDaniel and a lady came down on the court and yelled at the visiting team players as they were leaving the court after the game. A Southeast Melbourne player pushed a Townsville fan, but the team left the arena without any major altercation outside of verbal exchanges between the fans and visiting players. After the game McDaniel said that Kerle had called him a nigger and that the name-calling had precipitated the spitting incident. Kerle denied calling McDaniels any names.

A similar situation developed in the hotly contested Utah-North Carolina game in the 1998 NCAA Tournament. Makhtar Ndiaye of NC and Utah's Britton Johnsen exchanged words with Ndiaye spitting at Johnsen. After the Utah 65-59 victory, Ndiaye accused Johnsen of calling him the n-word. The Utah player denied the accusation, Coach Rick Majerus supported his player, and subsequently Ndiaye admitted that the name-calling did not occur. The Ndiaye-Johnsen controversy in San Antonio, Texas, sounded very similar to the McDaniel-Kerle problem in Townsville, Australia. Emotional outbursts in the heat of competition were primary with racial name calling, real or imagined, as the secondary reaction.

Mark Bragg, the Townsville coach, said that Brian Goorjian, the SE Melbourne coach, "turned the situation around" in the press and a public verbal exchange between Rob Nugent, the Melbourne club's General Manager, and the Townsville mayor ensued. It was reported nationwide that Nugent called Townsville "the red-neck capital of Australia." Mayor Tony Mooney was outraged, refuted the claim, and said that Nugent himself had never been to Townsville and therefore could not possibly know anything about the matter. Nugent admitted that he had never been to Townsville, but would stand by his comments. NBL chief executive John Rimazs attempted to smooth the matter over and, from the safety of his office in Melbourne, asserted, "It's (the argument) not in the interests of basketball…Townsville has great supporters, etc."

Off the basketball court and also recently, when I was in Australia on business, I noticed in a Sydney paper an article written by an African communications student. She described a threatening situation which occurred one evening while watching the magical lights from the Sydney Harbor. Her walk was interrupted by an intruder who came up behind her and said he had never fucked a nigger before and would like to.

I was re-reading the African girl's story and her experience as I stood in line to buy a ticket for a play at the Opera House. This regrettable and disgusting incident had occurred in Sydney, Australia, one of the world's truly great cities. It was still on my mind when I entered the theater to attend playwright Davidson Williamson's drama *After the Ball* performed by the Sydney Theater Company. I had a brief dialogue about race that day at the theater with an Australian lady.

It was a June 1998 matinee performance of a play which portrayed Australian family life in Melbourne in the 1950s. The father in one of his heated discussions with his wife mentioned something to the effect that the

Asians were taking over the country. At the intermission, I commented to the lady sitting on my right about my interest in David Williamson's work and the play in general.

I cautiously mentioned the scene in which the father expressed concern about the number of Asians in Australia. I found that she was Australian, had grown up in Melbourne in the 1950s, moved to Sydney at the age of 18 to take a job, and had lived there since. I told her in brief about my perceptions of race and racism in the U.S., the U.K., and in Australia. I asked her about the recent Royal Commission Report, which had confirmed the police abuse to Aboriginals in custody. She was aware of the report and was in no way defensive on this matter, but said candidly, "Yes, of course, racism exists in Australia. It is a two-way street, you know. Things will get better, but racist feelings exist on all sides."

Thus, while I would agree that "this (Australia) was not America" - *both* countries have their own societal problems to resolve, one of which can be called racial. I again pose the rhetorical question, "Where are the Aboriginal players in the Australian National Basketball League?" Is not the NBL a microcosm of the Aborigines' progress in Australia in general? The African student's story, the Asian comment in the play, the Royal Commission Report, and racial issues in general were on my mind, as I also thought back to the events prior to C.J. Bruton's return to Australia and his new job in the NBL.

C.J. Bruton on His Own

Green Bay Packer coach Vince Lombardi talked about discipline to his players and emphasized sacrificing to achieve team victory, the ultimate goal. I heard lecturer Scott Peck, also a psychiatrist and man-of-the-cloth, explain discipline as developing the ability to delay rewards and gratification, and that with *total discipline* all problems could be solved. Hopefully C.J. Bruton could become one of the exceptions among professional athletes and one who had learned and accepted the importance of a disciplined life. He had made notable progress in the area of taking responsibility for his own actions while in the U.S. If he could continue to grow in this area, it would give him a huge advantage in his pro basketball career and his life off the court. However, it would be a treacherous path. It would not be easy.

The decision had been made. C.J. was returning to the Australian NBL after the disappointing NCAA ruling. After it was decided that he would skip the 1997 Portland veterans' camp, even though he had been offered an NBA non-guaranteed contract, I worked out the Brisbane business details with Bullet general manager Terry Ryan. I also called Sharm Scheuerman to arrange for C.J. to play with Athletes in Action on a college tour in the fall of 1997 prior to the Australian season. On successive nights in November

1997, Athletes in Action beat Temple; lost to Cincinnati by 3; lost to North Carolina; lost to Iowa; and lost to Wisconsin. The competition gave young Bruton a head start on conditioning for the Australian pro season as well as a chance to examine his spirituality on the Athletes in Action tour, which became his U.S. "college career."

I attended the Athletes in Action-University of Iowa exhibition game at Carver-Hawkeye Arena in November 1998 to watch C.J. Bruton play against the Iowa Hawkeyes. When I saw him running around the arena lobby organizing tickets for about fifty people from Indian Hills College an hour before the game, I knew that he was not focused to play against a game-hungry Big Ten team on its home court in its season's opener. As I expected, Bruton struggled and to his credit made some plays, but overall had a dismal game.

In the post-game radio interview, Iowa Coach Tom Davis said that C.J. Bruton had not played well today, but that he had played six or seven consecutive games and looked tired. However, Davis assured the radio audience that Bruton was a capable player and should not be judged harshly on the basis of that exhibition. That was a fair, dignified statement. In 13 years at Iowa I have never heard Davis speak, regardless of the situation, in any other way.

I appreciated and respected Tom Davis' vindication of C.J. in that interview. The thinking behind the decisions made in this phase of C.J. Bruton's career had always been what was best for the player in terms of his total development - career, physical, mental, emotional, and spiritual. Athletes in Action reinforced these priorities and was a good choice at this juncture.

Even though C.J. Bruton was not allowed to play American Division I college basketball, he did play in the top junior college program in the United States under two-time National Coach of the Year, Terry Carroll. Bruton was the leader of the 1996-97 National title team which went 37-1 and started the school's championship tradition. In 1997-98 even without Bruton, Indian Hills rode their 38-0 record to another national title. Carroll was 269-50 over his nine seasons as a junior college head coach - that's a .843 winning percentage - and presented the Ottumwa school with basketball teams which were able to produce the national record of 72 consecutive victories and a 75-1 record over two years. Only his player graduation rates at the two-year school, with strong input from Assistant Mike Cappachio, exceeded his won-loss percentage: 73 of 75 Indian Hills players had reportedly earned associate degrees through the 1997-98 season. C.J. Bruton had experienced and contributed to excellence, a privilege reserved for very few in any area of their lives.

The day finally had arrived for C.J. Bruton to return to Australia. He had given the two years in school his best shot. He had done well both on and off the court. As we drove to the airport on Nov 29, 1997, in a steady Iowa autumn rain, I asked, "C.J., what do you remember most about your two years here?" He answered immediately: "I learned a lot about myself and how important it was to get honest, with myself and others." Then the Bruton smile as he hesitated and looked back at me before continuing through the departure gate headed for his first season as a real professional basketball player. He had searched hard to find what would work for him and he discovered the power of honest, sincere daily effort. If he stuck with it, matured, and toughened-up, he just might be an NBA player someday. Or he could possibly make the Australian Olympic team for Sydney 2000, which would be a great achievement and one of his primary objectives. If not, Spain, Italy, and France could also offer intriguing possibilities. I felt that it didn't matter where, but it did seem to matter to C.J. at this juncture *how* he lived his life, and he had taken some important steps in learning how to use his gifts to achieve personally and athletically.

I walked through the airport back to my car in the parking lot thinking of C.J. Bruton's whirlwind two years in the U.S. - his arrival, academic struggles, and personal problems followed by an awakening, with significant personal growth, change of behavior, and exceptional athletic achievement. He arrived as a child without a clue and he left as a young man with the tools, if he used and developed them, to live a good life and to influence others positively. I felt indebted to Terry Carroll and Indian Hills, and I was grateful that I had been here to give C.J. some direction, as I had understood well his problems from my own struggles.

The rain persisted as I drove back toward the city center of Des Moines. I absentmindedly dialed the car phone to my office voice mail and heard among the messages - "Message for Dave Adkins. This is Trish Bruton, at home in Perth, and I would like to discuss Austin. He just turned 17 and he really needs to get away from home and go to college. Do you have any ideas?"

◻*18*◻

EPILOGUE

In the NBA, normal player-club activities stopped. David Stern, the league's commissioner, once again was faced with the daunting challenge of "taking back our game." Damage control had turned into a full-time task for Mr. Stern. The club owners and the N.B.P.A., the player's union, were engaged in a bitter labor dispute with official work stoppage. The 1998 "summer of discontent," followed by fall and winter as the dispute wore on, had the potential to destroy the National Basketball Association.

The media mentioned "race" as an issue in the NBA labor negotiations. It seemed at times as if it was a race by both sides to kill the pro game. While the labor-management struggle took center stage in the NBA, few Americans probably really cared what happened. The $120 million player contracts, etc. have severed ties with mainstream U.S.A. The NBA dispute would not affect water supply, gasoline prices, or air travel. It meant only that the small percentage of U.S. citizens who watched the NBA will have to find a new afternoon TV program during a couple of months of the year. *But, alas, the two sides did come to an agreement and embarked upon plans for an NBA season with a limited number of games - and then Michael Jordan retired.*

Other developments saw Latrell Sprewell, the player who attacked and choked Coach P.J. Carlesimo, suing The League for $30 million for discrimination. A judge dismissed this lawsuit, but Sprewell wouldn't let go and sued again. The national, and international media, jumped on a story in a major U.S. publication about NBA players fathering children out of wedlock, apparently a common practice. An article cited one pro star with seven children by six different women, a league-leading statistic. Shaquille O'Neal, the Lakers star, was the only NBA news on October 16, 1998. He was "called for a charge" by a 23-year-old woman employee at Disney World in Florida. *Money Players* reported with alarming credibility the involvement of Michael Jordan and Isaiah Thomas in high-stake gambling activities with unsavory characters.

There was even trouble in the broadcast booth. Marv Albert, the authoritative and sometimes annoying voice of NBA basketball, was involved in a humiliating sex scandal and had to vacate his high-profile television position. Also, *The Dallas Morning News* reported an investigation into alleged sexual misconduct with female employees by Terdema L. Ussery, the chief executive officer of the Dallas Mavericks. Charles Barkley, who reportedly stopped drinking for a while, continued to make periodic appearances in the nation's newspapers for involvement in various bar room indiscretions. When Sir Charles retires, Chris Webber could be an able replacement in public controversy. Webber was fined at the airport in San Juan for possession of marijuana. Some NBA referees even got into the bad-behavior act. NBA whistle-blower Donald Vaden was charged with downgrading his first-class airline tickets and keeping the difference without reporting the extra cash as taxable income. Other NBA game officials were also involved.

On the positive side of the NBA ledger, Coach Phil Jackson and Coach Jerry Sloan set a new standard for self-control and quiet, effective leadership on the bench in the 1998 National Basketball Association Playoffs. Their disciplined approach to coaching at the highest level could impact bench behavior down-the-line from the pros to the nation's high schools.

Larry Bird's return to the NBA with the Pacers under-scored the "players' coach" style of running a team and reinforced the emphasis on self-control in leadership. Calbert Cheaney of the Washington Wizards quietly contributed $650,000 toward the construction of a gymnasium at his Evansville, Indiana, church. Grant Hill also donated to the building of an economic and spiritual center in Asheville, North Carolina.

The Lakers signed Jerry West, who never misses a play as a scout at pre-draft camps, to a new four-year deal as executive vice-president. The parade of ex-NBA personnel to the women's pro leagues continued. Frank Layden returned to coaching with the WNBA's Utah Starzz followed by Richie Adubato who took the reins with the New York Liberty. Orlando Woolridge was in the same league as coach of the Los Angeles Sparks. In the other women's pro circuit, the ABL, K.C. Jones (New England Blizzard) and Jim Cleamons (Chicago Condors) held head jobs, until the ABL went under financially. Clyde Drexler took the head job at his alma mater, the University of Houston. Coach Tim Floyd resigned at Iowa State to take the basketball operations director job in anticipation of the head coaching job with the Chicago Bulls. Larry Eustachy of Utah State immediately stepped into the ISU job. However, Pete Mikeal, the MVP at the National Junior College Tournament, decided against Iowa State after the C.J. Bruton debacle. The 6'6 Mikeal, Bruton's teammate at Indian Hills Community College, signed at Cincinnati and would have made a huge difference in ISU's fortunes.

"Outside the NBA" the National Basketball League of Australia celebrated its 20th year and elected its inaugural Hall of Fame class which included Calvin Bruton, Sr. (player, coach), Barry Barnes (coach), Bill Palmer (player, administrator), Herb McEachin (player), and league founder, Dr. John Raschke. The United States sent an all-star team coached by Rudy Tomjanovich of the Houston Rockets to the World Championships in Greece. The NBA labor problems forced a last-minute change of plans with Dream Team IV replaced by a squad of Americans from the CBA and European pro teams. Predictably, it wasn't enough to win the gold medal, but to the team's credit it did not come home empty-handed. Coach Tomjanovich surprisingly ranked their bronze medal along with his two NBA titles with the Rockets.

There was no live television coverage of the World Championship Tournament. However, the finals of the 1998 Goodwill Games from New York were telecast. Although not in the World Championships or Olympic category, Clem Haskins did a great job with his group of talented collegians in whipping Australia in the championship. Hubie Brown, the ex-coach and usually astute NBA television analyst, didn't seem to be up for the Goodwill event. From start to finish and for 45 consecutive minutes of action including the overtime, Hubie referred to the great Australian International, Andrew Gaze, as *Andrew Glaze*.

An update on characters and others pertaining to *A Journey in Overseas Basketball* is shown below:

Ron Adams left his Portland scouting job for a full-time assistant coaching position with George Karl at Milwaukee.

Stan Albeck was named an assistant to Lenny Wilkins at Atlanta.

Ron Altenberg was treated in the Cornell College "Hall of Fame" as if he were just another good athlete.

Mario Albuquerque was working in the computer department of a bank in Lisbon, Portugal, and playing tennis with other former Mozambique players on weekends.

Victor Alexander was under contract with Maccabi Tel-Avis in 1999.

Hurl Beechum rediscovered his European heritage and qualified as a Bosman Rule player in Germany. He set a FIBA record with 12 treys in a single league game.

Tony Bennett was a player-coach with a club in Auckland, New Zealand.

Larry Bird was inducted into the Naismith Basketball Hall of Fame with his first pro coach, Bill Fitch, present.

Marty Blake named his son, Ryan, as assistant director of NBA scouting.

Mike Born had his own basketball business - running camps in the summer and playing in the I.B.A. in the winter.

Edd Bowers was retired and spending winters in Texas with wife, Eleanor.

Freitas Branco, the Portuguese referee, had assumed the role as President of the Mozambique Basketball Federation.

Austin Bruton came to the U.S. on his own at age 17 and won a full scholarship to Indian Hills Community College through his play at a Future Stars Camp. He was red-shirted for the 1998-99 season.

Calvin Bruton Sr. was remarried and working as a sales representative for a printing company in Perth, Australia. He also was doing expert commentary on Australian basketball telecasts.

C.J. Bruton played the 1998 season in the Australian pro league averaging 16 ppg for the Brisbane Bullets. He signed with the Wollongong Hawks for the 1998-99 NBL campaign. He was still Portland's property in the NBA and was planning to return to camp with the Blazers in 1999. He was working to earn a spot on the Australian team for the 2000 Olympics.

Trish Bruton-Newman completed a B.A. at the University of Western Australia and was working as a painter and sculptor in Perth, Australia.

Canberra Cannons of the Australian NBL were saved by a last-second sponsorship deal which averted closure in the 1998-99 season.

Mike Cappacio was named head coach at Indian Hills Community College succeeding Terry Carroll, who went to Iowa State as an assistant. *Mike Marquis* of Marshalltown CC joins the IHCC as associate head coach.

Steve Carfino was married and working on various basketball shows on television in Sydney, Australia.

David Carmichael was directing his various business enterprises, including the Townsville Crocodiles, from his office in Townsville, Australia.

Terry Carroll resigned as head coach of Indian Hills Community College with 72 consecutive victories and two national titles as his legacy. He took an assistant's job at Iowa State under new coach Larry Eustachy.

David Claxton was named assistant coach at Wollongong in the NBL.

The CBA, Continental Basketball Association, fielded 9 teams for the 1998-99 season.

Larry Creger was still living in Culver City, California, and working as a consultant to the L.A. Summer Basketball League.

Although not exactly the same as point-shaving in basketball, the international sport of *Cricket* was having its own problems with dishonesty among its participants. Australians Mark Waugh and Shane Warne, big names down-under, admitted taking payments ($3,000+ each) in 1995 for providing bookmakers with inside information on weather and field conditions for Australian matches in Pakistan.

Bruce Chubick was playing for Telecom Club of Lisbon and living in Portugal with wife, Wendy, and son, Trey.

Ken Cole was organizing U.S. tours for various Australian basketball teams. His business, One-on-One, was based in Baton Rouge, Louisiana.

Ricky Davis, who played one season at Iowa, was drafted by Charlotte. He joined Raef LaFrentz as the second former Iowa high school prep player taken in the NBA's first round in 1998.

Tom Davis, veteran college coaching standout, was apparently forced out at Iowa after 13 productive years on the job.

Mike D'Antoni, former NBA player and Italian League coach, was named head coach of the Denver Nuggets. He inherited an 11-71 season from Bill Hanzlik. D'Antoni hired *John Lucas* and *Mike Evans* as assistants.

Jerry Dennard was married to Robyn. They have two children and were living in Adelaide, Australia.

Cameron Dickinson was playing for the Wollongong Hawks in the Australian NBL.

Drake University, 5-50 over past two seasons, appeared to be ready for a break even season, and survival, under Coach Kurt Kansaskie.The Bulldogs broke a 39 conference game losing streak upsetting pre-league favorite, Creighton, to open the 1998-99 Missouri Valley Conference season.

Mike Dunlap became the head basketball coach at Metropolitan State University in Denver, Colorado.

Augusto Duquesne was living in Toronto, Canada.

Larry Eustachy moved from Utah State to Iowa State to replace Tim Floyd.

Belinda Fedrick was working for FIBA in Munich, Germany.

FIBA, world governing body of basketball, voted in a landmark decision on December 1, 1998, to throw out rules limiting the use of foreign players in pro competition. Immediate reaction: lower salaries for U.S. players and a more viable financial atmosphere for foreign clubs. The new rule would reduce the value of a Bosman Rule player.

Bill Fitch was temporarily retired in Houston, Texas.

Kevin Fite continued his work as the NCAA's overseas-player eligibility expert.

Tim Floyd didn't leave the cupboard bare for Larry Eustachy, but not bountiful either with one draftable player, Marcus Fizer, returning. The Brutonless backcourt at Iowa State went 12-18 overall and 5-9 in Big 12 play in Floyd's last season (1997-98) in Ames, Iowa. As the Bulls new head coach, Tim Floyd was also facing some empty shelves.

Gar Forman had followed Tim Floyd to Chicago apparently as a scout. No more NCAA worries for either of them.

Alexander Franco, former journalist and coach in Lourenço Marques, was publishing a sports paper, *Stadium*, and doing daily sportscasts on CFMT-TV in Toronto.

Gary Garner took the head job at Division I Southeast Missouri State.

Andrew Gaze, signed by the Spurs in '99, has led the Australian NBL in scoring each year and was pointing to the 2000 Olympics - possibly his last major international event as a player.

Lindsay Gaze was still coaching *his* club, the Melbourne Tigers, in the Australian NBL.

Neil Gliddon continued as Director of Coaching with the South Australia Sports Institute based in Adelaide.

Bobby Hansen has established himself as a basketball announcer on WHO Radio in Des Moines to supplement his business career with Kirke-VanOrsdel.

Marc Hansen was writing his weekly sports columns for *The Des Moines Register.*

Chuck Harmison assumed G.M. job with the Wollongong Hawks of the NBL.

Jack Hartman, highly successful college coach at Southern Illinois and Kansas State and disciple of Henry Iba, died of a heart attack in 1998.

Elliot Hatcher, after a good year in the Australian NBL, was waiting for another overseas opportunity while working in Wichita.

Shane Heal, Australian point guard, continued to shoot the three-pointer in Europe and exploded for huge games. The NBA must be watching.

Dan Hickert was living with his wife and family in Perth, Western Australia.

Indian Hills Community College went into the 1998-99 season with 72 consecutive victories. They tied UCLA's record of 88 straight wins on January 6, 1999, and then broke it with their 89th against Northeast Oklahoma on January 8.

The International Basketball Association has expanded to 10 teams and now stretches from Billings, Montana to Mansfield, Ohio. *Darryl Dawkins* at Winnipeg and *Kevin Mackey* at Mansfield were name basketball people riding the IBA pines during games and Greyhound en route.

Chet Kammerer became a scout with the Miami Heat.

George Karl was fired at Seattle, but subsequently signed a $20 million deal as head coach of the Milwaukee Bucks.

Brian Kerle, Australia's winningest NBL coach, was back on the bench with the Brisbane Bullets.

Simon Kerle was playing for Coach Ian Stacker at Townsville.

Raef LaFrentz, from Monona, Iowa, was the third player taken in the 1998 NBA Draft. Out of Kansas, he was a big one that got away from Iowa and Iowa State.

Tates Locke continued to scout for the Portland Trailblazers.

Tom Maher continued as coach of the Australian National Team (women).

Lourenço Marques, Mozambique, now called Maputo, was once a beautiful seaport city and blend of European and African cultures. Devastated by the terrorist war and failed collectivism, the city was still dangerous for visitors and slowly, ever so slowly, was making limited progress. It would never be the same.

John Lucas was named assistant coach with Denver in the NBA.

Luis has disappeared, but I know he is watching.

Clarisse Machanguana of Maputo, Mozambique, starred at O.D.U. and was first-round pick of the San Jose Lazers.

Mike Mashak took over as head coach with the LaCrosse Catbirds, replacing Don Zierden.

Jim McGregor has retired in Palm Springs, California.

Wayne Monaghan was working as a player agent for women in Hobart, Australia.

Kevin McKenna continued to work as an assistant to Dana Altman at Creighton University.

Lynn Nance was working as the head coach of the Southwest Baptist University Bearcats in Bolivar, Missouri.

The *NBA lockout* continued to eliminate major events in the ill-fated 1998-99 season. A disinterested and annoyed public watched training camp, opening day, Christmas games, all-star game, etc. disappear down the drain. *It finally ended.*

NCAA was smarting from order to pay $67,000,000 to restricted earnings coaches. However, preferring to pay their own lawyers rather than the coaches, the Overland Park crowd appealed - but lost. The U.S. Supreme Court refused to hear the appeal.

Nick Nurse, who coached Birmingham to the 1996 English title, had taken the head job in Manchester. The Giants club was under U.S.-based ownership headed by Scott May, former Indiana great and NBA vet.

Greg Norman, back from an injury, was playing golf and making money.

Northwestern University of the Big Ten Conference saw two of its former basketball players, *Dion Lee* and *Dewey Williams*, sentenced to prison terms for a point-shaving fiasco in 1995.

Lute Olson continued to lead his powerful program at the University of Arizona.

Jim Paxson left Portland to became an executive with the Cleveland Cavaliers.

John Pfitsch retired as head soccer coach at Grinnell College.

Rod Popp won his first CBA-Australia title in 1998 at Cairns.

Paul Rogers left Real Madrid in Spain after the 1997-98 season to sign with the Perth Wildcats and is a member of the Australian National Team for *Sydney 2000*.

Jim Rosborough continued as the top assistant coach at the University of Arizona.

Derek Rucker was playing for the West Sydney Razorbacks in the Australian NBL.

Orv Salmon was considering leaving his insurance business to become an overseas coach.

Nelson Serra, former Sporting of LM star, was the head coach of Clube Telecom of Portugal.

Sharm Scheuerman was working as director of player personnel with Athletes in Action.

Malcom Simpson was the retired president of the Adelaide 36ers and ran his company, Champion Travel, from his Adelaide, Australia office.

Jim Sleeper was working as *Dan Panaggio's* assistant with the CBA's Quad City Thunder. Sleeper had back-to-back CBA titles to his credit at Oklahoma City and Quad.

Gene Smith continued as the Athletic Director at Iowa State.

Phil Smyth, former Australian Boomer and Canberra star, coached the Adelaide 36ers to the NBL title in his year as coach in 1998.

Jerry Tarkanian won a $2.5 million settlement from the NCAA after a lengthy battle. Tark has also been in the news regarding the quality and character of some of his players at Fresno State.

Mike Thibault, former head coach with the Omaha Racers, followed George Karl from Seattle to Milwaukee as full-time assistant coach.

David Thompson hit 73 points in an NBA game and led NC State to the NCAA title in 1974 yet was once bankrupt due to drug habit. He has rallied with a reported 10-years of clean-sober living.

Bill Tomlinson was at the helm of the Sydney Kings hoping Acey Earle could bring some magic to the Crescent City.

Leon Trimmingham continued to move up in overseas professional basketball. He was currently with DAIWA in Japan with U.S. interest from Toronto Raptors on the basis of pre-lockout camp play.

Troy Truvillion, who is French and directed by his agent, Paco, continued to draw a nice paycheck in French Pro A competition.

Rudolf Vanmoerkerke hired Dirk Bauerman, the German National Team coach, to lead the Sunair Basketball Club in the Belgian league. Mr. V. continued to live, of course, in Oostende, Belgium.

Rudy Washington, the former Drake coach, asserted himself as Commissioner of the Southwest Athletic Conference. He suspended Prairie View A&M from conference play as that school's band started a brawl with the Southern University marching band in a pre-game (football) fiasco.

Pat Whalen, former Hobart Devil assistant coach, has assumed scouting duties for the N.Y. Knicks in Australia from his Broome, Western Australia, office.

Harry Wrublewski, the president of the Birmingham Bullets in the English League, put the team on the market and announced plans to return to home in Sydney, Australia.

Michael Wrublewski continued his quest for an NBL title as president of the Sydney Kings in Australia.

BIBLIOGRAPHY

I. Books

Agnew, Ivan. *Kiwis Can Fly*. Auckland: Marketforce, Ltd., 1976.

Alexander, Douglas. *Holiday in Mozambique*. South Africa: The Rustica Press, 1971.

Ashe, Arthur R. Jr. *A Hard Road to Glory*. New York: Warner Books, Ltd., 1988.

Baldwin, James A. *"Stranger in the Village"*: The Oxford Book of Essays by John Gross. New York: Oxford University Press, 1991.

Bauer, Douglas. *Prairie City, Iowa: Three Seasons at Home*. Iowa State University Press, 1979.

Bee, Clair. *The Chip Hilton Sports Book Series*. 23 volumes.

Bogues T. and Levine D. *In the Land of the Giants*. Canada, USA: Little, Brown, and Co., 1994.

Bradley, Bill. *Life on the Run*. New York: Vintage Books. 1995.

Bruton, Cal w/Ian Brayshaw. *The Black Pearl: No Regrets* Australia: Griffin Press, 1991.

Challen, Paul. *The Book of Isaiah: The Rise of a Basketball Legend*. Toronto: ECW Press, 1996.

Clarke, Marcus. *For the Term of His Natural Life*. Sydney: Reader's Digest Services Pty Ltd., 1987.

Conrad, Joseph. *LORD JIM*. Ref. *Joseph Conrad*: Chronicle. (Zdzislaw Najder). New York: Quality Paperback Book Club, 1992.

Denby, David. *The Great Books*. New York: Simon and Schuster, 1996.

Douchant M. and Nantz, J. *Inside Sports Magazine: College Basketball.*
Visible Ink Press: Detroit. 1997.

Ferris, Eric. *A Season with Coach Dick Bennett.* Madison: Prairie
Oak Press, 1997.

Gaze A. and Smith P. *On the Road with Andrew Gaze.* Sydney:
Pan McMillan Australia. Pty. Ltd., 1995

George, Nelson. *Elevating the Game.* New York: Harper Collins, 1992.

Halberstam, David. *The Breaks of the Game.* New York: Knopf, 1981.

Halberstam, David. *The Children.* New York: Random House, 1998.

Hall, James Norman. *This Side of Paradise.*

Harris, Bret. *Boom: Inside the NBL.* Australia: Pan McMillan
Publishing, 1992.

Hill B. and Baron R. *The Amazing Basketball Book: The First 100
Years.* Louisville: Devyn Press, 1988.

Issel D. and Martin B. *Parting Shots.* Chicago: Contemporary
Books, Inc., 1985.

Kakfa, Franz. *The Metamorphosis and Other Stories.* New York:
Barnes and Noble Books, 1996.

Karl G. w/ Yeager D. *This Game's the Best.* New York: St. Martin's Press, 1997.

Kesey, Ken. "One Flew Over the Cuckoo's Nest" *Masterpieces of
American Literature.* New York: Harper-Collins, 1993.

Keteyian A., Araton H., and Dardis M.F. *Money Players.* New York:
Pocket Books, 1997.

Levinson, Daniel J. *Season's of a Man's Life.* New York: Ballantine
Books, 1978.

Locke T. and Ibach B. *Caught in the Net.* New York: Leisure Press, 1982.

McGregor J. and Rapoport R. *Called for Traveling*. New York: Mac Millan Publishing, 1978.

McGivern, Gene. *Here's Johnny Orr*. Ames: Iowa State University Press, 1992.

McPhee, John. *Levels of the Game*. New York: The Noonday Press, 1991.

Merriam Webster's Biographical Dictionary. 1995.

Miller, Arthur. *Death of a Salesman*.

Molloy, Paul. *Where Did Everybody Go?* New York: Doubleday, 1981.

Monteleone, John J. *Branch Rickey's Little Blue Book*. New York: Macmillan, 1995.

Newitt, Malyn. *A History of Mozambique*. Indiana University Press, 1995.

Packer, Billy. *Hoops*. Chicago: Contemporary Books, Inc., 1986.

Patton, Jim. *Il Basketball D'Italia*. New York: Simon and Schuster, 1994.

Peck, Scott. *The Road Less Traveled*.

Pilger, John. *Hidden Agendas*. Australia, UK: Vintage-Random House, 1998.

Pilger, John. *Secret Country*. New York: Alfred A. Knopf, 1991.

Pluto, Terry. *Falling From Grace*. New York: Simon and Schuster. 1995.

Raterman, Dale. *Big Ten: Conference of Excellence*. Champaign: Sagamore Press, 1996.

Rosen, Charles. *Cockroach Basketball League*. New York: Donald I. Fine, Inc., 1991.

Rosen, Charles. *The House of Moses All-Stars*. New York: Seven Stories Press. 1996.

Rosen, Charles. *Barney Polan's Game*. New York: Seven Stories Press. 1998.

Shaughnessy, Dan. *Ever Green*. New York: St. Martins's Press, 1995.

Turnbull, Buck. *From the Press Box*. Ames: Iowa State University Press, 1996.

Vaillant, G.E. *Natural History of Alcoholism*. Mass: Harvard University Press, 1983.

Wilder, Thorton. "Our Town" *Masterpieces of American Literature*, (F.N. Magill). New York: Salem Press, 1993.

Wolfe, Thomas. *You Can't Go Home Again*. New York: Harper-Collins, 1992.

Yeager, Don. *Undue Process: The NCAA'S Injustice for All*. Champaign: Sagamore Publishing Co., 1991.

II. Technical Basketball References

Adidas Blue Ribbon College Basketball Yearbook: 1985-1998.
Athlon Sports College Basketball: 1997-98.
Big 8 Conference Men's Basketball Media Guide: 1994-95.
Big 12 Conference Men's Basketball Media Guide: 1997-98
Big 10 Conference Men's Basketball Media Guide: 1994-95.
CBA Guide and Register: 1997-98.
ESPN Sports Almanac: 1998.
FIBA Media Guide: 1996-97.
Giganti del Basket: Italy. December 1992 edition.
Inside Sports Magazine: College Basketball: Mike Douchant. 1997.
History of Basketball in Portugal: Albano Fernandes. 1977.
Leventhal NBA Draft Report: Don Leventhal. 1995-98.
Missouri Valley Conference Men's Basketball Media Guide: 1992-93.
Monter Draft Report: Chris Monter. 1995-1998.
NBL Media Guide: Australia. 1997-98.
One on One: Australia. 1997-98 monthly editions.
Official NBA Encyclopedia. 2nd Ed. New York: Villard Books, 1994.
Official NBA Guide: 1997-98. St. Louis: The Sporting News Pub.
Official NBA Register: 1997-98. St. Louis: The Sporting News Pub.
Street and Smith College Basketball Yearbook: Various Editions.

Super Basket: Bologna, Italy. 1992-93 monthly editions.
The Sporting News College Basketball: Various Editions.
Todo Basquet: Uruguay. 1993-94 monthly editions.
The World Basketball Club Almanac: Various editions, archives.

III. Articles

Burnham, Jeff. *The Cedar Rapids Gazette*. "Rosen Tried to Close Door on C.R. Police." December 31, 1989.

Charlip, Julie and Don Williamson. *The Wichita Eagle*. "Big Mo's Story. January 15, 1978.

Charlip, Julie and Don Williamson. *The Wichita Eagle*. "It's Supposed to be a Fair Trade. . ." January 16, 1978.

Fatsis, Stefan. *The Wall Street Journal*. "NBA Proves Foreign to Some." November 7, 1997.

Hansen, Marc. *The Des Moines Register*. Three-part series on C.J. Bruton Case. November 9, 10, 11 of 1997.

Hansen, Marc. *The Des Moines Register*. "NCAA's Credibility Is Criminal." February 1, 1998.

Harris, Bret. *The Australian*. "King's Star Makes Point Over Position." June 3, 1998.

Koolbeck, Mike and Miller, D.R. *The Cedar Rapids Gazette*. "Rockford Coach Runs Afoul of Law." December 30, 1989.

O'Brien, Richard and Hersch, Hank. (ed.) *Sports Illustrated*. Scorecard: "Foreign Affairs." June 23, 1997.

Oden, Bev. *Sports Illustrated*. "David Thompson, Hall of Famer" December 7, 1998.

Powers, John. *The Boston Globe*. "Wheelers and Dealers." July 5, 1987.

Wahl, Grant and Wertheim, Jon L. *Sports Illustrated*. "Paternity Ward." May 4, 1998.

Williamson, Don and Charlip, Julie. *The Wichita Eagle.*
6-part series from January 15, 1978 - January 20, 1978 on
death of Bob Elmore.

Wolff, Alexander. *Sports Illustrated.* "Foreign Legions." January 26, 1998.

IV. Special Events

After the Ball. Sydney Theatre Company Production written by
David Williamson. Sydney Opera House. 1997.

Chariots of Fire. 20th Century Fox and Allied Stars, Enigma
Productions. Film. 1981.

Diversions and Delights. Vincent Price as Oscar Wilde. Brisbane,
Australia. 1980.

Hair. Broadway Play Presented by Michael Butler. 1970. American
Conservatory Theatre. San Francisco.

He Got Game. Spike Lee film. 1998.

Hong Kong Tennis Association Program. December 28-29, 1969.
Cragengower Cricket Club. Hong Kong.

My Dinner with Andre. By Wallace Shawn and Andre Gregory.
Screenplay by Louis Malle, 1981.

John Ruan Celebrity Golf Exhibition. 1983. Wakonda Country Club:
Des Moines.

South Pacific Tennis Classic. October 8-14, 1979. Milton,
Queensland. Australia.

That Championship Season by Jason Miller. 1974. Garrick Theatre: London.

The Club by David Williamson. January 18, 1979. Theatre Royal:
Sydney, Australia.

World Championship Basketball Tournament. 1994. Toronto.

World Team Tennis Official Program. 1977. Kemper Arena: Kansas City.

V. Personal Interviews and Relevant Conversations

Albuquerque, Mario. Lisbon, Portugal: February 2, 1998.
Artime, Javier. Madrid, Spain: February 5, 1998.
Bruton Sr., Calvin, Sr. Perth, Australia: 1998 (Telephone)
Bruton, C.J. Des Moines, Iowa: 1997.
Carmichael, David. Townsville, Australia: 1997.
Costa, Leonel. Lisbon, Portugal: January 30, 1998.
Creger, Larry. Culver City, California: July 25, 1998 (Telephone)
Dickinson, Cameron. Wollongong, Australia: 1997.
Dukes, Mark. *The Cedar Rapids Gazette*. Kansas. 1998. (Telephone)
Harris, Bret. Wollongong, Australia: 1998.
Monter, Chris. Minneapolis, Minnesota 1998 (Telephone)
Morrison, Paul. Des Moines, Iowa: July 28, 1998 (Telephone)
Nurse, Nick. Oostende, Belgium: 1998. Des Moines, Iowa: 1998
Olson, Lute. University of Arizona: 1998. (Telephone)
Pfitsch, John. Grinnell, Iowa: April 28, 1998.
Salmon, Orv. Des Moines, Iowa: 1997-98.
Seminoff, Kirk. *The Wichita Eagle*. Kansas. April 6, 1998. (Tel)
Serra, Nelson. Lisbon, Portugal: 1997-98.
Vanmoerkerke, Rudolf. Oostende, Belgium: January 27, 1998.
Wrublewski, Harry. Birmingham, England: 1997.
Wrublewski, Michael. Sydney, Australia: 1997.

VI. Special Interview

Thompson, Scott. Cornell University. 1997. by Marc Hansen.

APPENDICES

APPENDIX A: BIOGRAPHICAL INFORMATION ON THE AUTHOR (DAVE ADKINS)

Born: Grinnell, Iowa
EDUCATION:
Grinnell High School
Cornell College: Bachelor of Arts Degree
Northeast Missouri State University: Master of Arts Degree
Middle Tennessee State University: Doctor of Arts Degree
LANGUAGE STUDY:
Portuguese: Leif College- Pretoria, South Africa
                Individual Study - Rejane Orticelli Thomassen
                Novo Hamburgo, Brazil
Spanish: Individual Study - Paloma Soria Mate-Kodjo
                Madrid, Spain
BASKETBALL JOBS
Current: Overseas Basketball Services
Head Coach - Hobart Devils - Australian NBL
State Director of Coaching - Queensland, Australia
Coaching jobs - Sporting Club of Lourenço Marques, Mozambique
             - Academica Club of Lourenço Marques, Mozambique
             - Desportivo Club of Lourenço Marques, Mozambique
Graduate Assistant Coach - Middle Tennessee State University
Head Coach-Athletic Director- Kubasaki High School-Okinawa
Head Coach- Prairie City High School - Iowa
Head Coach - West Liberty High School- Iowa

APPENDIX B: OVERSEAS BASKETBALL SERVICES PLAYER PLACEMENT LIST
(PARTIAL LIST)

NBL-Australian Pro League   AAABL- Amateur Summer League

George Abrams (Eastern Washington - Australia AAABL)
Jeff Acres (Oral Roberts - Australia NBL)
Mick Allison (Rockhurst - Australia AAABL)
Rick Allison (Rockhurst - Australia AAABL)
Paul Anderson (Southern Cal College - Australia AAABL)

Brian Banks (Nebraska - Australia NBL)
Jim Bartels (Iowa - France)
Mike Bell (Oklahoma - Germany, Chile)
Ronnie Bellamy (UNNC - New Zealand)
Greg Bergland (Biola - Australia AAABL)
Chester Brown (Middle Tennessee - Africa: Mozambique)
Charles Brunson (Australia AABL)
Calvin Bruton Sr. (Wichita State - Australia NBL)
Calvin Bruton Jr. (Indian Hills CC - Australia NBL)
Eric Bundgaard (St. Olaf - Africa-Mozambique)
Eric Cardenas (Oklahoma Christian-Portugal)
Steve Carfino (Iowa - Australia NBL)
Mark Cassidy (New Mexico Highlands - Australia AAABL)
Kirk Chastain (Wm Jewell - Australia AAABL)
Bruce Chubick (Nebraska - Belgium, Portugal)
Shelly Clark (Illinois - France)
Dan Clausen (North Dakota - Australia NBL)
Gordon Clemens (Franklin College - Australia AAABL)
James Crawford (Cumberland - Australia AAABL-NBL)
Donnie Creamer (Winthrop - Australia AAABL)
Ronnie Creamer (Winthrop - Australia AAABL)
Donnie Ray Cruise (McMurray College - Australia AAABL, NBL)
Jimmie DeGraffenried (Weber State - France, Sweden)
Jerry Dennard (Iowa - Australia NBL)
Cameron Dickinson (Grand View - Australia NBL) (Australian)
Mario Donaldson (Drake - Australia NBL)
Tony Dorsey (Southern Tech - England, Germany)
Tad Dufelmeir (Loyola-Chicago - Australia NBL)
Jene Dunbar (St. Augustine - Australia CBA, Finland)
Wayne Engelstad (Cal-Irvine - Australia NBL)
Chris Ensminger (Valparaiso - Portugal, Finland)
Mike Epps (Pfeiffer College - Australia AAABL)
Patrick Fairs (Texas - Australia NBL)
Curt Forrester (Stetson - Australia NBL)
Carl Gonder (Augustana, SD - Australia WABL)
Ricky Grace (Oklahoma - Australia NBL)
Chuck Harmison (Iowa State - Australia NBL)
Elliot Hatcher (Kansas State - Australia NBL)
Tim Hatchett (South Dakota - Australia SABL)
Kelvin Henderson (St. Louis - Australia NBL)
Dan Hickert (Kansas State - Australia NBL)
Mark Hiatt (Hastings College - Australia AAABL)

Gary Hopkins (Prairie View - Australia AAABL)
Larry Hotaling (William Penn - Australia WABL)
Lenzy Houston (Tusculum College - Australia AAABL, CBA)
Joe Hurst (NW Missouri - Australia NBL)
Craig Jackson (NE Oklahoma State - Australia AAABL)
Terry Johnson (Middle Tennessee - Africa: Mozambique)
Bill Jones (Northern Iowa - Australia NBL)
Larry Jones (Boston University - Finland, New Zealand)
Ricky Jones (Clemson - Australia NBL)
Wayne Kreklow (Drake, Boston Celtics - Australia NBL)
Andre LaFleur (Northeastern - Australia NBL)
Bennie Lewis (Southern Illinois-Edwardsville - AAABL, NBL)
Rod Littlepage (Drake - Portugal)
LeRoy Loggins (Fairmont State - Australia NBL)
Chad McClendan (Appalachian State - Australia NBL, Latvia)
Wayne McDaniel (Cal- Bakersfield - Australia NBL)
Brad Miley (Indiana State - Australia NBL)
Eric Moore (University of Pennsylvania - France, New Zealand)
Jeff Mosher (Rockford College - Australia AAABL)
George Morrow (Creighton - Australia NBL)
Eric Mounts (Cedarville College - Australia AAABL)
David Nelson (Ft. Lewis State - Australia AAABL, NBL)
Dwayne Nelson (Newberry - Australia AAABL, NBL)
Yohance Nicolas (Phillips University - Latvia)
Phil Nolin (Oregon College - Australia AAABL)
Kevin Ollis (Spring Hill College - Australia AAABL)
Ray Owes (Arizona - Australia NBL)
Lawson Pilgrim (Hendrix College - Australia AAABL)
Jason Reese (Northern Iowa - Australia NBL)
Dylan Rigdon (Arizona - New Zealand, Australia NBL)
David Robinson (UMKC - Australia NBL)
Melvin Robinson (St. Louis - Taiwan)
Billy Ross (Appalachian State - Australia CBA, England)
Derek Rucker (Davidson-Australia NBL)
Jeff Santasiero (Nyack College - Australia AAABL)
Tom Shafer (Iowa State - Australia NBL)
William Shain (Erskine College - Australia AAABL)
Rodney Smith (Texas-San Antonio - Philippines)
Melvin Thomas (Texas-Pan American - Australia NBL)
Marcus Timmons (Southern Illinois - NBL, Philippines, Latvia)
Leon Trimmingham (Briar Cliff - NBL, Germany, Venez., Japan)
Troy Truvillion (Eastern Montana - Australia WABL)

Alonzo Weatherly (Denver University - Australia AAABL, NBL)
Greg Wolf (Pittsburg State - Australia AAABL)
Chuck White (Purdue - Australia NBL, CBA)
Donald Whiteside (Northern Illinois, NBA - Australia NBL)
Corey Williams (Arizona - Philippines)
David Winslow (Northeast Missouri State - Australia NBL)
Pop Wright (Drake - Australia NBL)

APPENDIX C: THE GEORGE WASHINGTON
UNIVERSITY 1997-98 UNOFFICIAL
FOREIGN PLAYER ROSTER

Name	Country
Roey Eyal	Israel
Andrei Krivonos	Russia
Francisco de Miranda	The Netherlands
Antxon Iturbe	Spain
J.J. Bade	Canada
Daniel Soares	Brazil
Pat Ngongba	Central African Republic
Seco Camara	Portugal
Alexander Koul	Russia
Yegor Mescheriakov	Russia

APPENDIX D: FOREIGN PLAYER LIST
1996-97 NCAA-I COMPETITION

Note: This is only a partial, unofficial list of Division I NCAA players listed in the 1996-97 college rosters compiled by *The World Basketball Club Almanac,* and overseas basketball publications. List does not include all foreign players in Division I - NCAA competition, nor does it include any players from NCAA II, III and NAIA competition.

Player	Country	U.S. College
Adebayo, Sunday	Nigeria	Memphis
Adderley, Blair	Canada	Appalachian St.
Adler, David	Israel	South Florida
Ahlbom, Jarkko	Finland	Brigham Young
Aidietis, Giedrius	Lithuania	Monmouth

Alkaus, Zaid	Jordan	Buffalo
Allouche, Danny	Israel	Missouri
Aluma, Peter	Nigeria	Liberty
Anderson, Michael	Denmark	Rhode Island
Arigbabu, David	Germany	Rhode Island
Arsic, Peca	Yugoslavia	Delaware
Aurianthal, H.	Canada	Wisconsin
Aurianthal, Ralph	Canada	St.Francis
Avebe, Jean	Cameroon	Boston U.
Aw, Boubacar	Senegal	Georgetown
Awojobi, Tunji	Nigeria	Boston U.
Aybar, Ramon	Dominican Rep.	Florida Int.
Baldanshin, Rafael	Russia	American U.
Balgac, Rob	Serbia	Mount St. Marys
Bami, S.	Nigeria	Liberty
Barbic, Yann	France	Loyola, Chicago
Barnes, Stephen	U.K.	N.W. Louisiana
Barrett, Elvin	Jamaica	South Alabama
Beamer, B.	Canada	Niagra
Beckett, Tim	Canada	Hofstra
Behicevic, Haris	Bosnia	Tennessee-Chat.
Belin, Sebastian	Belgium	Marist
Berkovitch, T.	U.K.	Eastern Michigan
Beyina, Maurice	Central African Rep.	Dayton
Bigus, Rafal	Poland	Villanova
Boucard, D.	Canada	Fairfield U.
Brade, J.J.	Canada	Geo. Washington U.
Brown, Shawn	Canada	Virginia Tech
Bucero, Jeronimo	Spain	Manhattan
Callender, M.	U.K.	Middle Tennessee
Camera, Seco	Portugal	Geo Washington
Cautzor-Schroder, M.	Switzerland	Western Illinois
Crespo, Javier	Spain	Bowling Green
Chitikov, Alex	Russia	Eastern Michigan
Christopolus, Andy	Greece	Northeastern Ill.
Ciosici, Stephan	Romania	Lafayette
Correa, Michael	Brazil	San Diego State
Cyrus, C.	Canada	St. Bonaventure
Dalton-Brown	Trinidad	Cal-State S.B.
Davis, Garth	U.K.	East Tennessee
DeMiranda F.	Holland	Geo. Washington U.
Dia, Ya-Ya	Senegal	Georgetown

Dickel, Mark	New Zealand	UNLV
Domani, Dmitri	Russia	St. Joseph's
Donovan, Michael	U.K.	Miami
Dumic, Vladan	Bosnia	Houston
Duncan, Tim	U.S.V.I.	Wake Forest
Ewodo, Norcisse	Cameroon	Davidson
Egan, Luke	Australia	Eastern Washington
Espinosa, J.	Venezuela	St. Francis
Evtimov, Vassil	Bulgaria	North Carolina
Farrington, Roger	Bahamas	Arizona State
Femerling, Pat	Germany	Washington U.
Formanek, George	Czechoslovakia	South Carolina
Fowler, John	Australia	Louisiana Tech
Fox, Clinton	Australia	Boise State
Foyle, Adonal	Grenadines Is.	Colgate
Francis, G.	Canada	Fairfield U.
Gieseck, Bjorn	Germany	Butler
Goodman, J.	Bahamas	Loyola-Chicago
Grassili, L.	Italy	Columbia U.
Halbauer, D.	Croatia	Davidson
Hamilton, Sherm	Canada	Virginia Common.
Hatton, B.J.	Puerto Rico	Marist
Haslam, Chris	U.K.	Wyoming
Henry, Michael	U.K.	Montana State
Hoffmann, Harry	Germany	Santa Clara
Iturbe, Iker	Spain	Clemson
Ivaz, D.	Yugoslavia	Samford
Janulis, M.	Lithuania	Syracuse
Jobity, Kevin	Canada	Niagra
Joseph, Abel	Canada	Marquette
Journo, Shay	Israel	Centenary
Jovanovic, Luke	Slovenia	South Florida
Jurkunas, Andrius	Lithuania	Clemson
Juskowick, J.	Poland	Winthrop
Kaba, Jacky	Liberia	Seton Hall
Kane, B.	Senegal	Manhattan
Karavanic, Walter	Croatia	Bucknell
Kaukenas, Rimas	Lithuania	Seton Hall
Kelley, U.	Bahamas	Arizona State
Kemna, Karsten	Germany	Iona
King, K.	Bahamas	Portland
Kos, Steno	Australia	Wright State

Koul, Alexander	Russia	Geo. Washington U.
Krieger, Vincent	Netherlands	UNC-Asheville
Kruiswyk, R.	Canada	San Diego St.
Kuehl, Alexander	Germany	UNC-Charlotte
Landgren, Olof	Sweden	LaSalle
Leban, B.	Slovenia	New Mexico State
Lugo, Ricardo	Venezuela	St. Francis
Lyte, Richard	Canada	SE Missouri State
McCullough, Todd	Canada	Washington U.
Marie, Cedric	France	Nicholls State
Marks, Sean	New Zealand	Cal-Berkeley
Martinez, Fred	Puerto Rico	Middle Tennessee
Matthew, Bryan	Antigua	Iona
Milisa, Nate	Croatia	James Madison U.
Minlend, Charles	Cameroon	St. John's
Mirich, Nik	Australia	George Mason
Misyunchenko, K.	Russia	The Citadel
Mitchell, Ryan	Canada	S.F. Austin-Texas
Monday, Paul	Nigeria	Arkansas State
Morales, E.	Spain	Evansville
Morris, David	Nigeria	Arkansas State
Mujezinovic, H.	Bosnia	Indiana
McAndrew, Craig	Australia	Virginia
Najera, Eduardo	Mexico	Oklahoma
Nondas, Paul	Greece	St. Louis
Ndiaye, Makhtar	Senegal	North Carolina
Nees, Mark	Germany	U.S.F.
Newton, Mark	Canada	Duke
Ninkovic, Dayon	Yugoslavia	Bowling Green
Nordahl, T.	Australia	Pacific
Ode, David	Nigeria	Texas-SA
Okam, Felix	Nigeria	Ala-Birmingham
Okon, Dominic	Nigeria	Loyola-Chicago
Oloko, A.	Nigeria	Tenn-Chatt.
Olowokandi, M.	U.K.	Pacific
Ourguis, Khali	Belgium	Illinois St.
Ovcina, E.	Yugoslavia	Syracuse
Owinje, Godwin	Nigeria	Georgetown
Owoiya, T.A.	Nigeria	Nicholls St.
Pazdrazdis, Alvyd	Lithuania	McNeese St.
Pennisi, Mick	Australia	Eastern Mich.
Peral, Ricardo	Spain	Wake Forest

Peruzzo, F.	Italy	South Florida
Petrovic, N.	Yugoslavia	St. Joseph's
Petrovic, Sasa	Yugoslavia	Oregon St.
Quesada, Dario	Spain	Texas A&M
Rigby, Cameron	Australia	Bradley
Rogers, Paul	Australia	Gonzaga
Rouwhorst,Koen	Holland	Bowling Green
Ryan, Steve	Australia	Colorado
Sanchez, Juan	Argentina	Temple
Santiago, Daniel	Puerto Rico	New Mexico
Savvidis, Alex	Greece	Georgia St.
Sawyers, Dave	Canada	Canisius
Schoone, Marc	Holland	St. Bonaventure
Touomou, Ray	Cameroon	Rider
Touomou, Joseph	Cameroon	Georgetown
VanVelzen, R.	Netherlands	Illinois St.
Vasilijevic, Pero	Australia	Kansas St.
Zwikker, Serge	Netherlands	North Carolina

APPENDIX E: Foreign Players Stripped of All NCAA Eligibility in 1997

C.J. Bruton	Australia	Iowa State

APPENDIX F: SPORTS ILLUSTRATED REPRINT OF BRUTON ARTICLE

Reprinted courtesy of *Sports Illustrated*, June 23, 1997. Copyright 1997, Time Inc. "Foreign Affairs" all rights reserved.

FOREIGN AFFAIRS (pp. 18-19)

When C.J. Bruton, a 6' 2" point guard from Australia, signed a letter of intent with Iowa State earlier this year, he was upfront about his basketball experience. Yes, in 1994 he had played for money with the Perth Wildcats of Australia's National Basketball League, but not for much ($11,000) and not with particular distinction (limited minutes in only 22 games). He knew that other Australians, including several former Perth players, had competed in the NBL and then gone on to successful careers at U.S. colleges. No big deal, right?

Wrong. Bruton, who led another Iowa school, Indian Hills Community College, to this year's junior college national title, was recently declared ineligible by the NCAA, which deemed him a professional. But according to Dave Adkins, a former agent for Cal Bruton, C.J.'s father and a one time Australian pro star, C.J.'s case should be no different from those of dozens of other foreigners who, after playing for money abroad, have petitioned the NCAA and gained eligibility. He points in particular to Andrew Gaze, an Australian who boosted Seton Hall to the 1989 NCAA championship game months after leading the NBL in scoring. "He was paid much more than C.J., he was a better player, and he was older," says Adkins. "We don't understand this at all."

"They told me that I'm considered a professional player and that they weren't going to let me in," says Bruton, 21. "At first I was shocked. But I figured I could appeal the decision, and I was confident it would be O.K." In fact, he *couldn't* appeal, though he wrote twice to the NCAA to explain his position. Only a school can appeal, and Iowa State, against coach Tim Floyd's wishes, chose not to do so because, an Iowa State source said, officials did not want to buck the NCAA. The Cyclones' athletic director, Eugene Smith, did not return calls from SI.

Though Bruton says he wants to complete college, he was left with little choice but to declare for the June 25 NBA draft, in which he could be picked in the second round. Most likely, he will play next season in Australia or in the CBA. For now, he's suiting up in a summer league in Ottumwa, Iowa.

Rodney "Pop" Wright
shutting down Larry Bird
in 1979 Drake-Indiana St.
game

Photo courtesy of *The Tribune Star* of Terre Haute

Jerry Dennard at 6'9 shows ball handling skills. 1988 Hobart.

Photo courtesy of *The Mercury* (Hobart, Australia)

**NCAA Midwest Regional All-Tournament
Team** at South Dakota State University 1961.
Front row: Cornell Lackey (Prairie View A.M.),
Dave Adkins (Cornell College).
Back Row: Don Jacobsen (South Dakota State),
Zelmo Beaty (Prairie View),
Don Slattery (South Dakota State).

Photo courtesy of Cornell College

BASQUETEBOL
UM NACIONAL
E TANTO!....

4

Terry Johnson, ex-Middle Tennessee State University, skies
in first round of 1973 National Championship of Portugal
played in Luanda, Angola. Sporting player to right
(horizontal stripes) is Mario Albuquerque and Sporting
player #5 is Nelson Serra.

1972 All-Star Tour of Mozambique and Angola. Front row: Richard Almstedt, Kit Jones and Jim Jones. Back row: Dave Adkins, Mahlon Saunders, Rob Clark and Dale Dover.

5a

5b

Sporting Club of Lourenço Marques 1973 National Champions of Portugal. Front row: Tomane, Nelson, Pecito, Simongo and Massagista. Back row: D. Adkins, Terry Johnson, Vitor, Rui Pinheiro, Mario Albuquerque and Ramao.

Luanda, Angola, 1973. Victory ride for Coach Dave Adkins after coaching Sporting Club to National Championship of Portugal with 102-77 win over Benfica of Lisbon.

Rui Pinheiro of Sporting shoots over
Richard Almstedt. Jan Hoeks at left with
glasses. 1973 "Freitas Branco" game.
Lourenço Marques.

Cal Bruton in his all-star prime
with the Geelong Cats.
Australia, 1981.

Photo courtesy of Cal Bruton
and the Geelong BBC

Cameron Dickinson with Townsville Suns of Australian NBL in 1995. Townsville, Australia.

Photo courtesy of *Townsville Bulletin.*

Agent and three great players.
Center-bottom: Derek Rucker, left:
D. Adkins, right: Clarence Tyson,
top: Cameron Dickinson. 1996

Photo courtesy of *Townsville Bulletin*.